Republic of
Korea

CASSELL BUSINESS BRIEFINGS

Republic of
Korea

Judith Cherry

KOREA BUSINESS SERVICES

⊥
CASSELL

Cassell
Villiers House
41/47 Strand
London WC2N 5JE

387 Park Avenue South
New York
NY 10016-8810

First published 1993

British Library Cataloguing-in-Publication Data
A catalogue entry for this book is available from the British Library.

ISBN 0-304-32636-4

Typeset by Colset Private Limited, Singapore
Printed and bound in Great Britain by
Biddles Ltd, Guildford and King's Lynn

Contents

PART FOUR

Culture

PART FIVE

The Economy

PART SIX

Doing Business in Korea

PART SEVEN

Directory

PART EIGHT

Appendix

About the Author

Judith Cherry was instrumental in setting up the Korean Studies Unit (now the Institute for Korean Studies) at Sheffield University and between 1980 and 1987 she taught courses there in Korean language, history and politics. During this period, she also made regular contributions to BBC broadcasts, providing analysis of current affairs in Korea, and co-authored the Linguaphone Korean course.

In 1987, Judith joined the Research Department of Salomon Brothers International, with responsibility for all written research and presentations on the Korean economy and financial markets. She returned to Sheffield at the end of 1990 in order to set up Korea Business Services. Judith is currently a member of the British Overseas Trade Board Asia-Pacific Advisory Group and the Korea Trade Action Committee.

Preface

Over the past forty-five years the Republic of Korea (ROK) has undergone rapid political, social and economic change. The next decade will see further important developments, most notably in the economic and financial spheres, as the ROK government pursues its policies of internationalization, deregulation and liberalization. To keep pace with these changes, this book will be revised at regular intervals and updates in electronic form made available on application to the publisher.

Although every effort has been made to ensure that the statistics used in this book are accurate and consistent, the reader should be aware that discrepancies among the various statistic sources in the Republic of Korea are relatively common.

US dollar equivalents are given for wŏn. Unless otherwise stated, the exchange rate used is W787/US$1, which was valid on the last day of trading in 1992. Metric and imperial equivalents are provided for all measurements.

I should like to thank Ruth Grayson, Jeff Gosling and Trevor Rolls for their comments and suggestions, Helen Evans for her assistance in Seoul, Mr Kim Hae-gŭn for his never-ending help and support, and also Mark Badger for his assistance with the computer.

Judith Cherry
March 1993

PART ONE

Introduction

THE REPUBLIC OF KOREA

1 General Overview

For a great many Westerners, the Republic of Korea is still very much an unknown quantity. What little is known relates mostly to the Korean War, student demonstrations, low-priced automobiles and the Seoul Olympics. There is a great deal more to South Korea than that.

Although the Republic itself is less than fifty years old, the history of the Korean peninsula stretches back over five thousand years. The division of the peninsula in 1945, which split in two a nation that had been unified since the seventh century AD, is symptomatic of Korea's history as a whole.

Too often, important decisions taken about Korea's future have not been made by the Koreans themselves – the peace negotiations conducted by China with Japan after the Japanese invasions of Korea in 1592, the battle for supremacy over Korea among China, Japan and Russia in the early twentieth century, and the division of the peninsula by the Allied Powers in 1945 are good illustrations of the Korean saying, 'When the whales fight, the shrimp's back gets broken.' Korea, as a small but geopolitically important country, has often found itself at the mercy of external forces and interests.

South Korea's rapid economic development over the past four decades has given its people a strong sense of national pride and a determination that the political and economic future of the country will be decided by the South Koreans themselves. South Korea has already assumed a leading role among the Newly Industrializing Economies, and is close to achieving its dream of advanced nation status.

Rapid industrialization and westernization have resulted in dramatic and often painful changes in South Korean society. Nevertheless, the values instilled over the centuries through the influence of Confucianism remain intact – the importance of the family, respect for the elderly, and the desire for education. The South Koreans have also maintained their artistic and cultural identity, which has been influenced by and yet remains distinct from that of neighbouring China and Japan.

Being well informed is a key element of success in business. In the case of a rapidly developing country like South Korea, being informed about the economy makes obvious sense; new opportunities are constantly arising as the South Koreans look for export markets and import sources, and seek foreign partners who can provide the advanced technology that they need to keep moving forward.

Being culturally aware is also extremely important. A common error made by many businessmen and women visiting the Far East in general, and South Korea in particular, is to assume that doing business in such a truly foreign market is simply a matter of common sense. They play by the same rules, apply the same logic, and expect the same responses as they would back at home.

Knowing the rules by which the South Koreans play, understanding their logic, and anticipating their responses will help you to succeed when doing business in the Republic of Korea. Showing sensitivity to Korean beliefs and values and demonstrating an understanding of Korean business practices will not only create a lasting good impression with your South Korean counterparts, but also prove invaluable in building and maintaining long-term business relationships in the Republic of Korea.

2 Gazetteer

LOCATION

The Korean peninsula occupies a position at the eastern end of the Asian continent, between 124°11′ and 131°53′ E longitude and 33°06′ and 43°01′ N latitude. The peninsula, which is roughly 600 miles (960 kilometres) long and 135 miles (216 kilometres) wide at its narrowest point, covers a total area of 85,256 square miles (220,813 square kilometres) – slightly less than that of Great Britain. There are more than 3,000 contiguous islands, of which approximately 200 are inhabited.

The peninsula is bounded to the north by the Amnok (Yalu) and Tumen Rivers, which form the boundary between Korea and the Chinese land mass; the last 10 miles (16 kilometres) of the Tumen River also serve as a boundary with the former Soviet Union. Japan lies 128 miles (205 kilometres) to the east across the Eastern Sea (Sea of Japan), and the Shantung peninsula lies 118 miles (189 kilometres) to the west over the Yellow Sea. The Korean Straits lie to the south of the peninsula.

The peninsula is divided roughly at the 38th parallel by the 2.5-mile (4-kilometre)-wide Demilitarized Zone (DMZ), which has separated the communist Democratic People's Republic of Korea (DPRK) from the democratic Republic of Korea (ROK) since 1945. The division of the peninsula in 1945 left South Korea with the majority of arable land, and North Korea with the lion's share of the peninsula's limited natural resources.

In 1991, the Republic of Korea, which occupies the southern part of the peninsula, covered an area of 38,031 square miles (99,300 square kilometres) – roughly the same size as Portugal or the state of Indiana – or approximately 45 per cent of the total land area. The land area has increased in recent years, due to reclamation work; in 1991, it expanded by 101 square miles (261 square kilometres).

In 1991, forests covered 66.2 per cent of the Republic of Korea; paddy fields accounted for 12.8 per cent of the land, dry fields 8.8 per cent, rivers 2.9 per cent, building sites 2.0 per cent, roads 1.9 per cent, ditches 1.6 per cent, and grave-yards 0.3 per cent. Of the total area, 19.3 per cent was owned by the state. With only a small proportion of arable land, all available land in the south is intensively cultivated.

TOPOGRAPHY

More than two-thirds of the Korean peninsula is mountainous; the most common rocks are granite and gneiss, but there are also abundant igneous and sedimentary rocks, including lime-stone and sandstone. There are neither strong earthquakes nor active volcanoes on the peninsula.

The principal mountain range on the Korean peninsula extends southwards along the east coast, forming the 'back-bone' of Korea and creating an internal division between east and west. Lateral branches spread out from the main range towards the south-west of the peninsula. The mountains are mostly low, with the highest, Mount Paektu in North Korea, reaching 9,055 feet (2,744 metres); there are no mountains above 6,600 feet (2,000 metres) in the southern part of the peninsula. The southern and western mountain slopes gradually descend into the coastal plains of South Korea.

The west and south coasts are characterized by many indentations and irregularities, with numerous islands and harbours. The west coast has exceptionally high tides – the port of Inch'ŏn boasts the second highest tidal movement in the world (29 feet or 9 metres). There are only a few islands along the steep eastern coast of the peninsula, which has deep waters, rocky outcrops, and comparatively few good harbours.

There are many rivers on the Korean peninsula, the major-ity of which are found in the south and the west. These are an important source of water supply for agriculture and hydro-electric power generation, but only the Naktong River north of Pusan can serve as a navigable waterway. The most important rivers in the west are the Amnok, Han and Taedong, all of which empty into the Yellow Sea. The Tumen River in the east flows into the Eastern Sea at the border with the former Soviet Union.

CLIMATE

There are four distinct seasons, covering roughly the same months as in Britain. Spring begins in late March or early

April, and is characterized by mild and windy weather with occasional drizzle. This is the blossom season, with cherry, forsythia and azalea flowering in abundance. Temperatures begin to rise in June, and July and August are hot, humid and wet. The summer monsoon brings heavy rain to the peninsula: more than half the annual rainfall occurs between June and August, with 30 per cent often occurring in the month of July alone.

Autumn is rather short, clear and dry – perhaps the most pleasant season of the year, and the time to enjoy the brilliant blue skies and spectacular foliage in the mountains along the east coast. Although the winter is cold, with temperatures typically remaining below freezing throughout January and February, spells of milder weather relieve the bitter cold – the phenomenon known to the Koreans as 'three cold and four warm days'. Snow is particularly heavy in the northern provinces.

The humid, East Asian monsoonal climate is influenced by both the Asian continent and the surrounding seas. The continental climate is more pronounced towards the north, while the ocean's influence is felt more in the south. The climate is also affected by the mountains; the east coast, sheltered by the mountains from the north-westerly winter winds, is warmer than the west, which faces continental Asia and is vulnerable to the influence of monsoons throughout the year.

The climate is characterized by extremes of heat and cold; the range of temperatures for the South Korean capital Seoul between the coldest and hottest months of the year is about 28°C (82°F). The average winter temperature is generally below freezing, while that for the hottest month of summer is above 25°C (77°F). However, temperatures in excess of 30°C (86°F) are not unusual. The extremes of temperature are more pronounced in the north and the interior than in the south or along the coasts. The average minimum temperature on the southern coast in winter is −5°C (23°F), compared with −23°C (−9°F) on the Kaema plateau in North Korea.

The average annual rainfall varies from 20 inches (500 millimetres) in north-eastern inland areas to 60 inches (1,500 millimetres) on the southern coast.

FLORA AND FAUNA

The geographical location of the Korean peninsula makes it a good natural habitat for a large number of plants and animals. A variety of alpine plants is to be found in the north and in mountainous areas; the central region and the western low-lands have temperate vegetation, and warm-temperate plants

7
∎

grow in abundance along the southern coast. Korea's largest island, Cheju-do, is famous for its subtropical vegetation.

In the north of the peninsula are found coniferous forests, while mixed and broadleaf forests are found in the centre and south of the peninsula respectively. Common trees include the alder, birch, elm, pine and willow; fruit trees include the apple, chestnut, ginko, pear and persimmon. Vine fruits and other temperate and subtropical plants and shrubs grow in profusion all over the country.

Animal life in the northern region of the Korean peninsula is closely related to that of Manchuria, Siberia, Sakhalin and Hokkaido. Highland species include the roe-deer, the brown bear and the lynx. Fauna of the southern lowlands, which includes the black bear, the river deer and the mandarin vole, is more closely related to that of southern Manchuria, central China and Japan. Some animal species, including the Manchurian weasel, the striped hamster and the bat, are found only in North Korea. Domestic animals include cats, dogs, horses, oxen and common farm animals.

Located along the main migration route for birds that breed in Manchuria and Siberia and winter in Japan, the Korean peninsula is visited annually by a variety of migratory birds such as geese, teals, swans and white egrets. Among the most common of the 400 species of bird recorded are the crow, magpie, heron, oriole, lark and pheasant. Predatory fowl include the rare Steller's sea eagle and the white-tailed sea eagle.

The government of the Republic of Korea has designated 23 species Natural Monuments, including the white-bellied black woodpecker, the great bustard, the musk deer and the Chindogae (Korea's indigenous dog). It has also designated 20 birds, 2 mammals and several insect species as endangered species.

POPULATION (LINGUISTIC AND ETHNIC DISTRIBUTION)

The Koreans are a homogenous ethnic group of Mongolian descent. According to archaeological research, linguistic studies and legends, tribes living in Central Asia thousands of years ago began to migrate to Manchuria and Siberia; some of those migrants travelled as far east as the Korean peninsula, where they settled as a homogeneous race, independent of their neighbours. This homogeneity was consolidated after the unification of the peninsula in AD 668 by the Shilla kingdom, and the Koreans have developed one language and one culture, remaining unified until the end of World War II.

Although many people make the mistake of assuming

that Korean culture would be indistinguishable from Chinese or Japanese culture, the Koreans *are* distinct from their neighbours in their culture, language and national characteristics. The Korean peninsula acted as a conduit for the flow of culture from China to Japan, as the Koreans adopted and adapted Chinese religion, art, philosophy and government practices before passing them on. The Koreans have fought to maintain their own cultural and political identity in the face of extensive contacts with China over centuries, countless foreign invasions and, eventually, colonization by the Japanese in 1910.

As a race, the South Koreans are highly nationalistic and fiercely proud of their achievements. They are competitive, tenacious, disciplined and resilient, with a warm, generous nature and an earthy sense of humour. Referred to by themselves and foreigners alike as 'the Irish of Asia', they love singing and drinking and are renowned as being more outgoing and emotional than many of their Asian neighbours.

THE FLAG OF THE REPUBLIC OF KOREA

The flag, called the *t'aegŭkki*, symbolizes peace, unity, creation, brightness and infinity.

The flag design comprises a circle divided into two equal and comma-shaped parts, one blue and one red. This symbol is known to many as that of yin and yang (Korean: *ŭm* and *yang*) – the red upper section symbolizes the yang (positive) forces, while the blue lower section represents the yin (negative) forces. The whole symbolizes the dualism, balance and harmony inherent in the universe – male and female, night and day, good and evil, etc.

The four trigrams, one in each corner of the flag, represent the four elements that make up the universe – heaven, earth, fire and water.

The national flower of the Republic of Korea is the Rose of Sharon (Korean: *mugunghwa*).

POLITICAL ADMINISTRATION

The Republic of Korea comprises nine provinces: Kyŏnggi, North and South Ch'ungch'ŏng, North and South Chŏlla, North and South Kyŏngsang, and Cheju Island. The provinces, which are administered by governors, are further divided into 67 cities, 137 counties (*kun*), and townships (179 *ŭp* and 1,260 *myŏn*). The cities are subdivided into wards (*ku*) and districts (*tong*). For almost three decades, the government appointed local officials; in 1991, however, direct elections were held for municipal and provincial assemblies. Elections for provincial governors and mayors, due to take place in 1992, were postponed until the mid-1990s.

There has traditionally been a strong rivalry between the eastern and western provinces of the Republic. Economic development and industrialization have focused on the Kyŏng-sang provinces, which have also been the power base for the ruling party. In contrast, there has been less development in the Chŏlla provinces, the stronghold of the main opposition leader, Kim Dae-jung. The Kwangju Uprising of 1980 (see: History), in which at least 200 citizens were killed by government forces, hardened those divisions and has remained a key issue in South Korean politics. Following the events of 1980, the government expressed its commitment to providing compensation and promoting the development of the region.

There are six special cities which are metropolitan areas with the status of province and administered by mayors. These are:

- **Seoul** (population: 10.5 million in 1989) is the capital city and the commercial, legal, educational and cultural centre of the Republic. Industries located in Seoul include light and medium engineering, electronics, textiles, and pharmaceuticals. Although Seoul covers a tiny proportion of the total area of the Republic (0.6 per cent), almost one quarter of the population lives there. In 1994, Seoul will celebrate its six hundredth anniversary as the capital city of Korea.

- **Pusan** (population: 3.7 million), the largest port and the second largest city in the Republic, is home to a wide range of industries including textiles, ceramics, shipbuilding, electronics, light and heavy engineering, and plywood.

- **Taegu** (population: 2.2 million) is an important manufacturing base for textiles, nylon, light industrial goods and metal working.

- **Inch'ŏn** (population: 1.6 million) is the largest port on the west coast, with light and heavy engineering, glass manufacturing, plywood, and oil refining.

- **Kwangju** (population: 1.2 million) is a centre for textiles and industrial equipment companies.

- **Taejŏn** (population: 868,000) is the site for the 1993 Expo.

Other industrial centres of note are the cities of Ulsan (shipbuilding, automobiles, oil refining, petrochemicals and fertilizers), P'ohang (steel and non-ferrous metals) and Yŏsu (oil refining, petrochemicals and fertilizers). The Republic's principal ports are Pusan, Inch'ŏn (see above), Kunsan and Mok'po.

3 History

According to Korean legend, Hwanung, the son of the Divine Creator, came down to earth with three thousand companions, proclaimed himself king, and ruled the universe. During his rule, a bear and a tiger petitioned the king to be allowed to become humans. The king told them that their wish would be granted if they lived in a cave for one hundred days, eating only mugwort and garlic. The tiger failed to accomplish the task, but the bear succeeded and turned into a woman, whose son, Tan'gun, is the mythical founder of Korea. Tan'gun is said to have formed a single kingdom in the year 2333 BC – the national holiday on 3 October celebrates the founding of the nation on this date – and ruled until 1122 BC. This kingdom was later known as Ancient Chosŏn, the first of the tribal leagues to be established on the peninsula.

The Emperor Han Wu-ti of China made an unsuccessful attempt to invade Ancient Chosŏn in 109 BC, but succeeded the following year. Placing the newly conquered territory under Chinese administration, the Emperor divided it into four counties, with administrative headquarters at Lolang, Chenfan, Hsuantu and Lintun. These commanderies served as centres for early contacts and trade with the Chinese empire. Here Koreans were exposed to Chinese systems of government and administration, as well as language, philosophy and art. However, the Chinese quickly lost control of three of their outposts; only Lolang remained under Chinese control for four hundred years.

The fourth century BC saw the emergence of many other tribal leagues, which were eventually consolidated into three kingdoms: Koguryŏ in the north, Paekche in the south-west, and Shilla in the south-east. Koguryŏ (37 BC–AD 668) quickly emerged as a strong military state, controlling two-thirds of the peninsula and a large part of Manchuria. Koguryŏ drove the Chinese out of the last remaining commandery at Lolang in AD 313 and ruled from (modern-day) P'yŏngyang until AD 668. Paekche (18 BC–AD 660) was founded near present-day Seoul, but later moved down to the south-western part of the peninsula. Shilla (57 BC–AD 935) was the last to develop, located in the south-east of the peninsula.

The establishment of the three kingdoms brought a degree of stability to the peninsula and stimulated cultural development. Although separate political entities, Koguryŏ, Paekche and Shilla were related ethnically and linguistically. All three established hereditary monarchies and governments administered by members of the aristocracy.

The influence which China had begun to exert over Korea through contacts with the four commanderies became pervasive during the Three Kingdoms period. All three kingdoms were greatly influenced by Chinese culture, adopting (to varying extents) the Chinese bureaucratic system of government, accepting and patronizing Buddhism (which arrived from India via China), and adopting the tenets of Confucianism. Following the introduction of Buddhism, Korean monks who were sent to China for study brought back ideas on architecture, sculpture and other arts as well as Buddhist texts.

The introduction of Confucianism, with its emphasis on the study of the Confucian Classics, had a significant influence on intellectual life, and contributed to the rapid spread of the Chinese language and writing system among the upper classes. Chinese-style schools were established to teach the Classics and the Confucian canon to the sons of the nobility.

Due to its geographical location, Shilla was the last to adopt these foreign ideas, and retained its tribal customs and ideas to a greater extent than did Koguryŏ and Paekche, adapting Chinese models of government and administration to suit its own circumstances and customs. It was during the first half of the sixth century that specialist government offices began to appear, with a clear distinction between military and civil functions.

However, the formation of the three kingdoms also led to military conflict. In the latter part of the sixth century, China launched four unsuccessful attacks against Koguryŏ before making an alliance with Shilla, which enabled it to overthrow Koguryŏ. After Chinese and Shilla forces attacked and conquered Paekche, it became clear that the Chinese intended to ignore Shilla's part in the victory, and treat all the conquered Korean land as part of the Chinese empire.

Shilla began military operations against the Chinese in AD 671, drove the Chinese forces out of the former Paekche territory, and then allied with the defeated Koguryŏ people to drive the invaders out of the Korean peninsula. The peninsula was thus united under Shilla rule, and remained one nation with a single language and culture for the next twelve centuries.

The early Unified Shilla period was one of peace, prosperity, stability and great cultural achievements. The study of the Chinese Classics and Confucianism flourished and the first national university was established in the capital city of Kyŏngju. Buddhism was accepted as the state religion, and became a dominant force in the kingdom's spiritual and cultural life; this was the golden age of Buddhist art, particularly sculpture.

Unified Shilla reached the peak of its prosperity and power in the mid-eighth century AD. The fall of the dynasty set a pattern of dynastic decline repeated over the centuries in Korea; internal power struggles at court, corruption and decadence among the ruling classes, crop failures, increasingly difficult rural living conditions, and peasant uprisings. Unified Shilla was overthrown by the rebel leader Wang Kŏn in AD 918, with the king surrendering seventeen years later.

The Koryŏ dynasty (918-1392), like the Unified Shilla before it, began with a period of political stability and cultural development. In addition, the new rulers instigated a programme of reform and reorganization. The capital was moved from Kyŏngju in the south-west to (modern) Kaesŏng in the north, the better to keep watch over the country's northern frontier, and defences were strengthened in order to repel possible invaders. A policy of land reform was implemented to improve the peasants' lot – each farmer was given a plot of land to cultivate during his lifetime – and measures were taken to curb the power of the aristocracy.

All private armies were disbanded and the military were excluded from important official posts. The bureaucracy was divided into military and civil wings, with the top officials in each section forming the upper classes. The term *yangban*, which is sometimes still used by more elderly Koreans as a term of respect, meaning literally 'two noble groups', dates back to this era of military and civil nobility.

The Chinese government model was further assimilated with the institution of civil service examinations in 958. As in China, the subject matter of the examinations was the Confucian Classics and commentaries, but, unlike in China where the examinations were (in theory) open to men of all classes, in Koryŏ the aristocracy enjoyed a virtual monopoly over education and access to government posts. Those members of the ruling classes who were most proficient in the Confucian disciplines were appointed to the top official posts; thereafter promotion depended on social status and seniority.

Buddhism remained a dominant ideological and cultural influence, and monks rose to positions of importance as advisors, tutors and consultants to the state.

As had happened in the Unified Shilla period, court intrigue and factional fighting began to weaken the royal household. In the midst of the chaos, members of the military, angered by the civilians' supremacy at court and prejudice against their own class, carried out a coup in 1170. The constant struggle for power eroded the government's ability to deal with the new threat posed by the rise of the Mongols in the Central Asian steppes.

Koryŏ was plagued by Mongol attacks from the early part of the thirteenth century through to the end of the dynasty in 1392. Koryŏ's formal diplomatic relations with the Sung dynasty in China were perceived as a threat by the Mongols, who crossed the Yalu river and invaded the Korean peninsula in 1231. The Mongols continued their harassment of Koryŏ for the next forty years, finally making it a vassal state in 1270. The Koreans were forced to adopt Mongolian institutions and customs, and paid taxes which helped to finance the Mongols' unsuccessful attempts to invade Japan in 1274 and 1281.

Having conquered China in 1279, the Mongols established themselves as the Yuan dynasty. For the next one hundred and fifty years, Koryŏ was subordinate to the Yuan dynasty. Princes were forced to marry Mongol princesses, and gifts and hostages were sent to the court in Peking. The Koreans did receive some benefits from their contacts with the Mongols, who, unlike the Chinese, were receptive to foreign culture and ideas. The Mongols' invasion of Persia brought them into contact with Arabic culture, and they, in turn, introduced it to the Koreans. Thus Koryŏ was exposed to the advanced cultures of the outside world, including astronomy, mathematics, medicine and the western calendar.

During this period Buddhists carved the entire Buddhist Cannon on 81,258 woodblocks as a pious act to secure Buddha's help in repelling the Mongol invaders. (The blocks, known as the Tripitaka Koreana, are currently housed at Haein Temple, near Taegu.) The spread of Buddhism and Confucianism, both of which were dependent on written texts and records, stimulated the development of movable type in 1234. The other major achievement of the Koryŏ dynasty was celadon pottery, a ceramic ware with a greenish-blue glaze. Celadon was originally imported from China, but the Korean potters developed and refined the techniques to a degree that won the admiration of the Chinese (see: The Arts).

With the waning of the Mongols' power from the mid-fourteenth century, power struggles erupted at court and rebellions broke out all over China, culminating in the over-throw of the Mongols and the establishment of the Ming dynasty in 1382. In 1388, General Lee Sŏng-gye was ordered to lead an army against the advancing Ming forces: – seeing this as futile, General Lee turned back and overthrew the Koryŏ dynasty. In 1392, he established the Yi dynasty; this, the last Korean dynasty, lasted for more than five hundred years, ending in 1910.

The new ruler of Korea pledged allegiance to China, in return for which the Emperor chose a name for the new dynasty – in fact, the old name of Chosŏn (literally, 'Land of the Morning Calm'), the other name by which this final dynasty is known. The capital was transferred from Kaesŏng to Hanyang (modern Seoul) in 1394, and the new ruler moved swiftly to introduce social, political and economic reforms.

Although Buddhism and Confucianism had co-existed peacefully for centuries, in the latter years of the Koryŏ dynasty there had been increasing animosity between the adherents of these two beliefs. This was aggravated by the arrival from China of a new interpretation of Confucianism – Neo-Confucianism – which emphasized the family as the basis of society, and criticized men for abandoning their responsibilities to become monks. The Neo-Confucianists were also openly critical of the wealth and power wielded by the monasteries. As Confucianism gained ascendancy, the power of the Buddhists weakened, and religious leaders were excluded from participation in state affairs.

Neo-Confucianism was adopted as the state ideology and quickly became the basis of the government, education, daily family life and ethical and moral standards of the Korean people. It continues to exert a strong influence over modern South Korean society (see: Society).

Once again, the early part of the dynasty saw a period of cultural creativity, crowned by the rule of King Sejong (r. 1418–50). It was during his reign that a number of scientific inventions and cultural achievements were attained, the most significant for the Koreans being the invention of their own alphabet, *han'gŭl* (see: Language).

However, before long, the same problems that had beset earlier dynasties began to reappear. Early land reforms did not last, and with the growth of non-taxable estates belonging to the royal family and the bureaucracy, heavier levies on taxable land drove increasing numbers of farmers to abandon their land and join the large estates as workers. The growth of the *yangban* class was so rapid that it was impossible to find official posts for all successful examination candidates. The resulting factional struggles, aggravated by the Confucian concepts of clan loyalty and the duty of sons and grandsons to carry on their fathers' fights, led once again to power struggles within the court and bureaucracy.

The government, thus weakened, was ill equipped to cope with the new threat of a unified Japan. Relations with Japan had been suspended in 1555, following years of attacks by Japanese pirates along the Korean coastline. In the last years of the sixteenth century, Hideyoshi Toyotomi sent envoys to re-establish relations with Korea, with the aim of obtaining free passage for his troops through Korea and on to invade China. The Korean court refused and Hideyoshi retaliated by invading Korea. The seven-year war which followed ended when the Japanese troops withdrew from the peninsula, but left the Korean countryside in ruins. The Koreans enjoyed a brief moment of glory during the war, when Admiral Yi Sun-shin and his 'turtle-boat' armada conducted a series of brilliant naval operations in the Korean Straits, destroying many Japanese ships. The 'turtle-boats' were, in fact, the world's first iron-clad battleships.

China's participation in the war had left its own government weakened in the face of the growing power of the Manchus. After the Manchus overthrew the Ming dynasty in 1627 and established the Ch'ing dynasty, Korea became a vassal state once again, forced into a 'little-brother' relationship and sending hostages and gifts to the Peking court.

The Korean court's response to these events was to attempt to close the country off to the outside world, choosing to believe that everything foreign was barbaric. This policy of self-imposed isolation, which was to earn Korea the epithet 'the Hermit Kingdom', lasted until the beginning of the twentieth century.

In the continuing economic chaos, confusion within the government intensified with the mounting factional struggles. Revenues fell as the bureaucrats expanded their private estates, and the Confucian disdain for private commerce and manufacturing restricted the growth of commerce and trade. In its penury, the government began to offer government office to anyone capable of supplying grain and funds – as a small class of merchants began to establish itself, it was possible to buy one's way into the upper class.

The late eighteenth century saw the first direct contacts with the west, as Catholic missionaries entered Korea along with explorers and traders. However, Korea's geographical isolation and the cultural chauvinism of its ruling classes, who believed that nothing worthwhile could come from countries other than China, meant that Korea's contacts with the west were largely restricted to indirect influence through

China. Although western scientific ideas were slow to be accepted in Korea, western religions quickly found favour with the poor and oppressed. The increasing economic distress of the peasants made the promise of a peaceful life after death attractive to the common people. Fearing the spread of a religion which, in many respects, ran counter to the teachings of Neo-Confucianism, the government responded by persecuting both missionaries and converts.

The movement against the academic (classical Chinese) learning espoused by the Neo-Confucians and in favour of more practical studies, which had begun in the seventeenth century, came to prominence in the eighteenth century. The supporters of this movement criticized the Neo-Confucians' preoccupation with the past and with formalism, and demanded an empirical, practical approach to government.

The latter half of the eighteenth century was a period of great instability in Korea, as factional warfare and power politics frustrated any constructive efforts at political and economic reform. The most powerful man in the court was the Taewŏn'gun, the regent ruling on behalf of the 12-year-old boy who succeeded to the throne in 1864. The Taewŏn'gun was a staunch adherent of Confucianism and a firm supporter of the isolationist policy adopted by earlier rulers. He refused to allow contact with foreign ideas and turned his back on the new realities that conflicted with his beliefs. Under his rule, foreign missionaries were persecuted and ordered to leave the country; the nine priests who refused were executed, along with 8,000 Korean converts.

Although the French government sent a fleet to exact revenge for the killings, the ships were forced to withdraw. The sinking of the American merchant ship the *General Sherman* in 1866, and the routing of an American flotilla that approached the Korean coast in 1871 further convinced the Koreans that their country was invulnerable to foreign attack.

It was in the late nineteenth century that Korea's neighbours began to take an active interest in developments on the peninsula – Japan, eagerly seeking overseas markets for its new industries, was anxious to prevent the domination of Korea by any nation other than itself. Clashes between Japanese survey vessels and the Koreans were eventually resolved, with the signing of a Treaty of Peace and Amity between Japan and Korea in 1876, which led to the opening of the ports of Pusan and Inch'ŏn to foreign vessels. Other foreign nations were quick to demand similar concessions, and a treaty with the United States in 1882 was followed by agreements with Great Britain, Germany, France and Italy.

The accession to the throne of the young King Kojong and

the retirement of the Taewŏn'gun led to a small measure of reform in Korea. The king and his queen, Min, were eager to obtain information about foreign countries, and to find a way to accept the benefits of modernization without falling prey to the foreign nations that sought to control Korea. The Chinese government still wanted to keep Korea in its traditional vassal relationship, and resented Japanese interference in what it regarded as its own sphere of influence. Russia had been demanding, without success, formal relations with Korea since the 1860s in its quest for warm-water ports in the Far East. A treaty was negotiated and ratified in 1886.

An army revolt in 1882 gave the first clear sign of the rivalry among neighbouring nations to gain control over Korea. As the rebellion got out of control, the Taewŏn'gun was recalled to rule the country. The Chinese moved swiftly to kidnap the Taewŏn'gun and send him to China; Queen Min was restored to power, supported by a strong Chinese military presence in Seoul. However, China's ability to support and protect Korea was diminished by its own struggle to maintain its sovereignty in the face of western encroachment.

There quickly followed an attempted coup by pro-Japanese reformists assisted by Japan. They captured the king and announced the formation of a new government and the instigation of sweeping reforms. The coup ended in failure after just three days as the Chinese military presence in Seoul proved too strong for the pro-Japanese faction to overcome. Both Japan and China agreed to withdraw their troops from Korea and give each other prior notice of intent to station them there in the future.

The Tonghak rebellion in the closing years of the nineteenth century proved to be the catalyst for the final showdown between China and Japan. Farmers' protests at intolerable living conditions, punitive taxes and inequitable land distribution erupted into a popular uprising which threatened the existence of the government in Seoul. Many of the rebel leaders were adherents of Tonghak (Eastern Learning), a new religion which had appeared in 1860 and which called for new values appropriate to modern conditions.

The government's initial response had been to arrest and execute the leaders. The news that the rebels were marching on Seoul caused panic in the capital, and foreign warships were ordered into the port of Inch'ŏn to protect foreign residents in Seoul. Reports that the rebels were beginning to form an army prompted the government to ask the Chinese for help – the Japanese responded by sending troops into Korea under the pretext of protecting the Japanese legation.

Although Japan's declaration of war on China was ostensibly to repel Chinese aggression, Japan's decisive victory in the Sino-Japanese War helped it to consolidate the foothold it had already gained in Korea. The Treaty of Shimonoseki in 1895 proclaimed Korean independence from China and gave Japan a free hand on the peninsula. With Chinese influence gone, Japan began to make demands on Korea and obtained a series of agreements which virtually placed Korea under Japanese rule.

Japan gained the rights to build telegraph systems and railways in Korea, all ports on the south-west coast were opened to Japanese vessels, and a treaty of military alliance between the two countries ensured a source of supplies for the Japanese army. Under Japanese supervision, the government, judiciary and education systems were reformed. Japanese advisors were appointed to every government ministry and the Korean military was placed under Japanese control.

The anti-Japanese faction in Korea gained some comfort from the fact that pressure from western nations, including Russia, had forced the Japanese to return the Liaotung peninsula, taken by them after the war, to Chinese control. Queen Min now began to look to Russia as a possible ally against the Japanese. With Russian support, the Koreans grew bolder and dismissed pro-Japanese officials from the court. In October 1895, however, Japanese troops ransacked the royal palace, murdered Queen Min and captured the king. They then proceeded to install a pro-Japanese government headed by King Kojong, despite protests from the Koreans.

The following year, the Russians captured the king and took him to the Russian legation, thus depriving the Japanese of a legitimate head for their government. The formation of a pro-Russian government gave the Koreans a few years of freedom. In an attempt to assert the sovereignty of Korea, the king changed his title to emperor, and the name of the country to Taehan Cheguk (the Korean Empire).

The Independence Association, formed around this time by a group of US-educated young men, aimed to reassert Korean independence and called on the government to sever ties with Russia. The Association, led by Sŏ Jae-p'il and Syngman Rhee, published Korea's first modern newspaper and raised funds for the Independence Arch, which still stands in the western suburbs of Seoul. The government quickly became alarmed at the group's radical activities, and the leaders of the Association were arrested or exiled.

In 1904, Japan declared war on Russia and sent troops into Korea despite the Korean government's declaration of neutrality. The defeat of Russia in 1905 removed from the scene the only nation that had dared to oppose Japan's aim of supremacy in Korea. The Treaty of Portsmouth, signed between Japan and Russia, recognized Japan's dominant political, economic and military interests in Korea, and gave Japan total control over Korea's foreign relations. All diplomatic relations were to be handled by the Japanese. Japanese diplomats would look after the interests of Koreans overseas, Japan would take the responsibility for fulfilling all the provisions of existing treaties between Korea and other nations, and Japan would appoint a resident-general to work with the Korean emperor, and serve as the ultimate authority on Korea's foreign affairs. The Korean army was disbanded.

This move prompted little response or criticism from other nations. Many felt that the Japanese were merely attempting to help a backward nation whose repeated failures to implement political and economic reforms could, ultimately, affect the stability of the whole region. Although Emperor Kojong sent secret envoys to plead Korea's case in the United States and at the international peace conference in The Hague in 1907, the envoys, who had no right to international representation, were not allowed to address the conference. Their private lobbying was sympathetically received but did not result in action.

In 1910, Japan moved to formalize its annexation of Korea through an official agreement, signed by the Japanese resident-general and the Korean prime minister. Under this annexation treaty, the emperor 's status was to be reduced to that of a king, the country's name was to be changed to 'Chosen' (the Japanese pronunciation of 'Chosŏn'), and all existing treaties between Korea and other nations were declared null and void. King Kojong was forced to abdicate, and his second son, Sunjong, became the twenty-seventh and last king of the Yi dynasty. The establishment of a governor-general in Korea to act as agent for the Japanese government brought Korean independence to an end.

The Japanese colonial period (1910–45) is still remembered with great bitterness by older Koreans. It was a period in which the Japanese robbed the Koreans of their independence and political freedom, attempted to eradicate their national identity and culture, and deprived hundreds of thousands of Koreans of their means of living.

Under the new administration, Japanese officials enjoyed a virtual monopoly of the higher administrative posts; Koreans were appointed only to lower offices. The administration was headed by the governor-general, who exercised almost complete power over the government, judiciary and police. He maintained a tight rein over political activities through the secret police and Japanese army, and quickly curbed any signs of dissent or unrest.

Before the annexation in 1910, the Japanese had already taken steps to allow Japanese nationals freely to purchase land in Korea, and had also enacted currency reforms to facilitate transactions between Korea and Japan. The number of Japanese in Korea rose from 20,000 in 1897 to 170,000 in 1910; the Japanese immigrants took over fishing, lumber and mining rights on the peninsula, and obtained communications and railway concessions.

From 1910 onwards, Japanese control over the Korean economy tightened. A land survey was conducted, under which landowners had to register their land with the authorities. Many Korean farmers, either ignorant of the new law or simply illiterate, lost their land to Japanese settlers. While it cannot be denied that the steps taken by the Japanese to develop the Korean economy did create a modern industrial infrastructure for Korea and greatly improved the rural economy, the policy had the ultimate aim of creating an economy which could complement that of Japan, under Japanese ownership and management. The development of industry, communications and transportation on the peninsula served mainly to support the Japanese economy and, later in the colonial period, the Japanese military.

The loss of their independence was perhaps the single most important factor in creating the Koreans' sense of nationhood. Resistance to Japanese rule was constant and bitter. At the end of World War I, the Koreans were given new hope by the American president Woodrow Wilson's endorsement of the principle of self-determination. The idea that the manner in which a nation is governed should be decided by its people seemed strikingly relevant to Korea. Resistance workers saw an opportunity to focus world attention on Korea's plight and force Japan to abandon its colonial rule, and planned nationwide demonstrations to mark the occasion of King Kojong's funeral.

More than two million Koreans took part in the nationwide demonstrations on 1 March 1919, during which their leaders read a declaration of independence and called on Japan to withdraw voluntarily from Korea. They proclaimed to the world that Korea had been annexed against the wishes of its people, and declared that Korea had the right to exist as a free and independent nation.

The Japanese reacted violently. More than 6,500 demonstrators were killed, over 15,000 were injured, and more than 46,000 were arrested for their part in the peaceful demonstrations. Although the movement was a failure in that it did not win Korea's freedom, it gave the Koreans a strong sense of national identity and showed the Japanese that the Koreans would not accept rule by force. Many of the independence movement's leaders fled overseas to establish resistance movements in Manchuria, Siberia, the United States and China. A provisional government in exile, led by Syngman Rhee, was established in Shanghai, and drew up a constitution based on a presidential form of government, with an elected legislature and freedom of speech, religion, association, press and petition.

Japan's assimilation policy was applied to the Koreans from 1937 until the end of their rule in Korea. The policy aimed to wipe out Korean culture and make the Koreans think, talk and act like native Japanese. Accordingly, Korean-language newspapers and magazines were banned, the use of the Korean language was prohibited in offices, businesses and schools, and Koreans were forced to take Japanese names and worship at Shinto shrines. The Korean flag and traditional Korean dress were outlawed, and members of the Korean Language Society were imprisoned on charges of fomenting unrest.

In 1931, Japan had declared war on Manchuria; in 1937, the war with China began. Korea assumed a new importance for the Japanese as a strategic base and source of supplies for the war effort. Improved agricultural techniques and better irrigation had boosted yields, and between 1917 and 1938 Korean rice exports to Japan rose more than tenfold, reaching 50 million bushels. Korea became a major supplier of rice for Japan, while the Koreans themselves faced food shortages. Cattle were requisitioned and all metal implements confiscated for the munitions factories. While the Japanese prospered, the Koreans' standard of living deteriorated and thousands of Korean farmers left their land and moved to Manchuria or Japan.

The Koreans' situation worsened further after Japan entered World War II. Hundreds of thousands of Korean men were drafted into the Japanese army or taken to Japan for forced labour in mines and factories. Tens of thousands of young Korean girls were also drafted into the Japanese army as 'comfort girls', nursing the Japanese wounded by day and providing sexual favours for the Japanese soldiers at night. By the end of the war, more than two and a half million Koreans were engaged in forced labour in Korea and a further 724,000 had been taken to Japan.

During the course of the war, the Allies had made several pledges that, once the war was over, Korea would become free and independent 'in due course'. When Korea was liberated from Japanese colonial rule on 15 August 1945, it seemed that Korea would at last become a sovereign nation in its own right.

When Japan surrendered, the Allies decided to split the

Korean peninsula into two zones, under Soviet control in the north and American control in the south, as a temporary arrangement until elections could take place and a Korean government could be formed. This 'temporary arrangement' led to a division of Korea which has lasted to the present day.

In December 1945, the United States, the United Kingdom, the People's Republic of China and the USSR agreed among themselves to place Korea under a five-year, United Nations-supervised trusteeship which would help the Koreans to prepare for independence. This news outraged the Koreans, who staged violent demonstrations against the idea of another five years of foreign administration. In spite of this, an American–Soviet Joint Commission was formed in 1946 to consult with political parties and social organizations in Korea, and prepare for the establishment of a provisional government. However, meetings through 1946 and 1947 failed to produce any results, and the prospect of integrating the two zones seemed remote.

Between 1945 and 1948, the southern half of the Korean peninsula was administered by the US Military Government. Despite the intense political activity and rapid formation of political organizations, both communist and democratic, after liberation, the Military Government did not recognize any Korean political authority. The Americans placed Koreans in charge of the national administration, with US advisors to assist them, and set up administrative, judiciary and legislative branches of government, which then assumed the normal responsibilities of a national government.

This period saw a rapid hardening of the political and ideological division between north and south. Korean conservatives who did not wish to live in a Soviet-style system migrated to the south, where the military government favoured the establishment of a right-wing administration, while communist and left-wing party sympathizers moved to the northern part of the peninsula.

The problem of the reunification of the peninsula was put before the United Nations (UN) in 1947, and it was agreed that UN-supervised general elections should be held on the peninsula in May 1948. In the event, however, the UN commission was denied access to the northern half of Korea and the elections took place in the south only. A constituent assembly was formed, with 100 seats reserved for future delegates from the north, should the situation improve at a later date.

THE FIRST REPUBLIC (1948–60)

The new state was designated Taehan Min'guk (the Republic of Korea – ROK), and a new Constitution was promulgated in July 1948, one month before the formal foundation of the nation. Syngman Rhee was elected the first president of the Republic of Korea, and the ROK government was declared by the UN General Assembly to be the sole legitimate government on the Korean peninsula. The response from the north was swift; within weeks the communists announced the establishment of the Democratic People's Republic of Korea (DPRK).

In the months that followed, most of the Soviet and American troops withdrew from the peninsula, and the US government made provision for aid to be supplied to the Republic of Korea to assist in the development of its economy and the training of its armed forces.

At dawn on 25 June 1950, North Korean armed forces invaded the Republic of Korea. They took the capital, Seoul, three days later. In response to the UN's condemnation of the aggression and its call for military and other assistance for the ROK, sixteen nations sent troops to the peninsula as members of the UN forces under General Douglas MacArthur. In September 1950, UN forces recaptured Seoul after an amphibious landing behind enemy lines at Inch'ŏn, and pushed back up to the 38th parallel.

The entry into the war in November of 30 divisions of a Chinese 'volunteer' army in support of the North Koreans forced the UN forces to pull back, and Seoul fell once more. By May of the following year, the battle had been taken back again to the 38th parallel, and truce talks began that summer, while the fighting continued. The signing of an armistice treaty in July 1953 left the boundary between the two nations roughly where it had been three years previously, but this time with a 4-kilometre-wide strip of no-man's-land (the Demilitarized Zone) as a buffer between north and south.

Shortly after the armistice was signed, the US and ROK governments concluded a Mutual Security Treaty, which became the cornerstone of the United States' military commitment in South Korea.

At the end of the war, the Republic of Korea faced various problems. With only an armistice signed rather than a peace treaty, there was still the threat of war with the north. The division of the country at the 38th parallel in 1945 had left the north with most of the nation's industry and what limited natural resources the peninsula possesses, while the south had the bulk of the agricultural land. The devastation caused by war had obliterated the attempts made since 1945 to build an economic structure in the south; farmers were leaving their ruined land for the cities, and social and economic problems were intensified by large numbers of war widows, refugees and homeless people.

Despite the nation's mounting economic and social problems in the immediate postwar era, President Rhee appeared to be preoccupied with consolidating his own power base and planning for the reunification of the peninsula on his own terms. Rhee's increasingly authoritarian and dictatorial style of government, together with his railroading of amendments to the Constitution and other laws to prolong his term of office, led to rising popular discontent with the government. The blatant rigging of the 1960 presidential election sparked off violent demonstrations and clashes between citizens, students and the police, and the discovery of the body of a student murdered by the police touched off massive student demonstrations on 19 April 1960. As the demonstrations spread through the country, the government declared martial law.

In a scenario that was to be parallelled in the democracy movement of 1987, it was the support of the middle classes for the student demonstrators that gave them their victory. In the face of continuing demonstrations by students and ordinary citizens alike, President Rhee resigned on 27 April 1960, and preparations were made for a general election.

THE SECOND REPUBLIC (1960–1)
Following the collapse of the Rhee regime, the Constitution was amended to provide for a parliamentary form of government, headed by a prime minister with a figurehead president. The former opposition Democratic Party replaced Rhee's Liberal Party as the ruling party, and its leader, Chang Myŏn, became the first prime minister of the Second Republic.

The new government was inexperienced and proved weak and inconsistent in its handling of the political and economic problems facing the country, and Chang Myŏn failed to win the support of the people. The students, elated by their role in toppling the Rhee regime, continued to be politically active; their demands for direct negotiations with North Korean students and their plans to march to the border for direct talks echoed calls from newly established left-wing groups for contacts with the north. The government was unable to respond to the situation or formulate a clear policy of its own.

In the end, it was the military that took action. In post war South Korea, military academies offered opportunities for good education, administrative and technological training through contacts with the United States, exposure to western management skills, and access to modern communications. The graduates were typically bright, nationalistic and well disciplined, and, therefore, it has been argued, best placed to take over the government. As their disenchantment with the government and fears of a left-wing uprising grew, plans for a coup began to take shape.

On 16 May 1961, armed forces led by Major-General Park Chung-hee overthrew the Chang administration and seized power in a bloodless coup. The military junta declared martial law, dissolved the National Assembly, imposed press censorship, suspended party political activities and took over the reins of government. Yun Po-sŏn, who had served as president in the Second Republic, was persuaded to stay on in that capacity. The Supreme Council for National Reconstruction was established as the new legislative body, to be headed by Major-General Park until such time as power could be transferred to a civilian government.

The six-point pledge made to the people by the new administration expressed a positive and uncompromising opposition to communism, respect for the United Nations Charter, a desire for close ties with the United States and other free nations, a promise to eradicate corruption, and a commitment to develop the economy and pursue unification. A transfer to civilian rule would be effected once the revolutionary mission had been accomplished.

The presidential system of government was revived in December 1962, and new political parties began to form early the following year. However, the purging of some 2,600 politicians in 1962 reduced the number of experienced men on the scene. Prominent among the new political parties was the Democratic Republican Party (DRP), organized by the coup leaders while political activities were (in theory) suspended.

The opposition was split into half a dozen small parties. Their inability to compromise and unite against the DRP proved to be their downfall. The opposition parties fielded several candidates in the 1963 presidential election; their failure to offer a single opposition candidate undoubtedly cost them the election. As it was, Park Chung-hee retired from the army, declared his candidacy and won with 42.6 per cent of all votes cast.

THE THIRD REPUBLIC (1963-72)

The transition from military to quasi-civilian government was completed with the holding of general elections in November 1963. Once again, opposition disunity ensured a victory for the ruling party. President Park thus began a sixteen-year rule which was characterized by rapid economic development and broadening diplomatic relations, most notably the normalization of relations with Japan. However, it was also characterized by an increasingly authoritarian, centralized system of government.

President Park's first priority was to build a strong nation, capable of withstanding the continuing threat from North Korea. It was his belief that an increase in the nation's standard of living would protect it from the possibility of communist insurgence. At this stage of the Republic's history, the development of democratic political systems was, in his view, of secondary importance. Park therefore implemented the first in a series of five-year economic development plans which were to transform the South Korean economy (see: The Economy – General Overview).

The early years of Park's rule were marked by an increase in diplomatic activities; the number of countries having diplomatic relations with the Republic rose from 17 in 1962 to 77 ten years later. Talks with Japan, begun by the military junta in 1961, continued through the early 1960s, despite vehement opposition at home. The anti-government, anti-Japanese protests led to a brief spell of martial law in the summer of 1963, but did not prevent the establishment of full diplomatic and economic relations in 1965, twenty years after Japan's colonial rule ended. Japan paid the Republic of Korea an indemnity of US$300 million for the harm suffered during the colonial rule, and extended a further US$300 million in long-term loans to assist in the implementation of South Korea's economic development programme.

Relations with the United States were boosted by the contribution made by South Korea to the American war effort in Vietnam. Once again, there was strong opposition at home. A breakthrough was achieved in inter-Korean relations, with a joint statement issued on 4 July 1972 declaring the opening of talks aiming to achieve peaceful reunification (see: Relations with North Korea).

Like Rhee before him, Park amended the constitution to prolong his term of office beyond the two terms therein allowed, and was re-elected in 1967 and 1971. Key figures in the national opposition at this time were Kim Young-sam and Kim Dae-jung, who have continued to exert a strong influence over the South Korean political scene since those days.

The rapidly deteriorating situation in Vietnam, combined with changes in the United States' policy towards Asia (typified by the ping-pong diplomacy with China in the early 1970s) and mounting anti-government feeling at home, prompted President Park to declare a state of national emergency in December 1971. Martial law was declared ten months later.

The president asserted that strong measures were needed to cope with the critical international situation and to strengthen the military preparedness of the nation. Moreover, he maintained that it was essential that he be able to exercise the special powers granted under martial law to cope with crises that might arise as a result of international developments. The president also justified his actions on the grounds that institutional reform of the nation's political system was needed – once martial law was declared, the National Assembly was dissolved and all political activities were suspended.

The draft constitution presented to the nation by President Park allowed him to be re-elected indefinitely, not by direct popular vote, but indirectly, via an electoral college – the National Conference for Unification. The president also gained the right to appoint one-third of the members of the National Assembly (having lost its majority in the Assembly in the previous elections, this move assured the ruling party of a majority in future elections), and the privilege of exercising emergency powers at will. This Yushin (literally: Revitalizing Reforms) Constitution was adopted in a national referendum on 21 November 1972.

THE FOURTH REPUBLIC (1972-9)

Two years after the adoption of the new Constitution, President Park exercised his newly acquired emergency powers. All activities opposing or criticizing the new Constitution were prohibited, universities were closed and rallies banned, dissidents were jailed and deprived of their civil rights. Despite the restrictions, there was growing opposition to the Park regime and there were increasing calls for the repeal of the Yushin Constitution.

The kidnapping of opposition politician Kim Dae-jung in Tokyo by the Korean Central Intelligence Agency (KCIA) heightened the tensions between the ruling and opposition parties. Kim, who had been actively campaigning against the Park regime in America and Japan, was taken back to Korea and imprisoned. An assassination attempt against the president, in which his wife was killed, and the public outrage expressed at this, appeared to soften Park's stance. He agreed to hold a national referendum on the Constitution, and promised to resign should the vote go against him. His rule was upheld, but the anti-government protests continued.

By the time that President Park ran for his sixth term of office in 1978, South Korea's political problems were reaching a critical point. In March 1979, former president Yun Po-sŏn and Kim Dae-jung were again placed under arrest. The opposition New Democratic Party (NDP) appointed Kim Young-sam as its new president, but Kim's anti-government activities prompted moves to expel him from the Assembly and suspend him from the presidency of the NDP. The subsequent demonstrations against the Park regime were the most serious since 1960. South Korea's growing political crisis was being compounded by economic gloom – the oil shock, a disastrous crop failure and runaway inflation (see: The Economy).

On 26 October 1979, Park Chung-hee was assassinated by the Director of the KCIA, Kim Chae-gyu, who later said that he killed the president to put an end to Park's one-man rule. Premier Choi Kyu-ha was immediately sworn in as acting president, and was subsequently elected president by the electoral college. The ruling DRP appointed Kim Jong-p'il as its new party president. Political prisoners released at this time included Kim Dae-jung; his reappearance on the political stage set the scene for the renewed rivalry among the Three Kims – Kim Jong-p'il (leader of the DRP), Kim Dae-jung and Kim Young-sam, who vied for supremacy within the opposition NDP.

In the period of political and social confusion that followed the assassination, a group of junior generals, led by General Chun Doo-hwan, staged what amounted to a coup within the military, by accusing their superiors of complicity in the president's death. While Choi fulfilled his role as acting president, pending a debate on and the revision of the Constitution, Chun exercised power behind the scenes, through the Special Committee for National Security Measures, which he chaired. The committee moved quickly to ban all political activity and close party headquarters, dissolve the National Assembly, and shut down the nation's universities and colleges. Once again, the students rose up to protest, demanding the lifting of martial law, the withdrawal of the military, and democratization.

Demonstrations calling for a new Constitution, an end to martial law, and the resignation of Chun as acting director of the KCIA culminated with a rally of some 72,000 citizens in Seoul on 15 May 1980. The government's response was to extend the limited martial law throughout the country and arrest the Three Kims. News of Kim Dae-jung's arrest sparked off demonstrations in Kwangju, the provincial capital of South Chŏlla Province and Kim's stronghold. The protests escalated into a full civil uprising, in which the people of Kwangju took control of the city and fought the police. The movement was crushed by paratroopers on 22 May, leaving hundreds dead and wounded.

With the resignation of President Choi Kyu-ha on 16 August, a movement to elect Chun president got under way. Chun, who had recently retired from the army, was duly elected president by the electoral college, and was inaugurated on 3 March 1981. Kim Dae-jung was indicted, both for anti-state, pro-communist activities and for allegedly inciting riots in Kwangju, and was sentenced to death.

THE FIFTH REPUBLIC (1981–8)

The aims of the new administration were publicly stated as the realization of democracy, the construction of a welfare state, the attainment of justice, and the implementation of educational reforms. The new Constitution guaranteed a peaceful transfer of power at the end of President Chun's seven-year term, by prohibiting him from standing for re-election. Furthermore, the incumbent president was not allowed to benefit from any changes made to the election law during his term of office.

The Fifth Republic began with some reforms – the four-hour nightly curfew was lifted, restrictions on overseas travel were eased, and (Japanese-style) school uniforms were abolished. Colleges and universities were reopened, and freedom of political activity was declared. More than 5,000 political prisoners were freed and the death sentence imposed on Kim Dae-jung was commuted to life imprisonment. In May 1984, the Council for the Promotion of Democracy was formed, and the following year, the opposition New Korea Democratic Party (NKDP) was inaugurated.

The outstanding achievements of the Chun administration were winning the right to host the 1986 Asian Games and the 1988 Summer Olympics and the resumption of talks with North Korea, which, though making little real progress, did result in exchange visits by arts troupes and by family members separated since the Korean War (see: Relations with North Korea). The end of Chun's administration also saw the first peaceful transfer of power in the nation's history. The economic success story which had its roots in the early 1960s continued, culminating in the recording of the nation's first significant trade and current account surpluses in 1986.

As economic development continued apace, there were increasing calls for political reform and democratic developments to match the economic gains. Students and the opposition were increasingly critical of the slow progress towards democratization and began to demand direct presidential elections. Although President Chun agreed to negotiations with the opposition on the issue of amending the Constitution and the electoral laws, disunity among the opposition and the inability to reach a consensus prompted him to announce that the laws would not be reformed before the 1987 presidential elections took place.

Discontent at this announcement and dismay at the nomination of retired general Roh T'ae-woo as the ruling Democratic Justice Party's presidential nominee produced a violent reaction. As in 1960, the middle classes joined the students in their condemnation of what was perceived to be a move to prolong rule by the military for another seven years. In the face of mounting social unrest, Roh suddenly announced that he would make his candidacy conditional on the implementation of democratic reforms, including the holding of direct presidential elections and the release of political prisoners.

In making this move, Roh was clearly gambling on the inability of the opposition to field a single candidate for the race. It was a gamble that paid off: unable to decide which of them should represent the opposition, both Kim Dae-jung and Kim Young-sam entered the race. With the opposition vote split, Roh won the election with just 37 per cent of the vote. The peaceful transfer of power from Chun to Roh was the first in the Republic of Korea's history, and was a landmark in the nation's progress towards democracy. Although the Roh administration was, at least in its early days, quasi-civilian in that many of its members were retired military officers, the prospect of another military coup within the Republic faded with the progress made towards a more democratic system of government.

THE SIXTH REPUBLIC (1988–93)

Despite continuing allegations by the opposition that the presidential elections were rigged, Roh T'ae-woo was inaugurated as president of the Republic of Korea in February 1988. The revised constitution limited him to a single, five-year term of office.

The Roh administration is likely to be remembered for its accomplishments in the field of diplomacy rather than for its economic achievements. The phase of economic restructuring into which the Republic entered after the 1988 Olympics has been associated with a period of trade and current account deficits, high inflation, and sluggish exports (see: The Economy – General Overview). Dissatisfaction with the ruling party's handling of the economy was cited as a major concern for voters in both the National Assembly and presidential elections in 1992.

However, President Roh's 'Nordpolitik', or opening up of relations with former communist nations, has proved immensely successful – diplomatic relations were established with the (then) Soviet Union in 1990 and with the People's Republic of China in 1992. The latter years of the Roh administration also saw talks between the North and South Korean prime ministers, and the signing of an Agreement on Reconciliation, Non-Aggression, Exchanges, and Cooperation in

December 1991 (see: Relations with North Korea).

The failure of the Democratic Justice Party (DJP) to win a majority in the National Assembly elections in April 1988 gave the opposition the power to launch an investigation into allegations of corruption and abuses of power made against former President Chun and members of his administration. (Such was the groundswell of public feeling against Chun that he was unable to fulfil his dream of attending the opening ceremony of the 1988 Olympics.) Chun's brother was put on trial and sentenced, more than a dozen other relatives were arrested, and Chun himself was forced to testify before the nation and make a public apology for his misdoings, before handing over his wealth and going into exile in the Korean countryside.

The DJP regained its majority in the Assembly in February 1990 through a surprise merger with two of the nation's opposition parties. The ruling party merged with the Reunification Democratic Party (RDP), led by Kim Young-sam, and the New Democratic Republican Party (NDRP), led by Kim Jong-p'il, to form the Democratic Liberal Party (DLP). The new party was headed by President Roh, with the two Kims and Park Tae-joon serving as co-chairmen. The merger underscores the fact that, in Korean politics, policies matter far less than personalities; only a few former RDP law-makers refused to join their leader within the ruling party.

The move was seen by many observers as a bid for power by RDP leader Kim Young-sam, who joined the ruling party in the hope of gaining its nomination for the 1992 presidential election. His bid was successful in June 1992.

For a while, the merger left the other opposition leader, Kim Dae-jung, and his Party for Peace and Democracy out in the cold. However, mergers with the New Democratic Union and the Democratic Party in 1991 brought Kim back into the political arena as co-chairman of the Democratic Party with Lee Ki-taek. The party's policies were close to those of the other parties – supporting unification, a free market economy, and democratization – but with greater rhetoric in its opposition to corruption, big business, and trade pressure from advanced nations, and support for the poor and underprivileged.

Public disillusionment with the ruling DLP's economic management and its intra-party squabbles robbed the DLP of its majority once again in the 1992 National Assembly elections, although the party was finally able to squeeze ahead of the opposition in the Assembly by recruiting a few pro-government independents. (The fact that National Assembly members almost always vote along party lines makes having even the slimmest majority a basis for power.)

The 1992 National Assembly elections saw a notable event in the emergence of the United People's Party (UPP), an opposition party established by the honorary chairman of the Hyundai Group, Chung Ju-yung. The tycoon had been openly critical of the government and its policies, and the feud which subsequently developed between the Hyundai group and the government in 1992 (see: The Chaebŏl) was said by many to have its roots in Chung's political aspirations.

The UPP's platform was the fair and progressive reform of politics, the promotion of economic exchanges with North Korea, the realization of economic justice through the promotion of national welfare, and the creation of a clean environment. Chung was particularly critical of the government's economic policies, and claimed that he would rescue the country from danger and turn the economy around, just as he had built up the Hyundai empire.

The birth of the UPP and of the Saehan (New Korea) Party, with which it later merged, was made possible by growing public mistrust of and disenchantment with the 'old politics' typified by Kim Dae-jung and Kim Young-sam. Less than two months after its formation, the UPP won 24 seats in the National Assembly elections, after which Chung declared that he would run for the presidency.

The run-up to the presidential elections in December 1992 brought with it some political surprises. In August 1992, President Roh severed his ties with the ruling party and formed a 'neutral' cabinet, in order to ensure fairness in the electoral process. There was speculation that the real reason behind the move was the president's desire to distance himself from Kim Young-sam, who was already flexing his muscles and challenging Roh's authority.

Kim Young-sam won the December election with 42 per cent of the vote; both Kim Dae-jung, who garnered 34 per cent of the vote, and Chung Ju-yung, who took a 16 per cent share of votes cast, retired from politics after the election.

Kim Young-sam represents a new breed of president in South Korea, if not a new generation. He will be the first president of the Republic not to come from a military background, and the first to come from an area other than the ruling party stronghold of North Kyŏngsang Province. The Roh administration achieved much in the fields of democratization and diplomacy – Kim's government will face the task of economic restructuring, and Kim Young-sam will face the challenge of consolidating his position within a party that he joined barely two years before his election as president.

PART TWO

Politics

SOUTH KOREA IN EAST ASIA

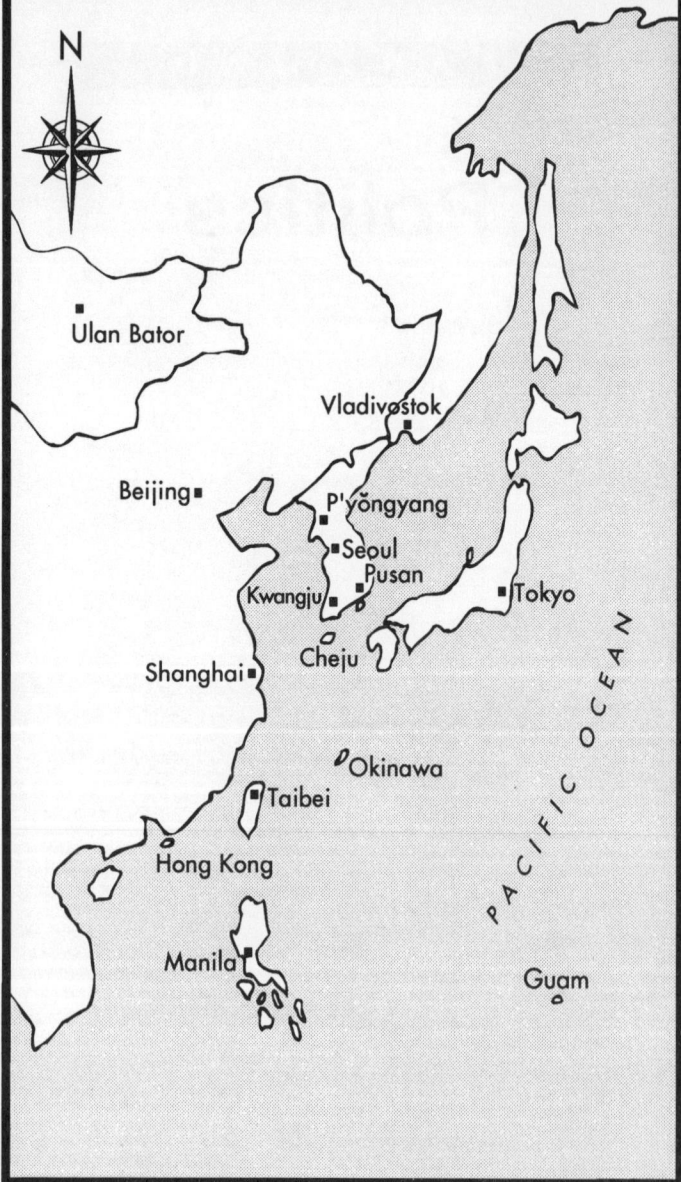

N

- Ulan Bator

- Vladivostok

- Beijing

- P'yŏngyang

- Seoul
- Pusan

- Kwangju

- Tokyo

- Cheju

- Shanghai

- Okinawa

- Taibei

- Hong Kong

- Manila

- Guam

PACIFIC OCEAN

4 Introduction

HISTORY OF SOUTH KOREA'S POLITICAL DEVELOPMENT

The presidential elections of 1988 saw the first peaceful transfer of power within the Republic of Korea in its 40-year history; the presidential elections of 1992 saw the election of the first civilian leader in three decades.

The first three administrations to govern the Republic were all brought to an end by unconstitutional means (see: History). The Syngman Rhee government was toppled by a student revolution in 1960, which was the culmination of public discontent at corruption and abuse of power by the president. A short-lived attempt at parliamentary government failed to get to grips with the nation's social and economic problems, and fell swiftly to a military coup in 1961. The military junta was succeeded by a quasi-civilian, authoritarian, presidential regime, which lasted for eighteen years, until the assassination of President Park Chung-hee in 1979.

Although there were some moves towards democratization during the early years of President Chun Doo-hwan's administration (1981–8), it was in his final full year as president that the Republic of Korea took its first real steps towards a more democratic system of government. Democratic reforms promised by Chun's protégé and the ruling party's presidential candidate, Roh T'ae-woo, paved the way for a revision of the constitution that provided for greater freedoms and direct popular presidential elections.

The first peaceful transfer of power, from Chun Doo-hwan to Roh T'ae-woo, took place in 1988. While falling short of establishing a truly civilian government – Roh and several of his administration's top officials were former army officers – it was a landmark in South Korea's political development.

Although the government's subsequent attempts to create a Japanese-style, mammoth ruling party through the establishment of the Democratic Liberal Party failed when it lost its majority in the 1992 National Assembly elections, the ruling party maintained its grip on power with the success of its candidate, Kim Young-sam, in the 1992 presidential elections.

The year 1992 marked another stage in the transition of Korea's political system. Local elections for municipal and provincial assemblies were held for the first time in 32 years, as a first stage in the decentralization of government. The second two stages – elections for provincial governors and mayors – were postponed until the mid-1990s owing to government concern over the impact that a series of elections would have on the economy.

CHARACTERISTICS OF SOUTH KOREAN POLITICS

Since 1948, South Korean politics have been characterized by a strong, authoritarian leadership, personality-dominated politics, right-wing political tendencies, and brinkmanship.

In the three decades following the establishment of the Republic, Syngman Rhee and Park Chung-hee set the pattern for a *strong, authoritarian leadership* in South Korea. The ambition and vision of these two men prompted them to take all measures, constitutional and otherwise, to prolong their terms of office indefinitely. So strong was the memory of these two regimes that many found it hard to believe that Chun Doo-hwan would honour his commitment to one term in office. The peaceful transfer of power from Chun to Roh in 1988, while marred by subsequent allegations of and investigations into corruption and abuse of power by Chun, set a new pattern for Korean politics.

The change in 1992 to a government led by a non-military man is seen by many as an irrevocable step away from the military-dominated politics of the past. The fading 'threat from the north' which gave justification to authoritarian policies in the past, greater political stability and a higher standard of living in the south, together with the worldwide trend away from communism should mean that the chance of further military intervention in Korean politics is receding.

The influence exercised by Kim Young-sam and Kim Dae-jung over the past thirty years illustrates the fact that Korean politics focus more on *personalities* than policies. The strong allegiance felt by party members to their leader, and the loyalty to personality rather than platform, was amply illustrated by the fact that, when Kim Young-sam switched over to the ruling party in February 1990, only eight of his party's members refused to join him in the Democratic Liberal Party.

Criticism of slow progress in South Korea's political development has often focused on the need for a new breed of politicians, to break way from the 'old-style' thinking of men like the two Kims. However, Kim Young-sam's victory in the 1992 elections ensured his place at the forefront of South Korean politics for a further five years. Kim Dae-jung's defeat forced him to resign from the National Assembly and announce his retirement from politics.

Given the uncompromising anti-communist stance adopted by South Korea's leaders in the early years of the Republic and the continuing absence of a truly left-wing party on the political scene, there tends to be little to choose between the policies of the ruling and opposition parties. All the major parties can be classified as *right-wing*, supporting democratization, a free market economy, and unification with North Korea.

South Korean politics continue to be characterized by lack of compromise and *brinkmanship*, which in turn have created a poor opinion of politicians among the electorate. Fisticuffs and schoolroom behaviour in the National Assembly, reports of financial scandals and pocket-lining, and allegations of vote rigging in the 1992 National Assembly elections were a significant factor in the poor voter turnout for them. Some cited this as an important factor in the strong showing made by the newest party, the United People's Party, which promised a fresh approach to politics.

PRESSURE GROUPS

The late 1980s and early 1990s have seen an increase in the formation of pressure groups, and the activities of ruling and opposition politicians alike have come under close public scrutiny. Among the most vocal pressure groups are the students, who continue in the tradition of their *sŏnbae* (predecessors at school), acting as the conscience of the nation and drawing public attention to what they believe are the political and economic evils of the day. Idealistic rather than realistic or practical, they continue to attract foreign media attention to their cause, be it opposition to Japanese colonialism and American trade pressure or support for democratization and reunification (see: Education).

However, past experience has taught that, unless supported by the middle classes, as happened in 1960 and 1987, the students are no more than an irritation. Support for their cause has waned following the death of seven riot policemen on a Pusan university campus, and the torturing to death of a student suspected of being a government spy. It is always worth remembering that, in many cases, the student radicals of the 1960s are the civil servants and businessmen of today.

Other important pressure groups are the farmers (especially concerning the GATT Uruguay Round negotiations), the newly empowered labour unions, and foreign governments. However, the importance of the military, a dominant pressure group in the 1960s and 1970s, is now fading.

5 The Constitution

The Constitution of the Republic of Korea was adopted on 12 July 1948, and has undergone nine revisions since then, the most recent being in 1988. The current version of the Constitution was the result of discussion and negotiation between the ruling and opposition parties; the previous eight amendments were passed unilaterally by the ruling party of the time. The most recent revision also differed from previous ones in that they were effected with the express intention of prolonging the rule of the incumbent president.

The content of the current Constitution, which took effect with the inauguration of President Roh T'ae-woo on 25 February 1988, was, to a great extent, the outcome of the democracy movement which took place in South Korea in 1987. Debate on constitutional reform began in 1986, with the ruling party favouring a cabinet system, and the opposition parties lobbying for direct presidential elections. However, in April 1987, President Chun announced that the discussions were to be postponed until after the Summer Olympics in 1988 – by which time another presidential term would have begun. The violent demonstrations which followed this announcement led to a promise of democratic reform by the ruling party's candidate for the presidential election, Roh T'ae-woo (see: History; Politics – Introduction).

Final agreement on a draft revision was reached in September 1987, and the new Constitution was approved by the National Assembly and passed in a national referendum the following month. Key features of the Constitution of the Sixth Republic are:

- a return to the direct presidential elections, suspended in 1971. The president is to be elected by the people, to serve a single, five-year term of office, and serves as the chief executive and the head of state of the Republic of Korea (see also: The Executive). Re-election is prohibited by law, and any subsequent amendments to this provision will not apply to the incumbent president.

- the curtailment of presidential powers. Although the presidential system of government is upheld by the Constitution, the powers of the chief executive have been reduced (in comparison with those exercised during the Park and Chun administrations), while the powers of the National Assembly have been increased. The president no longer has the power to dissolve the National Assembly, but the Assembly does have the right to recommend the removal of the prime minister and the members of the State Council, either as a group or individually. The president's general power to issue emergency decrees has been withdrawn; he may issue extraordinary orders with the power of law relating to the budget and finance only. The National Assembly now has the power to audit and inspect affairs of state.

- better protection of human and civil rights. The basic law provides for greater freedom of assembly, association and speech, and also gives workers the right of free association, collective bargaining and industrial action.

- enhanced separation of powers. The revision aims to clarify and strengthen the divisions between the administrative, legal and executive branches of government.

- ban on press censorship. Regulations governing the establishment of mass media outlets such as newspapers and magazines are eased under the new law.

- guarantee of the political neutrality of the armed forces.

6 The Executive

The president of the Republic of Korea is elected by universal, direct, secret ballot to serve a single, five-year term of office. The president serves as the head of state in domestic and foreign affairs, and also heads the executive branch of the government.

The president is the commander-in-chief of the armed forces and chairman of the State Council (Cabinet). He has the power to appoint or dismiss the prime minister, cabinet ministers and other senior officials; he may proclaim martial law, has the power to grant amnesty, and to commute or restore civil rights, as prescribed by law. In addition to the powers he exercises, the president has clearly defined responsibilities. He is bound to safeguard the constitution and the independence, territorial integrity and continuity of the state, and also assumes the duty of pursuing the peaceful reunification of the Korean peninsula.

The president issues presidential decrees concerning matters delegated to him by law; issues of key importance to the nation (such as matters relating to national defence and unification) are subject to national referenda.

All citizens who are eligible for election to the National Assembly, and who have reached the age of 40 years or more on the date of the presidential election, are eligible to be elected president. If two or more candidates receive the same number of votes in a presidential election, the matter is put to a vote in an open session of the National Assembly. In the event that only one candidate is presented at the election, he or she cannot be elected unless he or she receives at least one-third of the total eligible votes.

The prime minister of the Republic of Korea is appointed by the president, with the approval of the National Assembly. The prime minister administers the executive branch of the government and is accountable to the National Assembly for government policy. In his capacity as vice-chairman of the State Council (see below), he advises the president and makes recommendations concerning the appointment or dismissal of State Council members. The prime minister also supervises the administrative activities of the individual ministries.

The most important organization within the executive branch of the government, and the highest policy-making organ in the country, is the State Council or Cabinet. The State Council, which is chaired by the president, with the prime minister serving as vice-chairman, comprises between 15 and 30 members, including the two deputy prime ministers (who concurrently serve as ministers of the Economic Planning Board and the National Unification Board), the heads of the executive ministries, and two ministers of state. Council members are appointed by the president on the prime minister's recommendation, and may serve concurrently as National Assembly members.

Within the Republic of Korea, legislative power is exercised exclusively by the National Assembly. The Constitution requires that the unicameral assembly comprise no fewer than 200 members; currently there are 299, of whom 224 (two-thirds) are elected by popular vote, to serve a four-year term. After the election, the remaining 75 seats are allocated proportionately among the political parties which gained five or more seats, based on the number of elected law-makers per party. One speaker and two vice-speakers are then elected by the Assembly members to serve a two-year term.

There are two types of legislative session, regular and extraordinary. Regular sessions, which last for 100 days, are held once a year. Extraordinary sessions, which last for 30 days, may be convened at the request either of the president or of one-quarter of the National Assembly members.

The Assembly has the power to propose, deliberate, approve or reject bills introduced by members of the Assembly, the president or the administration. The Assembly also deliberates and approves the annual and supplementary budgets, which are drawn up and submitted to it at least 90 days before the beginning of the new fiscal year. Bills passed by the Assembly are sent to the president for promulgation. They may be returned to the Assembly for further consideration should the president object to the content of the bill, but, if passed again with a two-thirds majority, become law in spite of any continuing objections. Bills also automatically become law if not promulgated or returned to the Assembly within fifteen days. However, the president may exercise a veto over new legislation.

Revisions made to the Constitution in the late 1980s strengthened and expanded the Assembly's powers. Members now have the authority to inspect affairs of state and government activities, and approve emergency orders issued by the president. Members also have the right of consent to ratify or reject treaties with foreign countries, and to concur in the declaration of war, the despatch of Korean troops overseas, the stationing of foreign armed forces within the Republic, and the conclusion of peace treaties. The president's powers to take emergency action in times of natural disaster (such as floods or typhoons) or serious fiscal or economic crisis, and to declare martial law in times of war, are subject to the consent of the Assembly. Without that consent, the orders must be rescinded.

The Assembly may impeach the president for violation of the Constitution, or pass a vote of no confidence in the prime minister or members of the State Council. (The dismissal of the prime minister automatically results in the dismissal of all members of the State Council.)

Political groups which comprise more than twenty Assembly members may form a negotiating group within the National Assembly. There are also a number of standing committees, including Legislation and Justice, Foreign Affairs, Home Affairs, Economics and Science, and Commerce and Industry. Special committees are formed as and when it is deemed necessary.

THE PRESIDENTIAL AGENCIES

These are as follows:

- The National Security Council comprises the president, the prime minister, the two deputy prime ministers, the Minister for Foreign Affairs, the Minister for Home Affairs, the Minister of Finance, the Minister of National Defence, the Director of the Agency for National Security Planning (see below), and one standing member. Its function is to discuss all diplomatic, military and domestic policy which relates to national security before it is deliberated upon by the State Council.

- The Agency for National Security Planning, formerly the Korean Central Intelligence Agency, was established to collect information, both within and outside the Republic, in order to plan and coordinate the government's intelligence and security activities. The Agency focuses particularly on information relating to communist espionage and subversive activities, and the director of the Agency is accountable only to the president.

- The Board of Audit and Inspection is an independent watchdog body, which audits and reports on the accounts of central and local government agencies, state-run corporations and related organizations.

THE MINISTRIES
These are as follows:

- The Economic Planning Board (EPB) has responsibility for the overall planning of the economy, the formulation and execution of the national budget, and the administration of inward and foreign investment, research and technical development, and economic cooperation with foreign countries and international organizations. The minister concurrently serves as one of the nation's two deputy prime ministers.

- The Ministry of Agriculture, Forestry and Fisheries administers loans to these three sectors, and handles all related issues, including the marketing of produce, prevention of diseases, and the registration of land.

- The Ministry of Communications handles postal affairs, exchanges, savings, pensions, and national life insurance.

- The Ministry of Construction establishes and coordinates plans for the development and control of national land, the development and renovation of land and water resources, the production of materials, preparation of budgets, and supply of labour for projects including housing, highways, ports and harbours.

- The Ministry of Culture is responsible for all matters relating to culture, the arts, publications and religion.

- The Ministry of Education supervises the formulation of the nation's education policies.

- The Ministry of Energy and Resources has responsibility for the exploration, exploitation, production and importing of energy and resources.

- The Ministry of the Environment formulates and implements policies aimed at preserving the national environment and preventing environmental pollution.

- The Ministry of Finance (MOF) is responsible for the government's financial affairs, including finance-related legislation, currency and foreign exchange, national accounts, control of state-owned properties, taxation and customs. The MOF controls the Office of National Tax Administration, the Office of Monopoly, the Office of Customs Administration, and the Securities and Insurance Bureaux, and directs and supervises the special banks and those in which the government holds the majority share.

- The Ministry of Foreign Affairs has jurisdiction over matters concerning diplomacy, trade and other treaties with foreign nations, international agreements, and the protection of the interests of South Korean nationals abroad.

- The Ministry of Government Administration supervises the administration of the State Council, personnel management of government officials, pensions for public officials, and other matters which are not administered by other central government agencies. The ministry also manages the National Archives.

- The Ministry of Health and Social Affairs deals with issues relating to public health, the prevention of epidemics, hygiene and sanitation, welfare and family planning.

- The Ministry of Home Affairs is responsible for local administration, the management of referenda, the handling of national emergencies, the protection of the lives and property of South Korean nationals, the administration of national registers and the naturalization process. The ministry also supervises the National Police Headquarters.

- The Ministry of Information collects and disseminates information relating to national and international affairs. It also conducts surveys of public opinion and supervises the national media.

- The Ministry of Justice handles prosecutions, penal administration and the prison system, entry to and exit from the Republic, the protection of human rights, and the administration of civil and criminal justice.

- The Ministry of Labour manages and coordinates labour-related affairs, including working conditions, training, social welfare for workers, insurance and labour disputes.

- The Ministry of National Defence handles all aspects of South Korea's military affairs, encompassing the army, navy, air force and homeland reserves.

- The Ministry of Science and Technology promotes the development and application of science and technology, and manages industrial and technical manpower.
- The Ministry of Sports promotes and manages national sports.
- The Ministry of Trade and Industry (MTI) has responsibility for commerce, foreign trade (including import and export regulations), industry, trademarks and patents, and industrial standards. (The Ministry of Trade and Industry merged with the Ministry of Energy in early 1993.)
- The Ministry of Transport has responsibility for land, marine and air transportation as well as tourism. It also supervises the Office of National Railroads and the Korea Maritime and Port Administration.
- The National Unification Board conducts research into issues related to the reunification of the Korean peninsula, and is responsible for national education and public information on these matters. The minister concurrently serves as one of the nation's two deputy prime ministers.

There are, in addition, two ministers of state, one handling national security, foreign and domestic policy, and one with responsibility for social and cultural affairs.

7 Major Political Parties

THE DEMOCRATIC LIBERAL PARTY (DLP)

Inaugurated:	**February 1990**
Party president	**Kim Young-sam**
Seats won in the 1992 National Assembly elections	**149**

The DLP was formed in February 1990 through a merger between the ruling Democratic Justice Party (DJP) and two opposition parties, the Reunification Democratic Party (RDP) and the New Democratic Republican Party (NDRP). This followed a period in which the opposition parties had dominated the National Assembly through a combined majority.

The merger was little more than a marriage of convenience – the ruling party regained its majority in the Assembly, and the former leader of the RDP, Kim Young-sam, ultimately gained the ruling party's nomination for the 1992 presidential elections. In the 1992 National Assembly elections, however, the ruling party lost its majority, winning 149 seats out of a total of 299, but subsequently managed to regain a slight lead by persuading independent law-makers to join the DLP.

Kim Young-sam won the 1992 presidential election with a 42 per cent share of the votes cast, and will serve a five-year term of office, beginning in February 1993.

During the election campaign and immediately following his victory, Mr Kim pledged himself to lead a campaign to cure what he termed the 'Korean maladies' – rampant corruption, social decay and the floundering work ethic.

On the economic front, Kim Young-sam pledged that his

administration would bring inflation down to 3 per cent from the current level of 5 per cent, and would lower bank and market interest rates to a single-digit figure. Investment in research and development would be boosted to 5 per cent of GNP by 1998 from the current level of 3 per cent, the tax system would be reviewed, support for small-and medium-sized businesses would be increased, and the use of real names in financial transactions would be made mandatory.

In order to redress the imbalance between the urban and rural sectors, measures would be implemented to develop farming and fishing towns, and a total of W42 trillion (US$53 billion) would be invested in rural areas over the next decade. The new administration would also oppose the liberalization of rice imports.

Mr Kim promised to make all efforts to halt North Korea's nuclear programme, and to take steps to further reunification, including cross-border exchanges and visits for families separated since the end of the Korean War, exchanges of correspondence, and the creation of an open meeting place at the border village of P'anmunjŏm.

THE DEMOCRATIC PARTY (DP)

Inaugurated	**September 1991**
Executive chairman	**Lee Ki-taek**
Seats won in the 1992 National Assembly elections	**97**

Following the creation of the DLP in February 1990, the opposition Party for Peace and Democracy (PPD), led by Kim Dae-jung, found itself in a weakened and vulnerable position. The PPD therefore merged, first with a dissident group to form the New Democratic Party (NDP), and then with the opposition Democratic Party (DP). The DP was itself only formed in June 1990 by a group of eight law-makers as a protest against the DJP–RDP–NDRP merger. Kim Dae-jung and Lee Ki-taek served as executive co-chairmen of the revamped party.

The DP candidate for the 1992 presidential elections was Kim Dae-jung, who came in second, with 34 per cent of the votes. Following his defeat, Mr Kim announced his resignation from the party and the National Assembly, and his retirement from politics. Mr Lee Ki-taek agreed to serve as executive chairman until a successor to Mr Kim could be elected at the party's national convention in March 1993. Mr Lee was elected representative chairman at the convention.

During his campaign Mr Kim promised that he would form

a 'pan-national' cabinet, including a substantial proportion of politicians from other parties, in order to ensure an era of 'grand national reconciliation'. Mr Kim also promised an era of clean politics with no place for corruption, and said that he would introduce a parliamentary cabinet system, if that was the wish of the people.

Mr Kim's economic policies focused on narrowing the gap between classes, regions, and small and big business. His election promises included the curbing of inflation, the fair distribution of wealth, the promotion of harmonious labour–management relations, the implementation of tax reforms, and support for small- and medium-sized businesses. He also pledged his support for implementing a real-name system for financial transactions.

THE UNITED PEOPLE'S PARTY (UPP)

Inaugurated	**January 1992**
Party president	**Chung Ju-yung**
Seats won in the 1992 National Assembly elections	**31**

The United People's Party was formed in January 1992 by Chung Ju-yung, at that time the honorary chairman of the Hyundai Group. One month later, the party merged with the Saehan Party, which had also been established in early 1992 by former dissident Kim Tong-gil. The UPP merged again with the New Korea Party in November 1992, just ahead of the presidential elections, but the merger was nullified in January 1993.

Chung Ju-yung stood as the UPP candidate in the 1992 presidential elections; he came third, with 16 per cent of the vote. Although he subsequently affirmed his intention to remain as party leader, he announced his resignation from politics in February 1993.

During the presidential campaign, Mr Chung presented the UPP as a new force in Korean politics, which would replace old-fashioned politics with new and innovative ideas. His bold pledges included achieving 3 per cent inflation within a year of taking office, registering a US$30-billion trade surplus within three years, and achieving reunification within five years. He expressed his support for a change to a parliamentary cabinet system of government, and promised that this would be implemented within three years of his taking office.

Mr Chung called for a change to a civilian-led economy and promised measures to lower interest rates, save struggling small- and medium-sized enterprises, cut real estate prices, and enforce the use of real names in financial transactions. He had long been critical of the Roh administration's major projects, and pledged to postpone the construction of the new airport and high-speed rail link, which, he argued, would hinder the process of economic recovery and exacerbate the trade deficit. More surprisingly, as the founder of one of South Korea's largest and most successful conglomerates, he spoke of the necessity of breaking up the chaeböl in order to turn the subsidiary companies into world-class corporations.

On the domestic politics front, Mr Chung, like Kim Dae-jung, promised to form a coalition cabinet in order to resolve the problems of regionalism. Mr Chung also vowed to pursue a positive unification policy, seeking reunion with North Korea through 'natural absorption', as the north eventually evolves into a free market economic system. In the meantime, however, his administration would strengthen security ties with the United States to prepare for any surprise attack by the North Koreans.

8 The Judiciary, Law and Order

THE JUDICIARY

Judicial power within the Republic of Korea is exercised by the Supreme Court (the highest tribunal in the nation), high courts (which are intermediate appellate courts) and district courts (including the Family Court). The Constitutional Court, Family Court and Court-Martial have jurisdiction over legal matters in specific areas. There is no jury system in the Republic of Korea.

The Supreme Court comprises the chief justice, who is appointed by the president subject to the approval of the National Assembly, and thirteen justices, recommended by the chief justice and approved by the National Assembly. Whereas the chief justice serves a single six-year term, other justices may be reappointed for additional terms of office. All other judges are appointed by the chief justice, with the consent of the Supreme Court Justices' Council. The retirement age is 70 for chief justices, 65 for justices, 63 for chief judges of appellate courts, and 60 for all others.

The Supreme Court is the ultimate authority in the review of the constitutionality or legality of administrative decrees, regulations and dispositions. Appeals against verdicts passed in courts-martial and in civil and criminal cases in the nation's lower courts are referred to the Supreme Court for examination and a final decision, which is indisputable. The Supreme Court also acts as the final tribunal in the review of sentences passed in courts-martial, and has sole jurisdiction in proceedings involving the validity of national and local elections. Decisions made by the Supreme Court form judicial precedents, which are binding on all lower courts. The Supreme Court comprises fourteen justices, including the chief justice, who hear cases either as a Grand Bench (all fourteen) or as Petty Benches (three or four).

The Republic's four high courts, located in Seoul, Pusan, Taegu and Kwangju, hear appeals against verdicts given in civil and criminal cases in the district courts. The high courts also have original jurisdiction as a trial court of the first instance in cases contesting administrative actions. Cases are heard by a collegiate body of three judges, with one of the three presiding.

The thirteen district courts are located in the nation's major cities and exercise jurisdiction over all civil and criminal cases in the first instance, with the exception of cases which fall under the jurisdiction of other courts (for example, election disputes and family cases). District courts also have jurisdiction over a variety of non-contentious cases, such as bankruptcies, liquidations, and registration of real estate. Cases at the district court are heard by either one judge or a collegiate body of three judges, depending on the nature and gravity of the case. Judges for the lower courts are appointed by the chief justice with the approval of the Conference of Supreme Court Justices. Within each district, there are also branch courts and circuit courts.

The Family Court has jurisdiction over all cases relating to matrimonial problems or concerning minors. There is only one Family Court in South Korea, located in Seoul. Family matters elsewhere are heard by the appropriate district court. Sessions of the Family Court are held in camera to protect the privacy of those concerned. Cases involving juveniles are heard by one judge; other domestic cases are usually referred to conciliation proceedings first, and only sent for trial if conciliation fails.

The Constitutional Court was established in 1988, and comprises nine members appointed by the president to serve a six-year term. Of the nine, three are recommended by the National Assembly, three by the chief justice, and three by the president. This special court is empowered to rule on the constitutionality of laws passed by the National Assembly, to scrutinize petitions relating to the Constitution, and to impeach high-ranking public officials, including the president and the prime minister. The court may even dissolve a political party, if its activities are deemed contrary to the fundamental democratic order. A major function of the court is to protect human rights, by allowing petitions from individuals whose basic rights have allegedly been violated by the exercise or non-exercise of public power.

Disputes relating to the division of power among the central government, government agencies and local autonomous organizations are also referred to the Constitutional Court.

The Court-Martial exercises jurisdiction over all crimes committed by members of and civilians attached to the armed forces. It also has the power to try civilians charged with espionage and other military- or security-related offences.

Compared with other nations, the amount of litigation in South Korea is somewhat low. Traditionally, Koreans have preferred to take recourse to the law only as a last resort, as a public confrontation of this sort would inevitably lead to the destruction of the relationship involved. In other words, they prefer informal means of resolving disputes rather than resorting to formal court procedures.

The basic codes of law are the Constitution, the Civil Code, the Commercial Code, the Code of Civil Procedure, the Criminal Code, and the Code of Criminal Procedure. Other forms of written law include statutes passed by the National Assembly, presidential declarations and ministerial directives.

LAW AND ORDER

The National Police was established in 1945, and for the next 30 years was headed by the Director of the National Police Bureau. In January 1975, it was upgraded to the National Police Headquarters, and in August 1991 to the National Police Administration. The organization is now headed by an official of vice-ministerial rank.

Despite the commitment of successive governments to crack down on crime, criminal offences, including traffic violations, drug abuse, human trafficking, gang warfare and financial scams continue to be reported. The increase in juvenile delinquency and substance- and drug-abuse in recent years is a major cause for concern in South Korea. In 1988, there were 97,550 reported cases of juvenile delinquency; and in 1992, it was reported that 12 per cent of juveniles were habitual drug-takers.

The government plans to expand the size of the police force through the late 1990s as part of its policy of enhancing social stability and reinforcing the fight against crime. The ratio of law enforcement officers to citizens will fall from 1:516 in 1991 to 1:358 by 1996, and the 112 emergency telephone system will be expanded to cover the whole nation by 1996. (The system currently operates only in the nation's six largest cities.) The number of substations and police boxes will be increased, and sophisticated fingerprinting and car-number-plate analysis equipment will be introduced to speed up checks on criminal records.

9 The Military

The failure to sign a peace treaty at the end of the Korean War in 1953, the continuing tension between North and South Korea, and the perceived or real threat of another invasion by the DPRK have resulted in massive spending on defence by both the South and North Korean governments over the past four decades.

In 1991, South Korea spent W8 trillion (US$10 billion) on national defence, an amount approximately equivalent to 4 per cent of its GNP, and 25 per cent of its annual national budget. In 1990, North Korea reportedly allocated the equivalent of roughly one-quarter of its far smaller GNP (US$23 billion) to defence.

Since the signing of the armistice agreement in 1953, the Republic of Korea has been protected by both South Korean and American military forces under a combined command structure.

The Republic of Korea has a national conscription system, under which almost all men spend three years in the military. In addition to its standing armed forces, the Republic of Korea also has Homeland Defence Forces, made up of male civilians who give between 68 and 100 hours a year to the forces. Each community has its own Civil Defence Corps, which protects lives and property in time of enemy attack or during situations affecting public peace and order. The total number of civilians registered with the Homeland Defence Forces and Civil Defence Corps is estimated at 3.4 million.

The United States currently maintains 38,000 troops on South Korean soil; the number of troops has been reduced in recent years and further cuts are likely, in line with the US government's policy of reducing defence costs. That said, the United States government remains committed to the defence of the Republic of Korea, and will not withdraw its troops from the peninsula until requested by the ROK government to do so.

Figures published in 1992 by the ROK Ministry of Defence show that North Korea has larger armed forces in total (995,000 against 655,000), more army and air-force personnel (868,000 and 82,000 against 540,000 and 55,000 respectively), more tanks, armoured personnel carriers, artillery and mortars than the Republic of Korea. The DPRK also enjoys a marked numerical superiority in terms of ground-attack aircraft, transport planes, and interceptors. Although the north has more submarines than the south (24 against 1), the south holds an advantage in numbers of naval manpower, destroyers, frigates and helicopters.

The numerical advantage enjoyed by the north is offset to a great degree by the quality of military hardware and the advanced technology possessed by the ROK armed forces. However, with Seoul lying just 22 miles (35 kilometres) from the DMZ, the disposition of the DPRK armed forces is a continuing cause for concern. It is thought that the North Korean forces are prepared for a blitzkrieg, with a high proportion of assault commandos and good bridge-laying capability. Fears have also been expressed in recent years over North Korea's nuclear capability – some analysts maintain that the north will be able to produce a nuclear device by the mid-1990s (see: Relations with North Korea).

The new alliances forged between the Republic of Korea, the former Soviet Union and the People's Republic of China limit North Korea's military options. Without support from its two erstwhile allies, the north would be forced to make a solo attack on the combined ROK–US armed forces. While this is not impossible, it grows harder to imagine it as a feasible unification option for a country desperate to forge links with Japan and the western world. Nevertheless, the south continues to upgrade its defence capabilities, with the aim of being able to defend itself without American help by the mid-1990s. An increasing proportion of the defence budget is being allocated to research and development, focusing on the production of next-generation rifles, combat aircraft, various guided missile systems and so forth.

10 Foreign Relations

The past decade has seen a remarkable change in the Republic of Korea's attitude towards diplomatic relations, from a strong anti-communist posture in the 1960s, through a willingness to open relations with non-hostile communist countries in the 1970s, to the establishment of full diplomatic relations with the majority of countries in the former eastern bloc.

Over the past 45 years, South Korea has joined numerous international organizations, including the United Nations (UN), the Asia-Pacific Economic Council (APEC), the International Monetary Fund (IMF), the International Bank for Reconstruction and Development (IBRD), the International Labour Organization (ILO), and the Asian Development Bank (ADB).

For more than twenty years following the establishment of the Republic of Korea, its diplomatic relations were influenced to a great extent by North Korea's diplomatic activities, as the ROK government endeavoured to set up embassies or consulates in all non-communist countries where the DPRK had a diplomatic presence. In 1973, President Park Chung-hee announced that his government would develop links with all nations, including those under communist regimes, that were not hostile to South Korea.

The greatest changes came in the late 1980s, when President Roh T'ae-woo's government implemented its northern policy ('Nordpolitik'), aiming to promote commercial and political relations with North Korea and its communist allies. In the years following the 1988 Olympic Games, the Republic of Korea established diplomatic relations with all the former eastern bloc countries except Albania and Cuba. After decades of hostility, South Korea finally established diplomatic relations with the former Soviet Union in 1990 and with the People's Republic of China in 1992.

The achievement of the goal of broader contacts with the eastern bloc was made easier by the fact that North Korea's erstwhile allies had begun to perceive South Korea as a nation in its own right, rather than as a lackey of the American government. Moreover, South Korea's economic success offered an excellent role model for their own economic development. The mood of pragmatism within the eastern bloc meant that the need for technology, capital and markets took precedence over consideration for North Korea's finer feelings.

In 1992, the Republic of Korea maintained diplomatic or consular relations with 163 nations. Amongst these, the Republic's relations with the United States, Japan, the People's Republic of China, and the former Soviet Union merit special attention.

THE UNITED STATES

The military and economic support given to South Korea by the United States over more than four decades has formed the cornerstone of US–ROK relations. The leading role played by American armed forces in the Korean War, and the aid and loans made available to South Korea in the early stages of its economic rehabilitation and development, created a strong bond between the two nations.

The United States continues to maintain a significant military presence in South Korea; in 1992, there were 38,000 American troops stationed there. Immediately following his victory in the American presidential elections, Bill Clinton reaffirmed his country's commitment to the defence of the Republic. Although the Clinton administration may reduce the troop levels in South Korea, the US military will remain on South Korean soil for as long as the ROK government feels that its presence is necessary.

Although many South Koreans see the stationing of American troops in their country as a necessary safeguard against an attack by DPRK forces, the North Korean authorities and South Korean radical students maintain that the US military presence is a major stumbling block to reunification. The annual US–ROK military exercises, 'Team Spirit', are regularly used by the north as a pretext for suspending inter-Korean dialogue.

As the South Korean economy developed and expanded, the United States became an important trading partner as well as a military ally. Exports to the United States accounted, on average, for a third of South Korea's total annual exports between 1981 and 1990; in 1986, 40 per cent of the nation's exports went to the American market.

The relationship between the United States and South Korea has been through a number of changes over the past forty-odd years. In the 1950s, South Korea received substantial amounts of American aid to finance its postwar rehabilitation. Between the 1960s and the 1980s, South Korea's status changed from aid recipient to debtor, as the ROK government borrowed the funds needed for its economic development plans.

The economic boom experienced by South Korea in the latter half of the 1980s placed the nation in an unfamiliar position – in 1986, for the first time its history, South Korea recorded a surplus in its trade with the United States. Two years later, the surplus had swelled to more than US$8 billion. Although the surplus has shrunk in recent years, and South Korea's efforts to diversify its export markets have resulted in a lesser degree of dependence on the American market, the United States remains an important trading partner.

The relationship has not been without its problems; indeed, the past few years have seen an increase in anti-American sentiment, especially among the younger generation, who have no memory of the help given by the US government in the postwar years. Close associations in the past between the US government and unpopular, authoritarian regimes in South Korea, increasing pressure upon the Republic to open its markets to American goods and services, and protectionist measures against South Korean products in the US marketplace have led to friction and tension.

The US government has accused South Korea of unfair and restrictive trade practices in the past, and a number of South Korean companies have faced anti-dumping suits in the American market. There are fears that the Clinton administration will pursue a tougher trade policy and that the Super 301 provisions of the 1988 US Omnibus Trade and Competitiveness Act, which expired in 1990, may be revived in 1993. However, trade relations have improved over in recent months, and there is also optimism that some South Korean companies or industries will be able to negotiate cooperation agreements with American partners.

The relationship between South Korea and the United States clearly shows the contradictions in the South Koreans' view of themselves – on the one hand as a nation in their own right, on the verge of achieving advanced nation status, and no longer to be considered as a 'little brother' to the United States, but at the same time as a developing nation in need of special treatment and concessions from the United States and other advanced nations.

However, given the two nations' common interests in the defence of the peninsula and the maintenance of peace and stability within the region, and also given their strong trading links, the Republic of Korea's relationship with the United States will remain of prime importance over the years to come.

JAPAN

Relations with Japan are prickly at best. Some South Koreans maintain that their people's hatred and mistrust of the Japanese goes back to the Hideyoshi invasions in the sixteenth century, but possibly the real roots are in Japan's colonization of Korea between 1910 and 1945 (see: History).

There is still a great deal of bitterness and bad feeling against the Japanese for their harsh treatment of the Koreans during the colonial period. Although diplomatic relations with Japan were restored and reparations made by the Japanese government in 1965, the tension shows little real sign of abating. Issues such as the claims for compensation made against Japan by former 'comfort girls' (Korean women who were drafted into the Japanese army in the 1930s and 1940s to serve as prostitutes), and the Japanese government's refusal in the past to recognize as Japanese nationals the descendants of Koreans forcibly settled in Japan during the colonial period and still living in Japan, have badly strained ROK–Japanese relations.

The South Koreans' attempts to force an apology from the Japanese for their actions during the colonial period, and their dissatisfaction with official statements made on the subject, indicate that the resentment of and bitterness towards the Japanese will need more time to ease. The closest that the Japanese have come to an apology was a statement made by Emperor Akihito in May 1990, referring to his 'deepest regret for the suffering of the Korean people'.

Although the South Koreans may have a grudging respect for the economic success achieved by the Japanese, resentment at being referred to as a 'Second Japan', indistinguishable culturally and economically from their neighbour, exists and should be borne in mind by foreign visitors (see: Business Culture).

Once diplomatic relations were restored in 1965, Japan quickly became an important trading partner for South Korea and a prime source of technology and capital goods. The geographical proximity of and cultural similarities between the two nations make trading with Japan easier than with other nations, and, having been ruled by the Japanese for

35 years, the older South Koreans probably understand the Japanese better than any other people.

However, the trading links between Japan and South Korea have also proved a source of friction, as the trade deficit with Japan has regularly accounted for the lion's share of the Republic's trade deficits. In 1991, the deficit with Japan reached US$8.8 billion, while the total trade deficit stood at US$9.7 billion. The expanding trade deficit and Japan's reluctance to open its markets further to South Korean goods or to provide the advanced technology now needed by South Korean manufacturers are the main topics for debate at meetings between ROK and Japanese economic officials.

In addition to its economic links with South Korea, Japan is an important trading partner for North Korea, and there are reportedly more than forty factories in North Korea managed by pro-North Korean groups in Japan. Fears that North Korea may be edging closer to re-establishing relations with Japan were eased to some extent by the Japanese prime minister, Toshiki Kaifu's, assurances in 1991 that Japan would consult with the ROK government over its dealings with North Korea, and would not offer any financial compensation for the colonial period to the north until relations were normalized. (South Korea received financial compensation from Japan when relations were reinstated in 1965. See: Relations with North Korea.)

THE PEOPLE'S REPUBLIC OF CHINA

The establishment of diplomatic relations between the Republic of Korea and the People's Republic of China (PRC) in 1992 renewed a relationship that goes back to before the birth of Christ. For centuries, China was Korea's ally, its artistic inspiration and an important source of knowledge and culture (see: History).

However, for more than four decades after the establishment of the Republic of Korea, the relationship maintained between the PRC and North Korea precluded any ties with South Korea. The ROK government's policy of pursuing contacts with communist bloc countries in the late 1980s paved the way for the development of economic exchanges between South Korea and China and, ultimately, the establishment of full diplomatic relations between the two nations.

The reasons behind the rapprochement were mainly economic. South Korea wanted new export markets, cheap labour and raw materials, and China needed technology and capital.

The growth in economic contacts has indeed been rapid; bilateral trade, which stood at US$118 million in 1980, approached US$6 billion in 1991. During the first eight months of 1992, South Korean exports to China jumped by 77.8 per cent year on year to US$2.57 billion, while imports from China expanded by 16.4 per cent to reach US$2.55 billion. Bilateral trade for the whole year was estimated at close to US$9 billion, with China overtaking Germany to become South Korea's third largest trading partner, after the United States and Japan.

Although South Korean companies initially had high expectations of China as a potential market for their goods, the first few years of trade between the two countries resulted in trade deficits for South Korea, as Chinese companies exported inexpensive, low-quality goods to the South Korean market. The trade deficit, which reached US$1.1 billion in 1991, turned into a surplus the following year, but it remains to be seen whether this was due to a slump in imports to South Korea, rather than an improvement in export performance.

South Korea also began to experience a boomerang effect from its activities in China, as cheap goods manufactured in PRC–ROK ventures in China were exported to and took a sizeable market share in South Korea.

China, with its population of more than 1 billion, does have enormous medium- to long-term potential as a market for South Korean consumer goods, but currently lacks the necessary purchasing power. In the short term, therefore, China has more to offer the South Koreans in terms of cheap labour and natural resources, and there are good prospects for collaboration in light industrial ventures such as textiles, automobile parts and consumer electronics production.

In 1985, there was one case of South Korean investment in China, valued at US$185,000; by August 1992, cumulative investment by South Korean companies stood at US$237 million in 250 projects. Plans are under discussion for the construction of an industrial complex at Tianjin, which would house a hundred South Korean textiles and electronics companies.

The advantages for the South Koreans and the Chinese in doing business with each other is that their economies complement each other to a significant degree. The Chinese can provide abundant labour and natural resources, while the South Koreans can offer capital, technology and light industrial know-how. South Korean businessmen have said that their shared cultural background, similar security and trade interests, and common experience with the Japanese help to ease economic and commercial cooperation.

For the South Koreans, the risks involved in doing business in China include political uncertainty, different methods of business operating procedures, and a lack of understanding among the South Koreans of how the Chinese market operates. South Korean companies investing in China are also reported to be facing problems due to competition for skilled manpower, rising overhead costs, and conflicts with the Chinese on management issues.

THE FORMER SOVIET UNION

Diplomatic relations with the former Soviet Union were re-established in 1990, after a hiatus of some eighty years. As in the case of relations with China, economic considerations were as important as security and political concerns.

The establishment of full relations was also marked by South Korea's provision of a three-year financial package, which included a US$1.5 billion tied loan for the importing of Korean consumer goods. Economic relations between the two countries were expected to facilitate trade and promote investment and cooperative ventures combining Soviet resources, labour and advanced technology with South Korean capital and light industrial know-how.

Bilateral trade, which had begun in 1988, reached US$1.2 billion in 1991, with South Korean exports and imports totalling US$625 million and US$577 million respectively. Trade between the former Soviet Union and South Korea is forecast to reach US$10 billion by 1995.

The former Soviet Union offers a number of opportunities for South Korean investment including the development of the consumer goods industry and the improvement of infrastructure, as well as projects for cooperation, such as the development and exploitation of the former Soviet Union's abundant natural resources.

The relationship hit problems at an early stage, however, when, following the collapse of the Soviet Union, interest payments on the South Korean loans were not made. In early 1992, there were reports that South Korean companies were having problems obtaining payment for their exports, and in March of that year, the ROK government suspended approval for further exports of consumer goods under the tied loans scheme. In May 1992, the Russian government notified Seoul that it was unable to meet the interest payments; in August, it defaulted on the payments once again.

In November 1992, Boris Yeltsin became the first Russian leader to visit the South Korean capital. Following talks with President Roh T'ae-woo, the two leaders signed a treaty relating to economic, industrial, scientific and technical cooperation. Mr Yeltsin gave President Roh documents guaranteeing the repayment of loans and the payment of overdue interest; for his part, President Roh agreed to resume economic aid to Russia.

Mr Yeltsin also agreed not to supply offensive weapons, nuclear technology or materials to North Korea, and promised to re-examine the 1961 Mutual Assistance Treaty with North Korea, which requires automatic involvement by Russia in any war waged by the northern regime.

11 Relations with North Korea

POLITICAL RELATIONS

For 18 years after the signing of the Armistice Treaty in 1953, there were no official contacts between the Republic of Korea and the Democratic People's Republic of Korea. In 1971, Red Cross officials met to discuss reuniting families separated by the division of the peninsula, and, in July of the following year, the ROK and DPRK governments issued a joint communiqué, pledging their best efforts towards the peaceful reunification of the peninsula. However, there was little in the way of tangible results in the years that followed.

During the 1980s, there were intermittent contacts and talks on economic and humanitarian issues. Meetings aiming to foster family reunions, economic cooperation, sports exchanges, and inter-parliamentary debate achieved little more than the exchange of some separated families and performances by arts troupes for four days in 1985. Terrorist activities by the North Koreans, including a bomb attack on President Chun Doo-hwan and his entourage during a visit to Rangoon in 1983, and the blowing up of a Korean Air jumbo jet in 1987, heightened the hostility and mistrust between north and south.

However, changes in the international political scene in the late 1980s and the economic difficulties now facing North Korea have prompted new efforts at dialogue with the south. The collapse of communism and the establishment of diplomatic relations between South Korea, the former Soviet Union and the People's Republic of China have resulted in North Korea becoming increasingly isolated.

In the face of these changes, North Korea has been more active in inter-Korean dialogue and has also been making efforts to re-establish links with western nations and Japan.

The North Korean economy has contracted for three years in a row, and the north now faces the problems of a lack of exportable products, little hard cash for imports, and shortages of food, energy and other necessities.

The early 1990s saw the opening of talks between the North and South Korean prime ministers, which culminated in the signing of a number of agreements in December 1991.

The South–North Agreement on Reconciliation, Non-aggression, Exchanges and Cooperation called for the establishment of committees to discuss arms reduction, commerce, personnel and communications exchanges, and military trust-building. A military hotline was to be set up between Seoul and P'yŏngyang, a liaison office was to be established at the border village of P'anmunjŏm, and both sides agreed to exchange military information such as prior notification of troop movements. Agreement was also reached on the need to develop scientific, cultural and academic exchanges, promote the reunion of separated families, re-establish rail, road, sea and air routes between north and south, and set up postal and telecommunications links.

The premiers also signed an Agreement on the Formation of Three Sub-committees on Exchange and a Joint Declaration for the Denuclearization of the Korean Peninsula. Under the latter declaration, the two sides agreed not to 'manufacture, test, produce, introduce, possess, deploy or use nuclear weapons', to use nuclear energy for peaceful purposes, and not to possess nuclear fuel, reprocessing or uranium enrichment facilities. Both sides also agreed to inspections of each other's nuclear facilities.

The signing of these agreements was hailed as the first significant step towards reunification since 1945, and generated optimism over the prospects for a summit between President Roh T'ae-woo and North Korean Premier Kim Il-sung. However, euphoria among the South Koreans swiftly turned to suspicion, and fears arose that the north's enthusiasm for talks was only a ploy, masking more sinister motives.

In the early 1990s, reports began to circulate to the effect that North Korea was well advanced in a nuclear programme and would be able to manufacture nuclear weapons by the mid-1990s. There were reports that the north had two nuclear reactors at Yŏngbyŏn and was constructing a reprocessing plant, which could be used to separate weapons-grade plutonium from the reactors' spent fuel.

Although a signatory to the nuclear non-proliferation treaty, North Korea had persistently refused to allow inspection of its nuclear facilities, claiming that their purpose was power generation and not weapon manufacture. On 1 February

1991, North Korea signed the nuclear safeguard agreement of the International Atomic Energy Agency (IAEA), but continued to drag its feet on the issue of inspections, heightening concerns that the motive was to win time either to develop a bomb or to change the location of the nuclear facilities.

Although representatives from the IAEA did make inspections on four occasions in 1992, with the purpose of gradually verifying the existence and location of facilities and stockpiles of nuclear materials, at the end of the year North Korea threatened to refuse further entry to the inspectors, unless the south agreed to call off 'Team Spirit' (the annual ROK–US military exercises). North Korea has been invited to send observers to 'Team Spirit', but continues to regard the holding of the exercises as a provocative act, and has used this as a pretext to suspend dialogue on a number of occasions. For their part, the United States and South Korean governments said that they would call off the exercises if North Korea allowed full mutual inspections.

No agreement had been reached by the end of 1992, and the 12th Plenary Session of the North–South Joint Nuclear Control Committee, held in December 1992, made no progress on drafting inter-Korean nuclear inspection regulations. The United States, Japan and the European Community have all made it clear that future contacts with North Korea will hinge on a speedy resolution of the issue of nuclear inspections. The ROK government has also called off all contacts with the north pending a satisfactory outcome of the problem.

ECONOMIC RELATIONS

The failure to resolve the nuclear issue has slowed down the development of economic exchanges between North and South Korea. The ROK government's decision in October 1988 to allow South Korean companies to trade with the north has led to a substantial increase in trade between the two sides in relative, if not in absolute, terms. Trade between the north and south has risen from US$25 million in 1990 to almost US$200 million in 1992.

During the first eleven months of 1992, South Korean exports to the north amounted to US$11 million, while imports stood at US$183 million. Exports from the north to the south include anthracite coal, minerals and marine products; South Korea has exported a small amount of sugar, rice, and some colour televisions and polyethylene film to the north. Despite the current hiatus in inter-Korean relations, the ROK Ministry of Trade and Industry forecasts a steady growth in bilateral trade, which is expected to pass the

TABLE 1 Comparison of major economic indicators for South and North Korea, 1990

Item	Unit	South Korea	North Korea
Population	Million	42.8	21.7
GNP	US$bn	237.9	23.1
Per capita GNP	US$	5,569	1,064
Economic growth rate	%	12.8	2.8
Exports	US$bn	65.0	2.0
Imports	US$bn	69.8	2.6
Fiscal budget	US$bn	3.2	1.5
Grain production	Mm tons	7.2	5.5
Energy supply	Mm TOE	81.4	28.7
Steel production	Mm tons	25.4	5.9
Coal production	Mm tons	17.2	43.3
Iron production	1,000 tons	265	295
Number of automobiles	1,000 units	3,375	264
Defence budget	US$bn	9.8	5.0
AS % of GNP	%	4.1	21.5

Source: National Unification Borard.
Mm = million.

US$5 billion mark by the end of the century. Table 1 gives a comparison of economic indicators for north and south.

In the late 1980s and early 1990s, optimism over the prospects for an improvement in north–south relations and the relaxation in the ROK government's attitude towards trade with the north prompted the formulation of a number of investment plans by South Korean companies. Visits to North Korea by Hyundai honorary chairman Chung Ju-yung in 1989 and Daewoo president Kim Woo-choong in 1992 provided opportunities to explore possibilities for joint ventures in the north, for example in the fisheries, Oriental medicine, agriculture, building material, textiles, footwear and electronics sectors.

There was also excitement at the prospect of South Korean involvement in the construction of roads, ports and industrial complexes, and the development of tourist areas in the north, such as the famous Diamond Mountains. In third countries, a combination of South Korean technology and capital and North Korean labour could be used to develop natural resources and bid for construction projects.

However, business contacts were suspended in February 1992, due to disagreements over the nuclear issue, and the joint venture projects agreed upon by the North Koreans and Kim Woo-choong were put on hold. Although North Korea's Kim Dal-hyŏn visited Seoul in July 1992 for talks with his counterpart, ROK Deputy Prime Minister Ch'oi Gak-kyu, and agreed in principle to promote economic exchanges, the nuclear issue still proved a major stumbling block to progress. Similarly, the visit to North Korea in the autumn of 1992 by a delegation of South Korean government officials and businessmen to carry out feasibility studies for the proposed north–south industrial estate at Namp'o has not been followed by concrete measures.

FUTURE PROSPECTS FOR INTER-KOREAN RELATIONS

Positive factors which could accelerate the easing of tensions on the Korean peninsula include the collapse of communism and the establishment of diplomatic relations between South Korea and the north's erstwhile allies. North Korea's ailing economy and its need for financial, industrial and technical assistance appear to be prompting a more pragmatic approach to contacts with the free world. North Korea's recent approaches to Japan may well signal a desire to get help without the loss of face involved in accepting aid from the United States or South Korea.

With every year that passes, a change in power in North Korea comes nearer; Kim Il-sung, now in his eighties, has designated his son Kim Jong-il as his successor, but the transfer of power is by no means guaranteed. The rise to power of a more pragmatic group could accelerate the speed of change in the north and on the peninsula as a whole. However, some analysts argue that, should the North Korean economic situation continue to deteriorate, bringing further shortages and hardships, the possibility of an uprising against the Kim regime cannot be ruled out.

South Korea's increasing economic power has prompted the ROK government to relax its stance *vis-à-vis* North Korea to some degree, in terms of promoting wider economic contacts and allowing greater public access to information about the north. The fear of the 'threat from the north' and concerns that life in the north would prove attractive to the South Koreans are gradually fading with the passage of time.

At the time of writing, the nuclear issue is one of the biggest stumbling blocks to an improvement in relations.

Other barriers include the diametrically opposed approaches to reunification adopted by the ROK and DPRK governments, the mistrust and hostility that exist between the two sides, and the closed nature of North Korean society. While the DPRK government favours resolving military and political issues (principally the removal of American troops from South Korea) ahead of all other discussions, the south has consistently called for the building of trust and confidence through economic and cultural exchanges before attacking more complex issues.

The effects of forty years of hostility and propaganda will not easily be overcome; reports of terrorist activities and the digging of invasion tunnels under the DMZ by the North Koreans have reinforced fears of the north's real intentions toward the south. In October 1992, it was alleged that North Korean master-spy Li Son-sil had established a chapter of the North Korean Workers' Party in South Korea, and had master-minded its operations between 1980 and 1990, with the aim of communizing the peninsula by 1995. There are still fears that North Korea will attack the south before losing its advantage in conventional weapons – South Korea is building up its defences to match those of North Korea – and that the north will possess nuclear weapons in the near future.

Although the South Koreans now have greater access to information about life in the DPRK, the North Koreans are, by all accounts, still largely unaware of the true situation in the Republic of Korea. The realization that the south is a prosperous, technologically advanced and independent nation, rather than a cowering and impoverished country under the heel of the US military, would shake the foundations of Kim's regime.

REUNIFICATION BY ABSORPTION?

As mentioned above, it has long been the view of the ROK government that confidence can be established and built upon through economic exchanges. Indeed, as South Korea has grown and prospered, many have come to view economic cooperation as the key to unification, leading to a point where economic absorption of the north by the south would be feasible. It would, they argue, be easier to achieve reunification if North Korea were stronger economically and had been opened up to the outside world through trade and investment.

The reunification of Germany initially prompted opti-mism in South Korea that economic cooperation leading to reunification by absorption would indeed be a viable option. However, the German experience in the years following reunification has introduced a note of caution for the South Koreans, as they gradually realized the enormous potential cost of integrating the two economies. Although North Korean economic growth and development outpaced that of the Republic in the 1950s and early 1960s, it has been estimated that the northern economy now lags behind that of the south by as much as twenty years.

In January 1993, the ROK Ministry of Finance (MOF) issued a report which estimated the cost of reunification at US$980 billion over ten years, assuming that reunification took place in the year 2000. Although the MOF did not provide a breakdown of its estimates – previous forecasts by other organizations had ranged between US$250 billion and US$500 billion over ten years – the message was clear. With a GNP of around US$300 billion in 1992, the financial burden of reunification on South Korea would be immense. Although the ultimate goal – reunification of the Korean peninsula – undoubtedly remains the same, progress is now likely to be more measured in the light of lessons learned from Germany's experience.

The most prudent approach – assuming that there is no sudden change of leadership in the north – is clearly the gradual expansion of economic relations between North and South Korea. There are three possible forms of economic exchange: inter-Korean trade, joint ventures or direct investment in the north by South Korean companies, and north–south cooperative ventures in third countries.

North Korea would be a valuable source of raw materials for the south and, with its population of 22 million, a significant consumer market in the medium to long term. Joint ventures, either in North Korea or in third countries, would combine South Korean capital, manufacturing know-how and overseas marketing networks with North Korean labour and raw materials.

However, joint ventures would pose a number of problems for both South and North Korea. On the South Korean side, there is already a realization of the practical problems that exist in the promotion of economic contacts with the north: lack of reliable information about the North Korean economy, lack of legislative guarantees such as protection of invested capital and repatriation of profits, ideological and cultural barriers, shortage of hard currency in the north, differences in management style, low productivity, difficult labour relations and so forth.

In addition, there is the problem of the volatile nature of the North Korean regime, which would make long-term planning difficult. Despite the easing of the ROK government's anti-communist stance, many South Korean businessmen are still said to be fearful that contacts with the north could have them branded as communists.

Finally, the products of north–south ventures might face restrictions in countries such as the United States, where North Korea is still classed as an enemy nation.

On the North Korean side, Kim Il-sung faces a dilemma: the full opening of the country to foreign trade and investment would risk the destruction of the personality cult which has secured his position as leader over nearly five decades. Joint ventures, be they with South Korean companies or foreign companies, would bring North Korean workers into contact with the outside world. On the other hand, failure to implement economic reforms could lead to the collapse of the North Korean economy and the overthrow of his government. As a compromise, the North Korean regime may well attempt to emulate China, by gradually opening up its economy while maintaining tight control over domestic politics.

PART THREE

Society

12 Introduction

Over the last century Korean society has undergone dramatic and often painful transformations, suffering the impact of Japanese colonial rule, civil war, westernization and rapid industrialization. While, over the past four decades in particular, there has been a strong tendency among South Koreans to adopt western culture, styles of dress, and business practices, they remain essentially both Korean and Confucian. A veneer of westernization, though in some cases quite thick, will usually cover traditional values and beliefs, instincts and responses that are inbred and hard to shake.

TRADITIONAL SOCIETY

From the Yi dynasty onwards, Korean society has been governed by the Confucian system of ethics, which even today exerts a strong influence over social relationships, including those in the business world (see: Business Culture). The Confucian system defines relationships in terms of a hierarchical social structure, and emphasizes the importance of each individual knowing his or her place within that hierarchy and acting accordingly. Confucianism has been called a system of interaction among unequals, with correct behaviour being determined by gender, age, and social position (see also: Philosophy and Religion).

The five major relationships outlined by Confucianism remain the key to South Korean society. Sons should show respect, obedience and filial piety to their fathers, subjects should be loyal to their rulers, the young should revere the old, wives should be subservient to their husbands, and friendships should be governed by mutual trust.

Traditionally, within the family, the father was a true pater familias with absolute authority over the family members, as well as a duty to support and protect them. For his part, the eldest son had the responsibility of carrying on the family line, performing ceremonies to honour the family ancestors, and supporting his parents in their old age. The relationship between a father and his son and the respect of the young for the elderly are still central to the family and to South Korean society at large.

The Confucian precepts of the dominance of man over woman and women's duty as a home-maker and childbearer have been responsible in large part for the low status afforded to women in Korean society. Women were defined in terms of their menfolk, first as a man's daughter, then as a man's wife, and finally as a child's mother. Their function was to keep the home and raise the children and they enjoyed a certain amount of power within the home. However, in traditional society the majority of middle- and upper-class women were afforded few rights, received no education, and had only limited contact with the world outside their homes. (Economic realities made it necessary for low-class women to work alongside their men and have greater contact with the outside world.)

In passing, it is interesting to note that the vestiges of the Confucian requirement that the sexes be separated from the age of 7 can still be seen in the tendency of the South Koreans to socialize and even eat with their own sex.

The family remains central to South Korean society. Although recent years have seen a trend away from the practice of three generations (parents, children and grandchildren) living under one roof and towards nuclear families (parents and children living together), family ties remain strong. Genealogy is important. Families maintain detailed family trees. The fact that the family line can only be carried on through the male goes a long way to explaining the South Koreans' deep-seated preference for male children.

Traditional celebrations continue to be held, one of the most important being the *hwan'gap*, or sixtieth birthday, a landmark which dates back to the time when life expectancy was low. As recently as the 1960s life expectancy for males was only 51, while that for women was 54. High levels of infant mortality gave rise to celebrations of a child's first hundred days (*paegil*) and first year (*tol*) of life. Both are still an occasion for family celebrations.

Friendships and connections are also important in South Korean society. Aside from true friends whose company he enjoys, a Korean man will typically have a large network of contacts and acquaintances, linked by family, school or work, on whom he can rely for help, particularly in his work. Indeed, business matters are often based more on personal relations than on commercial considerations – a case of preferring contacts to contracts (see: Business Culture). A woman's network may include contacts who could prove useful in her husband's career or to the development, education and marriage of her children. The relationships are maintained on the basis of reciprocity and exchange, with favours being repaid and obligations never forgotten.

The importance of harmony in all relationships and social groups cannot be overstated. Generally speaking, the interests of the individual are considered secondary to the needs of the group as a whole, be it a family or a corporation.

CHANGES IN SOCIETY

As with any society, attitudes and beliefs are subject to continuing change. Social class is still loosely based on education and occupation, but there are now other determinants, such as income. Social class is no longer hereditary, and there is growing social mobility – an increasingly large number of South Koreans now consider themselves to be middle-class. While respect for education remains strong, public office is no longer seen as the most desirable occupation and the Confucian scorn for commerce is truly dead and gone.

Along with the breakdown of social classes have come the beginnings of individualism, a trend much lamented in some sections of society. There are complaints, for example, that workers are no longer willing to work for the good of the company (and ultimately the nation) alone, but want more money, more leisure, and a greater share of the benefits that economic development brings.

In Korea the traditional belief was that the current generation must make sacrifices for the sake of the next generation. This may well become an outmoded idea as standards of living rise and the South Koreans come to have a stronger feeling of economic security. The expansion of welfare services will also have an impact on family responsibilities, as the burden of supporting parents in their old age eases to some degree.

Perhaps the biggest changes in South Korean society in the years ahead will be in the role of women. There is a growing realization that a large and highly educated part of the nation's workforce has been under-utilized, and the combination of demographic changes and labour shortages could well result in the recalling of married women to the workplace.

The change in the status of Korean women began in 1886 with the establishment of the Ewha Haktang (now Ewha Women's University) by American missionaries, and women's participation in the enlightenment and independence movements. In 1948, the Constitution of the newly established Republic of Korea guaranteed women equal rights, and gave them the right to vote. Educational opportunities expanded and rapid industrial development created jobs for women.

The amendment of the Family Law in December 1989 went a long way towards improving the status of South Korean women, in terms of property inheritance, child custody in divorce, and domestic relations. Pressure groups continue to fight for further amendments to the Family Law – in particular the provision which states that the headship of a family can only be assumed by a man – and labour laws.

Although women are now more active in South Korean society, they still suffer from lower pay, lower status and less job security. Laws concerning equal employment opportunities, the rehiring of women after childbirth, promotion and retirement do exist, but they are only loosely enforced. In addition, women's expectations are still low: many of the secretaries and clerks in South Korean offices are university graduates whose aspirations are limited by the fact that they will be expected to leave work once they get married and have a family.

Management expectations can be seen in the training courses run for employees. Whereas male employees are trained to pass examinations and gain promotion, the aim of courses for female workers is to school them in etiquette and culture, and groom them to be 'flowers of the office' – quiet, courteous, attractive, obedient.

A number of women do run their own companies in South Korea, but it is still comparatively rare to see women rising to middle management positions. It is only in areas which are less hidebound by traditions, such as journalism, public relations and advertising, that women are rising above the lowest ranks.

Although marriage and childbearing remain the norm in South Korea, subtle changes are also occurring in this area of life. Arranged marriages are still prevalent, but more couples are embarking on what are known as 'love marriages'. The average age for first marriages has been rising slowly over the past decade, from 27 to 29 for men and from 23 to 26 for women. South Koreans still tend to abide by the concept of a 'marriageable age' and many are genuinely alarmed at and bemused by the concept of an individual living a single life.

The rate of divorce has been rising. One marriage in eight now ends in divorce, and the vast majority of South Koreans cite incompatibility as the reason for the break-up of their marriage. The decision to divorce is still hard for many women, who may face economic insecurity and risk the loss of their children should they take that step. Whereas remarriage for a woman was almost unthinkable twenty years ago, 6 per cent of divorced or widowed women now remarry.

In 1992, pressure groups successfully foiled an attempt to abolish the South Korean adultery law under which an adulterous spouse can be imprisoned for two years. (The sentence will be reduced to one year from 1995.) Opponents to this reform claim that the law is a woman's last safeguard against her spouse's infidelity, and argue that it must not be abolished until a greater degree of economic security and enhanced custody rights can be guaranteed for wives who divorce their husbands.

13 Demography

In July 1992, the Republic of Korea ranked twenty-third in the world in terms of population size, with an estimated population of 43.7 million. The nation's population density of 440 people per square kilometre ranked it third in the world, after Taiwan and Bangladesh. (The rankings exclude the city states of Hong Kong and Singapore.) In 1960, the population was 25 million, with a density of 254 persons per square kilometre.

Important demographic trends over the past three decades include: a slower rate of population growth, an increasing rate of urbanization, and a trend toward an ageing population.

POPULATION GROWTH

The annual population growth rate has slowed down markedly over the past thirty years, with the average annual growth rate dropping to under 1.0 per cent in the early 1990s from 2.6 per cent in the 1960s. The slow-down is due to a number of factors, the most important of which is the concerted effort by the government to curb population growth, by encouraging people to limit the size of their families by practising contraception.

The policy was largely successful – the proportion of women practising contraception rose to 70 per cent in 1986 from 32 per cent in 1970, and the average number of children per female fell to 1.7 in 1989 from 6.1 in 1960. However, the traditional preference for male children has hindered the full implementation of this policy. In South Korean society, it is the male who carries on the family line, and the eldest son who has the responsibility of caring for his parents in their old age (see: Society – Introduction). There have been cases of women aborting female foetuses in an attempt to comply with both the wishes of their family and the exhortations of the government, and abortion is still reportedly used as a method of limiting the size of families. For the campaigns in favour of one- or two-child families to be truly successful, there will need to be further improvements in the status of women, and an easing of the financial burden of caring placed on the male children in a family.

Other factors in the slow-down in population growth include the trend towards later marriages – the proportion of single women aged between 20 and 24 increased to 80.7 per cent in 1990 from 72.1 per cent in 1985 – and the increasing rate of urbanization.

URBANIZATION
The Republic of Korea is heavily urbanized; at the time of the 1990 census, almost half the population lived in the six largest cities. More than one quarter of the population (currently around 12 million people) live in the capital, Seoul, making it one of the ten largest cities in the world. The heavy concentration of population in and around Seoul, which is regarded as the business, financial, educational and cultural centre of the nation, has strategic implications, in that the capital is so close to the border with North Korea. Accordingly, the government has been encouraging the relocation of businesses and public offices and the construction of satellite towns outside the capital.

The urban population has grown at an average annual rate of 5 per cent since 1955, with 73 per cent of the increase in that period attributable to migration from rural areas. In 1990, 57 per cent of the people living in Seoul had migrated there from other cities or the provinces. At the beginning of the 1990s, farming and fishing communities accounted for less than 30 per cent of the total population. The employment opportunities created by rapid industrialization have drawn increasing numbers of people into the cities, leaving fewer people to work the land (see also: Natural Resources: Agriculture, Fishing, Forestry and Mining).

Migration has been showing signs of easing since 1989, due to the stabilization of real estate prices, and expectations of more balanced regional development in the wake of the implementation of local autonomy. In the 1970s, an average of 5 million people moved to another area each year; the numbers rose to an average of 8.8 million per year and peaked at 9.9 million in 1988. By 1991, the figure had eased down to 8.9 million.

POPULATION STRUCTURE
In terms of population structure, the 1990 census showed that around 45 per cent of the population at that time was aged

under 25, and more than 70 per cent was aged under 40. However, as the rate of population growth continues to decline, and the average life expectancy increases (see below), the proportion of young people will continue to fall, while that of the old will rise. In 1970, the under-14s and over-65s accounted for 42.1 per cent and 3.4 per cent of the total population respectively; twenty years later, the shares had changed to 25.8 per cent and 5.0 per cent respectively. This clearly has implications for a society in which care of the aged continues to be the responsibility of the family.

The increasing trend towards the nuclear family, as more young families choose to set up home on their own rather than live with parents, has contributed to a decline in the average household size, from 5.5 persons in 1966 to 3.8 persons in 1990.

Improvements in diet and health-care have led to an increase in the average life expectancy and a decline in infant mortality. In 1990, the average life expectancy was 67 for men and 75 for women; in 1960, the figure had been 51 for men and 54 for women. The rate of infant mortality fell to 12 per thousand in 1990 from 17 per thousand in the 1980s.

14 Philosophy and Religion

Korea's philosophies and religions have always reflected foreign influence, be it shamanism from Siberia, Buddhism from India, Taoism and Confucianism from China, Christianity from the west, or Islam from the Middle East. It has been said that the South Koreans tend to be pragmatic about religion, and will try most things once. Some modern Koreans may in fact follow three or four religions, observing Confucian ceremonies to honour their ancestors, consulting a fortune teller about the propitious date for a wedding, worshipping at a rock which is reputed to ensure the birth of a son, and offering a prayer at a Buddhist temple while hiking in the mountains.

SHAMANISM
One of the most ancient religions known in Korea is shamanism, which originated in Siberia and was brought to the peninsula in Neolithic times. Shamanism is based on the belief that the world is inhabited by good and evil spirits, and that the help of and protection from those spirits must be sought by humans through an intermediary or shaman (Korean: *mudang*). In that sense, shamanism took one step further the primitive Koreans' belief that natural objects were inhabited by spirits – animism – and that their clans were descended from an animal or a natural object – totemism.

Individuals wanting to avert bad luck, cure illness or ensure a safe passage to the next world would seek out a shaman to intercede with the spirits on their behalf. The rituals performed involved music, incantations and dance, with the shaman often entering a trance-like state and speaking with the voice of the various spirits. A number of shaman temples still exist today, even in the largest of cities, and the help of the shaman, who is usually a woman, is sought about more worldly problems – success in examinations or finding a husband, for example. Travelling through the countryside, it is occasionally possible to see 'devil posts' – large, wooden structures somewhat resembling totem poles, which were placed at the entrance to a village in traditional Korea to ward off evil spirits.

TAOISM

Another religion introduced to the Koreans in ancient times was Taoism. Although it never became a major religious force in Korea, its influence is still felt today through the common use of Taoist symbols. Taoism's emphasis on the cultivation of mind and body, and its search for blessings and longevity, are seen in the use of the Chinese characters '*pok*' (happiness) and '*su*' (long life) on innumerable household items. The ten symbols of longevity, including the deer, crane and pine tree, are likewise popular· decorative motifs, and the yin-yang sign at the centre of the national flag (see: Gazetteer) is itself a Taoist symbol. Geomancy (the determination of propitious locations for public buildings, homes and family graves), fortune telling and numerology all have their roots in Taoism, and are all still widely used by modern Koreans.

It was during the Three Kingdoms Period (57 BC–AD 668 – see: History) that more sophisticated religions – Buddhism and Confucianism – entered the peninsula via China. While these did not replace the local beliefs and practices, they spread rapidly and became a dominant influence on Korean society and government. For centuries, Buddhism and Confucianism coexisted peacefully with local beliefs and with each other.

BUDDHISM

The teachings of Mahayana (Greater Vehicle) Buddhism, which entered the Korean peninsula in the fourth century AD, aim to attain personal salvation by renouncing worldly desires. They show how to cultivate spiritual discipline and achieve enlightenment, which enables the individual to break the endless cycle of earthly suffering and reincarnation, and enter Nirvana or Paradise. When all have achieved Enlightenment and entered Nirvana, the world will come to an end.

Buddhism spread quickly in Korea. Temples and monasteries were built, and monks were sent to China and India to bring back sacred texts and holy relics. Eventually, Buddhism was adopted as the state religion by all three kingdoms, Shilla, Paekche and Koguryŏ. Under state patronage in the Unified Shilla and Koryŏ dynasties, the influence of Buddhism strengthened. Priests, who were among the educated élite, rose to become politicians and courtiers, acting as advisors to the court. This role and the increasing wealth of the monasteries brought criticism and accusations of corruption and worldliness. With the change of dynasty in 1392, and the rise of Confucianism, the fortunes of Buddhism waned. The idea of renouncing one's family in order to become a monk was abhorrent to the Neo-Confucians; the monasteries' land and wealth was confiscated, and monks were barred from public office.

Buddhism has been experiencing something of a revival in recent years – in the 1985 census, almost half of those South Koreans professing a religion were followers of Buddhism – the Buddha's birthday is celebrated as a national holiday, along with Christmas. There are currently two major Buddhist sects in South Korea: Chogye, which requires celibacy of its monks and nuns, and T'aego, which permits marriage.

CONFUCIANISM

For centuries, Confucianism was the basis of government and administration in Korea; although its influence in these areas has waned, it still provides a moral frame of reference for the South Koreans. More a philosophy than a religion, Confucianism is a code of morals, a system of education, ceremony and administration, which is concerned principally with the here and now, rather than the hereafter. As such, it can exist in tandem with other religions that provide a supernatural framework and cosmology.

Confucianism is essentially a system of subordinate-superior relationships – son to father, subject to ruler, younger to elder and woman to man – and places great emphasis on maintaining harmonious relationships within a strictly hierarchical society. Also of great importance are filial piety and respect for one's ancestors, and the continuation of the family line through male issue.

In China, the Confucian texts and commentaries became the basis of formal education. Any man aspiring to government was required to show his scholarship and cultivation by his knowledge of the Confucian Classics. Confucius' teachings therefore became the basis of Chinese government and administration. As the Three Kingdoms accepted Chinese learning and embraced Chinese systems of government, the influence of Confucianism spread throughout the Korean peninsula. In time, Confucian academies and a Confucian university were established, and the Koreans, like the Chinese, came to select their administrators and officials on the basis of their knowledge of the Confucian texts. In fact, the Koreans adopted Confucianism so eagerly and in so strict a form that the Chinese referred to Korea as 'the country of eastern decorum'.

The fall from grace of Buddhism and the rise to pro-minence of Confucianism from the fifteenth century onwards ensured its lasting and pervasive influence on Korean society. Although the dominance of Confucianism in Yi dynasty Korea could be said to have had a beneficial effect in terms of stability and security, it also had a negative impact on Korea's develop-ment into a modern nation. The emphasis on mastery of the Chinese Classics, calligraphy, painting and poetry as prere-quisites for government office and the lack of focus on more practical subjects seriously hampered Korea's development. The traditional scorn for trade and commerce, and the refusal to believe that anything worthwhile could emanate from coun-tries other than China, left Korea weak and unable to cope with the challenge presented by the arrival of the western powers at the end of the nineteenth century.

The Japanese colonization of Korea in 1910 effectively put an end to the Confucian form of government which had ruled the nation for more than five hundred years. However, the customs, habits and thought patterns remained and are still largely in place today. The desire for education, respect for the elderly, importance of family ties and relationships, domi-nance of the male, and emphasis on hierarchy seen in modern South Korean society all have their roots in Confucian thought (See also: Society – Introduction; Business Culture).

It is worth mentioning here, in passing, that perhaps the only foreign religion introduced to Korea not to take root was Shintoism. Japanese attempts during the colonial period (1910–45) to force their religious beliefs on the Koreans were a complete failure.

CHRISTIANITY

Christianity came to Korea relatively recently, in 1832, but has spread rapidly; in 1985, 38 per cent of Koreans who professed a religion were Protestant and 11 per cent were Catholic. For the first fifty years after its introduction to Korea, both mis-sionaries and converts to Christianity were subject to persecu-tion, but the principle of religious toleration was established following the signing of commerce treaties with western nations in the 1880s. The rapid spread of Christianity in Yi dynasty Korea was in part due to its emphasis on release from earthly suffering and heavenly rewards, which proved attrac-tive to the nation's peasants. The missionaries made a signifi-cant contribution to the modernization of Korea through the education and medical care which they provided, and gave strong and much-needed support to the Koreans under Japanese colonial rule.

ISLAM

Islam is the most recent world religion to enter South Korea. Introduced during the Korean War by Turkish troops, it has spread and there are now seven mosques and more than 20,000 converts in the Republic. The adoption of the Islam faith is said by some to be responsible for the development of South Korea's close ties with the Muslim world.

15 Education

Before the opening of contacts with the west towards the end of the nineteenth century, education in Korea was available only to boys, and focused on the study of the text and commentaries which form the core of Confucianism (see: Philosophy and Religion). Scholars were also expected to be proficient in the arts of calligraphy, painting and the writing of poetry. In traditional Korean society, women received no formal education.

The year 1883 saw the opening of the nation's first foreign language school, which employed three American teachers to train official interpreters. Ewha Haktang (now Ewha Woman's University) was opened by Methodist missionaries in 1886, and further colleges were established by foreign missionaries in the late nineteenth and early twentieth centuries. In addition, a system was established of primary and middle schools, teacher training colleges, foreign language institutes, technical and commercial colleges, and medical schools.

During its rule in Korea, the Japanese colonial government attempted to suppress the Korean language by making Japanese the official language for education and business. Access to education for Koreans was restricted, with only a small percentage able to obtain a college education.

The modernization of South Korea's education system began in earnest after the peninsula was liberated from Japanese rule in 1945. The past fifty-odd years have seen a rapid expansion of the education system; in 1991, students accounted for almost one-quarter of the population, and the literacy rate of 98 per cent far exceeded that of most advanced nations, including the United Kingdom and the United States. Enrolment in primary schools has been almost 100 per cent since the mid-1960s; enrolment in secondary schools has risen from

35 per cent in the early 1960s to almost 90 per cent in the early 1990s. The proportion of South Koreans aged between 20 and 24 years attending higher education institutes has risen from 6 per cent to 36 per cent in the same period.

The South Koreans' desire for education is strong, and stories abound concerning the financial sacrifices made by parents to ensure a good education for their children. A survey carried out in 1991 revealed that more than 50 per cent of high school students in Seoul and almost 30 per cent nationwide receive extra tutoring, at an average monthly cost of W250,000 (US$318). The total spending on extra-curricular education for middle and high school students in 1991 was W1.2 trillion (US$1.5 billion), an amount equivalent to 24 per cent of the government's education budget for the same year. The education portion of the budget generally accounts for between 20 and 22 per cent of the total, or equivalent to around 3 per cent of GNP.

Education policy is drafted by central government, which also gives advice and financial support to the regional Boards of Education. Education at the national, provincial and district level is the responsibility of the Ministry of Education, assisted by provincial boards at the secondary level, and by provincial and district offices at the primary level. The National Institute of Education has responsibility for the development of educational theory, while the planning and implementation of educational reforms comes under the jurisdiction of the Korean Educational Development Institute.

The current education system in South Korea follows the American 6–3–3–4 model, that is, six years of primary education (ages 6–11), three years of middle school (ages 12–14), and three years of high school education (ages 15–17), followed by further study at undergraduate level.

PRIMARY EDUCATION

Kindergarten education for 5- and 6-year-old children is widely available in the private sector. The right to an elementary education is guaranteed by the Constitution; six years of compulsory primary education are provided by the state. There are plans gradually to extend state-funded education to cover middle school tuition. (Currently, tuition fees are payable for middle and high school students.) In 1991, there were 8,421 kindergartens and 6,245 primary schools in South Korea, with a total of 157,906 teachers and 5.2 million students.

MIDDLE SCHOOLS

Entrance examinations for middle schools were abolished in the late 1960s, since when selection has been made by lottery from among the primary school graduates in each school's catchment area. The curriculum for the three years of middle school education includes the Korean language, mathematics, natural sciences, English, history, ethics and physical education. In addition, schools funded by religious foundations may teach religious education. In 1991, there were 2,498 middle schools in the Republic, with 92,348 teachers and 2.2 million students.

HIGH SCHOOLS

The entrance examination for high schools was abolished in 1974 and replaced by a government-supervised preliminary test. Successful students are then assigned to a local school by lottery. The new system aims to be more egalitarian and adopt a comprehensive approach, with classes of mixed ability rather than elitist institutions.

There are two types of high school in South Korea: general, three-year high schools and two-year, vocational high schools, including commercial, technical, agricultural, arts and navigation high schools. Vocational training is strongly promoted by the government in the interests of expanding the pool of skilled manpower. Subjects taught at this level include Korean language and history, a foreign language, ethics and morality, sciences, social studies, music and fine arts, and Chinese characters. In 1991, there were 1,702 general and vocational high schools in South Korea, with a total of 95,272 teachers and 2.2 million students.

The sheer size of classes makes teaching by rote virtually unavoidable. Although official targets for class sizes do exist – 45 in primary schools and 60 in middle and high schools – there are still schools which have to work a shift system.

HIGHER EDUCATION

Higher education in the Republic of Korea comprises universities, independent colleges, junior and normal colleges, and graduate schools. Higher education is more or less evenly divided between private and state-run institutions, with scholarships available for promising students. Undergraduate courses typically last four years and students may go on to master's or doctoral programmes after completing their undergraduate studies.

All students wishing to be considered for college or university entrance must apply to the institution of their choice and then sit a state-run preliminary examination. The marks received in that examination, together with the student's high school records and performance at interview, will determine the success of his or her application. In 1992, it was estimated that the ratio of applicants to places was 4:1. The government's allocation of students to a particular institution or field of study will often reflect the priorities of its education policies, such as increasing the number of science or engineering graduates.

In general, institutes of higher education have a free hand in choosing their curricula, but the following subjects are compulsory: Korean language and cultural history, philosophy, introduction to the natural sciences, physical education and a foreign language. In 1991, there were 560 higher education institutions in South Korea (junior vocational colleges, teachers' colleges, colleges, universities and graduate schools), with 43,821 teachers and 1.5 million students.

The importance of entrance to a top university cannot be overstated. Graduates from the best universities, which include the state-run Seoul National University and the private Yonsei, Koryŏ and Ewha universities, have traditionally enjoyed a significant advantage in later years, in terms of career, alumni networking and social status. However, the economic slump of the past few years and the reduction in job opportunities has meant that even graduates of the most prestigious institutions are not guaranteed a top job.

Cramming and the 'examination hell' are part and parcel of getting into university, and with a success rate of just one in three, many have to go through the process more than once. The financial burden placed on their parents to pay tuition fees adds an extra dimension to the pressure felt by high school students. Every year brings stories of suicides by students who failed to achieve their goals.

Once the hurdle of entrance to university has been overcome, students can look forward to at least four years of relative freedom and opportunity. For some it is a last chance to rebel before settling down to corporate and family life, for others a chance to earn money by tutoring next year's would-be entrants. The legalization of private tutoring in 1989 has provided undergraduates with a ready source of income and boosted their disposable income – just four hours' tuition a week can bring in W500,000 (US$635) per month.

In the late 1980s, more than 20,000 students were receiving education overseas. Three-quarters of these were studying in the United States, which remains the most popular choice for postgraduate study. There were almost 300 foreign lecturers working in South Korea, and approximately 250 Korean staff working in education institutes overseas. The ROK government offers scholarships to foreigners wishing to study at South Korean universities.

Student activism has always been a part of university life

in South Korea (see also: History; Politics) and, in Confucian terms, scholars have the responsibility of upbraiding the nation's rulers when their actions deserve criticism. The role which the students played in the overthrow of the Syngman Rhee regime in 1960 and the implementation of democratic reforms in 1987 cannot be over-emphasized (see: History). But these were both occasions on which the students had identified causes supported by the middle classes. Without that support, the demonstrations – be they anti-Japanese, anti-government, anti-United States, or pro-North Korea – may be noisy and disruptive, but they do not pose a real threat to social order. To the observer, they seem well orchestrated, with both students and riot police observing unwritten rules; the swing of feelings against the students after the death of seven riot police on Dongeui University campus in May 1989 and the public outrage when student radicals attacked the prime minister with flour and eggs in 1991 clearly showed when the students had overstepped their mark.

The government's rather paternalistic attitude has been that the students should concentrate on their studies and leave political activities to their elders. Expulsion from university can have far-reaching effects in terms of ability to get a job, or even to get married. For many, the demonstrations are a final display of defiance before settling down to family and corporate life.

But it is not only the students who have been raising their voices in protest. In May 1989, 200 teachers formed their own union in defiance of a government ban (teachers are considered to be quasi-civil servants, and therefore are banned from collective action). Their defiance led to disciplinary action and the dismissal from their posts of almost 1,500 union members. In 1992, the Teachers' Committee for Educational Reforms and Reinstatement of Dismissed Teachers was formed, and quickly enlisted more than 30,000 members. Despite the dismissal of the chairman and vice-chairman from their teaching posts, the committee continued its campaign.

Outside the formal education system, there is a good deal of activity in continuing and non-formal education. The government has established an adult education programme; evening classes, women's classes and a radio correspondence college are also available. Furthermore, one of the national television channels is set aside exclusively for educational programmes.

16 Housing

It is fair to say that housing is one of the few failures in the Republic of Korea's economic development. In 1991, the number of households in South Korea was 10.6 million, while the number of dwellings was 7.9 million, giving a housing supply ratio of 74.5 per cent. Although this represents an improvement over the level of 69.7 per cent recorded in 1985, it remains below the level of 78.2 per cent seen in 1970. Moreover, the 1991 statistics show a disparity between housing shortages in urban and rural areas; the urban housing supply ratio in that year stood at 67.3 per cent, compared with 95.9 per cent in rural areas.

During the 1970s and 1980s, net additions made to the national housing stock were insufficient to keep pace with the growth in the number of households. The increase in the number of households was due in large part to the shrinking average size of households, escalating urbanization and increasing mobility (see: Demography). This, combined with migration from rural to urban areas, resulted in an acute urban housing shortage; in the larger cities, many households were forced to share accommodation, while rental and purchase prices soared.

A survey carried out in 1991 revealed that, on average, it takes a South Korean couple 8.5 years to save enough money to buy their own home. The average cost of a home in 1991 was W37 million (US$47,000) nationwide and W50 million (US$63,500) in Seoul, against an average monthly income of W917,000 (US$1,165). The average dwelling size was 86.1 square feet (72 square metres). The survey also revealed that, while only 50.6 per cent of the population owned their own home, more than 400,000 people owned two or more houses, and over 1,500 owned more than ten properties. The 41–60 age group accounted for the largest share (57 per cent) of house-owners, with just 3 per cent coming from the 21–30 age group.

The housing shortage combined with other factors, such as the shortage of land for industrial use, the building of new satellite cities, and plans to develop the west coast as an industrial region, to produce a real estate boom. Average land prices, which had risen by 9.6 per cent in 1987, jumped by 21.7 per cent in 1988, and by 26.8 per cent in 1989. Between 1976 and 1990, land prices rose by 13.3 times nationwide, and housing prices by 7.1 times.

In July 1991, the most expensive land in South Korea was to be found in the central district of Myŏngdong in Seoul, where 1 square metre (1.2 square yards) was valued at W43 million (US$54,640). The most expensive residential real estate was to be found in Taehyŏndong, Seoul, valued at W10 million (US$12,700) per square metre; at the other end of scale, the cheapest land was to be found in an area of Kyŏngbuk Province, costing just W160 (US$0.20) per square metre.

The rampant real estate speculation prompted government action. The landownership system was reformed, limits were placed on the ownership of housing lots in urban areas, and the nation's conglomerates were ordered to sell off their idle land. In 1992, land prices fell for the first time since 1975.

One of the election pledges made by President Roh T'ae-woo in 1987 was the construction of an additional two million housing units during his term of office. (The current five-year plan calls for the housing supply ratio to be raised to 82 per cent by 1996.) Of the two million units, 900,000 were to be built in the public sector and 1,100,000 in the private sector.

A record number of housing units were completed in 1988 (320,000) and 1989 (450,000), and completions for the following three years were targeted as 450,000 in 1990, 400,000 in 1991, and 380,000 in 1992. However, this policy contributed to the economic problems facing the nation in the late 1980s and early 1990s, as shortages of labour and construction materials pushed up wages and prices, and the boom in the construction sector contributed to the overheating of the economy (see: The Economy).

17 Health and Welfare

HEALTH

In the 1960s, infectious diseases were the most frequent cause of death in the Republic of Korea. In the 1980s, the leading killers were cerebral diseases and cancer of the stomach, liver and lung. Statistics for the first years of the 1990s show that circulatory and respiratory problems, cancer and traffic accidents are responsible for the majority of deaths. Factors detrimental to the national health include stress – there have been reports of death due to overwork – heavy smoking and drinking, poor diet and lack of exercise.

In the late 1980s, the incidence of digestive complaints was greater than that of respiratory ailments, with a rate of 396 per 100,000 against 385 for respiratory problems. By 1990, these positions had been reversed, with a rate of 622 per 100,000 for respiratory ailments and 509 for digestive complaints. The rapid increase in respiratory problems is attributed to worsening air pollution and heavy smoking: in 1990, the South Koreans were ranked the fourth-heaviest smokers in the world (after the Japanese, Hungarians and Poles), with an annual per capita consumption of 2,200 cigarettes. Heavy smoking is also an important factor in the high incidence of cancer in South Korea.

South Korea has the highest mortality rate for liver cancer in the world, with 24 deaths per 100,000 being attributed to it. This high rate, which compares with 14 in Japan and 1.4 in both the United States and the United Kingdom, is attributed to heavy smoking, drinking and the hot and salty Korean diet.

South Korea also holds the world record for traffic fatalities. In the first eleven months of 1992, there were more than 220,000 traffic accidents in the Republic; more than 10,000 people were killed and almost 274,000 injured. The rate of 32 deaths per 100,000 people is slightly ahead of those recorded for Portugal (31), New Zealand (28) and the former Soviet Union (22). The rates for Japan and the United States are 13 and 21 respectively.

The ROK government has recently announced plans to establish hospitals in the nation's three largest cities for the exclusive use of road traffic accident victims. As the high ratio of fatalities has been blamed partly on the lack of proper emergency services, steps will be taken to improve response times (currently averaging 20 minutes against an international standard of 10 minutes), increase the number of patrol cars and emergency telephone lines, and train patrols to administer initial medical treatment. However, the problems of haphazard driving and low levels of traffic sense, which are also major contributory factors, will take longer to address.

The first diagnosis of the Human Immuno-deficiency Virus (HIV) in South Korea was made in 1985. In 1990, the number of people with the virus was 100; this had more than doubled to 235 by late 1992, and 26 people who had developed AIDS had died. AIDS is still looked upon by many as a foreign disease, with reports that most carriers had contracted the virus while travelling or working overseas, and had passed it on after their return to South Korea.

Mandatory testing was introduced in the late 1980s for foreign visitors falling into specified categories, such as those working in the entertainment business, and there have been cases of foreigners diagnosed as HIV positive being deported from the Republic. In August 1992, the ROK government implemented mandatory testing for those foreigners who gave themselves up to the authorities during a crack-down on illegal aliens, and deported those who refused to take the test. The authorities also considered seeking the cooperation of South Korean companies employing legal foreign workers in urging them to be tested for AIDS.

As far as occupational diseases are concerned, the results of medical check-ups conducted in 1991 revealed that 55.5 per cent of those diagnosed as having occupational diseases were hard of hearing and 42.4 per cent suffered from pneumoconiosis. There were also some instances of lead, mercury and chrome poisoning. In 1991 it was also reported that, on average, six people were killed and 81 severely injured at work every day, giving South Korea one of the highest industrial accident rates in the world. In 1991, a total of 2,299 workers were killed on site, and 29,854 were left physically handicapped as the result of an accident.

The majority of the accidents (38 per cent) took place in the capital and the surrounding Kyŏnggi Province. This was attributed to the fact that the majority of construction projects are under way in this region. Experts have also blamed the increase in the use of inexperienced labourers on construction projects (due to the shortage of workers in the industry), and on the rapid execution of the projects. In July 1992, the Haengju Bridge, being built across the Han River in Seoul, collapsed in mid-construction; initial reports blamed the collapse on faulty design and slipshod work.

In 1991, there were 637 hospitals (general, dental, special and Oriental medicine hospitals) in the Republic of Korea, with a total of 107,223 beds – a ratio of 248 beds per 100,000 people. There were almost 52,000 registered doctors (including doctors of Oriental medicine), giving a doctor-to-patient ratio of 838:1. In addition, there were more than 95,000 nurses, over 10,000 dentists, and in excess of 38,000 pharmacists in South Korea in that year. The introduction of nationwide medical insurance in 1989 has resulted in an increase in the number of visits made to the doctor by South Koreans. In 1990, the average was 6.4 visits per year; that is forecast to rise to 9.1 by the end of the century.

Under the provisions of the current five-year plan, the average life expectancy for males will rise to 70 years in 1996 from 67 years in 1990. The average life expectancy for females will increase to 77 from 75 during the same period. The infant mortality rate, which stood at 17.3 per thousand live births in 1980 and 12.0 in 1990, will continue to decline, to reach 7.0 per thousand by the year 2000.

WELFARE

In 1988, the government instituted a mandatory national pension scheme for employees of companies with a workforce numbering ten or more, under which 3 per cent of an employee's gross salary is contributed – 1.5 per cent is withheld from the employee's pay and an equal amount is contributed by the company. The pension scheme is optional for firms with fewer than ten employees, farmers, fishermen, housewives and the self-employed. By the end of 1989, 4.5 million South Koreans were members of the scheme, under which persons who have made contributions for twenty years or more receive a pension equivalent to 40 per cent of their final pay-check on retirement at 55 or 60. Companies must also provide a retirement allowance system, giving a lump sum payment of one month's pay for each year served to each employee who leaves or retires, be it voluntarily or forcibly.

In July 1989, the national medical insurance scheme was expanded to cover all South Korean nationals. Companies with more than five employees must participate in the government's health insurance programme – once again, the premium is split between employee and employer – and must also provide medical examinations on hiring and then at regular intervals.

In traditional Korean society, care for the elderly was the responsibility of the children, specifically the eldest son. Although the family remains the principal source of support for the elderly, increasing life expectancy and the trend towards the nuclear family have raised concerns about long-term care for the elderly. In 1989, there were 91 homes for the aged, of which 85 provided free care. However, the number accommodated in these homes accounted for only a minuscule proportion of the nation's old people.

The government provides support for those who need care at home, those who are 'economically incapable', the aged, the handicapped and veterans. However, the number of people receiving public relief is small, reflecting to some extent the tradition of the family taking care of its own. In late 1992, there were reports that as many as 1 million handicapped people had refused to register with the authorities. The main reason given was that there was little to be gained by registering – the government's budget allowed for just W41,800 (US$53) in grants per person – but many may be reluctant to make their handicap public knowledge. The government has instituted an employment scheme for the handicapped, but only 8,648 had found work by late 1992.

18 Emigration and Immigration

EMIGRATION

Before World War II, Koreans emigrated in large numbers to Manchuria and Japan; in addition, thousands were mobilized by the colonial government to work in Japanese factories and serve in the Japanese armed forces. The Koreans who stayed on in Japan after the war have fought a long and bitter battle to gain Japanese resident status for themselves and their descendants.

In the 1960s and early 1970s, an average of 40,000 South Koreans emigrated every year, many looking to escape from poverty and social unrest and start a new life in another land. Similarly the number of South Koreans marrying foreigners rose steadily from the 1960s and into the 1970s, peaking at 4,400 in 1978. The majority of these international marriages were between South Korean women and foreign men (often American servicemen), and in many cases, the couples emigrated to the husband's home country. Marriages between South Korean men and foreign women have been less common; the importance of carrying on the family line would have made it extremely difficult, if not impossible, for an eldest son to marry a foreign woman.

With the improvement in economic conditions and standards of living in the 1980s and early 1990s, the number of South Koreans emigrating and/or marrying foreigners declined; in 1991, 17,000 emigrated and 1,775 international marriages were recorded. However, in the first six months of 1992, the number of emigrants began to rise again, with 10,104 Koreans from 5,370 households emigrating, and the majority (7,200 people from 4,501 families) heading for the United States.

In the late 1980s, there were 500,000 Koreans living in the People's Republic of China (mostly in the former Manchuria), and 250,000 in the former Soviet Union. More than 100,000 Korean nationals were living in the United States.

IMMIGRATION

South Korea is remarkable for its homogeneity. There is only one ethnic minority in the Republic – 50,000 Chinese, who accounted for just 0.13 per cent of the total population in 1988. These are typically entrepreneurs, labourers and their descendants, who came to Korea in search of work, and have established their own neighbourhoods, schools and social clubs.

There are also some 38,000 American troops currently serving in the Republic as part of the United States' defence commitment in the region, and a growing foreign community of expatriate businessmen, students and missionaries. The number of illegal immigrants and workers is unknown, but has been growing as the labour shortage in the domestic market worsens (see: Migrant Workers).

19 Migrant Workers

At the time of writing, the ROK government continues to prohibit the hiring of foreigners for manual labour (except in a few, strictly regulated areas), in order to protect the work and wage rights of South Korean nationals. Companies in certain sectors, including financial and service, may employ foreign professionals, provided that they are doing work for which South Korean nationals would not be qualified. A short-term visa can be obtained for manual workers with specialized skills or with technical qualifications, but again with the proviso that they perform functions which cannot be carried out by South Koreans.

Until the late 1980s, South Korean companies enjoyed access to a large pool of cheap, well-educated labour. As a result of the economic boom of the late 1980s, substantial wage increases and a general rise in the standard of living, companies in certain sectors are finding it harder to recruit workers. There is an increasing tendency for workers to shun the so-called 'Three D' jobs – ones which are dirty, difficult or dangerous – in favour of work in the service sector, which offers higher pay and better working conditions. This has led to severe labour shortages in the manufacturing, mining and construction sectors, and increasing calls from affected companies to be allowed to import labour from abroad.

Although these calls have received support from organizations such as the Korean Employers' Federation, some critics of the proposal maintain that the problem should be tackled at home, by employing women, prisoners and the elderly, in preference to bringing in foreign labour. There are fears that foreign workers would be unable to integrate into society because of language and cultural differences, and that their employment would lead to racial conflict. Furthermore, they may fail to return home after their contract is finished, and take jobs away from South Koreans.

South Korean construction companies have been employing foreign workers on sites overseas for a number of years. With the construction boom at home and the increasing reluctance of South Koreans to work overseas, the percentage of foreign labourers in the total overseas construction workforce rose to 72.5 per cent in 1990 from 36.1 per cent in 1986. Companies engaging in joint ventures or direct investment overseas have also in many cases relied on local labour, rather than taking a South Korean workforce with them.

There is a large pool of labour available to South Korean companies, both in South-east Asia and among ethnic Koreans living in China and the former Soviet Union. Indeed, it is these groups from which most of the illegal workers currently in South Korea have come. The liberalization of travel in 1989 resulted in a massive outflow of tourists from South Korea to South-east Asia; the arrival of free-spending South Korean tourists encouraged many workers in the region to go to Seoul to seek their fortune. For the ethnic Koreans, there was, at best, the prospect of working and/or living with relatives and, at the very least, the advantage of being facially similar to the Koreans and thus able easily to mingle with South Korean workers. The average wage of W300,000–400,000 (US$381–508) per month was far better than the money they could make at home.

In October 1991, small- and medium-sized companies were allowed to increase the proportion of foreign technical trainees in the total workforce to 5–6 per cent from 1 per cent, and the permitted period of stay for these trainees was extended to one year from three months. The following month, companies with affiliates overseas or firms engaging in exports of industrial equipment were allowed to employ up to 50 foreigners (or 20 per cent of their total workforce) as vocational trainees. In December, the regulations were further eased, to allow up to 10 per cent of a company's total workforce to be composed of foreign technical trainees. The foreign workers would be issued a six-month visa, with one extension allowed for a maximum stay of one year.

In the summer of 1992, during a crack-down on illegal working, more than 61,000 foreigners gave themselves up to the ROK authorities. Of these, over 22,000 were ethnic Koreans and a further 19,000 were Filipinos; more than 42,000 were working in 'Three D' industries. Faced with the problem of deporting so many illegal aliens, the authorities allowed the majority with manufacturing jobs to stay on for a limited period, provided that they were guaranteed by their employer and were tested for AIDS.

In 1992, the government strengthened penalties for the illegal hiring of foreigners or acting as a broker for foreign workers to three years in prison and/or a W10 million (US$12,700) fine. However, the government also announced plans to allow up to 10,000 foreigners to obtain short-term visas for working in 'Three D' jobs, and allowed selected industries with poor working environments and low wages to employ more foreign trainees.

Despite fears of diplomatic problems with South-east Asian governments, the ROK authorities announced that priority in recruitment would be given to ethnic Koreans, who, they said, should be regarded as compatriots.

20 Requirements for Visitors

VACCINATIONS

Although vaccinations are not normally required for visits to the Republic of Korea, depending on the season, it may be advisable to have cholera, typhoid and hepatitis shots and obtain malaria tablets, especially if travelling outside Seoul. Up-to-date information should be sought from a general practitioner.

PROCEDURES FOR ENTRY INTO THE REPUBLIC OF KOREA

Some visitors to the Republic of Korea do not need a valid passport. Stateless persons or visitors from a non-recognized country may be issued with a Travel Document for Aliens, available from South Korean embassies or consulates abroad. Also, personnel under the jurisdiction of the Status of Forces Agreement (SOFA) are not required to obtain a passport prior to entry. The *laissez-passer* issued by the United Nations is recognized as a valid passport by the ROK authorities.

Possession of confirmed outbound air tickets entitles transit visitors to stay for up to fifteen days for general tourism purposes without a visa. This does not apply to visitors from countries whose governments are not recognized by the South Korean government or to visitors of South African nationality, holders of Hong Kong Certificates of Identity, bearers of Portuguese Certificates of Identity, and Japanese nationals. The limit in these cases is five days, after which a visa must be obtained. Japanese visitors may stay in Korea for five days or less without visas on condition that they have an onward ticket to a third country via South Korea or a ticket to Japan via South Korea. Members of group tours do not need to obtain individual visas.

Special visa exemptions exist between South Korea and the following nations, offering automatic 30-, 60- and 90-day visas, provided that nationals visiting from these countries do not engage in paid work while in the country:

- 90 days: Austria, Bahamas, Bangladesh, Barbados, Belgium, Chile, Colombia, Costa Rica, Denmark, Dominican Republic, Finland, France, Germany, Granada, Greece, Iceland, Ireland, Liberia, Luxembourg, Malaysia, Mexico, Netherlands, Norway, Pakistan, Peru, Singapore, Spain, Sweden, Surinam, Switzerland, Thailand, Turkey, United Kingdom
- 60 days: Italy, Lesotho, Portugal
- 30 days: Tunisia

Special-interest visas can be obtained for professional and business visits. To obtain these, the applicant must have an official letter of invitation to visit the Republic of Korea.

Long-term visas for stays exceeding 90 days require entry permits from the Ministry of Justice. Once the visa is granted, the holder must apply for a Residence Certificate at the local district immigration office within 90 days of arrival in South Korea.

Application forms for all visas and the visas themselves can be obtained from South Korean embassies or consulates overseas. Under normal circumstances, the processing of applications takes one week.

Visitors wishing to extend their visa must apply to the local immigration office at least one day before the visa is due to expire. Holders of tourist and 30-day visas must apply to the district immigration office for an extension, while holders of 60-day visas must apply to the Residence Control Division, and then apply for a Residence Certificate. It is not possible to change visa status from tourist to working in South Korea; applicants must leave the country and have the status changed at an ROK embassy or consulate in another country.

Immigration laws are strictly enforced in the Republic of Korea, with periodic roundups of illegal workers, who are then fined and/or deported.

CUSTOMS: ARRIVAL

On arrival in South Korea, an oral declaration is usually acceptable for accompanied luggage. A written declaration is required for valuables and unaccompanied luggage.

As in most international airports, there are green ('Nothing to Declare') and red ('Goods to Declare') channels for customs clearance. In practice, however, there may be little to choose between the red and green channels (which are, in reality, red and green queues) in terms of waiting time and thoroughness of checks, and visitors should be prepared for a wait.

Current regulations permit the entry of personal effects and articles acquired abroad (including gifts) up to the value of W300,000 ($880). Visitors may also bring into the country 400 cigarettes, 50 cigars, 200 grams of pipe tobacco and/or 100 grams of other tobacco (combined limit of 500 grams of tobacco), two bottles of alcohol (less than 1,520cc), and two ounces of perfume. Visitors with less than US$5,000 or the equivalent in foreign currency, and with no restricted or prohibited items (see below), may also pass through the green channel.

Restricted articles are items which are contrary to the National Constitution or which are considered detrimental to public security or traditional morals. Articles which may pose a threat to national security, such as classified documents and information, counterfeit money and securities, are also restricted. Certain items are restricted under the Gunnery, Knives and Powder Control Law, the Narcotic Law, and the Psychotropic Substances Control Law. Articles subject to quarantine (plants, animals and products from such) must be declared on arrival, as must wireless transmitters and receivers.

PROCEDURES FOR DEPARTURE FROM THE REPUBLIC OF KOREA

Holders of tourist visas, transit visas and entry visas for not exceeding 90 days do not need any additional documentation when leaving the country. An airport tax is payable at the port of departure (W7,200 [US$9.15] in 1992). Visitors who stay for more than 90 days must hand in their Residence Certificate to the Immigration Office at the point of departure. Single-entry certificates will be retained by the immigration authorities; receipts are issued for multiple-entry certificates, which must be collected on returning to South Korea from the Immigration Office at the original point of departure.

CUSTOMS: DEPARTURE

For visitors or residents wishing to re-enter South Korea, valuables such as watches, cameras, precious metals, jewels and furs, which will be used during the trip and then brought back into the country, must be declared prior to departure. Failure to do so could result in taxation on re-entry.

The export of certain items is restricted. These include cultural properties, such as crafts, paintings and sculptures, which can only be taken out of the country if they are judged to be of no historic or cultural value. Reproduction antiques (such as vases and wooden chests) pose no problem in this regard. If there are any doubts about the value of a particular item, queries should be addressed to the Art and Antiques Assessment Office in Seoul (telephone: 662-0106).

PART FOUR

Culture

Culture

21 Introduction

Throughout the centuries the Koreans have maintained a cultural identity influenced by, yet distinct from, that of neighbouring countries. Indeed, far from imitating Chinese culture, the Koreans adapted and blended it with their own culture, and played an important role in the transmission of Chinese culture to Japan.

A large number of cultural artefacts have been lost over time and countless historic buildings have been destroyed by war, most recently in the Korean War of the early 1950s. Recent years, however, have seen a revival of interest among South Koreans in their national cultural heritage. Efforts are being made to recover, restore and preserve cultural and historical treasures, and there is a nationwide search for artefacts from all eras. Although discoveries have been made throughout the country, undoubtedly the finest have been in the city of Kyŏngju, which was the capital of the Korean peninsula under the Shilla dynasty (AD 668–935).

The Law on the Protection of Cultural Properties, enacted in 1962, designates two broad categories of cultural asset: tangible and intangible. Tangible cultural assets are historic objects, including national treasures and treasured objects, and scenic places or sites of cultural and artistic interest. There are three scenic places protected by the law, and five sites with historic value: these include the city of Kyŏngju, mentioned above, and Pŏpchu and Haein temples. All the historical and cultural objects and sites are classified and numbered; for example, the South Gate (Namdaemun) in Seoul is listed as National Treasure No. 1.

Intangible cultural assets include forms, styles or techniques in the fields of art, drama, music and handicrafts, which are part of the nation's artistic tradition and heritage and uni-

113

que to the Korean people. These assets are usually associated with a person or group of people who have kept the traditions alive over the centuries. Examples of intangible cultural assets are the Pongsan masked dance, farmers' music, folk songs, bamboo crafts, and embroidery. It is only during the past three decades that research into these intangible assets has been carried out – skills and techniques are now carefully recorded for posterity and passed on to the younger generation. The government provides financial support and opportunities for performance or exhibition to the artists involved.

In 1989, there were 247 national treasures, 1,002 treasures, 325 cultural spots, 6 historical spots, 271 natural monuments, 90 intangible cultural assets, and 221 folklore materials.

The Korean Folk Village was created in 1977 to preserve and protect the nation's intangible cultural assets. Visitors to the village, located less than an hour's drive from Seoul, can see examples of all kinds of traditional architecture, from farmhouses to Buddhist temples, watch craftsmen at work making fans, calligraphy paper or bamboo items, and watch live performances of traditional dance and music.

The National Academy of Arts promotes the arts within the Republic of Korea, represents all artists, and deliberates issues related to the promotion of the arts. There are a number of fine museums throughout the country, including the National Museum (and its provincial branches), the National Folk Museum, and the National Museum of Modern Art. In recent years, a number of excellent theatres and concert venues have been built in Seoul, notably the Sejong Cultural Centre, the Seoul Arts Centre, and the Seoul Nori Madang, an open-air theatre for traditional music and dance performances.

22 The Arts

MUSIC AND DANCE

Traditional Korean music and dance can be classified in three main categories: religious (which accompanies Confucian and Buddhist rituals), court or ceremonial, and folk. Court music can be further subdivided into Korean music and that introduced from China. The instruments used to play this are also of both domestic and Chinese origin.

Traditional Korean music differs from western music in a number of fundamental respects, the most notable being that the music is based on a pentatonic or five-note scale rather than the eight-note scale used in the west. The characteristics of Korean dance are the use of the heel for stepping and turning, the gentle upward pulsing of the shoulders and floating of the arms, and the slow rising and sinking movements of the knees. Dance is an essential component of many traditional music performances.

Confucian ritual music (Korean: *aak*) is the most ancient type of music introduced to Korea from China. Just as the Koreans adopted and adapted Chinese systems of government and administration and studied the Confucian Classics, so they also adopted the music and dance which were performed to accompany Confucian ceremonies and rituals.

The music for these rituals is slow and solemn, and is played by two groups of musicians, one group seated on the terrace of the shrine and the other positioned at the rear of the shrine. The slow and graceful dance performed at these Confucian ceremonies dates back some nine hundred years. The number of dancers was determined by the importance of the occasion; for the most important ceremonies, there were eight lines of eight dancers. In traditional Korea, the bureaucracy was divided into two categories, civil and military;

during the performance, the dancers representing the civil officials carried a flute and a feather, while those representing the military officials carried a wooden shield and a hatchet. The dance is still performed twice a year at the Confucian University in Seoul (Sŏnggyun'gwan) and once at the Chongmyo royal shrine.

The main aim of **Buddhist dance and music** was as a prayer to Buddha to allow the souls of the dead to escape the cycle of rebirth and enter Nirvana or Paradise. Only four dances have survived until today: the Butterfly Dance (Korean: *nabich'um*), the Devil Dance (*moguch'um*), the Monks' Dance (*sŭngmuch'um*) and the Cymbal Dance (*parach'um*). Although many of the Buddhist dances performed in Korea originated in India, and were subsequently introduced to Korea through contacts with China, it is impossible to detect any Indian influence in the dances as performed today. The dances are often performed as part of a dance troupe's repertoire, as well as on certain holy days at Buddhist temples.

In addition to music and dance related to Buddhist and Confucian rituals, there are also a number of dances which form part of **shaman** rituals (see: Philosophy and Religion). The shaman's dance, which is performed in order to exorcise evil spirits, cure or avert illness and bring good luck, consists mainly of frenzied movements to the accompaniment of loud music. The shaman typically dances with two fans or performs acrobatic feats with symbolic objects such as knives and a tree of bells. These dances, too, are now performed by dance troupes as well as for religious purposes.

Many of Korea's **folk dances** have their origin in rural life and the agricultural cycle. The farmers' dance, the liveliest and most exuberant of all Korean dances, has been performed over the centuries to celebrate the planting and harvesting of crops. It is performed to the accompaniment of drums, gongs, oboes and squealing trumpets; the dancers themselves carry gongs and hour-glass drums. Dressed in white, with multi-coloured sashes and hats, the dancers give dazzling displays of acrobatic movements, all the while twirling long paper streamers attached to the crown of their hats. The most famous of the modern folk dance troupes is Samulnori, which has given its name to the revival of this style of music and dancing, and has performed to audiences all over the world.

Korean **masked dances** (Korean: *t'alch'um*) were originally folk plays combining music and dance, which were performed in the open air. In the play, the various characters, each wearing a distinctive mask, lampooned the corruption of the upper classes, the depravity of Buddhist monks, and the triangular love affair between a husband, his wife and his concubine.

Only one troupe now performs the *sandae* masked dance, and this dance has been designated an intangible cultural treasure. Recent years have seen a revival of interest in farmers' dances and masked dance on university campuses.

The Buddhist ceremonial drum dance was adopted as a folk dance in the early sixteenth century. In the Monks' Dance (Korean: *sŭngmu*), the dancers perform while playing hour-glass drums slung around their necks. In the Nine Drum Dance (*kugomu*), the performers play three drums each, which are suspended in front of them, to their left and to their right. The dancers playing increasingly rapid and complicated rhythm patterns, spinning and whirling between the drums.

Military music (Korean: *ch'uit'a*) was traditionally played to accompany parades or ceremonies such as the opening and closing of the city gates. The music was played by two sections of musicians: those playing louder instruments such as oboes, trumpets, cymbals, gongs and drums walked in front of the important person in a parade, while musicians performing on softer instruments such as flutes and hour-glass drums walked behind.

A form of improvised, solo music (Korean: *sanjo*) was played on a flute or zither, accompanied by an hour-glass drum. The length of the piece varied according to the mood and interplay between the performers. This remains one of the most popular forms of traditional music today.

In addition to the purely instrumental forms, there were also **vocal pieces**, such as lyric songs (Korean: *kagok*), narrative songs (*kasa*) and short lyric songs (*sijo*). All of these were performed by professional singers, accompanied by one or more musicians.

There are more than fifty **traditional musical instruments** which are still used in court and folk music performance in Korea. Many more are now obsolete or infrequently used. Unlike in the west, where instruments are classified as strings, reed, brass or percussion, instruments in Korea are classified according to the eight materials from which they are made. These are: metal, stone, silk, bamboo, gourd, clay, leather and wood.

Among the most interesting of Korean traditional instruments are the bronze bells (Korean: *p'yŏnjong*) and stone chimes (*p'yŏn'gyŏng*), which are used in ceremonial court music and Confucian ritual music. In the first of these, sixteen bronze bells are suspended from a wooden frame and struck with a hammer made of horn. The bells are all of equal size, the pitch of each being determined by the thickness of the metal. They have an exact counterpart in the sixteen L-shaped stone chimes, which are made of a stone similar to jade, and

117

are also suspended from a wooden stand. The pitch of the chimes is regulated by the ratio of the length of the shorter end of the L-shape to that of the longer end, and also by the thickness of the stone. The tone of the chimes is softer, and does not carry as far as that of the bells.

Gongs (Korean: *ching*) of various sizes are used in traditional music, most commonly in folk music, where small gongs played by the dancers are used to set the rhythm for the dance. Korean gongs are shaped like a shallow basin and held suspended from the hand on a cord. The gongs are then struck with a wooden stick or hammer to produce a loud, harsh sound.

The hour-glass drum (Korean: *changgo*) is probably the most popular of all traditional Korean instruments. The drum has two heads, which give it its hour-glass shape: the skin on the left head is thick, and is struck with the palm of the hand, producing a soft, deep sound, whereas the skin on the right head is thinner and is struck with a thin stick to give a sharper, harsher sound. The cords that stretch between the two heads can be adjusted to regulate the sound produced by the right head. The *changgo* can be played as a solo instrument or as part of an ensemble, and is often carried by dancers.

There are two popular types of zither among the traditional musical instruments: the six-stringed *kŏmun'go* and the twelve-stringed *kayagŭm*. The strings of the *kŏmun'go* are stretched over sixteen moveable bridges, and are tuned by twisting the round pegs securing the strings at one end of the instrument. The musician plays the strings with a plectrum held in the right hand, and uses the left hand to stop the strings at the bridges, producing a distinctive long, wavering vibrato. The *kayagŭm* can be used as a solo instrument, as an accompaniment for singing or as part of an ensemble. The musician either plucks the strings with the fingers or flicks them with the finger snapped from behind the thumb.

The two-stringed fiddle (Korean: *haegŭm*) is used in the performance of all music originally from China. Two strings are stretched between the instrument's open sound box and its tuning pegs; the hairs of the bow lie between the two. The fiddle produces long notes with a somewhat harsh and nasal tone.

The largest bamboo flute used in traditional music is the fixed-pitch flute (Korean: *taegŭm*), 30 inches long, with six finger holes. There is also a large hole covered by a membrane, which vibrates when air is blown through the instrument. This flute can be played both as a solo instrument, and in an orchestra, in which case the other instruments tune to the *taegŭm*.

The small flute (Korean: *tanso*), used only to play Korean

music, has six finger holes, including one on the underside of the instrument. The double-reed oboe (*p'iri*) is made from a bamboo cylinder, with eight finger holes, including one on the underside. The Chinese version of this instrument produces a heptatonic (seven-note) scale, whereas the Korean version produces a pentatonic (five-note) scale.

With the abdication of King Sunjong and the enforcement of Japanese colonial rule in 1910, **court music** was no longer required for state functions. However, the traditions were preserved and performing skills were passed down from generation to generation. Following the establishment of a modern republic in 1948, the court music became part of the nation's cultural heritage. The National Classical Music Institute was established, providing for musicians to be trained in the performance of court music.

Western music was introduced to Korea by western missionaries towards the end of the nineteenth century in the form of hymns and other church music. The first western orchestras were formed during the Japanese colonial period (1910–45), since when a number of symphony orchestras, chamber music groups and opera companies have been formed. In recent years, young musicians have been influenced by western rock and pop music, although the development of these musical styles has been carefully monitored by the authorities, fearful of the perceived connotations of drug-abuse, permissiveness and anti-social behaviour.

Modern dance was introduced to Korea in 1926 by the Japanese dancer Ishii Baku, who taught most of the Korean dancers who later became famous in modern dance. Today, modern dance troupes in South Korea perform western ballet, modern interpretations of traditional dances, and new creative dance. Although many of the nation's dances had fallen into obscurity by the early 1970s, there has been a revival of interest in traditional dance over the past two decades, and á number of the dances have now been designated national cultural assets.

The visitor wishing to see a short display of some of the best in traditional Korean music and dance can spend an evening at the Korea House during his or her stay in Seoul.

DRAMA

Although rich in music and dance traditions, it cannot be said that Korea has a strong tradition of dramatic art, comparable to Chinese opera and Japanese *Noh* or *kabuki*. Drama was scorned by the Confucians as being trivial, and Korea lacked an urban middle class which could support the development of theatres.

As has been mentioned above, folk dramas satirizing the lives and shortcomings of the upper classes were popular in traditional Korea and are experiencing a revival nowadays. Puppet plays were popular in the Yi dynasty (1392–1910), the most representative being *kkoktukaksi*, a play presented by a travelling group of musicians and puppeteers. As in the masked dances, the aim of the play was satirical, and dance and music were an important part of the performance. *Kkoktukaksi* is still occasionally performed today.

The first modern drama was staged in Korea in 1909 by a Korean who had returned from exile in Japan. The new drama movement grew, with newly established drama groups presenting both foreign plays and their own original works. However, the groups were forcibly disbanded by the Japanese, as cultural life in Korea was all but suspended during the 35 years of Japanese rule in Korea.

Five years after liberation from Japanese rule, the Korean National Theatre was established in Seoul in 1950, and drama in South Korea has continued to develop under the influence of both Korean and western styles and themes. The development of drama has received a boost in the past few years from the implementation of democratic reforms which have allowed greater freedom of expression than under previous regimes. Prior censorship of scripts was virtually abolished in 1988, and official permission is no longer necessary to form an acting company or drama group. As in many countries, however, live drama has been adversely affected by the advent of television drama, film and video.

The first Korean kinodrama (a play with motion picture inserts) was produced in 1919; the first silent film was made in 1923, and the first 'talkie' twelve years later. The motion picture industry, which was used by the Japanese as a propaganda tool during the colonial period, stagnated for more than three decades after Liberation, due in large part to strict government censorship and the advent of television.

The improvement in technical abilities during the 1980s, the gradual relaxation of censorship, and growing public dissatisfaction with the television diet of soap operas and historical melodramas has led to a revival of interest in the cinema. South Korean film makers are now gaining recognition and winning awards at international film festivals.

There are currently more than ten all-purpose theatres in South Korea, the largest being the Sejong Cultural Centre and the National Theatre. The Seoul Arts Centre, which covers 234,000 square metres, will, when completed, comprise a concert hall, calligraphy hall, art gallery, art library, festival hall and cultural theme park. Seoul also has a traditional amphitheatre, the Nori Madang, which stages performances of traditional and folk entertainment, and a large number of small theatres.

LITERATURE

Traditionally in Korea, education was restricted to the upper classes, and focused on the study of the Chinese Classics and commentaries upon them, which formed the curriculum for the national civil service examinations. Scholars, therefore, learned the Chinese language and memorized Chinese characters in order to master the texts and pass the examinations. Until the Korean alphabet was invented in the fifteenth century, the only means of writing down the Korean language was a system called *idu*, which used Chinese characters to convey either the meaning of a word or the pronunciation of a Korean grammatical particle (see: Language).

Records of historical and religious events account for most of Korea's early prose literature. Among the best known works are: the History of the Three Kingdoms (Korean: *Samguk sagi*), written in the twelfth century, and the Historical Relics of the Three Kingdoms (*Samguk yusa*), written in the thirteenth century. Poetry was also written in Chinese characters – 'local songs' (*hyangga*) and 'popular songs' (*sogyo*) – and showed the influence of Buddhism, Taoism, Confucianism and shamanism.

The development of truly vernacular literature was only made possible by the invention of the Korean alphabet in the mid-fifteenth century. The first major work in the Korean script was *Yongbi Ŏch'ŏn'ga* (Songs of the Flying Dragons), compiled to celebrate the founding of the YC dynasty. The work, which includes heroic tales, foundation myths, folk beliefs and prophecies, marked the beginning of the native vernacular literature.

However, by that time, the Chinese language and writing system were so well-entrenched among the upper classes that the new system *han'gŭl*, was slow to take root. For the next five hundred years, *han'gŭl* was used mainly by the ladies at court and the lower classes, and few literary works were written using the Korean alphabet.

'The Myths of Kumo', a collection of short stories written by Kim Si-sŭp in the late fifteenth century, is generally regarded as the first example of Korean fiction. It was more than two hundred years later that the first work of Korean fiction written in *hangŭl* appeared, Hŏ Kyun's *The Tale of Hong Kil-dong*. Another pioneer in vernacular fiction was Kim Man-jun, who wrote of Korea's best-known novels, *The Nine Cloud Dream*, in 1689.

Love stories and heroic tales began to appear in novel form during the later years of the Yi dynasty, as well as satirical and romantic novels. The most famous and best loved of these stories were *The Tale of Shim Chŏng*, the story of a devoted daughter who offers her life to restore her blind father's eyesight, and *The Tale of Ch'unhyang*, a comedy concerning a girl, her lover and a villain. These are still popular today.

However, the novel failed to develop fully in Korea; many maintain that this was due to the lack of a middle class to support the publication of fiction. The peasants were illiterate and the upper classes held only Chinese poetry in high esteem. Favourite forms of poetry included the *sijo*, a three-line poem written in 45 syllables, with strict groupings between the lines. Common themes were loyalty to the king, love, separation, drinking, and nature. *Sijo* remains a popular poetic form today.

The eighteenth century saw the beginning of a movement away from Chinese themes and styles of writing, in favour of a more realistic style, reflecting the Korean world. In 1896, with the publication of the first Korean-language newspaper, the Korean alphabet became a part of everyday life in Korea. At the same time, the New Literature Movement began to develop, experimenting with new themes and literary styles, under western influences, most notably symbolism and lyricism. The role of literature was now seen as to enlighten, educate and liberate; poems, short stories, and essays with nationalistic themes or dealing with political and social issues were published, taking literature out of the court and on to the streets.

Attempts by the Japanese to eradicate the Korean language during their 35-year rule in Korea proved largely unsuccessful. Literary works were still written in *han'gŭl*, which became a vehicle for protest against colonial rule, and a means of preserving the national identity. Towards the end of the period, however, literary publications were almost at a standstill due to strict censorship.

Joy at Korea's liberation from Japanese rule was soon overshadowed by the political reality of civil war. Korean literature of the period was humanistic and pessimistic, with bitter criticism of the society at that time. Although western influences were dominant in the years following the Korean War, there was a revival of Oriental literature in the 1960s, and calls for a return to traditional techniques. Recent years have seen a steady growth in the publication of literary magazines and the emergence of new writers.

ART

Each of the Korean dynasties produced its own artistic master-pieces, from the golden jewellery of Shilla, to the celadon pottery of Koryǒ and the painting and calligraphy of Yi. The characteristics of traditional Korean art are a feeling of live-liness and earthiness, a strong sense of naturalism, a lack of concern for technical perfection, and the use of texture and grain.

The earliest **paintings** found in Korea date back to the Three Kingdoms period, and were discovered on the walls of Koguryǒ and Paekche burial tombs. The murals show vividly the daily life and rituals of the people, as well as depicting mythical animals, such as the four heavenly animals (black turtle, blue dragon, white tiger and red phoenix).. The only surviving example of Shilla painting is a saddle flap on which a white horse is shown flying through the clouds.

Painting in both China and Korea was closely associated with Confucian scholarship. In addition to his mastery of classic Chinese texts, a true scholar was also proficient in painting, poetry-writing and calligraphy. As in China, favourite subjects were the 'Four Gentlemen' (orchid, plum, bamboo and chrysanthemum), landscapes, portraits, animals and birds. Buddhism also influenced painting, perhaps most strongly in the Koryǒ dynasty, when many monks tried their hand at painting, taking religious themes as their subjects.

At first, Korean artists were strongly influenced by Chinese styles and themes, painting imaginary landscapes and scenes from court life. In the eighteenth century, however, artists broke with this tradition and began to paint actual scenes observed on their trips around Korea. Genre painting also became popular in the latter part of the Yi dynasty; artists painted scenes from everyday life, showing not only the lives of the upper classes, but also those of the commoners.

The tradition of folk painting (Korean: *minhwa*) dates back to ancient Korea. These paintings use unorthodox techniques and styles to depict nature and the life of the commoners.

Western-style painting was introduced to Korea during the Japanese colonial period, but few notable works were produced during this period. Modern art began to take root in South Korea in the late 1950s, and western influences such as those of surrealism and abstract art began to enter the Republic, as South Korean artists travelled and trained overseas.

With the exception of the carved wooden devil-posts which were traditionally placed outside villages to ward off evil spirits, most **sculpture** in Korea has been associated with and influenced by Buddhism. One of the most important and impressive examples of Buddhist sculpture in South Korea is to be found in the Sŏkkuram Grotto, near Kyŏngju, the capital of the Unified Shilla dynasty. An artificial cave in the hillside contains a 12-foot-high (3.5-metre) granite statue of the Buddha, surrounded by 37 figures placed in accordance with their rank in the Buddhist pantheon of deities. When the cave was open to the elements, the jewel set in the middle of the Buddha's forehead caught the first rays of the rising sun, which shone out, protecting all those around.

There are few examples of sculpture from the Koryŏ dynasty, and the ascendancy of Confucianism in the Yi dynasty led to the decline of Buddhism and its related arts.

Some of the earliest Korean artefacts discovered are pieces of **pottery** decorated with a comb pattern, dating back (at least) to the first millennium BC. Although very few pieces remain from the Paekche and Koguryŏ tombs, large quantities of unglazed stoneware have been discovered, dating back to the time of Shilla. The pottery is characterized by a grey colour and rectangular perforations in the pedestals of the pots. Glazed roofing tiles have also been found, which show that the Koreans had developed skills in glazing before the introduction of Chinese pottery.

The finest examples of Korean pottery are undoubtedly to be found in the Koryŏ-period celadon. The tenth to the fourteenth centuries were a golden age for ceramics in both China and Korea. At first the Korean potters were influenced by Chinese shapes and techniques, but gradually developed their own shapes, colours and skills. It is said that the Chinese considered Koryŏ celadon so perfect that it was declared to be one of the ten most wonderful things in the world – the other nine were all Chinese.

Korean celadon is characterized by its bluish-green glaze and by the natural objects reflected in the shapes and decoration; vases are shaped like gourds, and water-droppers like monkeys. Common subjects in decorations are cranes, ducks, clouds and willow trees. There is also a sense of humour and playfulness that comes through in the design and decoration of Korean celadon pottery; one well-known piece, an incense burner, has tiny rabbits for the feet.

The greatest achievement of the Korean potters was the inlay technique used for celadon, in which a design carved into the unglazed body of a pot was filled with black or white slip, giving a delightful and often intricate design under the glaze. The best-known example of this inlay technique is the Thousand Crane Vase, decorated with numerous circles, each enclosing a crane flying through the clouds.

The delicate forms and complicated designs of Koryŏ celadon were replaced by the more robust shapes and almost abstract decorations of *punch'ŏng* ware in the Yi dynasty. After the Japanese invasions of Korea at the end of the sixteenth century, many potters were kidnapped and taken to Japan, where their work exercised a strong influence over the development of Japan's ceramic tradition. Also of note in the later years of the dynasty were the blue and white wares, in the Chinese tradition, and plain white wares for ceremonial use.

A substantial number of Korean ceramic pieces were taken out of the country during the Japanese colonial period, and many Koreans maintain that private collections in Japan house more pieces than the National Museum in Seoul. The ceramic traditions carry on today in South Korea: potters produce both reproductions of famous masterpieces and original works, using either traditional or modern designs and shapes.

As examples of **metalwork**, a small number of Buddhist temple bells remain, the oldest of which dates back to the Unified Shilla dynasty. Korean bells are convex in shape, and are struck from the outside with a log or hammer. The top ring is usually shaped like a dragon; other decorations include studs below the shoulder of the bell and Buddhist motifs such as lotus flowers and flying angels.

The finest examples of metalwork in Korea are the gold crowns and jewellery (earrings, necklaces and belts) found in Paekche and Shilla burial tombs. The spectacular crowns, which were probably for ceremonial use, are constructed of thin sheets of gold formed into symbolic trees and antlers, with jade pendants and shimmering gold leaves. The crowns and jewellery are on display at the National Museum in Kyŏngju.

Turning to **architecture**, the oldest stone structures extant in South Korea are dolmens or burial monuments, dating back centuries before the birth of Christ. There are no wooden structures still in existence that are older than the late Koryŏ period, and many were destroyed by fire or war. Traditional Korean architecture was heavily influenced by Chinese styles, and the basic structural style hardly differs from that used in China. However, the construction of Korean buildings – palaces, temples and private houses – also aimed to achieve simplicity and harmony with nature.

The most famous example of traditional architecture in South Korea is Pulguk Temple in Kyŏngju, which has been restored to its former glory. Although the majority of new private and commercial buildings in Seoul are in a modern style, some are still built with traditional influences in mind; the Sejong Cultural Centre in Seoul in a good example of the blending of western and Korean architectural styles.

Seoul boasts a number of good museums and fine art galleries, some of which are now sponsored by business concerns – the Kŭmho Fine Arts Hall (Kŭmho Group) and the Hoam Fine Arts Exhibition Hall (Samsung Group), to name but two.

23 Language

The official language of the Republic of Korea is Korean, which belongs to the Altaic group of the Ural-Altaic family of languages. Other languages within that group are Turkish and Mongolian. Grammatically speaking, Korean has some relationship with the Japanese language.

INFLUENCES ON THE KOREAN LANGUAGE
The influence exerted by China over all aspects of Korean life in centuries past is also seen in the Korean language. The introduction and acceptance of Buddhist and Confucian texts in Korea in the early centuries BC, and the adoption of Chinese forms of government and administration, meant that education in Korea followed similar lines to that in China. That is, education centred on the study of the Confucian Classics and the commentaries upon them, and therefore required the knowledge of Chinese grammar and Chinese characters. For centuries, Chinese was the language of literacy in Korea.

Prior to the invention of the Korean alphabet (*han'gŭl*) in the fifteenth century, the Korean language was written down using a system called *idu*, which used Chinese characters to convey either the meaning of a word or the pronunciation of a Korean grammatical particle. This fact that this system was used is even more remarkable when one considers that Chinese and Korean bear no resemblance to each other grammatically.

Chinese words were absorbed into the Korean vocabulary, and even today a substantial portion of the vocabulary used in spoken and written Korean is of Chinese origin. These loan words, which comprise 60 per cent of the vocabulary used in South Korea, can be written either in *han'gŭl* or as the original Chinese characters; the characters retain their meaning but are given a Korean pronunciation. The mastery of the basic 3,000

Chinese characters is still a requirement in schools in the Republic of Korea; however, the use of Chinese characters has been eliminated in North Korea.

The Japanese also borrowed a substantial number of Chinese characters, which are still in current usage, having been given Japanese pronunciations. In all three languages, the written characters are identical in appearance and meaning, but the pronunciation is distinct, though often clearly related. For example the word 'library' is pronounced 'tosŏgwan' in Korean, 't'ushukuan' in Chinese, and 'toshokan' in Japanese.

Despite attempts by the Japanese to eradicate the Korean language during their colonization of the peninsula (1910–45), there was virtually no assimilation of the Japanese language during that period. More recently, an increasing number of western words have entered the Korean language, their acceptance being made easier by the fact that *han'gŭl* can be used to transcribe the majority of western words. Students of the language find it alternately amusing and frustrating to find that the word which they have been struggling to translate is, in fact, a transliteration of 'Kentucky Fried Chicken' or 'bargain sale'.

HAN'GŬL: THE CORRECT SOUNDS FOR INSTRUCTING THE PEOPLE

In the mid fifteenth century, a phonetic alphabet was devised which at last gave the Koreans the means of writing down their own spoken language. The alphabet – *han'gŭl* – was created at the request of King Sejong (see: History), and, at the time of its promulgation, had seventeen consonants and eleven vowels. The introduction of *han'gŭl* met with great resistance from the scholar-officials, and for centuries the alphabet was used mostly by women. *Han'gŭl* only began to gain widespread acceptance at the end of the nineteenth century, when the Independence Association (see: History) published a newspaper in the Korean alphabet. *Han'gŭl* was standardized in 1933 with fourteen consonants, ten simple vowels and eleven compound vowels.

In written Korean, the vowels and consonants are combined in syllabic blocks – the most simple being composed of one vowel and one consonant, the most complex being one vowel and three consonants – which are then grouped to form words. Mastery of the letters themselves is a relatively simple matter; greater effort is required to learn the changes in pronunciation that occur when certain letters are combined. The accurate pronunciation of Korean poses problems for many foreigners, as there are some sounds that do not occur in the English language, and which are difficult to master. It is, however, possible, with a small amount of effort, to learn enough Korean to make visiting Seoul and building business contacts much easier.

In Korean, the basic sentence structure is subject–object–verb. The fact that the verb always comes at the end of the sentence makes Korean one of the few languages in the world for which simultaneous interpretation is impossible. Adjectives and verbs are conjugated by adding suffixes to the verb stem which indicate tense, and, in the case of verbs, mood and voice.

Korean nouns have no gender, number or case; gender can be indicated by the use of a prefix attached to certain nouns, while number and case (that is subject, object, etc.) can be shown by the use of suffixes. There are no definite or indefinite articles (in English, 'a', 'an' or 'the') in Korean. For example:

ch'in'gu	a/the friend
chin'gu-ga	a/the friend (subject)
han'gungmal	Korean language
han'gungmar-ŭl	Korean language (object)
kongbuha	study (verb stem)
kongbuha-mnida	studies (present tense suffix)
ch'in'gu-ga han'gungmar-ŭl kongbuha-mnida	(My/The/A) friend studies Korean.
chaemi it	is interesting (verb stem)
chaemi innŭn	interesting (present tense modifier)
ch'aek	book
chaeg-ŭl	book (object)
sa	buy (verb stem)
sa-sssŭmnida	bought (past tense suffix)
chaemi innŭn ch'aeg-ŭl sasssŭmnida	(I/He/She/They, etc.) bought an interesting book.

Perhaps one of the most interesting aspects of Korean is the extensive use of honorific language. When speaking in Korean, one must use a level of respect appropriate to the person being addressed or the person being discussed. The language used to address a small child will differ significantly from that used to a friend, and that too will be different from that used to a senior colleague or elderly relative.

There are some verbs and nouns which have their own honorific equivalents, while other verbs rely on infixes (syllables attached directly to the verb stem) or honorific verb endings. A good example is the simple question, 'Have you eaten?', which would be translated as:

Chinji-rŭl chapsusyŏsssŭmnikka!   to a senior or elder

Pap mŏgŏssŏ!   to a friend

Korean is very much a living language: changes to spelling and grammar are made by the Ministry of Education from time to time, in order to make the language more logical and systematic.

Western transliterations (romanizations) are commonly used by Koreans for company and personal names, road signs, place names, products and so forth. Although the ROK government adopted a standard system of romanization in 1984, perhaps the majority of ordinary citizens have their own personal systems, which can lead to much confusion and mispronunciation. With names as simple as Kim and Pak being romanized as 'Ghymn', 'Park' and 'Bark', addresses in Korea take on a life of their own. The most notorious example for many years, before the government standardized all the road signs in Seoul, was the Independence Arch – pronounced in Korean (and now written) as Tongnimmum, but signposted everywhere in English as Dog Rib Moon.

Company names such as Hyundai and Samsung have been mispronounced so often by westerners, misled by the romanization, that Koreans themselves can often be heard using the same erroneous pronunciation. Hyundai is correctly pronounced *hyŏndae* – ŏ as in 'not' and *ae* as 'end' – while Samsung should be pronounced *samsŏng*, as in 'Sam' and 'song'.

As far as the spoken language is concerned, Seoul dialect is the equivalent of RP (received pronunciation) speech. Regional dialects do exist, some so strong that even Koreans have difficulty at first in catching the meaning. It would also appear that, during the fifty-odd years since the division of the peninsula, the languages used in the north and south have developed in slightly different ways. Apart from significant differences in vocabulary – 'Korea' is *Chosŏn* in the north, a word only used by elderly South Koreans, and which smacks of the name *Chosen* used by the Japanese – there are differences in dialect.

24 The Media

The development of the media in the Republic of Korea and the degree of freedom with which it operates have been closely related to the nation's political situation.

NEWSPAPERS AND MAGAZINES

Within weeks of liberation from Japanese rule, 68 newspapers had been established in the southern half of the Korean peninsula, including some communist publications. However, under the provisions of the United States Military Government Ordnance 88, many left-wing publications were closed down, as threats to national security. The years immediately following the establishment of the Republic of Korea saw a further decline in the left-wing media.

Ordnance 88 was abolished in 1960, bringing in almost unlimited freedom of the press. In the short period between the end of the Syngman Rhee administration in April 1960 and the military coup of May 1961, the number of periodicals rose to 1,378, including 112 daily newspapers and 237 wire services. The total dropped sharply to 344 after the coup, with the number of dailies and wire services falling to 74 and 12 respectively. Strong controls were imposed on the press; newspapers and news agencies were strictly regulated.

Similarly, after Chun Doo-hwan's rise to power in 1980, there were a number of 'voluntary' mergers between and closures of newspaper offices and publishing companies, resulting in a decline in the number of publications.

With the implementation of democratic reforms in 1987, the existing Press Law was abolished, ushering in a new era of freedom for the media. During the first eight months of 1988, the number of daily newspapers doubled to 60, and hundreds of new magazines were registered for publication. At the end of 1991, there were more than sixty daily papers and almost six thousand magazines (mostly monthly) registered with the Ministry of Information. Most of the newspapers published are evening editions, and two (the *Korea Herald* and the *Korea Times*) are published in English.

South Korean newspaper companies jealously guard their circulation figures; estimates in 1988 put total annual circulation at 13 million, or 31 newspapers per 100 people.

TELEVISION AND RADIO

In 1927, the Japanese colonial government established a broadcasting station for propaganda purposes; this was taken over by the United States Military Government in 1945, and operated as the Korea Broadcasting System. Other stations came into operation in the years that followed, including the nation's first commercial radio station, Munhwa Broadcasting Station, in 1959.

Under the provisions of the 1980 Basic Press Law, the nation's privately owned television and radio stations were handed over to state control, and the Korea Broadcasting Corporation was established as the sole agency for radio and television advertising (see: Market Entry).

After the change of government in 1988, there were four television networks operating in south Korea: KBS-1 (Korea Broadcasting Services), KBS-2, MBC (Munhwa Broadcasting Company), and a channel reserved for educational programmes. In 1990, a commercial television station, SBS (Seoul Broadcasting System), began broadcasting, and there are plans for an additional channel to begin operations in the early 1990s.

In recent years, the total number of radio stations operating in South Korea has risen to eight. New radio stations include the Buddhist Broadcasting System, the Christian Broadcasting System, and the 24-hour Traffic Broadcasting System.

The American Forces Korea Network continues to broadcast on VHF television and AM and FM radio in South Korea. Although this has, in the past, proved an invaluable way for many Koreans to practise their English aural comprehension, there have increasingly been calls for the transfer of the television station to a UHF channel.

25 Sport and Recreation

The South Koreans are keen on all kinds of sport, both indigenous and western. Korean traditional sports include *t'aek-wŏndo* and *hapkido* (Korea's native martial arts) and *ssirŭm*, a form of wrestling. Many traditional folk games still survive, and a National Folk Arts Contest is held each year at the end of October, with teams from the various provinces vying for honours.

The most popular western sports are baseball, soccer, tennis and golf. In addition to a number of amateur and high school teams, there are a number of professional baseball teams in South Korea, the majority of which are sponsored by business concerns. Tennis is enjoyed by South Koreans of all ages, as evidenced by the number of clubs visible around Seoul. Golf is a sport and a recreation, and has been an indispensable part of doing business; there are golf practice driving ranges all over the capital, and a number of golf clubs, the majority of which are extremely expensive to join. However, the popularity of golf was hit by the reform movement implemented by President Kim Young-sam after his inauguration in 1993, and is now considered to be an elitist pastime. Other popular western sports include basketball, volleyball, boxing and table tennis.

As the South Korean middle classes find themselves with higher disposable incomes and more free time, the leisure business has boomed. Ten-pin bowling, ice skating, fishing and hiking have long been popular leisure activities. Now an increasing number of South Koreans are also enjoying snow-skiing at a growing number of resorts in the northern part of the country, as well as water-skiing, windsurfing and yachting.

South Korean athletes have performed well in international events as well as at domestic meetings, and Seoul has played host to a number of prestigious international sporting events, most notably the 1986 Asian Games and the 1988 Summer Olympics.

In the 1992 Barcelona Olympics, the South Koreans came seventh overall with 29 medals: twelve gold, five silver and twelve bronze. They took gold medals in, among others, badminton, weightlifting, shooting, archery, wrestling and the marathon. For the South Koreans, the sweetest victory at Barcelona was that achieved by Hwang Yŏng-jo in the marathon. In 1936, the Korean runner Son Ki-jŏng won the gold medal in this event, but was forced to run for the Japanese team.

Despite efforts on numerous occasions to form a united Korean team to participate in international events, this has only proved possible on two occasions – a youth soccer competition in Portugal and the World Table Tennis Championships in Japan, both held in 1991.

The National Sports Festival, held each year in October, is the national version of the Olympic Games. Athletes, both local and second-generation Koreans living overseas, compete in 27 sports. The Children's National Sports Festival, Winter Sports Festival, and National Sports Festival for the Handicapped are also held annually.

Major sports facilities include the 652,000-square-yard (545,000-square-metre) Seoul Sports Complex, which houses two gymnasia, an indoor swimming pool, a baseball park, and a 100,000-seat Olympic stadium. The Olympic Park covers an area of 2,631,000 square yards (2.2 million square metres), and includes a velodrome, three gymnasia, an indoor pool and eighteen hard-surface tennis courts. An equestrian park and regatta course were also built in Seoul for the 1988 Summer Olympics, as was the yachting marina in Pusan.

PART FIVE

The Economy

26 General Overview

SUMMARY
The past four decades have seen the transformation of the South Korean economy from a small, stagnant agricultural subsistence economy into one of the leading Newly Industrialized Economies (NIEs), along with Hong Kong, Singapore and Taiwan.

This success story can be summarized in a few remarkable statistics; between 1962 and 1991, the South Korean economy recorded an average annual growth rate of 8.5 per cent. In those three decades, expanded from US$2.3 billion to US$281 billion, per capita GNP rose from US$82 to US$6,498 (at current prices), and exports soared from US$55 million to US$71.9 billion (at current market prices).

The nation's industrial structure has also undergone a transformation; the share of GNP taken by the manufacturing sector rose to 32.5 per cent in 1988 from 16.0 per cent in 1962, while that of the primary sector fell to 10.5 per cent from 36.6 per cent during the same period. In 1991, the shares were 27.5 per cent and 8.1 per cent respectively.

As the economy has developed, there has been a change in focus from the production of light industrial goods, including textiles, toys and footwear in the 1960s, through the development of the heavy and chemical industries – steel, shipbuilding, petrochemicals, heavy equipment, automobiles and so forth – in the 1970s, to technology-intensive industries such as electronics and semiconductors in the 1980s.

In the late 1980s the South Korean economy entered a new stage of industrial restructuring, with the aim of effecting another transformation. This time the move will be from rapid, export-driven growth to more stable and balanced growth, from low-tech to high-tech industries, from labour-intensive to capital- and technology-intensive production, and from regulation to liberalization.

THE 1950s

The division of the Korean peninsula in 1948 left nearly all the nation's power-generating capacity and almost two-thirds of its heavy industry in the northern half of the peninsula. Moreover, the Korean War (1950–3) destroyed what little industrial base had been created in the newly established Republic of Korea. In the aftermath of the war, the Republic faced a number of socio-economic problems including rapid population growth (compounded by the migration of refugees from the north during the war), high unemployment and a severe housing shortage.

The immediate postwar period was one of reconstruction and rehabilitation rather than growth – the lack of economic and administrative infrastructure and the political instability seen during the early postwar period made long-term economic planning difficult. Moreover, President Syngman Rhee's preoccupation with politics and reunification meant that there was little government focus on the economy.

There was no clear growth strategy other than the reconstruction of the nation's industrial base and infrastructure, and the promotion of domestic production to replace imports. With virtually no domestic savings to draw upon, the government relied heavily on foreign aid: between 1954 and 1959, 70 per cent of all reconstruction projects carried out in the Republic were financed by foreign aid, principally from the United States.

Between the end of the war in 1953 and the military coup of 1961, the economy recorded an average annual growth rate of 3.7 per cent, with per capita GNP expanding by just 0.7 per cent per annum. In 1962, per capita GNP was a mere US$82. The economy remained largely agrarian, with about two-thirds of the population working in the primary sector. Bilateral trade amounted to US$445 million in 1962, with US$390 million of the total being accounted for by imports. Commodity exports were almost negligible, accounting for no more than 1 per cent of GNP per year, and totalling just US$55 million in 1962.

Perhaps one of the most significant achievements of this period was the rapid expansion of educational facilities and the increase in enrolment at all levels. The number of college students rose from 8,000 in 1945 to 100,000 in 1960, and the literacy rate soared from 22 per cent to 72 per cent during the same period. These achievements laid the foundation for the rapid economic development seen in subsequent decades by creating a well-educated, literate workforce.

THE 1960s

The economic transformation that has taken place in South Korea began with the implementation of structured, medium-term economic planning in 1962. With the establishment of a new government following the military coup in 1961 came a shift in focus away from reconstruction and towards growth.

In the early 1960s, the South Korean economy was still in dire straits – per capita GNP was less than US$100, there were virtually no exports or domestic savings, and the population was growing at a faster rate than the economy. The fact that the south lagged behind the north in terms of per capita income, industrial production capacity, military strength and defence industry output raised fears of social unrest in the south or another invasion attempt by the north.

President Park Chung-hee's approach to economic planning was simple: the faster the economy grew, the stronger the nation would become, and the less chance there would be of invasion by the North Koreans or insurrection among the South Koreans. Accordingly, the focus of the government's efforts was to be economic growth, even at the expense of political development.

Faced with scant natural resources and a small domestic market, the Park government formulated an outward-looking development strategy which aimed to capitalize on the nation's one available resource – its people and the value they could add to imported materials. Development would be led by industrialization, and industrialization would be led by exports of mass-produced, light industrial goods. This would increase income and employment, and provide a sound base from which to develop the economy further.

The Republic of Korea's first formal economic plan – the First Five-Year Economic Development Plan – was adopted in 1962. Its basic goal was to create the economic base for export-oriented industrialization and self-sustained growth. The government was to take an active role in managing the economy, setting out its policies and objectives in a series of five-year plans.

One of the key features of the first plan was the formulation of a systematic trade policy, aimed at boosting the nation's exports. Incentives including tax exemptions, reduced public utility charges, low interest loans, and tariff rebates on imports for re-export were offered, and foreign loans were made available to companies to motivate them to move into the export sector. Exporters were given access to short-term export financing, and customs procedures were simplified to facilitate the importing of raw materials for re-export.

The government set export targets for each sector.

Companies that met or exceeded those targets received even more favours, while sanctions and tax investigations faced companies that failed to meet their quotas. The nation's newly emerging conglomerates, or *chaebŏl*, were encouraged to devote themselves to 'nation building through industrialization'. The incentives offered to the *chaebŏl* and the support that they in return gave to the government were the beginning of a long and mutually profitable relationship between the government and big business (see: The *Chaebŏl*).

Interest rates on bank deposits were almost doubled in an effort to encourage private saving, while rates on loans were kept low (often negative in real terms). Although these measures were successful – bank deposits doubled every year between 1965 and 1968, and the share of total investment financed by domestic savings rose from less than 25 per cent in 1962 to 61 per cent in 1971 – the Republic was still heavily dependent on foreign funds for domestic investment projects.

The shortage of credit made it possible for the government to allocate funds to sectors targeted for development, thus ensuring that available bank credit was put to productive use. Companies were encouraged to borrow to finance the rapid expansion of their production facilities and export capacity. This led to high debt-to-equity ratios for South Korean companies and, given the paucity of domestic savings, to large foreign debts for the government.

The success of the new economic policies is demonstrated by the statistics for the period. Between 1962 and 1971, the nation's GNP more than doubled, recording an average annual growth rate of 8.7 per cent in real terms. Per capita GNP expanded by 6.9 per cent per annum, compared with the average annual growth rate of 0.7 per cent recorded between 1953 and 1961. Foreign trade surged: commodity exports increased at an average annual rate of 40 per cent to reach US$1.1 billion in 1971, while imports grew at an average annual rate of 21 per cent, rising to US$2.2 billion in 1971. The decade also saw structural changes in the economy, with the share of GNP taken by the manufacturing sector rising to 22 per cent in 1971 from 16 per cent in 1962, and that of the primary sector declining to 27 per cent from 37 per cent in the same period.

THE 1970s

The development strategy followed in the 1970s aimed at modernizing the rural sector, which had fallen behind the urban sector during the process of rapid industrialization, and developing the nation's heavy and chemical industries in order to create a more sophisticated industrial structure.

In order to promote the development of the rural sector, the government launched the *Saemaŭl* (New Community) Movement in 1971. The movement aimed to boost production and productivity in rural communities, thereby raising the income of farming and fishing families. Although the programme was successful in its bid to boost rural productivity and income, the policy of providing price support for agricultural produce was a major factor in the chronic deficits seen in the national budget during these years.

Government policy regarding the development of the heavy and chemical industries was to replace imported intermediate materials (such as steel and non-ferrous metals) and capital goods with domestically produced items. These goods would then serve as a foundation for the development of new strategic export industries, such as shipbuilding, automobiles and petrochemicals. The government's decision to allow monopolistic production in certain of these industries was based on the view that this would achieve economies of scale and would protect the new industries until they could become internationally competitive.

A National Investment Fund was established to provide low-interest loans for investment in the heavy and chemical industries, and tax and financial incentives were offered for investment, R&D and training in the application of more sophisticated technology. The continuing shortage of credit enabled the government to keep a tight rein on the flow of funds, and gave economic planners leverage in implementing their goals. However, as domestic savings still fell far short of investment needs, foreign borrowings continued to expand, and the management of the nation's foreign debt emerged as a major policy issue.

The heavy investment in these new areas had some unwelcome side effects. In order to support the development of these technology- and capital-intensive industries, the government had to scale down its support for the labour-intensive industries which had seen such rapid growth in the previous decade. The focus on large-scale, capital-intensive projects in the heavy and chemical sectors encouraged the growth of large companies at the expense of small- and medium-sized concerns.

The development of the heavy and chemical industries boosted energy consumption in the industrial sector; this posed problems for a developing nation which was 100 per cent dependent on imported energy. As South Korean industry became increasingly energy intensive, the country became more and more vulnerable to fluctuations in international energy prices. The two oil shocks of 1973 and 1980 pushed up the nation's crude oil import bill to the equivalent of 9.2 per cent of GNP in 1980 from 2.2 per cent in 1972. Accordingly, the Wholesale Price Index soared by an average annual rate of 19.4 per cent between 1971 and 1980, hitting 42.1 per cent in 1974 and 38.9 per cent in 1980. (Wholesale prices had risen by an average annual rate of 12.2 per cent between 1962 and 1971.)

A shortage of skilled workers and soaring inflation in the late 1970s pushed up real wages by 29.2 per cent per annum between 1976 and 1979. This, combined with insufficient investment in quality improvement and product innovation in the light industrial sectors, led to an erosion of South Korea's competitive advantage in many labour-intensive export industries. A number of developing countries were beginning to compete in South Korea's main export markets, and they still had the advantage of low labour costs; wage increases averaged 9.4 per cent in Taiwan and 5.0 per cent in Singapore over the same four-year period. This is a scenario which was to be repeated a decade later, in the late 1980s and early 1990s.

By 1979, the economy was showing signs of strain. The loss of competitive advantage in export-oriented light industries came at a time when, although investing heavily in the heavy and chemical industries, South Korea had not yet established an international competitive edge in these sectors. Moreover, as the manufacturing sector expanded and the primary sector shrank, more people moved into urban areas in search of work, placing the urban infrastructure under increasing pressure.

The year 1979 saw the first decline in exports for two decades, and a fall in the GNP growth rate to 6.5 per cent, the lowest rate of increase since 1972. The assassination of President Park Chung-hee in October 1979, the second oil shock and a disastrous harvest were contributory factors to a negative rate of economic growth in 1980, when GNP shrank by 4.8 per cent year on year.

THE EARLY 1980s

The state of affairs that existed in 1980 was, to a great extent, the result of the economic development programmes pursued in the previous two decades. A major shift in policy orientation was clearly needed – away from growth and towards stabilization.

The new strategy adopted in the early 1980s focused on price stability, balanced economic growth and market liberalization. A policy of fiscal restraint was implemented and restrictions were placed on the annual money supply growth rate, which helped to bring the annual inflation rate down to 2.7 per cent in 1986 from more than 25 per cent in 1980. Efforts were made to keep wage rises at reasonable levels, with the result that the average increase in nominal wages fell to 8.2 per cent in 1986 from 23.4 per cent in 1980.

The role played by small- and medium-sized enterprises in the economy was to be enhanced by offering them incentives to boost their R&D investment and increase their marketing activities. This aimed to redress the imbalance which had been created between the giant corporations and smaller firms. Similarly, in order to promote more equitable distribution of wealth between the urban and rural sectors, efforts were to be made to move industrial facilities into rural areas and thus boost alternative or supplementary sources of income for farm families.

The new policy also made efforts to give the private sector greater autonomy, thus allowing market forces to play a greater role in the economy. This was partly in response to criticism that government incentives and initiatives, aimed at focusing and controlling development, had, in fact, weakened the economy and hindered the proper functioning of market mechanisms. The 1981 Anti-Monopoly and Fair Trade Act was enacted to eliminate monopolistic practices such as cartel arrangements and price fixing.

Finally, domestic markets were to be opened up to foreign goods and services as part of the government's commitment to liberalization and internationalization. The ratio of freely importable items rose to 91.5 per cent in 1986 from 68.2 per cent in 1979; average tariff rates fell to 19.9 per cent in 1986, and regulations governing foreign investment were eased to allow overseas investors to participate in domestic industries.

The result was an overall improvement in economic performance. The trade deficit narrowed to US$1.8 billion in 1983 from US$4.4 billion in 1979, and the current account deficit shrank to US$1.6 billion from US$4.2 billion during the same period. The annual rate of GNP growth recovered from minus 4.8 per cent in 1980 to 6.6 per cent in 1981 and 11.9 per cent in 1983. Such was the success of the new policy that revisions were made to the fifth economic plan, projecting higher GNP growth and lower foreign debt through the remaining years of the plan, and a current account surplus in 1986.

THE BOOM YEARS (1986-8)

The trend of lower inflation and smaller trade and current account deficits carried on into the late 1980s and paved the way for the spectacular growth seen in the South Korean economy in 1986, 1987 and 1988.

In 1986, the Republic of Korea recorded the first significant trade and current account surpluses in its 38-year history. (Current account surpluses of a few million dollars were recorded in 1965 and 1977.) The robust economic growth in the late 1980s – averaging 12.8 per cent per annum in real terms between 1986 and 1988 – was boosted by the 'Three Lows' or the 'Three Blessings'. Low oil prices assisted a country heavily dependent on imported oil, low interest rates eased the burden of debt repayments, and favourable exchange rates for the wŏn against major currencies made South Korean goods cheaper in export markets.

In 1987, South Korea recorded one of the highest growth rates in the world (13.0 per cent), and exports of textiles and electronic goods both passed the US$10 billion mark. Total exports surged by 36.2 per cent year on year to reach US$47.3 billion, and the current and trade account surpluses swelled to US$9.9 billion and US$6.3 billion (on a customs clearance basis) respectively. The government now found itself facing a new problem: that of containing the surpluses in order to ward off trade friction and increased protectionism.

The government therefore increased the liberalization of imports, allowed an expansion in offshore investment by local firms, eased restrictions on foreign exchange transactions, and accelerated the repayment of outstanding foreign debts, which dropped to US$35.6 billion at the end of 1987 from US$46.7 billion in 1985. In 1987, the domestic savings rate reached 37.4 per cent (compared with 23.5 per cent in 1980) and exceeded the domestic investment rate. This made possible a resurgence in investment as South Korea was able to finance investment from its own resources.

The year 1988 was the third consecutive year of double-digit economic growth. The stellar growth of 12.4 per cent far outshone the performance of other countries – 4.2 per cent average for the NIEs, 4.4 per cent for the United States, 3.6 per cent for West Germany and 5.7 per cent for Japan. The average annual growth rate recorded in South Korea between 1983 and 1988 was 11.2 per cent, one of the highest in the world.

By the end of the year, the trade and current account surpluses had swelled to US$8.9 billion and US$14.2 billion respectively. Outstanding foreign debt had fallen to US$31.2 billion, and an increase in foreign assets pushed the nation's net foreign debt down to US$7.3 billion, raising hopes that South Korea would become a net creditor nation by the end of the decade.

However, the South Koreans quickly became victims of their own success, as advanced nations that found themselves running a deficit in their trade with the Republic began either to impose import restrictions to halt the flow of South Korean goods, or to demand the opening of the Republic's markets to their own goods and services. Most vocal among the trading partners was the United States, which was (and remains) South Korea's largest export market, and was running a deficit of almost US$10 billion with South Korea in 1987.

Furthermore, the implementation of democratic reforms in 1987 (see: History) was followed by the free formation of effective trade unions for the first time in the nation's history. Collective bargaining led to high wage increases, far in excess of increases in productivity, which eroded the price competitiveness of South Korean goods in overseas markets. The prolonged and sometimes violent disputes that accompanied the wage negotiations affected both South Korea's production and exports, and prompted overseas buyers to look elsewhere in the region for a more stable and cheaper source of supply.

The rapid appreciation of the wŏn against major currencies further weakened the competitiveness of South Korea's exports at a time when competition from other NIEs was intensifying. South Korean exporters found themselves unable to compete on price in the lower end of the market, yet lacking the quality to challenge the Japanese at the top end of the market. At the same time, the liberalization of domestic markets brought a surge in imports of both capital and consumer goods.

The expansion of money supply and credit which had accompanied that in economic activities and investment in the late 1980s combined with the release of more than W1 trillion (US$1.3 billion at the 1987 market average rate) to finance the presidential election campaigns in December 1987 to aggravate inflationary pressures, which had begun to mount following a poor harvest, wage rises, and rising costs of imported raw materials. The government, having pledged itself to the expansion of national welfare programmes, including medical insurance and national pensions, now found itself trying to balance fiscal restraint with the need to expand welfare provision.

The effect of these factors was clearly demonstrated in the economic statistics for 1989: the rate of economic growth almost halved, falling to 6.8 per cent in real terms, and inflation at the consumer level approached 10 per cent. With exports edging up just 2.8 per cent year on year to US$62.4 billion, and imports jumping by 18.6 per cent to US$61.5 billion (on a customs clearance basis), there was a sharp decline in the trade and current account surpluses to US$912 million and US$5 billion respectively.

However, it is also true to say that South Korea had reached the end of that stage of its economic development where it could simply rely on mass exports of low-tech, mass-produced goods. South Korea's exports had been too sensitive to price considerations to weather the combined effect of currency appreciation and wage increases. To move on to the next stage of development, the South Koreans had to improve their product quality and upgrade their technology in order to move into the production of high-tech, high-value-added goods.

With the benefit of hindsight, one can see that a good opportunity was missed during the boom years: at a time when they should have been making long-term investments in R&D and technological development, too many South Korean corporations were looking for short-term profits in the booming real estate and stock markets.

THE EARLY 1990s

The years 1990 and 1991 saw an improvement in some of the factors that had an adverse impact on the economy in 1989. The steady depreciation of the wŏn helped exporters regain some of their lost competitiveness, and the spring wage negotiations were completed more quickly and smoothly than in previous years. Furthermore, export markets with long-term potential were opening up in the former communist bloc, which also offered opportunities in terms of outward investment and joint ventures.

The government's decision in the late 1980s to boost domestic demand, in order to compensate for the reduced contribution made to growth by the export sector, aimed to find a breathing space while industrial restructuring took place. This was seen as a temporary measure, while exporters regained their competitiveness by upgrading technology and improving product quality – the ultimate goal being a more balanced economy, with growth fuelled by both the export and domestic sectors.

The policy appeared to be successful; private consumption and domestic construction boomed, resulting in GNP growth rates of 9.3 per cent in 1990 and 8.4 per cent in 1991. However, this type of growth was seen by many as structurally unhealthy, based as it was on a boom in domestic construction and consumption, which was likely to be only a temporary phenomenon.

The boom in domestic consumption, fuelled by three years of high wage increases, higher disposable income and an improvement in living standards, did provide a market for domestically produced goods, but also boosted imports of foreign consumer products. Faced with shrinking export profit margins, trading companies turned their attention to the lucrative import business, satisfying consumer demand for brand-name luxury goods. This aggravated inflationary pressures as well as causing a further deterioration in the nation's trade and balance of payments situation.

Domestic construction activities were boosted by pledges made in the 1987 presidential elections, which included the construction of two million houses units and a variety of social infrastructure projects. The boom quickly led to shortages of manpower and materials, which pushed wages and prices even higher, and the profits made by real estate speculators became a major cause of social discontent.

There was even talk of the economy overheating as the real rate of economic growth exceeded the potential rate of growth. Within two years, the government was taking action to curb 'excessive' consumer spending and cool down the 'overheated' construction market.

Frugality campaigns were carried out by the media and quasi-official organizations, discouraging the purchase of luxury items, and there were reports of police, tax and customs investigations against individuals indulging in extravagant lifestyles. Complaints from trading partners led to assurances from the ROK government that the campaigns were not anti-import campaigns but rather movements aimed at encouraging more rational consumer behaviour. Restrictions were placed on the construction of commercial buildings, and a number of infrastructure projects and public works were also delayed in an attempt to take the heat out of the market.

Imports continued to expand in 1990 and 1991, boosted by the increase in private consumption and the demand for capital goods needed in the process of restructuring. The rate of growth slowed from almost 30 per cent in 1987 to 13.6 per cent in 1990, but then picked up again, reaching 16.7 per cent in 1991. The rate of growth for imports continued to outpace that of exports; growth rates in 1990 and 1991 were 4.2 per cent and 10.5 per cent. (Exports in 1991 were boosted by the opening of new markets in Latin America, South-east Asia and the former communist bloc.)

The trade account went back into the red in 1990, with a deficit of US$4.8 billion, which swelled to a record US$9.6 billion the following year (on a customs clearance basis). The current account similarly returned to a deficit, recording red-ink figures of US$2.2 billion and US$8.8 billion in 1990 and 1991 respectively.

PROSPECTS: THE SEVENTH FIVE-YEAR ECONOMIC DEVELOPMENT PLAN (1992–6)

Targets for the Seventh Plan published by the Economic Planning Board in April 1992 call for an average annual GNP growth rate of 7.5 per cent during the plan period, with per capita GNP at current prices rising to US$10,440 in 1996 from US$6,685 in 1992. Exports and imports are projected to expand to around the US$135 billion mark by the end of the plan period, bringing the trade account into balance. A current account surplus of US$6.5 billion is forecast for 1996. The inflation rate will average 4.5 per cent over the five years, the unemployment rate will stand at 2.8 per cent in 1996, and the ratios of domestic savings and investment to GNP will be 36.0 per cent and 35.0 per cent respectively.

The basic aim of the Seventh Plan is to transform the South Korean economy and lay the groundwork for the reunification of the Korean peninsula. This will be achieved by stimulating technological and managerial innovation, boosting R&D spending to 3–4 per cent of GNP by 1996, increasing expenditure on social infrastructure and easing labour shortages. As far as social development is concerned, the plan will develop rural areas, improve social welfare, enhance socioeconomic equity, expand the nation's housing stock and curb real estate speculation.

The coming years should see a trend towards less government intervention in the economy in order to give greater rein to the operation of free market principles. The economic planners are also seeking to promote greater competition among businesses and ease the concentration of economic power among large corporations and business groups. The plan also envisages a greater role for the Republic of Korea in the global economy; responses to the Uruguay Round will be formulated and membership of the Organization for Economic Cooperation and Development (OECD) may be sought during the period of the plan.

THE CHALLENGES AHEAD

The implementation of the plan will be helped by a number of factors. In the early 1990s, there were signs of a cooling down in both construction activities and private consumption, which would lead to slower economic growth. The trade and balance of payments situation should be helped by a slow-down in import growth rates for capital goods, as the process of restructuring nears completion, and an increase in exports, as new markets are opened up. There are hopes for a continuing improvement in labour relations, and expectations that productivity increases will once again exceed wage increases from 1992 onwards.

However, South Korea also faces a number of challenges, both internal and external, in its bid to become an advanced industrialized economy. These include regaining export competitiveness, reforming the nation's financial infrastructure, resolving infrastructure problems, easing labour shortages, and establishing and maintaining smooth labour relations. In addition, the ROK government will have to try to accommodate calls for liberalization from major trading partners and the demands of pressure groups at home, and find a way to restore the public's confidence in its ability to manage the economy.

One of the most pressing tasks facing the South Koreans is the attainment of balanced economic growth. In terms of trade, this means finding a happy medium between the heavy export dependency seen through the 1960s, 1970s and early 1980s and the overheated domestic consumption that has characterized the late 1980s and early 1990s.

Exports will continue to be important to the Republic of Korea; the challenge now for South Korean exporters is to regain their **international competitiveness**. The failure to invest in technology development, quality enhancement and product innovation in the late 1980s has left South Korean exporters struggling to compete – on price with other NIEs and on quality with the Japanese. In addition, companies in some export sectors are finding that they have to compete with high-quality Japanese goods made in South-east Asia and other countries with comparatively low labour costs.

The way forward for South Korean corporations is to develop or obtain advanced technology, boost productivity and improve product quality. In certain labour-intensive industries, investment is now being made in automating production facilities, which has the dual effect of boosting productivity and reducing vulnerability to labour disputes and stoppages. The need to break away from dependence on original equipment manufacture (OEM) exports, develop and market brand names, and improve after-sales service is being recognized.

In addition, South Korean companies have to look beyond 'quick-fix' solutions, such as favourable currency movements, and seek other means of boosting overseas shipments. Such means include the development of new export markets and the establishment of production bases within trading blocs such as the North America Free Trade Agreement (NAFTA) and the European Community (see: Exports and Imports).

In their search for technology, South Korean companies are increasingly facing technology protectionism. Advanced countries are now reluctant or unwilling to provide technology to countries which would then become their competitors. The choices for the South Koreans are either to develop the technology in-house, which takes time and money, or to obtain it through a joint venture or technical licensing agreement. An increasing number of South Korean corporations are looking at a third option – acquiring foreign companies with proprietary technology. The ROK government now actively encourages all forms of cooperative venture that will lead to technology transfer (see 'R&D', pages 158–60).

It has been said that the backwardness of South Korea's **financial infrastructure** will act as a major constraint on the nation's future economic development. The tight control which the government has exercised over the flow of funds within the Republic and the credit squeeze which appears to be a permanent state of affairs for South Korean corporations are often cited as factors in the nation's current problems.

Companies have tended to rely on bank loans rather than direct financing in the nation's capital markets, and access to credit has usually been determined by government policy. Although annual money supply growth rates have averaged 25 per cent over the past two decades, peaking at 39.7 per cent in 1977, most of the new money has typically been earmarked for government-sponsored infrastructure and agricultural projects, policy loans and the like, leaving precious little for South Korea's corporations. Moreover, interest rates remain high – the trading yield on Money Stabilization Bonds and the inter-bank call money rate reached 17.5 per cent at the end of 1991, while the trading yield on three-year commercial paper was 19 per cent – and companies unable to get funds through official channels are forced to use the unofficial curb market, where rates can be 5–10 per cent higher.

As desirable as it may be to automate production facilities, build a factory overseas, initiate marketing campaigns, and invest in R&D to create the next generation of products, none of this is possible without funding. Some financial analysts argue that full deregulation of the financial sector is needed in order to improve the efficiency of resource allocation and lower the cost of funds (see: Financial Infrastructure).

Insufficient investment in the nation's **infrastructure** over the past thirty years is now causing major problems in terms of traffic jams, bottlenecks, delays in shipment and unloading, and increasing distribution and storage costs. The government now plans to expand investment in social overhead capital investment from 3.7 per cent of GNP in 1990 to 5.0 per cent in 1996; major projects include the building of a second international airport for Seoul, the construction of a high-speed rail link between Seoul and Pusan, and the expansion of the nation's ports (see: Infrastructure).

The increasing tendency among South Korean workers to shun the 'Three D' jobs – jobs which are dirty, dangerous or difficult – has led to **labour shortages** in the construction industry and certain areas of the manufacturing sector. In addition, there are concerns that the nation will face a serious shortage of skilled labour in the near future. Debate continues over the need for and the wisdom of using foreign labour for jobs which the South Koreans are unwilling to do (see: Migrant Workers).

In the short to medium term, the government will take steps to enhance the quality of technical education and vocational training in the Republic, and establish industrial and technical colleges to train professional and technical personnel. The government also plans to increase the number of technical high schools to 50 per cent of all high schools by 1995, and make professional training available at other high schools.

Although there has been a marked improvement in **labour relations** in the early 1990s – in September 1991, the nation enjoyed its first dispute-free day in four years – the impact which the stoppages, strikes and pay awards had on the economy at the end of the 1980s will not quickly be forgotten. While it is true to say that a framework for negotiations between unions and management is gradually evolving, issues such as the implementation of a total wage system and the revision of the nation's labour laws have yet to be resolved (see: Labour).

In the years since South Korea recorded its first significant trade and current account surpluses, the nation's major trading partners have increased the pressure on the ROK government to open up the South Korean markets to foreign goods and services. The pressure for **liberalization** will continue, and the ROK government's situation is made more difficult by the emergence of lobby groups within South Korea. Among the most powerful and vocal of these groups are the nation's farmers, who are strongly opposed to the opening of South Korea's rice market. Among the most bitter of the liberalization debates is that concerning the opening of the rice markets (see: Exports and Imports; Natural Resources: Agriculture, Fishing, Forestry and Mining).

During the years of the Roh adminstration, there has been a marked **decline in public confidence** in the government's ability to handle the nation's economic problems. The government is too often perceived as vacillating and looking for quick-fix remedies rather than long-term solutions. One of the main tasks facing Mr Kim Young-sam during his presidency will be restoring the public's faith in the government's ability to manage the national economy.

BALANCE OF PAYMENTS (CURRENT ACCOUNT)

The Republic of Korea recorded a deficit on the current account of its balance of payments every year from 1962 to 1985 with the exception of a small surplus of US$12 million in 1977.

In 1986, the current account turned into the black with a surplus of US$4.6 billion, which had swelled to US$14.2 billion two years later. This remarkable improvement in South Korea's balance of payments situation was due in large part to soaring export earnings, stable oil prices and lower international interest rates. Furthermore, earnings from tourism more than doubled, thanks to an increase in inbound travellers at the time of the 1988 Olympic Games.

The ROK government, which had for years been struggling to curb the nation's current account deficit, now found itself faced with the problem of managing a rapidly growing surplus. As the surplus expanded, there were increasing calls from advanced nations for the ROK government to liberalize the South Korean markets. The government's response was to begin paying down the nation's foreign debt, allow an expansion of investment overseas by domestic corporations, and lift restrictions on international travel by South Korean nationals.

The current account surplus shrank to US$5.1 billion in 1989, reflecting a slump in the nation's trade balance. In the early 1990s, the balance of payments situation continued to deteriorate, as exports remained sluggish and imports expanded rapidly. In 1990 the current account went back into the red, with a deficit of US$2.2 billion. By the end of 1991, the deficit had reached a record level of US$8.8 billion.

In 1986, the **trade account** recorded a surplus of US$4.2 billion (on a free-on-board basis). The strong performance of South Korean exports in the late 1980s – overseas shipments expanded by 14.6 per cent in 1986, by 36.2 per cent in 1987, and by 28.4 per cent in 1988 – boosted the trade surplus to US$11.4 billion in 1988. Although imports were also expanding, the growth rate was slower than that recorded by exports.

In 1989, the exports growth rate slumped to 2.8 per cent, as South Korean goods became less competitive and worldwide demand weakened. Imports soared by 18.6 per cent, boosted by the continuing liberalization of the domestic markets, the private consumption boom, and increasing demand for parts, components and capital goods from local companies modernizing and upgrading their production facilities.

In 1990, the trade account went back into the red, with a deficit of US$2 billion; twelve months later, the deficit had more than trebled to reach US$7 billion. Although the rate of export growth had recovered to 10.5 per cent thanks to concerted efforts to diversify the nation's export markets, it could still not match the rate of expansion seen in imports (16.7 per cent), which continued to be boosted by facility investment and the boom in domestic consumption and construction.

The **invisible trade account** went into the black in 1987, with a surplus of US$977 million. The reduction in debt interest payments and an increase in receipts from tourism helped to boost the surplus to US$1.3 billion by 1988. However, the government's decision to liberalize overseas travel as a means of curbing the current account surplus prompted a boom in outbound tourism and a surge in foreign travel expenditure by the South Koreans. This was a major factor in the invisible trade surplus shrinking to US$211 million in 1989, and turning into a deficit of US$451 million in 1990.

Another factor was an increase in the deficit in the transportation account due to increasing payments for transportation, shipping, insurance and the like. In 1991, the year in which the tourism account recorded its first deficit in nine years, the invisible trade account deficit stood at US$1.6 billion.

Net unrequited transfers have shrunk from a surplus of US$1.5 billion in 1988 to a deficit of US$152 million in 1991. This largely reflects a decline in remittances from South Koreans living overseas and, in 1991, the financial contribution made to the Allies by South Korea during the Gulf War.

The **long-term capital balance** moved from a net outflow in the late 1980s to a net inflow of US$5.7 billion by 1991. The change has been due in large part to increases in the issuance of foreign exchange bonds and the inducement of foreign bank loans by South Korean development institutions.

The **short-term capital balance**, which was in deficit in the mid-1980s, moved to a surplus of US$3.3 billion in 1990, before falling back to a US$41 million surplus in 1991, due to the increase in payments for short-term trade financing. The overall capital balance registered a net inflow of US$4.2 billion in 1991.

BUDGET (PUBLIC FINANCE)

Responsibility for the preparation of the budget lies with the Economic Planning Board. The administration of the government's finances is the responsibility of the Ministry of Finance. Supplementary budgets revising the original budget may be submitted to the National Assembly at any time during the fiscal year.

The General Account budget executes all the administrative functions of the government, including the raising of revenues, the operation of the various ministries, and the execution of most of the government's economic and social activities. Revenues comprise income from the levying of national taxes, customs and stamp duties, and profits from government monopolies. Expenditures are broadly broken down into general administration, national defence, education, economic and social development, local finance subsidies, and debt reimbursement.

Special Account budgets are established for specific projects and, although in theory self-financing, often receive assistance from the General Account budget. Special Account budgets include budgets for the national railroad, grain management and government procurement.

The General Account budget has registered a surplus every year for the past two decades. The surplus peaked at W3.3 trillion (US$4.8 billion at the 1988 market average rate) in 1988, but shrank in the years that followed, to reach W1.3 trillion (US$1.7 billion) in 1991. The reduction in surplus was due in part to the decline in revenues from value added tax and customs revenues. Part of the surplus was used for subsidies to local government and the repayment of some of the government's debt; the remainder was carried forward to 1992.

In drafting the 1992 General Account budget, the main emphasis was put on improving the national infrastructure – the construction of expressways, the expansion of transportation networks and the promotion of subway projects – and restructuring the rural sector. The government set up a Special Account to prepare the rural sector for the liberalization of agricultural and fishery imports.

The General Account budget for 1992 was set at W33.2 trillion (US$42.2 billion), an increase of 5.8 per cent year on year. The budget accounted for 14.6 per cent of GNP, slightly lower than the level of 15.2 per cent recorded in 1991. The majority (97 per cent) of the revenue was to be derived from taxes (W32.4 trillion or US$41.2 billion), with other sources accounting for W838 billion (US$1.1 billion).

The high priority given to national defence in South Korea has resulted in the allocation of a significant share of the annual budget to military purposes. Over the past twenty years, defence expenditure has, on average, accounted for more than 30 per cent of the annual budget. As a percentage of GNP, defence spending has averaged 4.8 per cent of GNP. In the 1992 budget, defence spending continued to account for a significant share of the budget – more than a quarter of the total. The 1992 budget allocations were as shown in Table 2.

The drafting of the budget is a common cause of discord between the ruling and opposition parties. In recent years, the opposition have criticized the government for drafting

TABLE 2 Budget allocation, 1992

Area	W	US$	% of total
Defence	8.7 trillion	11.1 billion	26.3
Education	6.4 trillion	8.1 billion	19.4
Economic development	6.1 trillion	7.8 billion	18.5
General administration	4.1 trillion	5.2 billion	12.2
Local finance subsidy	3.8 trillion	4.8 billion	11.5
Social development	3.2 trillion	4.1 billion	9.8
Debt reimbursement	748 billion	950 million	2.3

expansionary budgets when fiscal restraint is called for. The government's response has been that, despite annual increases in the budget, the ratio to GNP has remained fairly constant at around 15 per cent.

CURRENCY

The national currency is the wŏn; coins are issued in W50, W100 and W500 denominations, and notes for W1,000, W5,000 and W10,000 are currently in circulation.

On 27 February 1980, the foreign exchange system was changed from one linking the wŏn to the US dollar, to one using a basket of currencies (which includes the special drawing rights or SDRs and currencies of the Republic's major trading partners), in which the US dollar and the Japanese yen were given the heaviest weightings.

Ten years later, on 2 March 1990, the Market Average Rate System was implemented. This system, under which daily foreign exchange rates are determined by the demand and supply in the market, is more closely related to market forces and has significantly reduced government influence on exchange rates. However, the permissible range of fluctuation by foreign exchange rates is still determined by the government.

The change in system came partly in response to criticism and pressure from leading trading partners, who suspected the ROK government of manipulating exchange rates in order to boost exports. The wŏn depreciated steadily against the dollar through the 1970s and early 1980s, falling from W398.90/US$ in 1972 to W890.20/US$ in 1985. In the 1990s, the ROK authorities, while still controlling currency fluctuations for the short term, will rely more on other methods, such as the removal of barriers to trade and the encouragement of imports, to manage its trade accounts with other nations (see: Financial Infrastructure).

In 1991, the average exchange rate for the wŏn was 760.80 against the US dollar, 1,380.14 against the pound, and 607.18 per 100 yen.

FOREIGN DEBT

Until the early 1960s, South Korea's somewhat limited economic development was financed mainly by foreign aid, principally from the United States and international development organizations.

Following the adoption of an export-oriented development strategy and the implementation of the first five-year plan in 1962, South Korea needed substantial amounts of funding for its ambitious industrialization programme. However, domestic savings were at a low level, and the rate of growth in savings was far outstripped by that in demand for funds. It was, therefore, inevitable that South Korea should come to rely heavily on overseas loans to finance its economic development programme.

The level of external debt rose rapidly between 1962 and 1985, with levels in the 1970s being boosted by investment in the heavy and chemical industrial sectors. In the early 1980s, higher international interest rates increased the cost of servicing the foreign debt, and the government continued to borrow, both to secure funds for investment and to finance the current account deficit. As the domestic savings rate dipped, the nation's gross foreign debt soared to US$32.4 billion in 1981 and peaked at US$40.4 billion in 1985, making South Korea the fourth largest borrower in the world at that time, after Brazil, Mexico and Argentina. In the same period, the nation's net foreign debt increased from US$24.5 billion to US$35.6 billion.

Although the exceptional performance of the Republic's economy during this period meant that the South Koreans had experienced few problems in securing additional loans, in the mid-1980s international bankers began to express doubts that South Korea would ever be able to pay up in full.

However, South Korea's foreign debt began to decline during the boom years of 1986–8, as foreign assets increased and the government was able to use a large share of the current account surplus to pay down the external debt. By 1989, gross foreign debt had fallen to US$29.4 billion and foreign assets had risen to US$26.4 billion, giving a net foreign debt of just US$3.0 billion. This remarkable improvement in the nation's foreign debt situation gave rise to optimism that South Korea would become a net creditor nation in 1990 or 1991.

That optimism was dented in the early 1990s, with the economy showing clear signs of a slow-down, and the current account going back into the red. At the end of 1991, gross foreign debt had increased to US$39.3 billion, while foreign assets had edged up to US$26.8 billion, giving a net foreign debt of US$12.5 billion.

INFLATION

South Korea has fought a running battle with inflation throughout most of its history. During the late 1960s and the early 1970s, annual consumer price inflation was normally in double figures; between 1973 and 1981, it averaged 19.6 per cent per annum. However, efforts made by the Chun administration (1981–88) to bring inflation under control were largely successful, aided by weak oil and commodity prices. During the five years to 1987, consumer and wholesale price inflation averaged 2.8 per cent and 0.2 per cent per year respectively.

The wage increases and the construction and consumption boom of the late 1980s aggravated inflationary pressures, and consumer prices, which had risen by 3 per cent in 1987, jumped by 7.1 per cent in 1988, and 5.7 per cent in 1989. Inflationary pressures increased during the first years of the 1990s, despite stringent efforts by the government to keep price rises in single figures. The measures included strict controls over or surveillance of prices of key goods and services. Policy makers have been torn between the desire for rapid growth and development and the need to curb inflation; in the early 1990s the focus has very much been on price stability.

Although official figures of 8.6 per cent in 1990, and 9.7 per cent in 1991, indicated that the rate of inflation at the consumer level had been kept below 10 per cent, many expressed the view that hidden inflation was pushing up the cost of living at a far faster rate. Premiums paid to taxi drivers over the rate recorded on the meter (increases in fares are controlled by the government) and the underweighting of housing prices and rental costs in the inflation index were cited as two examples.

MONEY SUPPLY AND MONETARY POLICY

In the early years of South Korea's economic development, monetary policy was used to promote economic growth and efficiency. However, following the runaway inflation of the late 1970s, the goal in the 1980s was to achieve price stability. Over the past decade, the government's conviction that curbing inflation is a prerequisite for sustained, long-term economic growth has prompted it to keep tight control over money supply and credit.

The central bank uses three instruments to control money supply: adjustments in the reserve requirement ratios, changes in the terms and conditions of the rediscount facility, and open market operations in specified securities, most notably Monetary Stabilization Bonds (MSBs). MSBs have been one of the principal tools of monetary control in the 1980s and early 1990s. These low-interest bonds have been issued in order to absorb excess liquidity, typically after expansionary periods such as elections and the annual Thanksgiving and New Year's festivals. Financial institutions are required to buy a specified amount of each issue, thus restricting the funds available for loan. As the proceeds are not spent, the effect is to withdraw money from circulation.

After approaching the 38 per cent level in the late 1970s, the rate of money supply (M2) growth declined in the 1980s, falling from 26.9 per cent in 1980 to 7.7 per cent in 1984. In the latter half of the 1980s, the average M2 growth rate was 18.9 per cent. In 1990 and 1991, M2 expanded by 17.2 per cent and 21.9 per cent respectively. (M2 is defined as currency in circulation, fixed-term and savings deposits, and demand deposits.)

The seemingly high rate of growth in money supply may seem inconsistent with continuing reports of a credit squeeze in South Korea. However, a large proportion of the increase in money supply is accounted for by government policy-backed loans and projects, leaving insufficient amounts to satisfy corporate demand. There are continuing calls from industry for an expansion in money supply, which would ease the credit squeeze and help bring down interest rates.

R&D

It may be said that the majority of South Korean companies only began to focus on R&D towards the end of the 1980s. Until that point, success had been assured by focusing on quantitative rather than qualitative growth; it was simply enough to continue mass-producing labour-intensive goods, which dominated the low end of the market.

The erosion of South Korea's international competitiveness and the emergence of competitors in the low end of the market forced South Korean companies to rethink their R&D strategies. In order to survive, let alone succeed, they had to move away from labour-intensive mass production of cheap goods, and focus on the capital- and technology-intensive manufacture of sophisticated, high value-added goods. The need for this strategy was heightened by the prospect of the opening of the domestic markets to foreign goods.

The advanced technology needed for this transformation could be acquired in one of three ways: technology transfer, acquisition of proprietary technology, or in-house development.

Concerns over the 'boomerang effect', through which the sale of cast-off technology comes back to haunt the seller in the form of cheap, mass-produced goods, have made advanced nations wary of transferring technology to South Korea. Advanced technology *is* available, but at a price, and the tightening of patent and copyright laws is making the evasion of royalty payments increasingly difficult. In 1991, a total of 582 technologies were introduced from foreign countries, principally the United States and Japan, at a cost of US$1.2 billion.

The fastest route is the acquisition of technology through mergers and acquisitions (M&A), but this depends to a great extent on the availability of target companies. The long-term solution is the local development of advanced technology.

However good the intentions, the stumbling block for all of this is money. Corporations which are struggling to find operating funds have little chance of mobilizing large sums of money for R&D, and are reluctant to borrow money at the current high rates of interest to fund in-house research programmes which will yield only long-term benefits.

In 1991, for the fifth year running, Samsung Electronics came top in the league table of R&D expenditure, with an investment of W474 billion (US$602 million). Second and third were Samsung Aerospace and Hyundai Motor, with investments of W107 billion (US$136 million) and W85 billion (US$108 million) respectively. Out of the top ten companies, four were in the automobile industry and five in the electronics sector. A 1991 survey of more than 25,000 manufacturing companies revealed that, on average, investment in R&D accounted for 0.1 per cent of turnover and 8.9 per cent of total expenditure. Total R&D costs in that year (including manpower, education, etc.) accounted for 2 per cent of GNP, compared with a proportion of 4–5 per cent in the United States and Japan.

This is not to say that progress has not been made. South Korea was the third country in the world, after Japan and the United States, to develop the 256K Dynamic Random Access Memory (DRAM) chip, and currently produces 16-Mega DRAM chips. South Korean researchers have developed ferrite crystals, which are essential for the production of video cassette-recorder tape heads, and Hyundai Motor developed the first domestically designed and manufactured engine in 1991 (see: Key Industries). A number of companies have established research centres, both at home and overseas.

The government has launched a high-profile campaign, which aims to boost R&D spending to 5 per cent of GNP in the year 2001, up from 2 per cent of GNP in 1991, and to promote the local development of more than 900 key technologies by 1995, at a total cost of W1.6 trillion (US$2 billion). In general, the government is focusing on the development of high-tech industries such as microelectronics, mechatronics, aviation, fine chemistry, genetic engineering and optical science. Specific products targeted for development include liquid crystal displays (LCDs), high-definition television (HDTV) sets, super-integrated semiconductor chips, and intelligent computers.

The government also plans to expand education and training, and efforts are being made to encourage South Korean scientists and engineers currently working overseas to return home.

Private companies are being encouraged to share technology and work together on specific R&D projects, in order to prevent duplication of research and make the best use of available resources. Although cross-licensing agreements are common in Japan, South Korean companies have been loath to pool their resources as far as technological developments are concerned.

However, in June 1992, Goldstar Co. and Samsung Electron Devices Co. announced that they had agreed to share 8,000 patented technologies related to the development of LCDs and colour picture tubes. In addition to this agreement, a number of joint research projects are currently under way, including the development of high definition television, the 64-Mega DRAM chip, and a variety of automobile components.

THE TAEJŎN EXPO, 1993

In August 1993, the Republic of Korea will become the first developing country to host an international exposition. The Taejŏn Expo, which will run for three months, is seen by its promoters as an opportunity to enhance further South Korea's international image and to show the nation's potential for continued growth. The Expo will also highlight South Korea's role as a bridge between advanced and developing nations, fostering cooperation and the exchange of information. On the domestic front, it will show the young people of South Korea the importance of science and technology and promote the city of Taejŏn as a centre of technology.

Invitations have been sent to 165 countries and 59 international organizations; the promoters are optimistic that more than 70 countries and 20 organizations will attend. It is estimated that more than 10 million people will visit the Expo during its three-month run.

The theme of the Expo is 'The Challenge of a New Road to Development' and its aim is to bring people together to share their industrial, technological and environmental experience. The Taejŏn Expo will emphasize industrial development in harmony with the environment; its subthemes are 'Traditional and Modern Technologies for World Development' and 'Towards the Improved Use and Recycling of Resources'.

Construction of the Expo Park began in 1991; when completed in May 1993, it will comprise an international exhibition area with 76 exhibition rooms, a permanent exhibition area, theme zones, a theme pavilion, and a 100-foot-high (93-metre-high) symbol tower. Once the Expo is over, the park will be preserved as a science park. Taejŏn is already home to the Taedŏk Science Town, an 11-square-mile (28-square-kilometre) site which houses government and private research institutes, promoting the common use of research facilities, personnel and information.

The Expo has not been without its critics, who maintain that it is too costly considering South Korea's current economic difficulties. The total cost is estimated at W593 billion (US$753 million), with W387 billion (US$492 million) allocated for construction and operation, and W206 billion (US$262 million) for infrastructure development and expansion. (The costs compare with an estimated US$8.9 billion for the 1992 Seville Expo.) The ROK government, however, maintains that the Expo will stimulate growth and help the nation face the challenges of the 1990s.

Table 3 (overleaf) shows the major economic indicators for the current Five-Year Plan.

TABLE 3 Major economic indicators in the 1992–6 Plan

Indicator	1992	1993	1994	1995	1996
Population (millions)	43.7	44.1	44.5	44.9	45.2
Growth rate	0.9 %	0.9 %	0.9 %	0.9 %	0.9 %
GNP[a]	$291.3 b	$315.2 b	$349.4 b	$399.3 b	$471.0 b
Growth rate	7.0 %	5.0 %	5.0 %	4.5 %	4.5 %
Per capita GNP[a]	$6,685	$7,177	$7,884	$8,930	$10,440
Industrial structure[b]					
Primary	8.1 %	7.7 %	7.3 %	6.8 %	6.4 %
Secondary	29.4	29.8	30.4	31.3	32.2
(Manufacturing	29.0	29.4	30.1	31.0	31.9
SOC[c] and others	62.5	62.5	62.3	61.9	61.4
Investment and Savings[d]					
Domestic SR[e]	34.7 %	34.8 %	35.2 %	36.1 %	36.6 %
Domestic IR[e]	38.2	37.1	36.3	35.4	34.8
Overseas IR	(2.7)	(1.6)	(0.4)	0.5	1.4

TABLE 3 *continued*

Indicator	1992	1993	1994	1995	1996
External transactions					
Exports[f]	$81.0 b	$92.0 b	$104.5 b	$119.0 b	$135.0 b
Imports[f]	90.5	99.5	110.0	122.0	135.0
Current account[g]	$(8.0) b	$(5.0) b	$(1.5) b	$2.0 b	$6.5 b
Ratio to GNP	(2.7) %	(1.6) %	(0.4) %	0.5 %	1.4 %
Net overseas assets[h]	$(18.0) b	$(21.5) b	$(21.5) b	$(18.0) b	$(10.0) b
Ratio to GNP	(6.2) %	(6.8) %	(6.2) %	(4.5) %	(2.1) %

[a] GNP and per capita GNP at current prices.
[b] Industrial structure at 1990 constant prices.
[c] SOC = Social overhead capital.
[d] Investment and savings at current prices.
[e] SR = savings ratio; IR = investment ratio.
[f] Exports and imports on a customs clearance basis.
[g] Current account balance at current prices.
[h] Net overseas assets at current prices.

Source: Economic Planning Board, April 1992.

PROSPECTS FOR 1993

Table 4 shows the economic outlook for 1993 compared with 1991 and 1992 figures.

TABLE 4 Economic outlook for 1993

Area	[1991]	[1992]	[1993]
GNP	8.4 %*	4.9 %	5.8 %
Total consumption	9.2	6.8	5.8
Private consumption	9.2	6.3	5.5
Fixed investment	11.9 %	(0.6) %	3.6 %
Facility investment	12.8	0.8	4.5
Construction investment	11.2	(1.7)	2.8
Merchandise exports	9.4	9.7	7.9
Merchandise imports	17.4	0.7	4.4
Current account	$(8.7) b	$(4.3) b	$(2.8) b
Trade account	$(7.0) b	$(1.7) b	$0.5 b
Exports**	71.9	77.0	83.6
Imports**	81.5	81.5	86.6
Raw materials	43.4	42.4	45.4
Capital goods	30.1	30.7	32.3
Consumer goods	8.1	8.5	9.0
Invisible trade and unrequired transfers	$(1.8) b	$(2.6) b	$(3.3) b
Wholesale prices	3.1 %	1.8 %	2.2 %
Consumer prices	9.3	4.5	5.3
Unemployment rate	2.3	2.5	2.7

* Growth rate over the previous year.
** Export and import amounts are on a customs clearance basis.
Source: Bank of Korea.

27 Natural Resources: Agriculture, Fishing, Forestry and Mining

AGRICULTURE: A HISTORICAL PERSPECTIVE

The principal goals of the South Korean government's agricultural policy over the past three decades have been to maintain a landownership system based on the owner-occupation of small landholdings, to keep rural incomes from falling too far behind urban wages, and to achieve self-sufficiency in food grains. The last goal has been made all the more difficult by the lack of arable land in south Korea. Less than 25 per cent of the land is available for agriculture, and the problem is compounded by the continuing loss of land to urbanization (see below).

In the years immediately following the liberation of Korea from Japanese colonial rule in 1945, the South Korean government acquired the land which had been owned by Japanese absentee landlords and sold it to tenant farmers and the landless. A maximum acreage was set for individual landholdings; plots which exceeded the new limit were also taken and disposed of in the same manner.

By 1952, 1.5 million farmers had become landowners; an egalitarian system of landholding has been maintained since then by limiting holdings of paddy land to 7.4 acres (3 hectares). In 1991, the farming population stood at 6 million, with the 1.7 million households each tending an average area of 3.1 acres (1.3 hectares). While this system was laudable in terms of social justice, it has had the drawback of fragmenting the nation's limited arable land into small plots, some of which were scarcely economically viable.

With the rapid development of the South Korean economy over the past four decades, and its transformation from an agrarian to an industrialized basis, the contribution made to economic growth by the agricultural sector has diminished.

In the 1950s, the primary sector contributed 40 per cent to GNP and accounted for 70 per cent of total employment. By 1991, 16.7 per cent of the nation's workforce was employed in a sector which contributed less than 10 per cent to South Korean GNP.

In addition, the total amount of arable land has fallen over the past two decades, from 6.2 million acres (2.5 million hectares) in 1972 to 4.0 million acres (1.6 million hectares) in 1991. This is due in large part to the fact that the rate of growth in demand for sites for industrial, commercial or residential construction far outpaces the rate at which land is being reclaimed.

Demand for labour in the cities and industrial centres, together with a widening gap between rural and urban incomes, has drawn young people off the land and into the cities. Falling agricultural output and growing population in the 1960s prompted concern over prospects for the agricultural sector and the nation's ability to feed itself.

In 1971, the government launched the *Saemaŭl* (New Community) Movement to encourage self-reliance, cooperation and thrift among rural communities. Administrative, technical and financial help was offered for projects which would boost farm incomes. Despite these efforts, the rural sector continued to lag behind the urban sector and was increasingly reliant on older labour.

However, in recent years, mechanization has done a great deal to ease the problem of labour shortages in the agricultural sector, and the consolidation of small farm holdings into larger plots has also made it more feasible to replace manual labour with machines. More than 80 per cent of the planting and harvesting of rice was mechanized by the early 1990s, and efforts continue to boost the ratio further.

AGRICULTURE: PRINCIPAL PRODUCTS

South Korea's main agricultural crop is rice; other important crops are barley, maize, fruit, vegetables and tobacco. In recent years, the cultivation for export of fruit and vegetables including tropical fruits such as pineapples and bananas, and cash crops such as silk, button mushrooms and ginseng, has increased.

Rice production in 1991 totalled 5.4 million tons. Production levels were forecast to fall by around 1 per cent in 1992, due to a reduction in land under cultivation, and the switch to less-productive, higher-quality strains of rice. Just as the total area of cultivated land has shrunk in recent years, the area of land devoted to rice cultivation has also been shrinking, from 3.1 million acres (1.3 million hectares) in 1987 to 3 million acres (1.2 million hectares) in 1991. Idle land has been appropriated by real estate developers, and some farmers have converted their paddy fields to grow other crops.

Although South Korea has been self-sufficient in rice since 1975, the nation's self-sufficiency in basic food grains has been declining over the past few years. Self-sufficiency in rice dropped to 102 per cent in 1992 from 108 per cent in 1989, and is forecast to fall below 100 per cent in 1993. The fall in the rate of self-sufficiency for barley has been far more dramatic – from 119.4 per cent in 1988 to 66.9 per cent in 1992. Cultivation of wheat in South Korea virtually ceased in 1987; average annual wheat imports swelled to 4.5 million tons in 1991 from 1.6 million tons at the end of the 1970s.

The growth of imports has been partly due to changes in consumer tastes, as South Korean society becomes more westernized. Recent years have seen a tendency, especially among younger Koreans, to eat western breakfasts of toast and cereal rather than traditional Korean breakfasts of rice and soup. The rapid increase in western-style bakeries, pizza parlours, hamburger bars and the like have also boosted demand for wheat. Another important factor in the growth of grain imports is the rising demand for raw materials for food processing and feed grains such as wheat flour and corn for the growing livestock industry.

The increase in the consumption of meat and dairy produce in the national diet has promoted the growth of the domestic livestock industry and boosted imports to South Korea. The past two decades have seen a remarkable increase in the number of livestock raised by South Korean farmers. In 1972, there were 36,000 dairy cattle, 1.2 million pigs and 24.5 million chickens in the Republic; in 1991, there were almost 500,000 dairy cattle, 5 million pigs and 75 million chickens.

Annual per capita consumption of beef and pork in South Korea, while still low by western standards, is gradually edging up, and reached 11.5 lb (5.2 kg) for beef, 26.0 lb (11.8 kg) for pork and 9.5 lb (4.3 kg) for chicken in 1991. Accordingly, the rates of self-sufficiency for beef and pork have dropped to 44.1 per cent and 84.2 per cent respectively in 1991, down from 100 per cent just four years earlier.

AGRICULTURE AND TRADE FRICTION

Imports of agricultural and marine products have risen sharply from the mid-1980s, in line with the gradual liberalization of the South Korean market. The most recently published schedule calls for the import of virtually all agricultural products to be liberalized by 1997. (The liberalization rate was 80.3 per cent in 1990.)

Although there has been a great deal of discussion between South Korea and its trading partners on liberalization in general, the most acrimonious disputes have centred on the opening of the country's beef and rice markets.

Negotiations continue over the opening of South Korea's beef market despite earlier agreements with the United States, Australia and New Zealand to operate a beef import quota system until the market is fully opened. In September 1992, the ROK government told United States government representatives that it would be impossible to open the market in 1997, as previously agreed, and that it would continue to set import quotas on the basis of previous years' average import volume. Imports, which averaged 86,000 tons per year between 1989 and 1991, have been given an additional boost by the ROK government's desire to relieve meat shortages in the domestic market and thus ease inflationary pressures.

In discussions on the opening of the South Korean rice market, the dispute centres on the General Agreement on Trade and Tariff (GATT)'s determination to 'tarrify' agricultural products. This would mean removing all non-tariff import barriers, including import bans, and replacing them with tariffs, which will then gradually be lowered over time.

While the ROK government has expressed its willingness to make concessions in the Uruguay Round negotiations over other agricultural produce, it remains adamant in its desire to protect the nation's farmers and keep rice on the list of non-trade concerns. The full liberalization of imports of basic foodstuffs like rice, the government argues, will have an adverse impact on the nation's 'food security', the environment, employment and Korea's traditional culture. For their part, GATT officials maintain that making exceptions for specific products in the negotiations could put the whole process at risk.

Should the ROK government fail to carry the day, 3–5 per cent (in terms of distribution) of the South Korean rice market would be opened, allowing imports of 200,000 tons per annum against a total annual distribution of 5.5 million tons. Given the relatively limited opening being considered, many find it hard to understand the South Koreans' determination to keep this market closed.

A total of six million people, or roughly 15 per cent of the total population, is engaged in agriculture in South Korea. The vast majority of farm households grow rice and derive more than half of their income from this one crop. However, South Korean farmers are not competitive, and have been softened by years of government protection and subsidies.

The government's policy of encouraging production by

buying rice at a high price from the farmers and selling it cheaply in the domestic market led first to self-sufficiency and then to surplus. The eleven years to 1991 saw continuous bumper harvests and increases in production at a time when consumption was declining. Per capita consumption of rice dropped by almost 10 per cent in ten years, falling to 262 lb (119 kg) in 1990 from 290 lb (132 kg) in 1980.

The result of this policy was a rapid increase in government stockpiles. In the early 1990s, there were more than 70 million bushels (25 million hectolitres) in government storehouses – the optimum level for the stockpiles is thought to be 38 million bushels (14 million hectolitres). Every year, the farmers call for an increase in the government purchase price for rice. In 1991, the price of local rice was more than five times higher than that sold on international markets. A 176 lb (80 kg) bag of Grade A rice was selling then for W120,400 (US$153) in South Korea, against a price of W21,250 (US$27) overseas.

Experts in South Korea forecast that, should imports of rice be liberalized and the tariff equivalents be lowered to 24 per cent for ten years, almost a quarter of the nation's farmers would be forced to give up rice cultivation. Apart from purely economic considerations, arguments are made to the effect that rice cultivation is part of Korean culture and that the liberalization of the market would have dire social repercussions. Many South Koreans identify with the interests of the farmers, as their families too were farmers only a generation or two ago.

The government's motives in opposing full market opening and the reduction of subsidies to farmers are also partly political; farmers now constitute a powerful and increasingly vocal lobby group in South Korea, and have not hesitated to take their protests out onto the streets. Following his victory in the 1992 elections, president-elect Kim Young-sam reaffirmed his opposition to the full opening of the nation's rice markets. However, some leading politicians in Japan, which is also under pressure to open its rice market, have recently been promoting the idea of agreeing to a limited market opening, in order to satisfy other countries in the GATT negotiations. Such an agreement would weaken South Korea's position in the discussions.

Between 1992 and the year 2001, the ROK government plans to invest a total of W10 trillion (US$12.7 billion) in the mechanization of agriculture and the modernization of farming facilities. Up to 1997, the focus will be on dry field farming and the cultivation of rice; during the latter half of the period, the focus will switch to facility-aided farming, including greenhouse cultivation. Farmers are also being encouraged to switch from rice to other crops, especially cash crops and higher-value fruit and vegetables, and to make efforts to boost productivity and cut production costs.

AGRICULTURE: THE RURAL–URBAN GAP

The focus on and investment in the industrial sector over the past three decades has been at the expense of the agricultural sector. While the industrial sector expanded at an average annual rate of 13 per cent between 1966 and 1988, the rural sector grew by just 3 per cent per annum during the same period. Accordingly, the ROK government has implemented a number of measures to narrow the gap between rural and urban incomes. During the period of the Seventh Five-Year Economic Development Plan (1992–6), the average annual income of farming households is projected to rise by 7.5 per cent per annum to reach W16,980,000 (US$21,575) in 1996. In 1990, the average annual income was W11,020,000 (US$14,000).

In recent years, the government has taken steps to boost non-farm income by creating additional job opportunities in rural areas. In the early 1990s, the proportion of total rural income constituted by non-farm earnings was 43 per cent, up from 34 per cent in the early 1980s and 37 per cent in 1989. However, this still compares poorly with farm households in Taiwan and Japan, where off-farm income contributes 64 per cent and 86 per cent of the household's earnings respectively. Furthermore, in South Korea, a substantial proportion of the non-farm income is contributed by children who have gone to work in the big cities.

The government has also made efforts to boost mechanization in the agricultural sector, by providing subsidies and loans for the purchase of machinery, including power tillers, rice transplanters, binding reapers and combine harvesters. In addition, farmers have been encouraged to form cooperative groups for the purchase and use of farm machinery.

FISHERIES

The seas around the Korean peninsula are rich in marine life, including many types of fish, shellfish and other sea animals and plants. In addition to fishing in the waters off the Korean peninsula, South Korean fishermen catch pollack and pike in the north Pacific, octopus and squid off West Africa, and shrimp off the coast of Brazil.

In 1991, the nation's fishing fleet stood at almost 100,000 vessels, with a combined tonnage of 977,000 gross. This has more than doubled over the past two decades – from 393,000 gross tons in 1971 – and the average boat size has increased to 9.8 tons from 5.8 tons during the same period.

Fish catches from marine fisheries (including adjacent waters, distant waters and whaling) have risen to more than 3 million tons in 1991 from 1.3 million tons in 1971. Catches from inland fisheries rose to 30,400 tons from 1,200 tons in the same twenty-year period.

As well as satisfying domestic demand, the fishing industry has been an important source of export earnings, with exports of fresh and frozen fish totalling US$621 million in 1991. Total exports of fishery products that year (including seaweed, canned fish, and tuna caught in foreign waters) amounted to US$1.6 billion.

Like the farming sector, the South Korean fishing industry now faces the prospect of opening up to foreign competition. In addition, fishermen face problems created by the establishment of 200-mile fishing exclusion zones in distant waters. In response to the latter development, the ROK government is actively encouraging the development of inland fisheries and aquaculture. It is also planning to develop new fishing areas, and to limit the direct introduction into South Korea of marine products caught by foreign ships. The operations of foreign vessels will also be restricted.

During the period of the seventh plan, the average annual income of fishing households is forecast to rise by 7.5 per cent per annum, to reach W15,450,000 (US$19,630) by 1996.

FORESTRY

Following the devastation of the Korean War (1950–3), the ROK government implemented a programme of reforestation, which raised the coverage ratio for the nation's mountains to 96 per cent in 1984 from 58 per cent in the late 1960s. A total of 89 million trees were planted in 1991, as part of the government's continuing drive to build up the nation's forestry resources. Nevertheless, the forested area in South Korea has shrunk by 2.1 per cent over the past two decades.

A total of 16 million acres (6.5 million hectares) of forested land was recorded in South Korea in 1990, 71 per cent of which was under private ownership, and 20.8 per cent of which was owned by the government. Public ownership accounted for the remainder. The forests currently comprise 46 per cent coniferous trees, 28 per cent mixed forest and 26 per cent deciduous trees.

In 1991, timber output was 1.7 million square yards (1.4 million square metres), giving a self-sufficiency ratio of 14 per cent. During the same year, imports of forestry products approached the US$2 billion mark.

171

MINING

The division of the Korean peninsula at the 38th parallel left the Democratic People's Republic of Korea in the north with the lion's share of the peninsula's mineral resources. There are almost three hundred minerals on the Korean peninsula; commercially exploitable minerals include gold, silver, copper, iron, lead, zinc, tungsten, kaolinite, molybdenum and barytes.

The chief metallic mineral to be found in the south is tungsten, with reserves estimated at 12.9 million tons. Although there are also deposits of important minerals, ores and base metals in the south, such as lead, zinc, iron, copper and aluminium, the amounts extracted are insignificant in relation to the Republic's consumption. Anthracite coal is South Korea's only indigenous fossil fuel; reserves were estimated at 300 million tons in 1987 (see: Energy Resources).

28 Human Resources

In 1991, South Korea's economically active population (men and women aged 15 years and over) numbered 19,012,000, an increase of 2.8 per cent year on year. The percentage of the total population accounted for by the economically active population has remained fairly stable over the past two decades, at between 57 per cent and 60 per cent.

In 1991, the total number of people employed was 18,576,000, with women accounting for 40 per cent of the workforce. White-collar workers accounted for 9.2 per cent of the total workforce; blue-collar workers and service-sector employees took shares of 34.9 per cent and 11.4 per cent respectively.

The jobless rate has declined steadily over the past two decades, falling from a peak of 5.2 per cent in 1980 to 2.3 per cent in 1991. When interpreting South Korean employment statistics, however, it should be borne in mind that anyone who works for more than one hour per week for wages is considered employed. In 1991, a total of 1.3 million people – 7 per cent of the total workforce – worked for fewer than 36 hours per week, and were therefore classed as 'underemployed'. If the 226,000 people who worked for fewer than 17 hours per week were added to the unemployment tally, the rate for that year would rise to 3.5 per cent from 2.3 per cent.

However, the falling unemployment rate disguises the fact that there are severe labour shortages in certain sectors. An increasing aversion to the 'Three Ds' has led to an increase in employment in the service industries, at the expense of the manufacturing and construction sectors (see also: Migrant Workers).

The shift in the nation's employment structure can be seen in the statistics showing employment by sector. In 1972, 48.2

173

per cent of the nation's workers were employed in agriculture and forestry; twenty years later, that share had fallen to 16.0 per cent. The share of the workforce accounted for by the manufacturing sector had risen to 26.6 per cent in 1991 from 13.6 per cent in 1972. However, the 1991 figure represented a drop from the level of almost 28 per cent seen in 1988. Employment in the service industry has risen steadily to account for a 48 per cent share of the workforce in 1991, up from 31.7 per cent two decades previously.

In 1991, it seemed to be the case that the higher one's level of education, the harder it was to get a job. The unemployment rate among elementary- and middle-school graduates was 1.1 per cent. The jobless rate increased in line with the level of education attained: the unemployment rate for high-school graduates was 3.2 per cent, while that for university and college graduates was 3.7 per cent.

29 Energy Resources

In 1991, the Republic of Korea was the tenth largest consumer of primary energy in the world. The South Koreans consumed 103.4 million tons of oil equivalent (TOE) of primary energy, including coal, oil and liquefied natural gas. Oil accounted for 58 per cent of total energy consumption in that year, making South Korea the eleventh largest consumer of oil and the sixth largest importer of oil in the world. In 1991, 18 per cent of the foreign exchange earned from South Korea's exports went to finance its energy imports; the continuing dependence on' imported energy is, therefore, an important determinant of the nation's current account status.

THE HISTORY OF ENERGY IN SOUTH KOREA
In the early 1960s, when South Korea embarked on its programme of economic development, the nation's energy resources were scarce and of low quality. In 1962, firewood and anthracite coal supplied 87.4 per cent of the nation's primary energy needs, with oil accounting for less than 10 per cent of the total. Total energy consumption in 1962 was 10 million TOE; per capita consumption was 0.39 TOE.

In the early 1960s, a top priority for the nation's economic planners was to secure sufficient energy sources to support their ambitious economic development plans. However, the rapid growth of the South Korean economy in general, and the development of energy-intensive heavy and chemical industries in particular, left the country heavily dependent on imported energy and therefore vulnerable to fluctuations in the supply and price of world resources.

In 1970, 47 per cent of South Korea's total energy requirements, including 60 per cent of requirements in the industrial sector, were met by imported oil; by the time of the second oil shock of 1979, the dependence on imported oil had risen to 62.3 per cent. South Korea's heavy dependence on imported oil, and almost total dependence on the Middle East for those imports, prompted a re-evaluation of the nation's energy policy, and a realization of the need to reduce dependence on imported oil.

The new energy policy formulated in 1980 called for the diversification of energy sources away from oil and the development of alternative sources of energy such as liquefied natural gas (LNG), liquefied petroleum gas (LPG) and nuclear power. The electricity generating sector in particular was identified as an area in which dependence on oil could be reduced by the use of alternative methods of generation.

Within ten years, the share of total electricity generation accounted for by oil-burning facilities had fallen sharply, to 13.9 per cent in 1988, from 81.8 per cent in 1979. Oil was imported from 22 countries, as opposed to just five in 1979, and dependence on oil from the Middle East fell to 62.4 per cent in 1988 from 99.9 per cent in 1979.

The nuclear age in South Korea began in 1978. A year later, nuclear power satisfied less than 2 per cent of the country's energy requirements; within ten years, that share had risen to almost 15 per cent, and in 1991, nuclear power accounted for 36 per cent of the nation's total generating capacity.

Although the government had managed to curb energy consumption in the early 1980s, in the wake of the two oil shocks, demand soared towards the end of the decade, reflecting the economic boom of 1986–8, the surge in private consumption, and the advent of the 'My Car' era (see: Key Industries). By 1991, total energy consumption had exceeded 100 million TOE, with per capita consumption rising to 2.4 TOE. The trend towards lesser dependence on imported energy had reversed, with dependence rising to 93.4 per cent by the first quarter of 1992, from 91.2 per cent in 1991 and 76.2 per cent in 1985.

For the past three decades, South Korea's economic planners have faced the challenge of ensuring energy security. They now also face the consequences of artificial pricing policies, which aimed to control inflation but also boosted energy consumption, and lax investment in power generating facilities in the 1980s, which has resulted in very low power reserve ratios.

ENERGY SUPPLY: INDIGENOUS RESOURCES

Low-grade **anthracite coal** is South Korea's only indigenous fossil fuel resource; in 1987, recoverable reserves were estimated at 300 million tons. Although the country was heavily

dependent on anthracite coal in the early stages of its industrialization, the coal mining industry has gone into a decline
in recent years. This has been due in great part to rising production costs, deteriorating production conditions and price
competitiveness, and the shift in consumer preference towards
higher-quality, cleaner fuels.

Only about 10 per cent of domestically produced anthracite coal is used for electricity generation; the main use of
anthracite coal in South Korea has been to make coal briquettes
(yŏnt'an), which were traditionally used for heating and cooking. However, consumer preferences for cleaner, more efficient
fuels have led to an increase in the use of gas for heating and
cooking, and consumption of yŏnt'an is declining steadily.

The ROK government's coal-mine rationalization policy,
implemented in 1989, aims to reduce coal production to an
optimum level by closing down uneconomic mines. Annual
production is forecast to fall from 15 million tons in 1991 to
less than 10 million tons by 1996. With annual current consumption levels standing at just 2 million tons, and demand
for anthracite coal still declining, the government plans to
build a 200,000-kilowatt thermoelectric power plant by 1998,
to absorb some of the slack in production.

To date, no commercially viable deposits of **oil** or **natural
gas** have been discovered in South Korea. However, there have
been encouraging indications of offshore natural gas deposits
and possibly some small deposits of oil. A number of South
Korean corporations are actively involved in the development
of oil and gas resources overseas; oil produced by these ventures currently accounts for about 2 per cent of South Korea's
oil requirements.

ENERGY SUPPLY: IMPORTED RESOURCES

South Korea currently imports crude oil, petroleum products,
LNG, anthracite, and bituminous and coking coal. In 1991,
energy imports amounted to US$12.5 billion, a year-on-year
increase of 16 per cent.

South Korea is almost totally dependent on imported oil
(a large proportion of which is still sourced from the Middle
East) and continues to import petroleum products to supplement local production. In 1991, South Korea imported 400
million barrels of crude oil and 110 million barrels of petroleum products, at a total cost of US$10.1 billion. LNG has
been imported since 1986; in 1991, South Korea imported 2.8
million barrels of it at a cost of US$521 million. Imports of
coal in 1991 totalled 30.1 million tons in volume and US$1.6
billion in value.

South Korea's dependence on imported energy has risen

177

steadily from 76.2 per cent in 1985 to 93.4 per cent in March 1992; this compares with dependency rates of 3.8 per cent in the United Kingdom, 17.4 per cent in the United States, 51.3 per cent in Germany and 87.0 per cent in Japan. The increase in dependency on imported energy in recent years is largely due to the decline in demand for coal, which can be produced domestically, and a surge in demand for oil, which must be imported.

ENERGY CONSUMPTION

Demand for energy has increased sharply in the past few years, boosted by expansion in both the industrial and residential sectors. Total energy consumption grew at an average annual rate of 9.9 per cent between 1986 and 1989; the rate of expansion jumped to 14.1 per cent in 1990, before easing somewhat to 10.9 per cent in 1991.

In the late 1980s, growth in energy consumption in the industrial sector was fuelled by rapid economic growth. In the 1990s, the trend towards the automation and electrification of manufacturing facilities is helping to raise consumption.

In the residential sector, the trend towards nuclear families has meant that an increasing number of young families are setting up their own homes, thereby boosting demand for electricity and heating fuels. Also, higher disposable incomes and changes in lifestyles have led to increased ownership of automobiles and electrical appliances. One example well worth citing is that of the increase in use of air conditioners: the number of units in use has jumped to almost 2 million in 1992 from 901,000 in 1989. On 23 July 1992, a new record was reached in national consumption of electricity, pushing through the 20-million kilowatt level, as the nation sweltered in a summer heatwave.

Lack of awareness of or concern over the need to conserve energy is another factor in the growth in consumption, as is the rapid expansion of construction of larger houses and skyscraper office blocks. It has been estimated that the land-mark 63 Building in Seoul uses as much electricity as a medium-sized provincial city. The energy efficiency of the manufacturing sector remains relatively low, a result of insufficient investment in energy-saving equipment, and the rate of generation from waste is low – only one waste-burning plant exists in South Korea, and just 7 per cent of Korean waste is recycled, compared with more than 70 per cent in Japan. Artificial control of prices by the government, in the interests of curbing inflation, has removed much of the urgency from conservation.

Total energy consumption is forecast to increase at an

average annual rate of 5.1 per cent between 1991 and 2010, to reach 166 million TOE in 2010. Per capita consumption is forecast to reach 3.1 TOE in the same year. South Korea's relative dependence on oil as a source of energy will decline to 42.6 per cent in 2010, in line with the continuing development of alternative energy sources. However, demand for oil will rise to 1.4 million barrels per day in 2010 from 550,000 barrels per day in 1986, pushing up the nation's energy import bill to US$25 billion in 2010 from US$4.5 billion in 1986.

ELECTRIC POWER GENERATION

The Korea Electric Power Corporation (KEPCO) is the sole supplier of electricity within the Republic of Korea. Should private investors produce electricity, it must be sold through KEPCO. However, the construction and operation of nuclear power plants is the sole preserve of the government.

There are three principal types of electricity-generating plant in South Korea: thermal power plants, which burn fossil fuels; hydroelectric power plants, which make use of dammed water; and nuclear power plants. In 1991, South Korea had nine nuclear power plants in operation, which produced almost half (48.3 per cent) of the electric power generated that year, giving South Korea ninth ranking in the world in terms of nuclear power generation.

South Korea's electricity generating capacity has increased rapidly over the past three decades, rising from 367,000 kilowatts (kW) in 1961 to 21.1 million kW in 1991. In 1991, thermal power plants (running on oil, coal or natural gas) accounted for 52.3 per cent of the total generating capacity (11,050 kW), while nuclear plants accounted for 36.1 per cent of the total (7,615 kW). The generating capacity of hydroelectric power plants in that year stood at 2,445 kW, or 11.6 per cent of total capacity.

The ROK government's energy policy aims to secure a stable supply of cost-efficient electric power through the promotion of economical coal and nuclear power plants. However, cheap pricing policies from the mid-1980s and changes in the pattern of energy consumption have resulted in a surge in demand for electricity which can hardly be met by the power-generating facilities currently in existence. Between 1989 and 1991, consumption grew at an average annual rate of 12.8 per cent to 20.7 million kW, while power generating capacity expanded at an average annual rate of 6.2 per cent to reach 21.1 million kW.

The slim reserve margins (the surplus between electricity generated and electricity consumed) can mean that, in certain peak periods (such as the height of summer, when air

179

conditioners are in common use), it is impossible to meet total demand. An additional surge in demand at peak periods can result in occasional blackouts in designated areas, and the failure of any one power plant would make it impossible to meet demand.

The reserve margin has dropped sharply in recent years, falling to 2.5 per cent in 1992 (and to just 2.2 per cent on one day in May 1991) from 18.7 per cent in 1989 and 8.3 per cent in 1990, and remains a cause for concern for the South Korean authorities. The optimum reserve margin is 15 per cent, but it can drop to 10 per cent without any major difficulties.

The government has, therefore, embarked on an ambitious plan to construct a further 85 power plants with a combined generating capacity of 45 million kW by the year 2006. At the end of 1992, KEPCO announced that seventeen new power plants would be in operation by 1995, increase the electricity supply by 8 million kW (see below).

OIL REFINING

The oil refining industry has been one of the most highly regulated of all sectors in the South Korean economy. The nation's heavy dependence on imported oil and the strategic importance of the refining industry to the economy as a whole prompted the government to place it under strict controls.

In the past, the government has kept prices artificially low, sometimes by imposing limits on the expansion of profit margins, has restricted entry to and expansion within the sector, and has regulated distribution. All of this has meant that the nation's five oil refining companies could coexist fairly amicably, with no competition.

However, in line with the government's policy of liberalization and internationalization, prices and distribution will gradually be deregulated and the sector will be opened up to foreign corporations. The South Korean oil refiners now have to face up to both domestic and foreign competition, and the ROK government will have to loosen its controls over this important industrial sector.

Imported crude oil is refined to produce a variety of products including gasoline, kerosene, diesel, heavy oil and Bunker-C oil. In line with the increasing use of these products as industrial feedstocks and sources of energy, South Korea's total refining capacity has grown from 35,000 barrels per day in 1964 to 1.1 million barrels per day in 1991. In 1991, production of petroleum products totalled 408,000 barrels, against demand of 424,000 barrels.

CITY GAS

Since the first imports of natural gas from Indonesia in 1986, the use of gas for heating and cooking purposes has increased sharply in urban areas. At the end of 1991, 12–14 per cent of households were connected to the city gas network, and consumption totalled 3.5 million TOE. Experts forecast that consumption will rise to 14 million TOE by the year 2006, with 65–75 per cent of households using city gas in that year. Gas will then account for 10 per cent of total energy supplied in South Korea, up from 3.4 per cent in 1991.

GOVERNMENT POLICY AND FUTURE PROSPECTS

The long-term plan formulated by the Korea Electric Power Corporation calls for an **expansion in electric power supply** from 21.1 million kW in 1991 to 34.4 million kW in 1996 and to 60 million kW in the year 2006. The nation's oil refining production capacity will be boosted to 1.2 million barrels per day from the current level of 1.1 million barrels, and the handling capacity for LNG will be enhanced from 2 million tons per year to 9 million tons by 1996.

A total of 60 new power plants will be in operation by the year 2001, with a combined generating capacity of 28 million kW. The new plants will comprise 9 nuclear units, 24 soft coal-burning thermal power plants, 8 LNG-fired plants, 16 hydraulic power plants, 2 oil-burning plants and 1 hard-coal-burning plant. In 2001, KEPCO forecasts that nuclear power will account for 34 per cent of total power generation, coal for 32 per cent and oil and other sources for 20 per cent.

By the year 2006, a further 25 power plants will be in operation – 9 nuclear power plants, 4 soft-coal-burning plants, 6 hydraulic plants and 6 LNG-fired plants. These 25 plants will have a combined generating capacity of 16.9 million kW. Total investment in the construction of the 85 new plants, which will boost total generating capacity to around 66 million kW by the year 2006, is estimated at W45.5 trillion (US$57.8 billion).

The search for sites for nuclear power stations may face some problems due to the increasingly vocal anti-nuclear lobby in South Korea. The government has plans to establish a Cultural Foundation for Nuclear Plants, which will serve as a channel for discussion of issues and concerns relating to nuclear power.

The plan also reflects a determination to reduce the nation's dependency on oil (thus reducing imports and boosting its trade position) and calls for a shift in the composition of energy supply by the year 2006. In that year, nuclear power plants will account for 40 per cent of the nation's total projected electric power generation capacity. Bituminous coal-burning thermal power plants will account for 30 per cent, and LNG-fired plants 17 per cent. Hydroelectric plants will account for 10 per cent of production and oil-burning plants just 3 per cent.

The government will continue in its efforts to diversify **oil** import sources, partly in order to reduce further the nation's dependence on oil from the Middle East. South-east Asia, North America and Africa have been targeted as possible sources for imports of crude oil. Efforts will continue to secure oil supplies through participation in overseas development consortia. In 1992, imports from these sources accounted for less than 2 per cent of total domestic demand. This is forecast to rise to 10 per cent by the end of this century.

Import sources for **natural gas** will also be diversified; the former Soviet Union, Australia, Alaska and Qatar may be added to the list of suppliers. A total of W866 billion (US$1.1 billion) will be invested in the natural gas industry up to the year 2006 in order to improve storage facilities and capacity, localize supply equipment, and upgrade related technology. The nationwide gas pipeline network will be completed by the year 2000.

Since the Gulf War in 1991, the ROK government has given high priority to the building up of stockpiles. South Korea currently has the capacity to stockpile 40 million barrels of petroleum and 112,000 tons of LPG. However, with the rapid increase in energy consumption, these stocks would last just 34 days; the construction of seven additional storage facilities will bring the stockpiles up to 60 days for government supplies and 30 days for private sector supplies by 1996.

The South Koreans' energy consumption rate is one of the highest in the world, due to the rapid expansion of industrial activities and the increase in the nation's standard of living. The Seventh Five-Year Economic Development Plan (1992–6) calls for an average annual growth rate of 7.4 per cent in energy consumption over the five-year period; this represents a fall of 3.2 per cent from the rate achieved during the previous plan period. In September 1992, the ROK Ministry of Energy and Resources announced its own **energy-saving plan**, which aims to lower the nation's energy consumption growth rate from the current level of 15 per cent to 8 per cent in 1996, 5 per cent in 2001, and 0 per cent thereafter.

Attempts to limit the increase in energy consumption have been hampered by low public awareness of the need to conserve energy and the reluctance of manufacturing companies to invest in new, energy-efficient facilities. Energy conservation campaigns to date have included measures such as restricting the operating hours of petrol stations, and banning private cars from the roads one day in ten on a rota basis. Public utility rates have been adjusted to penalize heavy users, and officials have been instructed to carry out assessments of energy use by more than 2,500 companies using more than 250 TOE of energy per year.

Controls over energy use in factories and public buildings are being strengthened; for example, the use of air conditioners at the government complex in Kwach'ŏn was prohibited in the summer of 1992, and recommended cooling and heating rates are now provided for public buildings.

However, just as important as the launching of energy conservation campaigns is the maintenance over the long term of the awareness of the need for conservation. In the past, the government has implemented strict conservation measures in times of crisis, such as the Gulf War in 1991, only to find that as soon as the emergency is over, the nation returns to its free and easy ways.

On the industrial front the government is actively encouraging investment in energy-saving equipment, through the provision of tax and financial incentives. Government expenditure on R&D will total W400 billion (US$508 million) between 1992 and 1996; efforts will focus on power technology, energy storage, and new and renewable sources of energy. Research will also be carried out into increasing the fuel efficiency of cars and lowering energy consumption by consumer electronics products such as air conditioners and refrigerators.

In 1992, the Ministry of Energy and Resources announced that seven energy-intensive industries, including steel, cement and petrochemicals, will be required to make efforts to reduce their energy consumption and to invest a total of W1.7 trillion (US$2.2 billion) in energy-saving R&D by 1996.

30 Key Industries

For South Korea, a country with meagre natural resources, attention has always focused on the manufacturing sector as the primary source of growth. The first decade of economic planning (1962–72) saw the development of export-oriented light industries such as textiles and footwear. In the 1970s, attention shifted to the growth of heavy and chemical industries such as shipbuilding and steel, and the 1980s and early 1990s have seen the development of technology- and capital-intensive industries, including electronics, automobiles and machinery.

From poor beginnings just over three decades ago, South Korea has established a strong presence in a number of key industrial sectors. In 1991, South Korea produced 1.5 million automobiles, ranking ninth in the world – ahead of the United Kingdom. In the same year, South Korea produced 26 million tons of iron and steel, accounting for 3 per cent of total world output, and ranking sixth in the world. In the shipbuilding industry, South Korea ranked second only to Japan, with 4.4 million tons built, and in the textile sector, South Korean apparel exports amounted to US$8.4 billion, giving them a 7 per cent world market share. In 1992, South Korea became the fifth largest ethylene producer in the world, with total production capacity of 3.3 million tons.

In looking at South Korea's key industries, certain themes are evident. Virtually every sector has suffered export setbacks in the late 1980s and early 1990s, due mainly to rising production costs, increasing protectionism in key export markets, and fierce competition from developing countries. Although a switch in focus towards the domestic market has helped some industries to offset the slump in export sales, the real answer lies in restructuring.

South Korea's manufacturing industries have now begun a painful process of transformation, from low-tech, labour-intensive production to the manufacture of high-tech, high value-added goods. Companies are looking for ways to reduce production costs, boost productivity, upgrade and improve production facilities, and increase investment in R&D. This will enable South Korean industries to produce high-tech, high value-added products at competitive prices, which must then be marketed and sold in as diverse a group of export markets as possible.

In addition to challenges overseas, most industries face competition in their home markets – from newly emerging competitors at the low end and from foreign companies at the top end. For some sectors, the prospect of the opening of South Korea's markets to foreign goods and services after years of protection and nurturing by the government is not a pleasant one.

Central to this restructuring process is the issue of funding; the modernization of production facilities, the development of new products and technologies, the opening up of new markets, and the marketing and advertising of brand-name goods all require finance. Weakening profitability leaves scant reserves for investment; high domestic interest rates and government restrictions on overseas borrowing create a reluctance to add to already heavy financial burdens.

AUTOMOBILES

The production of automobiles in South Korea began with the assembly of knock-down kits in the early 1960s. From those early beginnings, the industry has expanded and developed at a remarkable rate.

Production has increased rapidly from 28,819 vehicles in 1970 to 1,497,454 vehicles in 1991, making South Korea the ninth largest manufacturer in the world. South Korea's automobile manufacturers now produce a wide range of vehicles, from passenger cars to trucks and special vehicles, with an increasing diversity of models, the newest being the ranges of 'light' (under 800 cc) and 'sporty' cars. South Korean vehicles are sold locally and exported to leading markets such as the United States, Canada and Europe. In 1991, domestic sales of cars and commercial vehicles passed the one million mark for the first time (1,104,480), while exports totalled 390,361 units.

For most of its history, the South Korean automobile industry has been dominated by three companies: Hyundai Motor, Daewoo Motor and Kia Motors. In 1991, these top three manufacturers accounted for almost 95 per cent of automobile production in South Korea. Hyundai Motor dominates the market, taking a 52.4 per cent share of production in 1991.

Kia Motors' and Daewoo Motor's shares were 28.8 per cent and 13.5 per cent respectively. In June 1992, Hyundai Motor reached the five million production mark just 25 years after the company's inauguration.

All of the top three makers have forged links with foreign automobile manufacturers, to gain access to technology, key components, and marketing networks. Mitsubishi Motors has a 15 per cent stake in Hyundai, and has provided technology and parts to its Korean partner. Ford of the United States and Japan's Mazda both have minority interests in Kia, and Daewoo formed a joint venture with General Motors (GM) of the United States in 1977.

In mid-1992, it was announced that Daewoo's manufacturing relationship with GM would end, with Daewoo buying back GM's 50 per cent equity stake for US$170 million. There had been reports that GM had concerns over product quality and labour relations, while Daewoo was frustrated by GM's refusal to increase the venture's capital or to allow expansion into new export markets. Daewoo now has technology ties with Opel of Germany, and Isuzu, Suzuki, Nissan and Honda of Japan.

Following the liberalization of investment in the automobile sector in 1989, the number of producers has risen to eight. Daewoo Shipbuilding and Heavy Machinery now produces the Tico light car with assistance from Suzuki of Japan, while Hyundai Precision and Ssangyong Motor manufacture jeeps and recreational vehicles in technical tie-ups with Japanese and German automobile makers. (Mercedes-Benz bought a 5 per cent equity stake in Ssangyong in 1992.) Asia Motors, which is affiliated with the Kia Group, produces commercial vehicles with assistance from Eaton of the United States, Scania of Sweden, and Daihatsu and Hino of Japan.

In 1992, Samsung Shipbuilding and Heavy Industries received government approval to assemble cargo trucks using technology provided by Nissan Diesel. This raised concerns among the established manufacturers that Samsung's medium-to long-term aim may be to enter the passenger car market.

In the early 1990s, the automobile industry faces a number of challenges including flagging exports, weakening domestic sales, increasing competition from foreign cars in the local market, and sluggish investment in facility investment and R&D.

Exports

Until the mid-1980s, production was focused on sales to the domestic market, although a small number of cars were exported to the Europe. The successful penetration of the

North American market in 1985 by Hyundai Motor marked the beginning of a period of rapid growth for the automobile industry, which quickly joined textiles and electronics as a leading export sector.

In the late 1980s, sales to the United States were boosted by brisk demand for subcompact cars at a time when Japanese automobile manufacturers were switching their export priority from subcompacts to medium-sized cars. This provided the South Koreans with an opportunity to provide subcompacts to low-income buyers in the United States at competitive prices. In 1989, South Korean automobile exports reached 356,040 units, of which almost two-thirds (233,515 units) were sold to the United States.

However, in recent years, automobile exports have suffered from rising production costs and labour unrest. Between 1987 and 1990, annual wage increases averaged 19.2 per cent, putting the South Korean automobile workers' hourly salary on a par with that of Japanese workers, despite their lower levels of productivity. Between 1987 and 1991, there were 436 labour disputes in the automobile industry; total production losses for the period were W4.6 trillion (US$5.8 billion) or 520,277 vehicles, peaking at W813 billion (US$1.0 billion at the 1988 average market rate) in 1988.

Although labour relations at the automobile manufacturers have been improving in the past few years, there are still problems at automobile parts manufacturers. Out of the 67 labour disputes recorded in 1991, two occurred in the automobile industry, and 65 in the parts and components sector. The unrest in the components sector has an impact on the automobile industry as a whole, leading as it does to bottlenecks in the supply of key parts and components.

The South Korean manufacturers' tardiness in updating old models and producing new ones has also put them at a disadvantage in export markets, as have adverse currency fluctuations, which have made the South Korean models less attractive than their Japanese competitors.

Export sales dropped sharply in 1989 and 1990 but recovered somewhat to 390,000 units in 1991, thanks to the launch of new models, the depreciation of the Korean wŏn, and the opening up of new export markets. Sales to the United States peaked at 448,000 units in 1988 and have since declined rapidly, falling to 171,000 units in 1991. South Korea's share of the American market also dropped from 3 per cent in 1989 to 2.4 per cent in 1991.

In response to the slow-down in exports, South Korean automobile manufacturers have been making strenuous efforts to diversify their export markets, and reduce their dependence on the United States. These efforts appear to be paying off: during the first seven months of 1992, although exports to the United States, Canada and Eastern Europe fell by 37 per cent, 38 per cent and 69 per cent year on year, the rates of growth for exports to the Middle East and Latin America were 351 per cent and 304 per cent respectively. Exports to Western Europe jumped by 143 per cent and shipments to the Asia-Pacific region expanded by 57 per cent during the same seven-month period.

In recent years, South Korean automobile companies have been promoting exports of knock-down (KD) kits, which have the advantages of being subject to lower import duties than finished vehicles, and being able to be assembled overseas, thereby making use of cheaper labour. Furthermore, KDs offer a means of boosting exports to countries which ban or restrict the import of finished vehicles, and to countries with low levels of disposable income. South Korean automobile manu-facturers currently export on a KD basis to a number of coun-tries, including Thailand, Taiwan, the Philippines, Venezuela, Vietnam, Iran, India and Morocco.

In addition to diversifying their markets, the automobile companies are striving to establish or expand their sales net-works overseas and boost their marketing activities. Hyundai Motor already has sales companies in the United States, Canada and Germany; Kia Motors set up a sales subsidiary in the United States in 1992, and plans to establish others in Canada and (possibly) Japan. Daewoo Motor is currently using Daewoo Corporation's sales outlets in Nigeria and Algeria, with plans to establish dedicated sales companies in promising markets at a later date.

Unlike Hyundai, which has always marketed its cars under its own label through overseas dealer networks, Kia and Daewoo have, until recently, exported their passenger cars on an original equipment manufacture (OEM) basis, with Kia selling its Pride model as the Ford Festiva, and Daewoo exporting its Le Mans to be sold by GM as the Pontiac Le Mans.

Major manufacturers are also planning to establish plants overseas in order to circumvent the problems of rising labour costs, protectionism and labour unrest. For example, Hyundai already has a plant in Canada, and is reported to be planning further plants in Thailand, Iran and China. Kia Motors is looking at setting up assembly plants in the Philippines (for KD kits) and Vietnam.

Domestic sales

Following the trend which can be seen in the economy as a whole, manufacturers have been able, to a large extent, to compensate for flagging export sales by selling into the domestic market. The sharp rise in disposable income seen in the late 1980s, and the arrival of the 'My Car' era have given a huge boost to local sales. In 1987, exports accounted for 56 per cent of total sales; two years later, domestic purchases overtook export sales for the first time since exports reached a significant volume in 1986, taking a 68 per cent share of total sales. In volume terms, the growth was just as impressive; in November 1991, domestic sales hit the one million mark, or double the level recorded three years earlier.

In June 1992, 4.7 million vehicles were registered in the Republic of Korea, including 3 million passenger cars, and new vehicles were coming onto the road at a rate of more than 2,500 per day. The one million mark was passed in August 1985, two million in November 1988, three million in June 1990, and four million in October 1991.

However, the automobile companies are now facing the prospect of saturation in the domestic market, with a decline in the annual rate of sales growth from 46 per cent in 1989 to 25 per cent in 1990, and further to 16 per cent in 1991. Sales have been hit by frugality campaigns, rising gasoline prices, and government measures to restrict car sales due to problems with traffic congestion, pollution, and lack of parking facilities. Moreover, many analysts maintain that domestic sales are reaching their limit. In 1992, the automobile diffusion rate stood at 110 vehicles per thousand persons; the American and Japanese experience has shown that domestic sales begin to fall off once the diffusion rate reaches 100 per thousand.

In the early 1990s, workforces were cut, production curtailed, and vigorous sales promotions initiated to cope with rising inventories, which had reached 60,000 units by May 1992. This situation came hard on the heels of a sales boom, when producers were struggling to cope with backlogged orders; on the commercial vehicle side, for example, soaring demand due to the construction boom (see below) led to a rapid expansion in production capacity from 29,000 units to 48,000 units within two years. Demand dropped as the construction boom began to cool off, at least temporarily, leaving manufacturers with large inventories.

Imports

Although the domestic market has been open to foreign cars (with the exception of Japanese vehicles) since 1987, sales remain low. The number of foreign cars sold rose from 11 in

1987 to 299 in 1988, 1,414 in 1989, and 2,436 in 1990. More recently, high import tariffs and multiple layers of taxes, campaigns against excessive or conspicuous consumption, and fears of tax investigations into the financial affairs of big spenders have combined to dampen demand for high-priced foreign cars. In 1991, sales fell back to 1,791 vehicles.

R&D

In the past, South Korea's automobile companies have focused on expanding production capacity rather than on developing new technology. Moreover, shortages of funds have been an important contributory factor in sluggish investment in R&D. However, investment in R&D is essential to enable the South Korean automobile manufacturers to reduce their reliance on foreign technology and enhance their competitiveness in international markets.

South Korea's automobile companies are still heavily dependent on imported technology, relying on Japan and the United States for about 60 per cent of their imports. A total of 164 technologies were imported between 1989 and 1991; royalties amounted to US$30.1 million in 1989 (for 57 items), US$52.9 million in 1990 (again, for 57 items), and US$99.5 million in 1991 (for 50 items, 27 of which came from Japan). The average cost per item of technology has risen as companies have focused more on key technologies; in 1991, the average cost was US$928,300.

Moreover, the South Korean automobile manufacturers are heavily dependent on components produced in related industries such as steel, machinery, and electronics, which leaves them vulnerable to labour disputes in these sectors and to rising prices passed on by the parts manufacturers.

In addition to the development of parts and components, investment must be made in design and development of new models. The life-cycle of products in the industry is relatively short; in order to remain competitive, companies must develop a variety of models and respond more quickly to changes in consumer taste.

Despite the gloomy reports of a slow-down in R&D investment, progress is being made on the technical front. Hyundai Motor has already developed its own engine, and both Kia Motors and Daewoo Motor have embarked on engine development programmes.

Hyundai has successfully developed an anti-knock braking system, with technical assistance from the Bendix Corporation of the United States, a flexible fuel vehicle (FFV), which can run on a mixture of gasoline and methanol, and an electric car. The most recent test model of electric car, produced in 1992, has a top speed of 62 miles (100 km) per hour, and can run for 62 miles (100 km) on a single charge. Hyundai plans to commence commercial production in 1995.

Kia Motors and Daewoo Motor are working on the development of methanol and compressed natural gas (CNG) cars respectively. Kia has already developed a solar car with a maximum speed of 62 miles (100 km) per hour, which can run for up to 125 miles (200 km) on a single charge.

The Ministry of Trade and Industry's X-5 project, which was inaugurated in 1992, aims to take the automobile industry into the world's top five by the year 2000. The project planners forecast that R&D expenditure will be 5 per cent of sales of between 1992 and 1994, 5.5 per cent between 1995 and 1997, and 6 per cent between 1998 and 2000. The project aims to promote the acquisition of key technology, the development of independent technology, and the expansion of overseas manufacturing plants.

By the end of the project period, the nation's automobile production capacity will have risen to 4 million units, output will stand at 3.2 million units, and exports will total US$10 billion. The number of vehicles registered in South Korea will have risen to 13 million, and the automobile diffusion rate will have risen to 171 per thousand people.

However, in mid-1992, there were reports that all three major automobile manufacturers had scaled down their facility investment plans, in the face of rising inventories and sluggish sales. It now seems likely that plans to expand total automobile production capacity from 2.6 million vehicles in early 1992 to 3.7 million by the end of 1995 will likewise be scaled down.

In addition to the funding problems which face the majority of South Korean manufacturing companies, changes in methods of payment for vehicles are making it harder for automobile manufacturers to mobilize funds for investment. Changes in the terms and conditions for car loans have resulted in a sharp increase in the number of purchases on an instalment basis, which accounted for 85 per cent of total sales during the first eight months of 1992. This compares with a 19 per cent share in 1990 (the year in which the changes were effected) and 56 per cent in 1991. Payments spread over 24 to 36 months have left companies short of funds and have forced them to turn to short-term loans for working capital and investment funding.

CONSTRUCTION

In 1991 the construction industry recorded a growth rate of 46.1 per cent in terms of domestic and overseas contract awards, which increased to W40 trillion (US$50.8 billion). The growth rate was the second highest since 1978, when an expansion of 87.3 per cent was recorded. Growth was boosted by a recovery in overseas orders, thanks largely to the opening up of new markets, and large government-backed projects at home, including housing projects, infrastructure development, and land reclamation.

Overseas construction

The South Korean construction industry developed out of the need to rebuild the nation's infrastructure and establish production facilities after the Korean War (1950–3). In the 1970s, the focus changed to overseas projects as South Korean construction companies benefitted from the building boom in the Middle East, which was fuelled by oil profits. The experience gained by building roads, ports and factories at home enabled South Korean contractors to gain a huge share of the work available in the Middle East from 1974 onwards.

Total overseas orders jumped from US$15.6 million in 1967 to US$3.5 billion in 1977, before peaking at US$13.7 billion in 1981; orders from the Middle East soared to US$12.7 billion in the same year. Throughout the rest of the 1980s, however, overseas orders declined steadily, as Middle East contracts dropped to US$9.0 billion in 1983, US$1.3 billion in 1987, and US$0.9 billion in 1991, due to the deteriorating financial situation of some of the Middle Eastern nations. There was a temporary surge in 1990, thanks to the successful bid by a South Korean construction company for a US$5.6 billion project in Libya, but orders dropped back to US$3.0 billion in 1991.

In order to boost overseas orders, South Korean contractors have been making efforts to diversify their markets and reduce their dependence on the Middle East. Construction companies are now focusing on South-east Asia, which offers good prospects in the form of large-scale economic development and social overhead capital projects. In the first half of 1992, South Korean construction companies were awarded overseas contracts amounting to US$1.8 billion contracts. Of the total, 89 per cent (US$1.6 billion) came from South-east Asia, with just 11 per cent (US$199 million) accounted for by the Middle East. (In 1981, at the peak of the construction boom, the Middle East had accounted for 93 per cent of South Korea's overseas construction orders.)

Tourism development projects in Guam, Saipan and Papua New Guinea offer good opportunities, and South Korean construction companies are also looking for ways to break into Japan, North America, China, Vietnam, Cambodia and the former Soviet Union. However, South Korean companies have found it difficult to break into advanced countries such as Japan and the United States. In Japan, the South Koreans have found themselves in a Catch-22 situation, where they must have a performance record in order to bid for contracts, but cannot establish the record without a successful bid. Nevertheless, in 1992, Lotte Construction became the first South Korean construction company to win a direct order from Japanese. The main obstacle to success in former communist bloc countries is the lack of sufficient foreign exchange reserves to pay for the work in hard cash.

Although South Korean construction companies were optimistic about prospects for 1992 – the target for overseas orders was set at US$4.0–4.5 billion – the optimism was based to a great extent on confidence over the awarding of contracts in Hong Kong and Libya to South Korean companies. In the event, the Chingma Bridge contract in Hong Kong was awarded to a UK–Japanese consortium, after the Hong Kong authorities required Hyundai Engineering and Construction to put up a cash bond of more than US$300 million. The guarantee was required due to ROK government investigations into the affairs of the Hyundai business group.

Sanctions against Libya imposed by the United Nations may have an impact on work being carried out by South Korean companies on the multi-year, US$5.5-billion Great Man-Made River project in Libya. Phase Two of the project (awarded to the South Koreans) was the largest single construction contract in modern history; bidding for Phases Three, Four and Five was due to take place at the end of 1992. South Korean participation would be rendered difficult, if not impossible, by the continuing applications of sanctions by the UN. Hopes that South Korea would win a large share of the reconstruction orders after the Gulf War also faded with the realization that Iraq does not have the means to finance the construction work.

In January 1992, the ROK government announced its plans to develop overseas construction as a strategic industry. Measures to promote participation in overseas construction activities included the lifting of the automatic approval ceiling on overseas contracts from US$30 million to US$100 million for 13 Grade A and 243 Grade B construction firms. The government also plans to issue overseas licences every year instead of once every three years, in order to encourage greater participation.

Although hopes that cumulative overseas revenues, which amounted to US$96.4 billion between 1962 and 1991, would pass the US$100-billion mark in 1992 seemed over-optimistic, this level should be reached in 1993.

Domestic construction

The sluggish performance seen in the overseas construction market after the Middle East boom came to an end was offset to a significant degree by the rapid growth seen in the domestic market in the late 1980s and early 1990s.

The government's decision to encourage domestic consumption, in the form of both private consumption and domestic construction, in order to sustain economic growth gave a massive boost to the industry. The promotion of public projects, such as the construction of two million housing units during the presidency of Roh T'ae-woo and the large-scale investment in a variety of infrastructure projects, including the development of the west coast, the construction of a new airport, and the building of a high-speed railway between Seoul and Pusan, were all designed to boost the economy by stimulating domestic construction activities. Between 1987 and 1991, domestic construction activity expanded at an average annual rate of 37.7 per cent, and the share of GNP accounted for by construction more than doubled from 7.4 per cent in 1987 to 15.4 per cent in 1991.

Fears that the economy was overheating in the early 1990s led to a decision to cool down the domestic construction market, in which rapid growth had led to shortages of materials and labour, thus aggravating inflationary pressures. The construction boom and the scramble for land had also inflated real estate prices and widened further the gap between the haves and the have-nots. The government's measures have been largely successful; there were clear signs of a cooling down in late 1991 and early 1992. Although the government had placed restrictions on the construction of housing, commercial and recreational buildings from mid-1991, local contractors could still find work on civil construction projects. In June 1992, the government eased its restrictions on construction of commercial buildings and residential apartments and houses in Seoul and in cities with a population in excess of 300,000.

Many of the remaining restrictions are expected to be lifted in 1993, in line with the cool-down in the sector and the easing of materials and manpower shortages. The government also plans to remove quotas for housing construction in 1993, and may allow the construction of up to one million housing units. (The quota for 1993 under the current five-year plan is 550,000.) Construction activity in the hotel sector should pick up from 1993 as the nation prepares for 'Visit Korea Year' in 1994 (see: Tourism and the the Service Industry). Approval has already been given for the construction of 120 hotels; the builders are now waiting for the government restrictions to be lifted.

Prospects for the industry

With the exception of a few of the top firms, South Korean construction companies find it difficult to compete with western firms for high-tech and high-value-added construction work, demand for which is expanding. The South Koreans are hampered in their efforts to win contracts by their lack of technology, rising labour costs, and the difficulties they face in offering competitive financing packages due to government restrictions on overseas financing and high domestic interest rates.

The opening of the domestic market is scheduled for 1994. To meet the challenge from foreign contractors, the South Koreans need to rationalize their management and improve their technological capabilities. They may also seek joint ventures and subcontract work with European, Japanese and American companies in order to enhance their technological expertise, and form local consortia for big projects.

In 1992, the nation's large companies formed a private organization, the Council of Korean Construction Companies. The Council will take steps to promote the development of the industry ahead of the market opening and to boost the public image of the industry in the wake of a number of accidents in recent years, including the collapse of the Haengju Bridge in mid-construction in 1992.

ELECTRONICS

The history of the South Korean electronics industry goes back to the first local assembly of vacuum tube radios by Goldstar Co. in 1959. At that time, South Korean electronics companies lacked all but the most basic technology, and the local market was dominated by foreign firms. However, over the past three decades, South Korean electronics manufacturers, aided by foreign investment and technology transfer, have assimilated new technologies and mastered production processes at a rapid rate.

From their humble beginnings, South Korean electronics companies have developed to the stage where they now manufacture a wide range of sophisticated products for domestic and export sale. In the consumer electronics sector, leading companies such as Samsung, Goldstar and Daewoo produce a variety of high-tech items including camcorders, compact disc players and digital audio tape-recorders, in addition to the more traditional consumer electrical goods such as televisions, refrigerators and air conditioners.

In the industrial electronics sector, the South Koreans now have the capability to produce 32-bit personal computers, microcomputers, colour graphics terminals, laser printers, facsimile machines and telecommunications equipment. In recent years, the parts and components sector has seen the development of multi-layer printed circuit boards, integrated circuits, and state-of-the-art memory chips including the 16-Mega Dynamic Random Access Memory chip.

Between 1971 and 1991, annual production increased dramatically from W51.2 billion (US$138 million at 1971 market average rates) in 1971 to W13.4 trillion (US$17 billion). As in many other sectors, production was initially focused on the export market, rather than on local sales – in the two decades between 1972 and 1991, exports soared from US$140 million to US$19.3 billion. The share of total exports accounted for by the electronics sector also increased from 7.7 per cent in 1972 to 28.2 per cent in 1991.

The top ten electronics exports in 1991, accounting for 80 per cent of total electronics exports, are shown in Table 5.

TABLE 5 Top ten electronics exports, 1991

Export	US$	% year on year
Semiconductors	5.6 billion	24.6
Computers	2.1 billion	6.8
Audio equipment	1.6 billion	(9.1)
Colour televisions	1.5 billion	11.6
Videocassette recorders	1.3 billion	12.9
Magnetic tapes	900 million	4.4
Cathode ray tubes	900 million	20.4
Magnetic heads	600 million	(8.5)
Microwave ovens	600 million	19.6
Telephones	300 million	(17.7)

Consumer electronics

Among the three electronics sectors – consumer, industrial, and parts and components – the consumer electronics sector has the longest history and has seen the most rapid growth over the past three decades. However, in common with other South Korean industries, the sector has suffered a setback in exports in the late 1980s and early 1990s. The story was a familiar one; having enjoyed the advantage of access to one of the lowest-paid workforces in the world throughout the 1960s, 1970s and early 1980s, the rapid rises in real wages which occurred after 1987 pushed local wages well above those paid in newly emerging competitor nations such as Hong Kong, Taiwan and Singapore. The South Koreans were no longer able to compete on price in exports of labour-intensive, low-tech goods and lacked the technology to compete at the high end of the market.

The rate of export growth for consumer electronics exports, which had averaged more than 30 per cent in the 1980s, dropped sharply at the end of the decade, falling to 5.4 per cent in 1989. The downturn was largely due to the glut of and price cuts for consumer electronics goods such as videocassette recorders (VCRs), microwave ovens and colour televisions in the United States, South Korea's major export market.

There was also strong competition, both from the Japanese firms, which had maintained their price competitiveness through technical innovation and overseas production, and from other developing countries, which still enjoyed the advantage of low labour costs. Moreover, the South Koreans were paying the price for their success in penetrating export markets, as advanced nations took steps to limit the flow of South Korean electronic goods into their markets through tighter import regulations and higher trade barriers.

The response in the electronics sector was similar to that seen in other industrial sectors; that is, to sell to the local market while opening up other export markets and switching to production of high-tech, high value-added goods. An increasing number of companies have also chosen to relocate their low-tech, labour-intensive production facilities overseas, in order to take advantage of cheaper labour, and focus on high-end goods back at home. Manufacturing facilities overseas rose from 19 in 1990 to 24 in 1992, and are forecast to rise to 32 in 1992.

Domestic sales of household appliances have been boosted by the rapid rise in disposable incomes in the late 1980s and early 1990s; in addition to buying state-of-the-art home appliances, South Koreans began to purchase goods such as compact disc players, VCRs and personal computers – items which, just a few years ago, were beyond their means. The government's plan to build two million housing units during President Roh's term of office and the trend for young families to set up home on their own, rather than spending the early years of their marriage living with one set of parents, have also helped domestic sales of consumer electronics.

However, local companies are now facing problems even in selling to the local market, as the liberalization of imports has brought them into direct competition with well-known foreign brand products, and the market for conventional consumer electronics items is quickly becoming saturated. Leading manufacturers are trying to create demand by introducing new products such as 'fuzzy logic' washing machines and higher-quality, higher-value-added products. The 'big three' – Samsung, Goldstar and Daewoo – are reported to be increasing investment in R&D in order to develop high value-added products; in 1992, Samsung raised its percentage of R&D to 8 per cent sales – a level comparable with that seen among Japanese manufacturers.

During the first seven months of 1992, imports of consumer electronics showed a downward trend, with imports of colour televisions down by 60.3 per cent, VCRs by 36.3 per cent, washing machines by 10.2 per cent, and microwave ovens by 71.0 per cent. This was attributed partly to the development of new models by local companies, better technology and improved quality. It remains to be seen, however, what impact the lifting of bans on imports of audio and video equipment from Japan in 1993 will have on sales into the domestic market.

In order to maintain their presence in the consumer electronics field, South Korean electronics companies must continue to develop new markets, and make efforts to boost their own brand names overseas, rather than relying on OEM exports. New product development and after-sales service will also be important in maintaining market share. On the production side, there is a need to enhance productivity and improve quality control.

In common with many other sectors, the consumer electronics industry needs to promote technology development. Royalties for imported technology account for around 30 per cent of expenses incurred by manufacturers of consumer electronics goods in South Korea, who already suffer from a lack of funds for their own technological developments. Many are now seeking joint ventures or technical tie-ups with advanced nations in order to avoid huge investment costs and royalty payments. Electronics giants Samsung, Daewoo and Goldstar are reported also to be focusing on mergers and acquisitions (M&A) activities and seeking cooperative ties with local partners for sales networks in export markets.

Forecasts for 1992 called for a 9 per cent increase in exports to around the US$21 billion mark, thanks to increasing orders from emerging markets, such as Latin America and the Middle East. This would offset to some extent the sluggishness in exports to the United States, Japan and Europe, due to protectionism and new competition. The lowering of import barriers and tariffs in Latin America has prompted optimism that the region will soon become South Korea's second largest electronics export market, ahead of Europe. This is based on strong demand for conventional products, such as colour televisions, VCRs and refrigerators.

Industrial electronics

Over the past five years the rates of production and export in the industrial electronics sector have outpaced those seen in the consumer electronics sector; industry analysts forecast that, although South Korea will maintain a strong presence in the consumer electronics market, the industrial sector will play an increasingly large part in the electronics industry as a whole through the end of this century.

In 1988, consumer electronics accounted for 40 per cent of production in the electronics industry, with industrial electronics taking a 19 per cent share, and parts and components accounting for 41 per cent of the W17 trillion (US$24.9 billion at the 1988 market average rate) total. By the year 2000, the share taken by consumer electronics will have fallen back to 27 per cent, while the industrial electronics sector's share will have expanded to 33 per cent. Parts and components will continue to account for around 40 per cent of total production, which is forecast to reach W57 trillion (US$72.4 billion) by the end of the century.

Products manufactured in the industrial electronics sector include factory, office and home automation equipment, telecommunications equipment and robots; in recent years, the most notable success in the industrial electronics sector has been achieved in the area of computers.

In 1991, production in the computer section expanded by 3.8 per cent to W2.3 trillion (US$3.0 billion); domestic demand increased by 10.7 per cent to W1.8 trillion (US$2.3 billion), and exports grew by 6.8 per cent to US$2.1 billion. In that year, computers were the second-best-selling export item in the electronics sector (after semiconductors), accounting for 11 per cent of the total overseas sales.

By 1991, a total of 2.2 million 16-bit and 32-bit personal computers (PCs) had been installed and were being used in South Korea, a diffusion rate of 5.2 per thousand people. With PC sales rising to 757,899 in 1991, cumulative sales are forecast to pass the 3-million mark by 1995. Almost half the sales are to individuals and households, with 22 per cent accounted for by business enterprises and 9 per cent going to educational establishments.

Despite the impressive growth seen in volume terms in recent years, the technological level attained in the computer sector is comparatively low. Moreover, growth within the sector has been unbalanced, with attention and investment focusing on certain areas, such as personal computers, at the expense of others, including software, minicomputers and some peripherals.

In 1991, the rates of growth for domestic and export sales of computers were lower than those seen in previous years. Domestic sales were hindered by sluggish sales of educational computers, low investment in factory automation, and increasing competition from Taiwanese cheap imports at the low end of the market and American imports at the top end. Export sales suffered from the overall sluggishness of the computer business worldwide, especially in the United States, which accounts for the lion's share of South Korea's exports, and the computer manufacturers' failure to upgrade their models.

In order to boost exports, manufacturers are focusing more on high value-added products, such as 32-bit notebook computers and pen-based computers, and making efforts to develop new markets in Central and South America, South-east Asia and the Middle East. A high proportion of total computer exports is on an OEM basis, indicating a clear need for the South Koreans to boost their efforts at marketing and brand-name promotion.

South Korea's computer companies are hampered in their efforts to boost sales by the industry's slow pace of technology accumulation, which makes it hard for them to compete against new models brought to the market by competitors in advanced nations. To the extent that their past success has been built on borrowed technology and imported parts and raw materials, South Korean computer manufacturers now have to invest in R&D and the development of technology to safeguard their future.

Moreover, South Korean manufacturers still rely to a significant extent on imported peripherals and key components, including microprocessors and chips – in the PC sector, the import dependency for notebook computers is as high as 80 per cent. South Korea continues to suffer a trade deficit in its trade with Japan in parts and components.

In the early 1990s, it was estimated that, on average, royalties and patent payments accounted for 10 per cent of turnover for South Korean computer manufacturers. In addition to the expenses incurred, South Korean companies face the problem of the increasing reluctance of advanced nations to transfer technology to emerging competitors.

Parts and components: semiconductors
In 1991, semiconductors were the star performers, not only in the parts and components sector, but in the electronics industry as a whole. Exports of semiconductors jumped by 25 per

cent year on year to US$5.6 billion, and accounted for 29 per cent of total electronics exports.

Although many companies in South Korea assemble semi-conductors, there are only five manufacturers: Samsung Electronics, Goldstar Electron Co., Hyundai Electronic Industries, Korea Electronics, and Daewoo Electronics. In 1991, production by these five companies amounted to W2.4 trillion (US$3 billion), and total semiconductor production (including assembly) amounted to W5.1 trillion (US$6.5 billion); exports stood at US$5.6 billion. Targets for 1992 are W6.3 trillion (US$8 billion) for production (up 23 per cent year on year) and W5.5 trillion (US$7 billion) for exports (up 25 per cent).

Memory devices are South Korea's fastest growing electronics export line, in particular Dynamic Random Access Memory (DRAM) chips – commodity memory chips found in almost every electronic product, which currently make up about 10 per cent of world semiconductor manufacture. In 1991, DRAMs accounted for 50 per cent of semiconductor production by the top three manufacturers, and 70 per cent of semiconductor sales. Almost all the DRAMs were exported, with more than 33 per cent going to the United States.

In April 1992, three of South Korea's five semiconductor manufacturers – Samsung, Goldstar and Hyundai – were accused of dumping 1-Mega and 4-Mega DRAMs in the North American market, and a formal investigation was launched. Although dumping usually refers to the practice of selling at lower price than that charged in the home market or third countries, South Korea's top three manufacturers were accused of selling below their *production* cost.

In October 1992, the US Department of Commerce announced its preliminary findings, which were that all three South Korean manufacturers had sold DRAMs at less than a fair price – Samsung at 87.4 per cent below fair value, Goldstar at 52.4 per cent, and Hyundai at 5.9 per cent. Until a final ruling is made in 1993, the South Koreans will have to deposit the difference with the US Customs Service as a preliminary dumping duty. Samsung and Goldstar must make efforts to reduce the differential to 10 per cent and the South Koreans will probably have to conclude a Voluntary Restraint Agreement with the United States, as did Japan.

It now seems likely that the European Community will also introduce duties of around 10 per cent on South Korean DRAMs, and that the top three will have to sign price undertaking pacts, as did the Japanese in 1990.

In addition to facing problems arising from trade friction, the South Korean semiconductor companies are hampered by the slow pace of technology accumulation, their reliance on imported technology, and their heavy dependency on low-end chips.

In the past three years, South Korean semiconductor companies have signed 84 technical licensing agreements with foreign companies, half of which were concluded with the United States. The South Koreans are still 90 per cent dependent on imported production equipment and materials, most of it from Japan. This clearly leaves them vulnerable, and there are fears that Japan will try to get higher royalties for the technology transferred or slow down the transfer of processing equipment to impede the growth of the South Korean semiconductor industry.

To counter this, the South Korean semiconductor manufacturers have been increasing their investment in R&D and facility expansion. Targets for 1992 were set at W1.5 trillion (US$1.9 billion), an increase of 46.4 per cent year on year. Of the total, W1.2 trillion (US$1.5 billion) was to be spent on facility expansion (an increase of 50.8 per cent), with the remaining W331 billion (US$420 million) going to R&D.

As world demand for 1-Mega DRAMs gradually declines and demand for 4-Mega DRAMs increases, thanks to the development of new computers and upper-end machines including workstations, South Korean manufacturers have begun mass production of 4-Mega DRAMs. Production forecasts for 1992 were 119 million units – 60 million for Samsung, 34 million for Goldstar and 25 million for Hyundai. In addition, they would produce 190 million 1-Mega DRAMs and 48 million 256K DRAMs.

Samsung was the first South Korean semiconductor company to develop the 16-Mega DRAM, in 1990; test production began in 1992, and mass production is scheduled to begin in 1993. The top three companies are all constructing 16-Mega DRAM production lines, and forecast production of 1 million units in 1993. The market for 16-Mega DRAMs is expected to start to form from 1993 and grow to US$1.1 billion by 1997. Demand for 4-Mega DRAMs is forecast to peak at US$945 million in 1994, and decline thereafter.

In September 1992, first Samsung and then Hyundai announced the development of test models for the 64-Mega DRAM and forecast that commercial production would begin in 1995. A research project involving Samsung, Hyundai, Goldstar and the Electronics and Telecommunications Research Institute, and supported by the Ministry of Trade and Industry, had been established to develop the 64-Mega DRAM, with the understanding that all participants would announce the development together. Demand for the 64-Mega DRAM, which will be used in workstations, high-definition television, supercomputers, etc., is expected to grow from US$7 million in 1995 to US$7.5 billion in 1998.

Samsung has begun test production of the 32-Mega mask ROM (Read Only Memory) chip, used in fixed data storage systems, laser printers, workstations and laptop personal computers. Mass production is scheduled for 1993; the market for the chip is forecast to expand from US$70 million in 1992 to US$580 million in 1995. Samsung has also developed the 4-Mega Pseudo Static Random Access Memory (PSRAM) chip, used in telecommunications equipment, robots, laser printers, etc. The market for this chip is forecast to grow from US$40 million in 1992 to US$210 million in 1995.

The localization of raw and intermediate materials including lead frames, epoxy molding compounds, and wafers will give a boost to the industry; currently around 60 per cent of these materials are imported. In 1992, it was reported that business groups with semiconductor-related subsidiaries were beginning to move into the production of semiconductor materials.

Prospects for the industry

Negative factors affecting all sectors of the electronics industry in the early 1990s include rising labour costs, sluggish export and domestic demand, trade barriers, technology protectionism, and the industry's continuing heavy dependence on foreign technology. In order to boost sales, the South Korean electronics manufacturers have to reduce their production costs, develop high-quality, high value-added products, and increase the efficiency of their overseas marketing.

South Korea's electronics companies also face rising debts and royalty payments, falling profit margins (net profits averaged less than 2 per cent of sales in 1991), and funding shortages, at a time when investment in the development of new products and high technology is essential.

According to the Electronics Industry Association of Korea, investment in facility investment and R&D has been falling. Although 100 of its member companies set their 1992 investment targets at W2.4 trillion (US$3 billion), an increase of 10.6 per cent year on year, the amount was later scaled back to W2 trillion (US$2.5 billion), a drop of 8.5 per cent from 1991 levels. The slow-down in investment is attributed to tight funding, unclear business prospects, sluggish demand and worsening profit margins. Without a fundamental change in the government's policy on overseas borrowing and/or a thorough reform of the financial sector and capital markets, companies will continue to struggle to find funds for investment.

The Ministry of Trade and Industry's Electro 21 Project

(1992–6) aims to develop eighteen key technologies and core components, imports of which amounted to US$2.8 billion in 1991. The localization of these items would save an estimated W787 million (US$100 million) per year in royalty payments, cut production costs by W254 billion (US$323 million) over the five-year period, and boost the industry's localization ratio to 75 per cent by 1996. Items for development included application-specific integrated circuits, liquid crystal displays, and large-calibre silicon wafers.

The project will require funding of between W500 billion (US$635 million) and W800 billion (US$1 billion) over a five-year period, with contributions being made by both the government and the private sector. However, in August 1992, the project was scaled down by the government, which cited shortages of funds as one of the main reasons for its decision.

FOOTWEAR

The footwear industry played a significant role in South Korea's economic development through the 1960s and 1970s, and experienced particularly strong growth during the boom years of 1986–8. Over the past decade, the footwear sector has been a major contributor to the nation's export performance; between 1986 and 1990, footwear exports more than doubled from US$2.1 billion to US$4.3 billion.

In 1989, however, exports declined for the first time since 1962, and after peaking in 1990, slumped to US$3.8 billion in 1991. In the early 1990s, there were reports that most of the nation's footwear makers had been forced to shut down production lines permanently or temporarily, and 300 had gone bankrupt or were facing bankruptcy. By October 1992, a total of 26,000 jobs had been lost in the footwear industry.

Prospects for 1992 were gloomy; predictions by industry associations that exports would drop below the level recorded in 1987 to reach just US$3.3 billion appeared to be borne out by falling orders from overseas. In June 1992, orders from the top three international buyers – Reebok, Nike ·and L.A. Gear – hit a four-year low. Average monthly orders, which had dropped from 8–12 million pairs in 1990 to 5–7 million in 1991, stood at just 3.5 million in June.

The reasons for the decline are simple: the South Korean footwear industry is labour intensive (labour costs account for between 25 per cent and 30 per cent of total production costs) and highly export oriented, with more than three-quarters of production destined for overseas markets. The industry was, therefore, hit particularly hard by the problems of rising production costs and labour unrest which faced the South Korean economy in the late 1980s.

From 1987, rising wages weakened the price competitiveness of South Korea's exports, while labour disputes eroded foreign buyers' confidence in South Korea's ability to deliver the goods on time. This was especially true in the footwear sector. Soaring production costs pushed export unit prices up from US\$6.04 per pair in 1986 to US\$11.59 in 1991. Increasingly, foreign buyers looked to newly developing countries such as Thailand, Indonesia and the People's Republic of China as cheaper and more reliable sources of supply. Although a significant number subsequently returned to South Korea when the problems of quality deterioration and delayed delivery eased, the trend was still clearly towards sourcing low- and medium-priced footwear from South Korea's competitors.

South Korea's share of the United States footwear market fell from 68.8 per cent in 1988 to 30.8 per cent in the first five months of 1992; during the same period, the share taken by Chinese exports rose from 1.6 per cent to 28.4 per cent. Thailand and Indonesia increased their market shares from 4.3 per cent to 9.5 per cent and from 0.9 per cent to 20.0 per cent respectively.

In the domestic market, South Korean manufacturers were finding it increasingly difficult to compete with cheap imports from the People's Republic of China and South-east Asia; in the first half of 1991, imports from China jumped by 69 per cent year on year to US\$1.6 million. The year-on-year rates of increase for imports from Thailand and Indonesia were 117 per cent and 97 per cent respectively.

The South Korean footwear manufacturers were left with little choice but to relocate their low-end, labour-intensive production facilities to areas such as South-east Asia, which could still offer relatively cheap labour. At home, the industry is now concentrating on the production of high quality leather shoes and the development of brand-name footwear.

The industry is in urgent need of more investment in automation and technology development in order to produce high quality, high value-added products. The South Korean footwear companies' failure to invest in the 1980s has now come back to haunt them. Their situation is very different from that of the Italians, who have maintained their position as leading exporters through aggressive investment in factory automation and technology development. In the early 1990s, 45 per cent of Italy's footwear production was automated; the level in South Korea was just 7 per cent.

In the past, the vast majority of footwear exports (95 per cent in the late 1980s) have been on an OEM basis for such well-known foreign brands as Reebok and Nike. Although South Korea does produce its own brands of footwear – HS

Corp's LeCAF and Kukje Corp's Pro Specs – they have weak brand recognition due to lack of marketing and promotion. In such a fashion-sensitive industry, a known brand name is crucial to product differentiation. Own-brand sales have risen in recent years, reaching US$100 million in 1991 from US$35 million in 1986.

Now, in a bid to develop high price, high value-added, brand-name exports, new patterns, designs and materials are being developed, computer-aided design and manufacture are being introduced, and quality control is being strengthened. Obsolete manufacturing facilities are being replaced, and production lines are being automated.

The government has implemented a number of programmes aimed at preventing a further decline in the industry. These aim to promote the automation of existing production lines and encourage cooperation among smaller footwear manufacturers, while restricting expansion or new entries into the industry.

In January 1992, the ROK government announced that it had designated the footwear industry an 'industry rationalization business'. The government planned to release W200 billion (US$254 million) in loans to footwear companies, in return for which manufacturers were to make efforts to cut production costs, reduce their dependence on OEM exports, and strengthen their self-reliance efforts.

However, it was later reported that the footwear manufacturers' response had been lukewarm, with only 6 per cent of those eligible applying for loans in the first five months after the announcement.

MACHINERY

The machinery sector is unusual among South Korean industries in that it is largely domestic market-oriented; in 1991, more than 70 per cent of the industry's output went to the domestic market. South Korea's major export items in the machinery sector include standard and numerically controlled (NC) machine tools, construction and mining equipment, refrigeration and air-conditioning equipment, and air and water power machines.

Over the years, the growth of the industrial machinery and machine tool sectors has been boosted by the expansion in related local industries such as electronics and automobiles, and, more recently, by the trend towards upgrading production equipment and automating production processes. There has been a steady rise in domestic demand for increasingly sophisticated machine tools and industrial machinery.

Despite the domestic orientation of the industry, South

Korean manufacturers are unable to satisfy local demand, and the Republic is a large importer of industrial machinery and machine tools. This has resulted in a trade deficit for the machinery sector, which accounts for a heavy proportion of the national trade deficit. In 1991, the machinery trade deficit stood at US$9.9 billion, which was larger than the overall deficit for the nation that year.

The Korea Association of Machine Industries forecast that the trade deficit in the machinery sector would hit a record high in 1992, with exports rising by 15.3 per cent year on year to US$17.5 billion, and imports expanding by 16.0 per cent to US$29.1 billion, giving a deficit of US$11.6 billion.

Despite efforts to localize production and diversify import sources, South Korean machinery and machine tool companies remain heavily dependent on imports from Japan. The deficit in trade with Japan reached US$8.3 billion in 1991, and was forecast to swell further to US$9.8 billion in 1992, accounting for 85 per cent of the total machinery deficit in that year.

Industrial machinery

The industrial machinery sector began to develop in the mid-1970s, as the South Korean government promoted the development of the heavy and chemical industries amid the continuing rapid development of the national economy.

Between 1980 and 1991, production of industrial machinery – including construction and mining equipment, and manufacturing equipment for the consumer and durable goods industries – increased at an average annual rate of 24.9 per cent, rising from W696 billion (US$1.2 billion) at the 1980 market average rate to W11.3 trillion (US$14.3 billion) in 1991.

Only a small proportion of output – an average of less than 20 per cent since the mid-1980s – is exported. In 1991, exports rose by 24.0 per cent per year to reach US$2.6 billion. Imports of industrial machinery have expanded at an average annual rate of 17.7 per cent since 1980, reaching US$10.7 billion in 1991, equivalent to 13.1 per cent of the nation's total imports in that year.

Machine tools

The machine tool sector has seen brisk qualitative and quantitative growth since the mid-1970s, and its importance to the national economy has been boosted in recent years by the increasing trend towards factory automation.

Between 1980 and 1991, production of machine tools increased at an average annual rate of 23.2 per cent, rising from W57.4 billion (US$99 million at the 1980 market average rate) in 1980 to W628.0 billion (US$798 million) in 1991. As in the industrial machinery sector, only a small proportion of output is destined for overseas markets; in 1991, exports accounted for just over 20 per cent of machine tool production.

The level of accuracy and integration in machine tools manufactured in South Korea is lower than of those produced in advanced countries, and local producers are limited as to the size and variety of tools that they can manufacture. Although many products, parts and components are available locally, a large number of South Korean end-users prefer foreign goods, especially those imported from Japan, the United States and Germany, to locally produced items. A large proportion of domestic demand, both for finished products and core parts, is therefore satisfied by imports, the lion's share of which is sourced from Japan. Since 1985, imports of machine tools have soared, rising from US$343 million in 1981 to US$1.7 billion in 1991.

In 1991, machine tool exports were hit by weakening price competitiveness resulting largely from rising production costs, and domestic demand was sluggish due to the downturn in facility investment. The result was an increase in stockpiles of machine tools, which reached W60 billion (US$76 million) by the end of 1991, an increase of 70 per cent year on year. NC lathes, drilling and tapping machines, sawing machines and machining centres accounted for half the stockpile.

Precision instruments

Although the development of the precision instruments sector has been boosted by the growth of the electronics industry, it remains at a comparatively early stage in terms of technological capability. (Precision instruments include optical, medical and measuring instruments.)

Domestic demand has been boosted by an increase in modernized plants and equipment which require more and better measuring and diagnostic instruments. However, with the technical level of locally produced measuring and medical instruments still significantly lower than that found in advanced countries, South Korean companies continue to import sophisticated precision machinery, mainly from Japan and the United States. Between 1980 and 1991, imports increased at an average annual rate of 21.4 per cent, rising from US$417 million in 1980 to US$2.9 billion in 1991.

Prospects for the industry

Immediate prospects for the machinery industry in general are dampened by the continuing weakness in facility investment, which is hampering sales to the domestic market. Large-scale facility investments in the steel and petrochemical industries are complete or nearing completion, and investment in other manufacturing sectors remains sluggish. However, exports should be boosted by orders from the People's Republic of China and South-east Asia, where economic growth and capital investment are brisk.

The continuing reliance on imports to satisfy domestic demand for machinery has prompted the ROK government to focus on the development of the machinery industry. In the past, attention in the machinery sector has focused mainly on boosting production levels, rather than on improving technical standards; if the machinery industry is to continue to develop, the focus must shift to quality.

In order to reduce the machinery trade deficit, the government has designated 4,000 items of machinery, parts and materials for localization, and is actively encouraging investment in R&D and the development of key parts and non-finished products. Manufacturers are also now beginning to focus more on the production of high-tech products, including environmental equipment, precision machine parts and industrial robots.

Despite these good intentions, the industry's track record in R&D has not been good and progress towards localization has been slow. Under a plan implemented between 1986 and 1991, 4,542 machines and components were due for local production; in the event, only 2,157 or 47.5 per cent of the total were successfully developed. Moreover, R&D expenditure was sluggish in 1991, due to pessimism over the nation's economic prospects, tight funding, and increases in royalty payments for imported technology.

PETROCHEMICALS

The development of the petrochemicals industry in the 1970s aimed to foster the development of local industries by providing a balanced supply of basic raw materials.

The lifting of restrictions on investment in the petrochemicals industry in 1979 resulted in a remarkable expansion in annual production capacity, from 2.8 million tons in 1988 to 4.9 million tons three years later. The average annual growth rate for production during that three-year period was 21.0 per cent.

In 1991, exports amounted to 1.1 million tons, valued at US$1.6 billion. Exports of synthetic resins, including polypropylene, high-density polyethylene (HDPE), low-density polyethylene (LDPE), and PVC, rose by 103 per cent year on year to 961,000 tons, or 87.4 per cent of the total. In 1991, imports totalled US$3.4 billion, giving a trade deficit of US$1.8 billion.

In 1992, South Korea became the fifth largest ethylene producer in the world, as Hanyang Chemical Co.'s plant came on stream. The country's total production capacity in was boosted to 3.3 million tons; the four leading producers in the world are the United States (20.5 million tons), Japan (6.4 million), Germany (5.9 million) and the former Soviet Union (4.2 million).

For a number of years, local production could not satisfy demand, and the petrochemicals industry was looked upon as a guaranteed money-earner. However, the rapid expansion in production which followed the deregulation of investment in the industry in 1979 resulted in an oversupply of almost every product, and a drop in both prices and profitability. Industry analysts forecast a glut of almost 1 million tons in ethylene in 1992, and oversupplies of 440,000 tons for LDPE and 510,000 tons for HDPE, assuming the domestic market expanded by 10 per cent. New entrants to the industry have reportedly lost money, while the old-established manufacturers have been forced to sell their products at a loss.

With production rising faster than domestic demand and stockpiles mounting, petrochemicals companies have been turning their attention to exports. Between 1988 and 1991, exports rose sharply from 218,000 tons to 1.1 million tons, an average annual growth rate of 71.9 per cent.

Sales to South-east Asia have provided a great boost to exports, and the former Soviet Union and the People's Republic of China are looked on as good potential markets. South Korean petrochemicals companies are also exploring export opportunities in Europe and Middle East, two markets previously neglected due to additional transportation costs estimated at US$50–60 per ton. In addition to exporting petrochemical products, the South Koreans are looking at exporting technology, know-how and equipment to South-east Asia and the People's Republic of China.

In August 1992, exports outpaced domestic sales for the first time since the late 1960s, with exports totalling 179,000 tons and domestic sales reaching 173,500 tons. Another first was achieved in December 1992, when the industry recorded its first trade surplus, with exports of US$2.62 billion and imports of US$2.59 billion giving a small surplus of US$30 million.

The slower import performance was attributed to increases in domestic production, stabilized international prices, and the increased use of local basic oil derivatives and intermediate materials. On the export side, prices for synthetic resins were rising and South Korean companies' efforts to diversify their overseas markets were beginning to bear fruit.

However, although export growth rates have been high in volume terms, profitability has been eroded by falling prices worldwide, and the fact that the South Koreans are forced to export at low prices to offload growing stockpiles. In the first five months of 1992, exports rose by 166 per cent in volume terms but only by 66.7 per cent in value terms. A major problem for the South Koreans is that, as their production is naphtha-based, it is difficult for them to compete with production based on cheap natural gas.

Demand from South-east Asia is expected to decline in the short to medium term, as nations in the region bring their own petrochemicals plants on stream. Thailand will have its own naphtha-cracking centre in 1994 (annual production capacity: 350,000 tons), Malaysia will be self-sufficient in petrochemicals products by the end of 1992, and Taiwan is reported to be building a naphtha-cracking centre with an annual production capacity of 300,000–400,000 tons, due for completion by 1995. These countries can be expected to erect trade barriers as soon as they start to operate their own petrochemicals plants.

In 1992, the ROK government introduced an export recommendation system for petrochemical products, in an attempt to prevent excessive competition among South Korean companies in overseas markets. The system aims to coordinate the export prices and volumes of general-purpose synthetic resins, including polyethylene and polypropylene. The government's decision to exempt the two latest entrants to the industry, Samsung General Chemicals and Hyundai Petrochemicals, on the grounds that they are obliged to export more than 50 per cent of their output, has caused concern among the remaining companies, who fear that Samsung and Hyundai will undercut their prices in export markets.

The government also took steps in 1992 to restrict fresh investment in the industry, making public its plans to ban loans for investment in naphtha-cracking centres, and in plants for styrene monomer, synthetic rubber, and raw materials for synthetic fibres. The authorities also planned to curb investment in the manufacture of butadiene, toluene, xylene and synthetic resins. By curbing overlapping and excessive investment in conventional petrochemicals products, the government hopes to encourage local companies to focus on fine chemicals and advanced materials.

Despite the problems caused by excessive investment and oversupply, many companies are keen to expand further. Their reasoning is that they foresee a change in the supply–demand situation in 1995 which will require additional production capacity. As it takes two years to bring a plant on stream they should, they maintain, be expanding their facilities now.

R&D

In the past petrochemicals companies have been over-preoccupied with market share at the expense of profits. In such a capital-intensive industry, profits are needed to finance growth. Moreover, the South Korean petrochemicals companies are highly leveraged and heavily dependent on imported technology. Although there is a clear need to move from basic commodity chemicals to speciality chemicals, investment in R&D remains low; in 1989, the average R&D expenditure was 1.2 per cent of turnover, compared with 4.1–6.2 per cent in advanced countries.

In view of the slow growth in demand for synthetic resins, South Korean petrochemicals companies should be looking to introduce advanced technology and develop new products such as high molecular weight polyethylene, special vinyls for waterproofing, static electricity-proof vinyl tiles, and special grade polyethylene featuring heat resistance and high transparency.

SHIPBUILDING

South Korea is currently the second largest shipbuilding nation in the world, ranking only behind Japan. In 1991, total orders (domestic and overseas) reached 5.4 million gross tons, up 24.0 per cent year on year, while ship construction also increased by 24.0 per cent to 4.4 million gross tons.

The shipbuilding industry has developed rapidly over the past forty years. Up to the 1960s, it focused mainly on the production of inner coastal fishing boats and other small vessels for domestic use. The completion of the Hyundai Shipyard in 1974 was the real starting point for its growth.

The industry experienced rapid growth in the 1970s, when Japanese shipyards were hit by the effects of the strong yen. The South Koreans capitalized on their advantage of a plentiful supply of cheap labour, and gradually moved up into the number two position in the world. In the late 1980s, however, the South Korean shipyards' world market share fell as low as 16.7 per cent (from a peak of 30 per cent). Rising labour and raw materials costs and adverse currency fluctuations weakened South Korea's international competitiveness, and labour unrest undermined its credibility as a reliable supplier. At the same time, the South Korean shipbuilders faced increasing competition, as Taiwan and the People's Republic of China entered the market.

However, the industry received a boost in the early 1990s, as the Japanese yards reached capacity, and South Korean shipbuilders began to benefit from the overflow. In 1991, the South Korean yards did well in spite of a worldwide drop in new orders: although these fell by 16.9 per cent year on year to 20 million gross tons, orders received by the South Koreans jumped by 24.0 per cent to 5.4 million gross tons, the highest level since they entered the international market in the 1970s. In value terms, new orders jumped from US$3.6 billion in 1990 to US$5.6 billion in 1991, giving the South Koreans a 25 per cent world market share.

However, the pace of growth was not maintained in 1992. Orders for the year were estimated at 1.6 million gross tons in volume terms, a drop of more than 70 per cent from the previous year, and the lowest level seen in five years. Although new orders decreased, actual shipbuilding increased by 30.8 per cent between January and November 1992 to reach 4.4 million gross tons, thanks to brisk order receipts in the past few years and the stabilization of labour–management relations in the shipyards.

Should the slump in orders continue, the South Korean shipyards will face idle operations in 1994. In November 1992, the order backlog at the yards was 4.8 million gross tons, down 38.2 per cent year on year. The optimum level of backlog orders is said to be between 18 and 24 months – the level recorded towards the end of 1992 was not sufficient even for 12 months of operation.

The sudden downturn in orders was attributed to the continuing recession in the global shipping industry and the postponement of the replacement of old ships. According to some analysts, there is now an oversupply of ships, and prospects for new orders in 1993 are gloomy as the large number of ships ordered between 1989 and 1991 will continue to be delivered through the year. Competition is increasing as former eastern bloc countries, including the former Soviet Union, Bulgaria and Poland, switch production from warships to commercial vessels, and European countries including Denmark, France, Spain and Italy enter the market.

However, many industry observers see the current downturn as merely a short slump in a continuing boom. In the medium to long term, optimism over the prospects for the industry is engendered by the fact that more than half of the world's ships and almost three-quarters of its tankers were built before 1980, and will need to be replaced in the near future.

Furthermore, following the implementation of the Oil Pollution Act of 1990, new oil tankers and barges will be required to be built with double hulls, as a safeguard against accidents and ocean pollution, and existing ships will have to be replaced by double-hull vessels between 1995 and 2010. In addition to the prospects of extra work, the prices paid for the double-hull vessels are typically 15–20 per cent higher than those for single-hull vessels.

One cloud on the horizon is the prospect of trade friction with advanced nations such as the United States and the EC countries, which are pressuring the ROK government to reduce subsidies to the industry. The ROK government has provided substantial support to the nation's shipbuilders and the fate of the industry will be affected to a considerable degree by the outcome of the OECD multilateral trade negotiations, in which members are calling for an end to official subsidies and incentives.

The decision by OECD negotiators to introduce an anti-dumping system could seriously hurt the South Korean ship-yards, which rely heavily on exports. Moreover, their price competitiveness will suffer if they have to increase prices in order to avoid anti-dumping charges.

In response to this threat, South Korea's major ship-builders, including Hyundai, Samsung and Daewoo, are increasing their investment in R&D and taking steps to boost productivity, which include the introduction of computer-aided design and production systems. The South Korean ship-builders are also moving into repairs and maintenance of exist-ing vessels, and the production of ocean equipment needed for ocean oil development projects in South-east Asia and Africa. They are focusing too on diversifying their products away from oil tankers and bulk carriers and into high value-added vessels such as container carriers, chemical tankers and liquefied natural gas (LNG) and liquefied petroleum gas (LPG) carriers. The domestic builders have recently formed a consortium, in order to promote cooperation on large international bids.

Another problem facing the South Korean yards is the shortage of thick steel plate. In 1992, South Korean ship-builders had to import 500,000 tons, the bulk of which was sourced from Japan. Despite plans for an expansion of the thick steel plate production capacity of P'ohang Iron and Steel Company (POSCO) to 800,000 tons (see below), and the con-struction of new production facilities by Dongkuk Steel, the shipbuilding industry is likely to face shortages for a number of years to come. Although it is possible to import the steel plate from Brazil and Spain, Japanese delivery times are shorter and the quality better. This situation leaves the South Koreans vulnerable to changes in the price or supply of steel plate from Japan, their main competitor in the shipbuilding industry.

STEEL

The South Korean steel industry was originally established to meet domestic demand, principally from the automobile, shipbuilding and electronics industries. It was only in the late 1970s, with the expansion of production capacity, that exports assumed an important role in the industry. However, the rapid growth in domestic demand witnessed in the late 1980s limited the volume of steel products available for export, and analysts believe that, in future, the domestic market will drive the industry.

During the 1970s, the growth rate recorded in the steel sector was almost double that seen in the economy as a whole; in the 1980s, the rate was 1.4 times faster. In 1970, South Korean steel production amounted to 500,000 tons or just 0.1 per cent of total world production. South Korea's exports in that year totalled 400,000 tons, or 0.4 per cent of the world total. Twenty years later, South Korea's production and exports accounted for 3.0 per cent and 4.3 per cent of the world's total respectively; production stood at 23.1 million tons and exports at 7.2 million tons.

In 1991, South Korea was the sixth largest steel producer in the world, with total production of 26 million tons. The Republic ranked behind the former Soviet Union (133 million tons), Japan (110 million), the United States (79 million), the People's Republic of China (71 million) and Germany (42 million). In 1991, South Korea's per capita steel consumption stood at 605 kg and the nation's self-sufficiency ratio was 76 per cent.

The South Korean steel industry is dominated by POSCO. The company has made a huge contribution to South Korea's economic development by providing a stable supply of low-cost, high quality steel to leading industries, including automobiles, shipbuilding, machinery and electronics. POSCO was South Korea's first and remains its only fully integrated steel producer. The company accounts for more than 70 per cent of total steel production in the Republic, and enjoys a 60 per cent share of the local market. It has a monopoly in primary steel products and has established a strong position in secondary products such as cold-rolled sheets, galvanized sheets and special steels.

The construction of POSCO's first integrated iron and steel plant at P'ohang began in the early 1970s; within one decade, the plant's production capacity had soared from one million tons to more than nine million tons. The completion of four phases of the second plant at Kwangyang increased POSCO's crude steel capacity to 20.8 million tons in 1992.

Exports

In 1991, exports accounted for more than 30 per cent of South Korea's steel output. Although the United States has, in the past, been a major market for South Korean steel, in recent years the share of South Korea's steel exports accounted for by the United States has been declining.

In March 1992, the Voluntary Restraint Agreement regulating South Korean steel exports to the US market expired; although the Americans wanted to replace it with a Multinational Steel Agreement, which would remove government subsidies, multilateral talks failed to reach an agreement. A month later, the South Koreans implemented a Voluntary Export Restraint system under which they would impose unilateral and autonomous export restraints, rather than negotiating with the United States.

Despite these actions, the South Koreans found themselves facing dumping investigations in the United States; in August of that year, the US International Trade Commission (ITC) ruled that the American steel industry had been damaged by South Korean imports. Towards the end of the year, anti-dumping duties of 4.9–11.6 per cent were imposed on standard steel pipes, and of 2.5–7.8 per cent on stainless steel welded pipes. In addition, preliminary countervailing tariffs of 5.5 per cent on hot coil, 4.5 per cent on cold rolled steel sheet, 2.9 per cent on galvanized iron sheet, and 3.9 per cent on medium steel plates were announced.

The South Koreans are now looking to South-east Asia and the People's Republic of China to compensate for the drop in exports to the United States; in 1991, Japan and South-east Asia accounted for 64 per cent of all overseas orders, while the United States took a 20 per cent share.

Imports

Between 1987 and 1991, domestic demand for steel products increased at an average annual rate of 15.7 per cent, rising from 14.6 million to 26.3 million tons. Demand was boosted by brisk construction activities and the strong performance of steel-consuming industries. During that period, domestic production increased at a slower rate of 12.5 per cent per annum, leading to an increasing shortfall in steel for the local market. Imports rose from 2.9 million tons in 1987 to 5.6 million tons in 1991, an average annual growth rate of 18.0 per cent.

Imports showed signs of slowing during the early months of 1992, due to increased local production, a cooldown in the construction market and sluggish investment at home. In the first seven months of the year, South Korea recorded a small surplus in its trade in steel products, as exports rose 9.0 per cent to US$2.8 billion, and imports fell by 10.6 per cent to US$2.7 billion.

R&D

In 1991, investment in R&D by South Korea's steel companies amounted to W110 billion (US$140 million), a year-on-year decline of 8.5 per cent. The R&D expenditure was less than 1 per cent of turnover in that year.

In 1992, the ROK Ministry of Trade and Industry announced that it planned to earmark W5 billion (US$6.4 million) for the support of R&D in the steel industry. Tax favours for R&D would be introduced and tariffs on imported factory automation equipment would be reduced. The aim of the government's policy is to promote the localization of twenty key items and to increase the ratio of special steel production to total output. In 1989, special steel accounted for 6.2 per cent of total production; although the ratio had edged up to 7.8 per cent by 1991, it remains well below that seen in advanced countries. In the late 1980s, the ratio of special steel to total production was 19 per cent in Japan and 23 per cent in West Germany.

TEXTILES AND APPAREL

From its beginnings in the 1960s, the textile and apparel industry swiftly emerged as a major export industry, and, although recently overtaken by electronics as the nation's leading export sector, it continues to make a significant contribution to South Korea's exports and employment.

Textile and apparel exports hit the US$10 billion mark in November 1987. However, the annual growth rate for exports has slowed dramatically since the mid-1980s, falling from 24.7 per cent in 1986 to 5.5 per cent in 1991, and recording a negative growth rate of 3.1 per cent in 1990. In 1991 exports increased by 4.6 per cent year on year to US$15.3 billion. Exports of yarns and fibres grew by 12.8 per cent to US$1.3 billion and exports of fabric jumped 22.3 per cent to US$5.7 billion. However, exports of garments declined by 5.8 per cent to US$8.3 billion.

Forecasts for 1992 called for a 7.7 per cent increase in total exports to US$16.5 billion, a 10.9 per cent increase in yarn and fibres to US$1.4 billion, and a jump of 15.6 per cent to US$6.6 billion for fabric exports. Overseas orders for garments were expected to increase, pushing exports up by 1.8 per cent to US$8.5 billion. However, in the first ten months of 1992, exports were sluggish due to declining demand from the United States, Japan and Europe, and edged up just 3.8 per cent year on year to reach US$13.2 billion.

The decline in exports has been due to high wage increases, labour shortages, and increasing competition from developing countries. In common with many other industries in South

Korea, the focus in the past in the textile and apparel industry was on quantitative rather than qualitative expansion. Manufacturers now face the challenge of modernizing and upgrading their production facilities, and improving the quality of their products. Many observers now believe that the industry has reached the limits of its growth, and that it is unlikely to regain its status as a fast-growing, leading export sector.

Textiles

From an original base in cotton yarns and fabrics, South Korean textile manufacturers have moved into woollen and synthetic fibres and fabrics, and have also begun to develop products which are in demand in the industrial textiles market.

In 1991, South Korea produced 292,000 tons of cotton yarn, 65,000 tons of woollen yarn, and 770,000 tons of synthetic fibre yarn. Fabric production amounted to 702,000 square yards (587,000 square metres) of cotton fabric, 82,500 square yards (69,000 square metres) of woollen fabric, and 3.9 million square yards (3.3 million square metres) of synthetic fibre fabric.

Profitability in the sector has been deteriorating due to rising production costs and currency appreciation; South Korean manufacturers are heavily dependent on imported raw materials such as cotton, wool and chemical fibres, and the industry is, therefore, vulnerable to fluctuations in the prices of materials in international markets.

Prospects for the synthetic fibre sector, which accounted for 83 per cent of total fabric production in 1991, are good. Significant increases in export sales are forecast, thanks to increasing demand from the People's Republic of China, Southeast Asia, eastern Europe and the Middle East. However, the cotton sector is expected to decline in the coming years, in the face of mounting competition from countries such as the People's Republic of China, Pakistan and India, which enjoy the advantages of local raw materials and low wages.

Apparel

The apparel industry, which produces knitwear, sewn products and leather garments, is labour intensive and export oriented. Exports still account for about 70 per cent of the sector's output, and the share of total textile exports taken by garments has been as high as 70 per cent.

Between 1985 and 1991, production of knitted under and outerwear increased from 298 million to 419 million pieces. However, production of knitted outerwear (sweaters) alone dropped from 84 million to 52 million pieces during the same period. Exports of knitted, woven and leather apparel doubled between 1985 and 1990, rising from US$4.4 billion to US$8.9 billion, but then fell back to US$8.4 billion in 1991. Imports have increased steadily, from US$20 million in 1985 to US$424 million in 1991.

The downturn in export performance has been due in large part to rising production costs at home and increasing protectionism and competition in export markets. South Korea's apparel companies have been heavily dependent on a small number of markets; in 1991, the United States accounted for 36 per cent of all South Korean garment exports, while Japan and the European Community took shares of 30 per cent and 19 per cent respectively. The three largest markets accounted for 85 per cent of total apparel export.

South Korean manufacturers now face fierce competition in their export markets from the People's Republic of China, which has emerged as one of the world's largest apparel exporters. South Korea now ranks a distant second to China in garment exports to Japan; in 1991, South Korea's exports totalled US$1.5 billion against China's tally of US$2.8 billion.

Apparel makers, in common with other South Korean manufacturers, face cut-throat competition in the domestic market too – both from cheap imports at the low end of the market and from international designer labels at the top end. Moreover, domestic sales are suffering from oversupply and growing inventories.

Challenges facing the industry

The profitability of the textile industry is weakening due to low levels of technology and automation, rising labour costs, worsening labour shortages, and increasing financial expenses.

There is an urgent need to renovate or replace worn-out machinery; at the end of 1991, it was estimated that 42 per cent of the industry's sewing machinery, 49 per cent of its knitting machinery and 40 per cent of its dyeing facilities were obsolete. Investment is also needed to boost the automation rate, which was between 29 per cent and 45 per cent in the early 1990s, compared with 50–75 per cent in Japan.

According to industry sources, the number of workers in the industry has fallen from 785,000 in 1987 to 538,000 in 1992, and 15–17 per cent of jobs vital to the sector are now vacant. Other estimates put the labour shortage at 300,000 and call for an expansion of 30–50 per cent in the workforce. The industry is now calling on the government to allow it to employ foreign workers. In addition to the credit squeeze that faces many South Korean firms, textile and apparel companies face problems as local banks are increasingly reluctant to lend money to what is regarded by many as a sunset industry.

By the end of 1991, a total of W324 billion (US$412 million) had been invested by South Korean textile companies in 287 overseas projects, 246 of which were located in Southeast Asia and Latin America. The relocation of production facilities aims to take advantage of lower labour costs there and thus maintain export competitiveness in low-end goods. Factories in South Korea can then be used to produce items requiring high technology and skilled labour.

South Korean apparel manufacturers are particularly weak in design and label recognition. In 1991, 85 per cent of garments exported from South Korea were on an OEM basis. South Korean garment companies need to develop their own labels, improve their designs, and promote advertising and marketing overseas. Some manufacturers are already looking at installing computer-aided design (CAD) and computer-aided manufacturing (CAM) systems, adapting designs to suit international tastes, increasing their overseas activities, and establishing technical tie-ups with foreign fashion companies.

The ROK government is offering financial support to the industry, with the aim of making South Korea the world's largest supplier of textile products by the year 2000, with annual exports of US$30 billion in that year.

One of the main focuses of the government's support is the modernization of production facilities; in September 1992, the Ministry of Trade and Industry announced the implementation of a Five-Year Textile Facility Automation Programme, which will offer assistance to companies suffering due to labour shortages. The ministry also plans to establish a research institute to develop automation equipment for the sewing and dyeing processes. The government will provide W23.5 billion (US$29.9 million) in funds for the replacement of obsolete machinery.

31 The *Chaebŏl*

The South Korean economy is dominated by the *chaebŏl* – a small number of industrial conglomerates, consisting of large companies which produce a wide range of goods both for export and for sale in the domestic market. The *chaebŏl* have played a vital role in South Korea's industrial development over the past four decades, and, in doing so, have come to exercise a significant influence over the economy as a whole.

In June 1992, the Economic Planning Board's Fair Trade Commission (FTC) defined the *chaebŏl* as business groups with combined assets in excess of W400 billion (US$508 million); by that definition, there were 78 *chaebŏl*, comprising 1,056 subsidiaries. The FTC is reportedly planning to increase the basic standard to W600 billion (US$762 million) in 1993.

HISTORY OF THE *CHAEBŎL*

The history of the *chaebŏl* is relatively short. Few can trace their origins back beyond the beginning of this century, and many have their foundations in the Japanese colonial period (1910–45). It has been estimated that, during that period, 94 per cent of Korea's total economic assets were controlled by the Japanese. Although Koreans were employed by the Japanese in their factories and plants, they rarely rose to occupy managerial posts, and the activities of the few Koreans who were in business were severely restricted. After liberation in 1945, Koreans who had worked with Japanese-run companies were allowed to acquire the rights to take over the firms; by December 1948, more than 2,500 companies had been placed under Korean management.

In the period between liberation and the military coup of 1961, South Korean businessmen used American aid to set

221

up or expand their own companies, and companies such as Samsung, which had been established in 1938, quickly established a dominant presence in industries such as sugar refining, flour milling and weaving. Although many of today's *chaebŏl* existed as small companies before the Korean War (1950–3), their real origins lie in the ROK government's efforts to spur economic growth after the war, and particularly in the early 1960s.

In formulating his economic policies, President Park Chung-hee (1961–79) took the view that the best way to achieve rapid economic development was to identify target industries and give a few large, family-owned enterprises free rein to produce and export within these sectors. This concentration of economic power would be cost-effective, and the monopolistic or oligopolistic conditions would lead to economies of scale. For its part, the government would provide the necessary support for growth and expansion, assisting with control over labour activities, acquisition of technology and access to foreign markets.

The conglomerates thus became an important part of the government's export-led economic policies, with financial incentives and rewards offered to business groups which supported the government's policies and helped to achieve its economic targets. The conglomerates' development was controlled to a great degree by government priorities: the authorities' tight control over credit enabled it to direct corporate activities and encourage conglomerates to expand into specific areas.

The procurement contracts received during the Vietnam War, the oil dollars earned and international experience gained during the Middle East construction boom, and the government-supported development of General Trading Companies in the 1970s all contributed to the rapid growth of the conglomerates. Furthermore, in the 1970s and 1980s, they were allowed to acquire state-owned companies – one of the most notable acquisitions being the purchase of Korean Air by the Hanjin Group.

At the same time as they benefitted from the government's administrative and financial support, the *chaebŏl* chairmen were held personally accountable for the accomplishment of their allotted tasks, and the cost of failure was high. On the whole, however, the blend of supportive government policies, the entrepreneurial skills of the founders and the dedication of the workers proved a winning combination.

In 1991, the combined turnover of the top twenty *chaebŏl* was W170 trillion (US$216 billion), equivalent to 80 per cent of South Korea's gross national product.

CHARACTERISTICS OF THE *CHAEBŎL*

The main characteristics of the *chaebŏl* are as follows:

- **Family-controlled ownership and management**. The *chaebŏl* were typically founded as family firms by men who then dedicated their lives to the expansion of their businesses. 'Management by family' is still a strong tradition; the conglomerates are, as a rule, owned and controlled by one family, with management of the group or individual companies being handed down to sons or sons-in-law.

- **An authoritarian management style**. The chief executive officer of a *chaebŏl* has typically been the founder or a close relative. This father-like figure exercises virtually unchallenged power over all of the group's activities and assumes personal responsibility for the performance of the company and the well-being of its workforce. The role of the chairman is paramount and his decisions tend to be absolute. Although the management structure of South Korea's conglomerates is slowly beginning to change as a new generation takes over from the original founders, many *chaebŏl* have still not begun the transition to professional management (as opposed to family management) which has taken place in Japanese conglomerates, and which the ROK government is keen to encourage.

- **A wide range of business activities**. The *chaebŏl* typically have twenty or thirty subsidiaries involved in a wide range of business activities, including automobiles, construction, electronics, finance, petrochemicals and shipbuilding. Within the group, the subsidiaries will support each other, acting as subcontractors, suppliers and, in the case of the trading arms, export channels. There has been a strong tendency for the *chaebŏl* to invest in all industrial sectors which are perceived to be profitable, or in which they feel that they, as a major business concern, ought to have a presence. This has led to duplicated and excessive investment, cut-throat competition in areas such as petrochemicals, and ultimately, to overproduction and a fall in profitability for all producers. This tendency eventually prompted the ROK government to take steps to try to force the conglomerates to focus their attention and resources on a small number of core activities.

- **A close relationship with the government**. As mentioned above, in the early stages of Korea's economic development, the government and *chaebŏl* enjoyed a close and mutually beneficial relationship. The government provided administrative and financial support to the *chaebŏl*, which in turn developed their business activities in line with the government's economic policy guidelines. The conglomerates supported the government, but were also well aware that failure to attain government-set targets could lead to restriction or termination of access to finance and, ultimately, bankruptcy. The unequal relationship between South Korean conglomerates and their government, where the government formulates policies for the conglomerates to follow, differs from the relationship between the Japanese authorities and conglomerates, which is more one of consensus among equals. The *zaibatsu*, which number banks and other financial institutions among their subsidiaries, have a stable source of credit and are, therefore, less dependent on their government and more able to determine their own strategies than are their South Korean counterparts.

CHALLENGES FACING THE *CHAEBŎL*

The *chaebŏl* face a number of challenges in the early 1990s, one of the most important of which is a change in the government and public perception of the conglomerates and their position and role within the economy. In the late 1980s and early 1990s, the mood of both the government and the public began to turn against the *chaebŏl*.

Whereas in the past, the conglomerates have been looked upon as a driving force in the development of the national economy, there are now concerns about their increasing size and expanding wealth, and the degree of influence that they exert over the economy. Public criticism has mounted, focusing on the close relationship between the *chaebŏl* and the government and the massive benefits that have accrued to the conglomerates as a result of those links. The *chaebŏl* have been accused of engaging in reckless business diversification, triggering off real estate speculation, and competing against each other in the domestic market, rather than against foreign companies in the international markets.

There is also the view that the success of the *chaebŏl* has been achieved at the expense of small- and medium-sized companies. The suicide of a number of owners of small businesses in 1992 contributed to a rising consensus that the bigger the *chaebŏl* grow, the harder it is for small- and medium-sized enterprises to survive.

The entry of some of the *chaebŏl* into the non-banking financial sector has also caused concern in some quarters. In August 1992, the top 30 conglomerates owned a total of 50 non-banking financial subsidiaries, and controlled an estimated 50 per cent of secondary financial institutions. The concern is that their presence in the sector will give them privileged access to funds, despite the ban on their owning banks.

The government, having encouraged and supported the growth and development of the conglomerates over the past three decades, is now keen to reduce their influence in the interests of stabilizing the economy and ensuring a more equitable distribution of wealth and resources. It is taking steps – with varying degrees of success – to curb the conglomerates' access to new credit, control cross-investment among *chaebŏl* subsidiaries, and restrict diversification into new business areas.

The government has already taken steps to restrict bank loans to the *chaebŏl*, and has plans to freeze and then reduce cross-payment guarantees among the affiliated companies of the top 30 *chaebŏl*. The aim of this policy is to break the financial ties between the subsidiaries and make them financially independent.

Efforts have also been made to limit further diversification by the *chaebŏl* by stipulating that only three designated core businesses per conglomerate will be given access to new credit. The aim of this policy was to encourage the *chaebŏl* to develop a small number of world-class enterprises, rather than attempting to establish a presence in all industrial sectors. However, this had only limited success: for example, eleven out of the top 30 conglomerates chose petrochemicals as one of their core businesses. The *chaebŏl* were also careful to choose some companies in the early stages of development and thus in need of cash, rather than their well-established affiliates.

The government is now switching its focus and support towards increasing its financial and administrative support for small- and medium-sized enterprises (SMEs). In addition, large business concerns are being encouraged to hive off certain business activities to smaller enterprises. In time, the government hopes, the *chaebŏl* and SMEs will learn to work together and rely on each other.

The Hyundai affair

The swing in opinion against the *chaeböl* is perhaps best demonstrated by the continuing feud between the Roh administration and the Hyundai business group. In October 1991, an investigation began into allegations of tax evasion made against the Hyundai group and seven members of the founding family. The Office of National Tax Administration and the Securities Supervisory Board accused Hyundai's honorary chairman Chung Ju-yung of selling millions of personal shares in Hyundai group companies to his sons at less than the market price, without going through the Korea Stock Exchange.

In the past, the transfer of stock among *chaeböl* family members has often been used to pass on untaxed wealth from one generation to the next. The Hyundai family were accused of using this method to evade the payment of inheritance tax, and of failing to report the profits made through the irregular transfer of shares. Hyundai was eventually fined W136 billion (US$173 million) in penalties and back taxes.

Given that tax investigations have been used in the past as a means of keeping corporations and individuals in line, and that the Hanjin group had also come under investigation earlier in 1991 and had been fined W55.6 billion (US$71 million), some believed that this was a genuine attempt to begin enforcing the taxation of inheritance, focusing on the two *chaeböl* with the highest rates of family ownership – 42 per cent for the Hyundai group and 44 per cent for the Hanjin group.

However, others maintained that Chung Ju-yung was being punished by the government not only for failing to cooperate with official policy but for openly criticizing it – he had criticized the Roh administration's handling of the economy and had spoken out against one of its pet projects, the building of a high-speed rail link between Seoul and Pusan. It was also rumoured that Hyundai companies had failed to donate sufficient funds to the ruling party.

Perhaps most important of all was the belief that Chung was being punished for his political aspirations – he thereafter established his own political party, the United People's Party, which won 31 seats in the 1992 National Assembly elections, and ran for the presidency later that same year (see: Major Political Parties).

Following the incident, Hyundai companies reported difficulties in raising capital in the domestic markets; new bank loans were more or less frozen, and the Securities Exchange Commission rejected, for no apparent reason, applications from Hyundai affiliates for permission to issue corporate bonds. The Korea Exchange Bank postponed the guarantee of a would-be construction project in Libya.

In the spring of 1992, President Roh T'ae-woo ordered the authorities to take steps to prevent the unreported outflow of funds from business to political parties in the run-up to the National Assembly and presidential elections, and instructed financial institutions to monitor more closely the uses to which their loans were being put. Immediately following the presidential elections, charges were made that the Hyundai group had mobilized manpower and funds to support Chung's presidential bid.

Other challenges

Other challenges facing the *chaebŏl* in the early 1990s include deregulation and liberalization, the need to improve their financial structure, and pressure for the public listing of *chaebŏl* subsidiaries.

The increasing trend toward the **deregulation and liberalization** of the South Korean economy will pose a challenge to the *chaebŏl*, as their monopolistic or oligopolistic positions are weakened by the entry of domestic and foreign newcomers to the market.

The conglomerates' **financial structure** also gives some cause for concern. The collapse of the Kukje group in 1985 was attributed mainly to the group's unstable financial position, which, according to the government, had been aggravated by reckless expansion into too many areas. As mentioned above, rapid diversification into unrelated business areas has been a characteristic of *chaebŏl* development, and this has resulted in high levels of debt.

In the late 1980s and early 1990s, debt-to-equity ratios of 500 per cent and interest coverage ratios of 1.0–1.5 per cent were by no means uncommon; in 1991, the average debt ratio of the top 30 *chaebŏl*'s subsidiaries was in excess of 400 per cent. The average debt ratio of the 72 main enterprises was 435.2 per cent, while that of the 52 listed subsidiaries was 328.5 per cent. The average for all December year-end manufacturing companies in 1991 was 239 per cent. Companies with the highest debt-to-equity ratios were Daewoo Motor (2,355.7 per cent), Asiana Airlines (2,138.6 per cent) and Sammi Metal products (1,003.20 per cent). Companies with the lowest ratio were Dongkuk Steel (95.4 per cent), Kumho Petrochemicals (87.5 per cent) and Daelim Concrete (81.7 per cent).

The weakening of the *chaebŏl*'s relationship with the government, and official moves to give preferential financing to small- and medium-sized enterprises, will mean reduced access to finance for the conglomerates. As mentioned above, loans to the *chaebŏl* are being reduced, and steps have been taken to prevent their speculation in real estate – in early 1990, the government directed the *chaebŏl* to dispose of their idle, non-business land holdings – and restrict expansion into new business areas.

In 1991, controlling shareholders and family members still accounted, on average, for almost half the *chaebŏl* ownership. For Hyundai, the ratio was 67.8 per cent, for Daewoo 50.4 per cent, for Samsung 53.2 per cent, and for Lucky–Goldstar 38.3 per cent. In line with its policy of reducing the ratio of family stock ownership within the *chaebŏl*, the government aims to lower the average *chaebŏl* equity ownership ratio from the current level of 47 per cent to 30 per cent by 1996.

The *chaebŏl* are, therefore, coming under increasing pressure to allow their **subsidiary companies** to be listed on the stock exchange; currently an average of 80 per cent of affiliated companies are privately held. These moves are being resisted by many of the *chaebŏl* owners, who see this as leading to a dilution of family control and greater public financial accountability.

The planned tightening of the public disclosure regulations would give the public an insight into the financial workings of the *chaebŏl* which has thus far been denied them. Under South Korean law, companies are not obliged to produce consolidated accounts. As the *chaebŏl* appear reluctant to do so, it is difficult to find out exactly how financially interdependent the subsidiaries are, and to what extent they are linked by cross-shareholding and cross-guarantees – a situation which the government is keen to rectify.

As this situation clearly has serious implications should one of the companies go bankrupt, the Ministry of Finance plans to change the law and make the publication of consolidated accounts compulsory. However, the effect of this on the *chaebŏl* will be determined by the extent to which the government is able to persuade the subsidiaries to go public.

32 Infrastructure

The Republic of Korea has a network of 36,250 miles (58,000 km) of road, of which 76 per cent is paved. An expressway system extending 998 miles (1,597 km) creates a 'one day' travel network which, in theory, enables travellers to make a return journey to any part of the Republic within one day. In 1991, more than 4 million motor vehicles were registered in South Korea, bringing the number of vehicles registered per kilometre of paved road to 96, up from 59 in 1988 and 24 in 1965.

In 1991, a network of 4,039 miles (6,462 km) of railway track linked all major urban centres. The Seoul subway system, comprising four lines with a total track length of 73 miles (117 km), carried 1.1 billion passengers during the year. A smaller-scale subway system operates in the nation's largest port, Pusan.

The Republic of Korea has 47 ports with a combined cargo holding capacity in excess of 225 million tons. The nation's twelve airports, including three international airports at Kimp'o (Seoul), Pusan and Cheju, handled more than 16 million passengers and close to a million tons of cargo in 1991.

However, insufficient investment in infrastructure during the 1980s has led to acute traffic congestion throughout the Republic of Korea. Between 1980 and 1990, infrastructure investment averaged less than 2 per cent of GNP, at a time when the economy and foreign trade were expanding at average annual rates of 10 per cent and 12 per cent respectively. Official sources estimate that hundreds of millions of dollars are lost or wasted every year due to traffic congestion and bottlenecks at the nation's ports.

When not at a complete standstill, traffic crawls through Seoul, adding to both pollution and stress levels; at peak times, subways are crowded and buses resemble sardine cans. The 268-mile (428-km) journey from the South Korean capital Seoul

229

to its largest port, Pusan, can take up to 14 hours by express-way on normal days – and in the run-up to the Thanksgiving Festival in September 1992, the travelling time was 25 hours.

The rail link between Seoul and Pusan has reached maximum capacity, forcing distributors to put freight trucks on the already overcrowded roads, and Seoul's Kimp'o airport is expected to reach its maximum capacity of 160,000 flights and 12 million passengers per year in 1996. The shortage of loading and unloading facilities at South Korean ports now results in higher distribution costs (including warehousing charges), delays in production (due to bottlenecks in the supply of imported raw materials and semi-finished goods) and increased delivery times.

During the period of the Seventh Five-Year Plan, the ratio of investment in social infrastructure (roads, railways, sea ports, airports and water resources) is set to rise to 5 per cent of GNP in 1996 from 3.7 per cent in 1991. A total of W36–9 trillion (US$45.7–49.5 billion) will be spent during the five-year period to maximize the efficiency of the nation's transportation systems. Plans include the construction of two large inland container depots near Seoul and Pusan (covering an area of 1.2 million square yards – 990,000 square metres – apiece), and the establishment of a seaborne freighter service between Pusan and Inch'ŏn to ease road traffic congestion.

Within Seoul, the subway system will be expanded; the system is currently overwhelmed during the rush hours. The addition of four more lines by 1996 will increase the track length from the current length of 73 miles (117 km) to 208 miles (333 km). By 1996, the subway system will be handling 50 per cent of the capital's daily passenger traffic, and by the end of the century, following further extensions, 75 per cent of Seoul's passengers will travel by subway. The future growth of Seoul will be planned around the subway network, with stations serving as nuclei for new residential neighbourhoods, and the subways providing connections to railway lines. The aim is to confine more traffic to the suburbs, in order to ease the traffic congestion in the city centre.

The showpiece projects of the Seventh Plan, however, are the construction of the new airport and the building of a high-speed rail link between Seoul and Pusan. Although the Roh administration was criticized for going ahead with these expensive projects at a time when the economy was facing difficulties – the airport will cost a total of W10 trillion (US$12.7 billion) over 28 years and the rail link W5.8 trillion (US$7.3 billion) – the official response to these criticisms was that the expense was justified by the long-term benefits to the economy.

Work has already begun on the **new airport** on Yŏngjong Island, which will serve Seoul in the twenty-first century. The airport will be built on reclaimed land covering an area of 15.0 million square yards (12.5 million square metres), and is scheduled to be partially operational by 1997 and completed in the early twenty-first century. When completed in 2020, the airport will have an annual handling capacity of 100 million passengers and 7 million tons of freight. It will be constructed to prepare for the era of hypersonic jet transport, and may be used for international flights, leaving the existing airport at Kimp'o, which cannot be expanded due to the proximity of mountains and residential areas, to handle domestic flights.

Free Trade Zones covering a total area of 3.1 million square yards (2.6 million square metres) will be established within the grounds of the airport, and there are plans to build a business complex covering 1.8 million square yards (1.5 million square metres), incorporating exhibition and conference facilities, hotels and office buildings. Also under construction is an 'airport community' comprising residential and commercial sectors, entertainment and shopping facilities. New rail and road links will connect Yŏngjong Airport to the capital, Seoul.

The building of a **high-speed rail link** between Seoul and Pusan should do much to alleviate the acute traffic congestion on the one existing expressway between South Korea's two largest cities. It is estimated that the rail link will cut the travelling time between Seoul and Pusan to 100 minutes; with departures every three minutes, more than half a million passengers could use the link every day. When fully operational, the rail link would take 33,000 buses and 5,000 cars off the roads every day, allowing more freight to travel by road, as well as by conventional rail links.

This rail link will also allow more people to live outside and work in the capital, by bringing half the peninsula within commuting distance of Seoul. For example, travelling time to and from Taejŏn (the site of the 1993 Expo) would be cut from two or three hours to just 40 minutes.

The three foreign bidders for the high-speed rail link are France's Transportation Grande Vitesse (TGV), Germany's Inter-City Express (ICE) and Japan's Shinkansen (Bullet Train). The contract put up for tender by the ROK government is for 46 formations of high-speed electric cars (capable of travelling at 187 miles–300 km per hour), of which 44 will be assembled locally. The government is keen to acquire the technology to localize more than 50 per cent of the major components for the trains, with a view, eventually, to South Korean companies entering the high-speed train market.

33 Tourism and the Service Industry

OUTBOUND TOURISM

The South Koreans have a well-deserved reputation for working hard and taking few holidays. Until the late 1980s, the emphasis was very much on work rather than play; it was only after significant rises in disposable income, increases in paid holiday, and the lifting of restrictions on overseas travel that the outbound tourism industry really began to flourish in South Korea.

Until the early 1980s, tourism was restricted to inbound travellers because of South Korea's adverse balance of payments. South Koreans could only travel abroad for business, government or educational purposes. From 1983, South Koreans aged 50 or more were allowed to travel overseas for pleasure, but were restricted as to the length and frequency of their trips, the amount of money they could spend, and so forth. Nevertheless, between 1983 and 1987, an average of 500,000 South Koreans travelled abroad each year for business and pleasure.

The improvement in the balance of payments situation in 1986 and 1987 prompted the ROK government to ease its restrictions on overseas travel; the minimum age was lowered to 45 in 1987 and to 30 in 1988, and it was abolished in 1989. This led to a surge in outbound traffic, especially among students, the elderly, and the nation's *nouveau riche*, who had made money in the booming real estate and stock markets. Couples wishing to fly away for their honeymoon, two, found their horizons broadened from Cheju Island, off the south-west coast of the Republic, to South-east Asia, Hong Kong and Thailand.

In 1991, almost 2 million South Koreans travelled overseas: the most popular destination was Japan, which accounted for 49 per cent of the total, followed by the United States (16 per cent), and Taiwan and Hong Kong (7 per cent each). It is estimated that the number of outbound tourists will reach 7.5 million by 1999, making South Korea the second largest generator of tourists in Asia, after Japan.

However, the sudden surge in overseas travel has created a problem for the South Korean government. In 1991, South Koreans travelling overseas spent an average of US$1,750 during their visit, almost twice the average amount spent by foreigners visiting the Republic that year. The recording of the nation's first tourism deficit in nine years – US$339 million in 1991 – prompted fears that the ROK authorities would reimpose restrictions on overseas travel. Although travel bans were not imposed as such, some restrictions were implemented; for example, banning charter flights over the holiday period at the end of 1992.

INBOUND TOURISM

In 1962, a total of 15,184 foreigners visited South Korea, the majority being American businessmen and women. An average annual growth rate of 23 per cent through the 1970s pushed the number of visitors past the one-million mark in 1978; the two-million mark was passed ten years later. Tourism receipts rose from US$47 million in 1970 to almost US$3 billion in 1991, making inbound tourism a significant source of revenue for the South Korean government.

In 1991, more than 3 million foreigners visited the Republic, spending an average of W715,000 (US$910) during their stay. The Japanese accounted for half of the inbound travellers, while the Americans and the Taiwanese took second and third place respectively.

Inbound tourism should receive a boost from two major events in the early 1990s: the 1993 Taejŏn Expo (see: The Economy – General and Overview) and Visit Korea Year in 1994. The celebrations in 1994, which will centre on the six hundredth anniversary of the establishment of Seoul as the capital of Korea, aim to encourage foreigners to visit South Korea rather than just Seoul, and South Koreans to take their holidays at home.

The Republic of Korea has a great deal to offer the foreign visitor. In addition to places of historic and cultural interest, such as the ancient capital of Kyŏngju and the Korean Folk Village, and areas of outstanding natural beauty including Sŏrak Mountain, there are a number of modern tourist attractions. These include the Lotte World Magic Island Theme Park, Yongin Family Land, the Dragon Valley Ski Resort, and the Pukok Hawaii Health Resort, which offer a wide variety of leisure facilities to domestic and foreign visitors.

THE HOTEL INDUSTRY

In 1991, 424 hotels were registered in South Korea with a total of 42,489 rooms. Tourist hotels are graded with two to five *mugunghwa* (Rose of Sharon – South Korea's national flower); a total of 52 hotels with 17,113 rooms are classed as deluxe, or super deluxe for those having convention facilities and sophisticated safety facilities.

Two-thirds of the nation's deluxe hotels are located in Seoul, including a number of international chain and franchise hotels such as Westin, Hilton, Hyatt, Intercontinental and Swiss Grand. These hotels are usually owned by a South Korean company, and managed by an international hotel chain or group, with expatriates filling the top management posts. There is an increasing number of resort areas or hotel complexes in South Korea, including the Pomun Resort in Kyŏngju and the Chungmun resort on Cheju Island.

The restaurants and reception rooms in deluxe hotels continue to be used as venues for corporate entertaining, family celebrations and social gatherings. However, hotels in Seoul have recently been hit by the government's frugality campaigns; restrictions have included a ban on weddings at hotels, the closing of entertainment facilities at midnight, and the closing of health clubs and saunas one day per week.

Over the past decade, the convention industry has become an important part of the tourism and hotel industries. In addition to being advertised as a centre for culture, sightseeing and shopping, South Korea is increasingly being marketed as a convention centre at the hub of north-east Asia. South Korea has played host to a number of top conventions in recent years, including the IMF/IBRD Conference in 1985, the Rotary World Congress in 1989, and the World Scout Jamboree in 1991. Seoul will play host to the Pacific Asian Travel Association Conference and the twenty-first Congress of the Universal Postal Union in 1994.

In addition to the convention and exhibition facilities offered by hotels, there are excellent conference venues in Seoul, Pusan and Kyŏngju, including the Korea World Trade Centre, the Sejong Cultural Centre, the Seoul Arts Centre, the 63 Building and the Pusan Cultural Centre. The Korea Exhibition Centre (KOEX) also offers first-class exhibition and trade show facilities (see: Contact Addresses in South Korea).

34 Communications

TELEPHONE NETWORK
The telephone network in South Korea has developed rapidly over the past three decades, in terms of both its size and the quality of service offered. In 1962, there were 1,900 long distance transmission circuits and 167,570 telephone subscribers; thirty years later, there were more than 19 million telephone lines and over 15 million subscribers.

Investment in the telephone network began in earnest in the 1980s, largely in response to increasing demand from local businesses. Additional lines and digital switching systems were installed to create a nationwide automated telephone service, which was completed in 1987. International direct dialling (IDD) was introduced to South Korea in 1981, using AT&T's 4ESS system, and in 1991, Korea Telecom opened an international switching centre, using an AXE-10 switching system capable of handling 3 million international calls per hour.

In 1985, a joint research project involving the state-funded Electronics and Telecommunications Research Institute, plus domestic and foreign companies, developed the time division exchange (TDX) digital switching system for public telephone networks. Six years later, the TDX-10 switching system was developed, with the capacity to handle 100,000 telephone lines. South Korea currently exports TDX systems to more than sixty countries around the world.

A model system of the integrated services digital network (ISDN) was inaugurated in Seoul, Taejŏn and Cheju in 1991, offering a variety of services including telewriting and video-conferencing to around 500 subscribers. The network will be extended throughout the country during the mid-1990s.

In 1992, Korea Telecom inaugurated 'Netkeeper', an

automated control centre that monitors intercity and international telephone calls made in the Republic. The system, which is said virtually to eradicate the need for human involvement in directing telephone traffic, also reduces costs and improves the quality of service.

Also in 1992, an optic fibre cable network was introduced on a trial basis for local and international calls in South Korea's six largest cities – Seoul, Pusan, Taegu, Taejŏn, Kwangju and Suwŏn – at a cost of W5.4 billion (US$6.8 million). The network, which offers improved quality of voice and data transmission, also offers teleconferencing, G4 fax transmission, computer communications and other advanced telecommunications services. There are plans to extend the network throughout the country by 2015 at a cost of W10.6 trillion (US$13.5 billion).

By 1992, South Korea had the eighth-largest telephone network in the world, with more than 19 million telephone lines, or one line for every 2.2 persons. The number of lines is forecast to reach 22 million by the turn of the century. A total of 14.6 million subscribers was registered in the Republic in 1991; virtually every home now has a telephone, and all circuits are connected by automatic switching systems.

In 1991, there were 538,451 long distance lines installed in the Republic and 9,307 communications circuits (4,597 satellite and 4,710 undersea cable). International subscribers dialling (ISD) is currently available for direct calls to 171 countries. South Korea has already opened a number of undersea optic fibre cable networks, and has plans to extend these into a ten-nation network, linking the Republic with Japan, China, the former Soviet Union and South-east Asian nations by 1996.

The monopoly in telephone services within the Republic, which had been enjoyed by Korea Telecom since its establishment in 1981, came to an end when the privately owned Data Communications Corporation (DACOM) was allowed to enter the international telephone call business in 1991. This gave rise to what came to be known as the '001 and 002' war – 001 and 002 being the two companies' access codes for international calls. Although DACOM will be allowed to handle long-distance domestic calls in the near future, local calls will continue to be handled exclusively by Korea Telecom. Prior to these developments, DACOM had been the sole supplier of data communications services in South Korea; as a quid pro quo for the loss of its monopoly, Korea Telecom was allowed to expand into this area of business.

The result of the expansion of competition from a monopoly to a duopoly should be lower charges, a greater variety of services, and more rapid development of new technology.

The two companies were quick to announce new services, including credit card public phones, consolidated and detailed billing, language interpretation, and immediate pricing advice.

MOBILE TELECOMMUNICATIONS

The mobile telecommunications industry has seen rapid growth since the introduction of cellular phones and radio pagers in 1984. By 1991, cumulative sales of mobile telephones and pagers had reached 166,000 and 850,000 respectively; the totals are forecast to rise to 4.9 million and 7 million by the year 2001.

The growth of the industry has been boosted by the removal of restrictions on uses of radio frequencies and the worsening traffic situation in South Korea's major cities. From the late 1950s until the late 1980s, restrictions were placed on the use of frequency bands for any use other than military or official purposes, in the interests of national security. However, the easing of tensions between North and South Korea in recent years has led to a relaxation of the restrictions and has enabled the mobile communications industry to expand at a rapid rate. Traffic jams, which have become a part of everyday life in cities like Seoul and Pusan, have boosted demand for mobile telephones, which are now seen as an indispensable communication system.

Until the early 1990s the Korea Mobile Telecommunications Corporation (KMTC) enjoyed a monopoly in the wireless communications market as the sole supplier of mobile telephones and radio pagers. However, in 1992, the government decided to open up the market to limited competition, by allowing a second company or group of companies to offer mobile telecommunications services on a nationwide basis, and nine additional companies to enter the radio paging business in the provinces. The government also announced that KMTC, which is part owned by Korea Telecom, will be privatized by 1993, in order to promote fair and equal competition between the two providers.

By opening up the market, the government aimed to increase competition and thereby promote the lowering of charges and the introduction of new services. The significant amounts of investment needed in the expansion of switching systems and relay stations or cell sites in order to keep pace with the surging demand was also thought to be a factor in the decision. The prospects for the industry were deemed to be so good that no fewer than 440 companies (including twenty foreign firms) formed six consortia and entered the race. The low level of technology accumulated by the South Koreans in this sector necessitated the involvement of foreign partners: in the early 1990s, the localization rates for cordless hand phones, car phones and pagers were 15 per cent, 20 per cent and 30 per cent respectively.

The nomination of a second provider of mobile communications services ended in embarrassment for the government, when the announcement that a consortium led by the Sunkyong Group had won the contract was met with accusations of favouritism and nepotism. (The chairman of the Sunkyong Group is related by marriage to President Roh T'ae-woo.) Such was the furore that little more than a week after being nominated, Sunkyong waived its rights to the contract, which was declared null and void by the Ministry of Communications.

The decision was finally made to allow the Kim Young-Sam administration to award the lucrative contract after its inauguration in 1993 in order to avoid further suspicions that it was being used to win political favour ahead of the 1992 presidential election. However, that was not the end of the matter for Sunkyong, whose foreign partners threatened lawsuits and sought both compensation and royalties for technology transferred to the group ahead of the awarding of the contract.

SATELLITE COMMUNICATIONS

The first satellite station in South Korea was built at Kŭmsan in 1970. This was followed by a second station in 1976, and two satellite communication stations in 1985 and 1988. The stations provide high-quality transpacific telegraph, telephone and television connections.

In August 1992, the Republic of Korea became the twenty-second nation in the world to put a satellite into space. The scientific research satellite *Uribyŏl* (Our Star), launched from French Guyana by an Ariane rocket, was developed in collaboration with Surrey University in the United Kingdom. The satellite carries two high-definition cameras and an electronic mail system, and will perform a number of tasks, including taking photographs of the earth, measuring cosmic rays, and exchanging information with the earth station at Taejŏn. Through this collaboration, the South Koreans aim to acquire the technology to build a second satellite, to be launched in 1993 to coincide with the holding of the World Exposition in Taejŏn.

In October 1992, Korea Telecom opened a satellite link between the INTELSAT 5A satellite and earth stations in Pusan, Taegu, Taejŏn and Kwangju. (INTELSAT is a 120-member body operating satellites over major oceans on a charter basis.) Korea Telecom will use the INTELSAT services until 1995, when the South Korean broadcast satellite is due to be launched (see below). From 1993, the public will have access to a variety of fee-based services, including high-speed fax transmission, high-speed computer file exchange, and digital video transmission.

South Korea's first broadcast satellite, called *Mugunghwa* after South Korea's national flower, is due to be launched in 1995. The primary satellite will be launched in April 1995 and the back-up satellite six months later. Each satellite will have a capacity of 3,900 two-way voice circuits, three channels for direct broadcasting, and four video channels, and will cover an area extending from Manchuria in the north to Osaka, Japan, in the south. Once the satellite is in orbit, South Koreans who have a satellite dish will be able to access a variety of facilities including teleconferencing and high-speed data transmission, as well as enjoying enhanced radio and television broadcasts.

South Korea's lack of technology and trained and experienced manpower in the satellite field has made it necessary to forge links with foreign companies in order to develop the satellite programme. It is hoped that the project will lead to significant transfers of technology to South Korea's infant aerospace industry.

The programme comprises three phases: the building of the satellite body, the building of the launching equipment, and the development of equipment for the earth stations. Technology transfer was a key consideration in the awarding of the contract to GE Astrospace of the United States. The contract for the launch equipment was awarded to McDonnell Douglas of the United States.

DATA COMMUNICATION
During the late 1980s, DACOM established DACOMNET, a nationwide packet exchange system which enabled the rapid exchange of data through switchboards and computer networks. Although DACOM has been the sole provider of services such as electronic mail, information databases, videotex and value-added network (VAN) information, the partial liberalization of the sector in the early 1990s will bring DACOM into competition with both domestic and foreign firms.

THE LIBERALIZATION OF THE TELECOMMUNICATIONS INDUSTRY
The rapid growth of the industry and its huge potential for further development have led to increasing calls for its opening to foreign competition. The United States and South Korea have held talks on the telecommunications sector since 1989,

with the US delegation pushing for faster and broader access to the South Korean market. In 1989, the US Trade Representative designated South Korea a priority foreign country for trade negotiations in the telecommunications sector.

Under threat of retaliatory sanctions, the South Korean government made a number of concessions. The VAN market, which includes data access and processing, and information storage and handling, was partially opened to foreign companies in July 1991 – foreign companies may now take an equity stake of up to 50 per cent in a local VAN provider – and further liberalization is scheduled for 1994. The ROK government has also announced that the telecommunications equipment procurement market (386 items) and the telecommunications network equipment procurement market (265 items) will gradually be opened to foreign suppliers in the early 1990s.

FUTURE PROSPECTS

In the years ahead, investment, research and development in the telecommunications sector will focus on the enhancement of the quality of mobile telecommunications, ISDN technology, satellite telecommunications networks, packet switching networks, and optical fibre cable television (CATV) networks.

The government plans to invest W72.2 billion (US$92 million) between 1992 and 1996 in the development of mobile telecommunication technology, as well as offering financial and tax incentives for research and development in the area. Efforts will focus on the localization of key parts and components; currently, even major communication equipment companies simply assemble the product from imported components, and many import the finished products.

35 Environmental Policy

Over the past three decades the overriding concern of the ROK government has been economic growth and industrialization. The impact of this rapid growth on the environment, in terms of water and air pollution and the disposal of industrial waste, has received scant attention. During this period large South Korean companies did not invest in technology to dispose of their industrial waste products, and many small- and medium-sized companies lacked the funds to build and operate efficient waste-treatment facilities.

WATER POLLUTION

The quality of water near large cities and industrial complexes in South Korea is poor, and continues to deteriorate due to the disposal of untreated household sewage, industrial and agricultural waste. Only a small proportion of household and industrial waste water is treated before being discharged (28 per cent in the early 1990s). According to the ROK Ministry of the Environment, none of the coastal waters surrounding the Korean peninsula can be classified as suitable for drinking. The waters of the Masan Gulf are unfit even for industrial use, and some environmentalists claim that it is not safe to eat the fish caught in South Korea's coastal waters.

The quality of tap water in South Korea's cities is particularly bad; it was only in recent years that the ROK government allowed South Korean nationals to buy bottled water for drinking. Prior to that, bottled water was sold only to foreign visitors and expatriates in Seoul, who were advised against using tap water, even for brushing their teeth. The lax nature of anti-pollution regulations in South Korea was amply demonstrated in March 1991, when the source of drinking water for several million South Koreans was polluted by the dumping of 30 tons of untreated phenol resin (a powerful carcinogen) into the Naktong River.

AIR POLLUTION

On all but the clearest and brightest of days, a brown haze hangs over Seoul. The blanket of smog is clearly visible on the approach to the city by expressway. Major air pollutants are dust and sulphur dioxide generated by industrial facilities, and nitrates and carbon monoxide from vehicles. The continuing use of low-cost, high sulphur-content coal briquettes for cooking and heating is another major contributory factor.

According to a report published by the World Health Organization and the United Nations Environmental Programme in 1992, Seoul is the second most polluted city in the world, after Mexico City. Although the ROK Ministry of the Environment questioned the findings of the report and asserted that levels of pollution had fallen since the WHO and UNEP officials collected their data, environmentalists claim that levels, though falling, are still unacceptably high. In 1992, sulphur dioxide levels in the metropolitan area were 0.05 p.p.m., compared with the WHO recommended level of 0.021. Similarly, the level of total suspended particularates was 121 micrograms per square metre – the recommended level is 60–90 micrograms. The ministry has pledged to bring levels down to those recommended by 1996.

Acid rain, which had fallen only in Seoul, Pusan and Ulsan from the mid-1980s onwards, fell across 60 per cent of the nation between 1991 and 1992. Samples taken at 65 locations nationwide showed 16 per cent with a pH of 4.5 or less, 47 per cent with a pH of 4.5–5, and 37 per cent with a pH of 5 or above (a pH of 5.6 is neutral). The pH levels deteriorated from 5.7 to 5.3 in Seoul, from 5.9 to 5.1 in Pusan, and from 5.7 to 5.3 in Taegu during the period of the survey.

However, analysts expect pollution levels to fall as gas replaces coal as fuel for heating and cooking, stricter emission standards are enforced, and an increasing number of vehicles use cleaner fuels, such as unleaded petrol and liquefied petroleum gas (LPG). This optimism seems to be borne out by statistics showing a decline in the emission of air pollutants in 1991. Emissions of sulphur dioxide and carbon monoxide fell, as did the concentration of these pollutants in the air.

NOISE POLLUTION

In 1991, the level of noise pollution exceeded the permissible limit in all of South Korea's major cities. The permissible level is 50 decibels: Seoul recorded 61 decibels, Pusan 56, and Taegu 58; the lowest level recorded was 52 decibels. The high levels of noise were caused chiefly by heavy traffic and construction work. The acceptable level of 70 decibels for industrial areas was exceeded both in Seoul (78 decibels) and Pusan (76).

WASTE

In 1992, the amount of waste generated per day in South Korea as a whole reached 73,000 tons; in Seoul alone the total was 29,000 tons per day. The average amount per capita of waste is 5.1 lb (2.3 kg) per day nationwide and 6.2 lb (2.8 kg) in Seoul, compared with 4.0 lb (1.8 kg) in the United States, 2.2 lb (1.0 kg) in Japan, and 2.0 lb (0.9 kg) in Germany. Worth noting is the fact that leftover food accounts for more than a quarter of the daily rubbish, and the food thrown away each year is valued at W8 trillion (US$10 billion).

The majority of household waste (93 per cent) is disposed of in landfills; 1.8 per cent is incinerated, 0.6 per cent is stored for future disposal, and 4.6 per cent is recycled. The proportions for industrial waste are: landfill 33.4 per cent, incineration 3.0 per cent, storage 9.3 per cent and recycling 54.3 per cent. The largest refuse dump site in the Republic, located on Nanji-do Islet, was opened in 1978. By 1992, the mountain of garbage had risen to 85 yards (78 metres) above sea level, necessitating the opening of a new landfill site near Kimp'o, which is large enough to accommodate waste from 20 cities for 25 years.

THE GOVERNMENT RESPONSE

The past few years have seen an increase in government measures aimed at protecting the environment and making the South Korean industrial structure more energy-efficient. New environmental statutes were introduced in June 1990, replacing the old Environment Preservation Act; and, in 1991, amendments were made to strengthen the Solid Waste Management Act, the Marine Pollution Act, and the Natural Environment Preservation Act.

There have been calls for the Ministry of the Environment to enforce strict environmental impact assessments (EIAs) as quickly as possible, before other major industrial development projects get underway. However, regulations are often ignored, and laws are passed but not strictly enforced. In the past the ministry has seemed to have little real power to enforce its regulations, unlike the position in some western nations, where failure to comply with environmental regulations can result in the cancellation of a project. None the less, in late 1992, the ministry began to take action against firms which habitually violate environmental regulations, and placed 401 companies on an environmental blacklist.

In 1990, the use of liquefied natural gas (LNG) became mandatory for new apartments in Seoul with an area of more than 14 *p'yŏng* (55 square yards – 46 square metres), existing apartments larger than 35 *p'yŏng* (139 square yards – 116 square metres), and for public buildings which are heavy consumers of heating fuel. The use of leaded fuel will be banned in South Korea from 1993. Green-belt areas are being designated in urban areas, and both government offices and state-run firms are setting an example for the private sector by using recycled products.

The government has already launched a four-year plan (1992–6) to lower pollution levels. The plan includes the construction of additional sewage treatment facilities, waste water and sanitary waste disposal facilities. Steps will be taken to clean up the nation's four largest rivers by reducing the amount of waste discharged into them, thus raising the quality of the water to Grade 1 by 1996.

The government also plans to strengthen legislation to promote a resource-saving industrial structure, and to issue guidelines on packaging and the treatment of industrial waste. Conglomerates whose subsidiaries produce more than 30,000 tons of industrial waste per annum may be required in future to operate their own waste-treatment systems; industries producing more than 10,000 tons of waste will be encouraged to follow suit. Large buildings constructed in the future will be required to have ice-regenerative or gas-type cooling systems, rather than systems using chloroflurocarbons (CFCs).

The government will actively support the development of key environmental technologies through a ten-year programme extending to the end of the century. A total of W1 trillion (US$1.3 billion) will be invested in the development of new technology – W11.4 billion (US$14.5 million) will be spent on developing substitutes for CFCs, W815.5 billion (US$1 billion) on developing key know-how, and W100 billion (US$127 million) on developing new advanced materials.

THE CORPORATE RESPONSE

With changes in both domestic and international legislation concerning the environment, many South Korean companies face the prospect of developing alternative materials and replacing production facilities in order to escape censure and punitive actions. The Samsung business group has already taken steps to become more environmentally friendly; all companies within the group will stop using CFCs, coal and Bunker-C oil at their production facilities by 1996, and will establish joint disposal sites for industrial waste. The group used more than 3,000 tons of CFCs and produced 530,000 tons of industrial waste in 1991. New buildings will have cooling systems that do not use CFCs, and companies with their own power generating units will switch to LNG from coal and Bunker-C oil.

The concern over the use of CFCs, and the race to develop substitutes, have been prompted by South Korea's signing of the Montreal Protocol which aims to ban the use of CFCs by 1996. This will impact production and exports of products such as air conditioners, humidifiers and aerosol products in which CFCs are used. The Montreal Protocol will impose a limit of 6,000 tons of CFCs in South Korea in 1997 against an estimated demand of 96,000 tons. Levels for 1993 have been set at 10,252 tons of CFCs, a year-on-year drop of 39 per cent, and 2,660 tons for halons, down 50 per cent from the previous year.

Korean companies in sectors such as consumer electronics and automobiles now face choices: to develop their own substitutes for CFCs, use foreign technology and pay royalties, or import the substitutes from advanced nations and pass on the additional cost in higher export prices. The Korea New Chemical Corporation, which was established by Korea General Chemicals and Ulsan Chemicals, is one of a number of companies established recently to develop and mass-produce a substitute by 1994.

THE PUBLIC RESPONSE

Although the level of public awareness of the dangers of pollution and the environmental cost of the nation's economic development and industrialization has generally been low, the phenol resin dumping incident mentioned above caused widespread concern and led to a consumer boycott of goods produced by the business group responsible.

The importance of the 'Three Rs' – reduction, re-use and recycling – is now being stressed, and a variety of campaigns have been launched, including those promoting the recycling of paper, milk cartons and even electrical goods. A major newspaper has spearheaded a 'Don't Waste Wastes' campaign, reminding citizens that today's newspapers are tomorrow's resources (as recycled paper). The company has distributed paper bags for monthly newspaper collections, published booklets on recyclable waste, and sponsored pop music records to raise funds for further campaigns.

36 Financial Infrastructure

The South Korean financial sector comprises a diversified banking system, a wide range of secondary financial institutions, and a securities market.

Over the past three decades, the financial market has been closely controlled by the government, which has exercised tight control over many key areas, including the operations of both domestic and foreign banks, foreign exchange transactions, capital inflows and outflows, the introduction of new financial products, and local and foreign currency funding. As a result, the development of the financial sector has lagged behind that of the economy as a whole, and remains highly regulated and strictly compartmentalized with many institutions structurally weak and unable to compete on an international level. The current state of the financial markets has been cited as one of the greatest weaknesses of the South Korean economy. The chronic shortage of funds and high nominal and real interest rates are now constraining growth, as companies cannot obtain financing for facility investment or R&D. The high interest rates have been a key factor in a number of bankruptcies among small- and medium-sized firms, while the profitability of countless others has been eroded by the burden of debt.

There is a pressing need to reduce government intervention in the markets, guarantee greater autonomy for financial institutions, and allow market forces to determine the most efficient structure. The reform of the sector has, therefore, been identified as one of the most urgent economic tasks facing the nation.

During the process of South Korea's economic development and industrialization, it has generally been the case that available credit has not matched the demand for funds. Bank loans have typically been made available on a preferential basis to companies or sectors which, in the government's view, are vital to the nation's continuing development.

Corporations that are unable to obtain funds from the nation's commercial banks have three options: obtaining funds through direct financing (provided that the stock market is healthy and the government is not restricting listings or rights issues), borrowing from non-banking financial institutions, and borrowing on the curb market (an unofficial market offering and charging higher interest rates than the official market). Raising funds overseas has not been an option for the majority of South Korean corporations; only companies meeting certain strict criteria have been allowed to raise funds through equity-linked security issues in the international markets.

Each major South Korean company is assigned to one domestic commercial bank – its 'prime' bank – which must authorize any loans for which the company applies to other banks, both domestic and foreign. Loans are usually made on the basis of collateral rather than credit worthiness, as there is no authoritative credit rating agency in South Korea.

The ROK government is committed to the gradual liberalization and deregulation of the financial markets and has announced a schedule for the liberalization of the markets (see Table 6), which will be finalized in 1993.

The final stage of the plan will see the full liberalization of interest rates, the removal of credit controls, the opening of the bond market, the deregulation of the money markets, and the liberalization of international capital transactions, including foreign borrowing.

DOMESTIC BANKS

In 1991, there were thirteen nationwide city banks, ten provincial banks and six special banks in addition to the central bank, the Bank of Korea.

A number of new banks have been established since the early 1980s: the Shinhan Bank was set up by South Korean residents in Japan in 1982, and the Koram Bank, a joint venture between South Korean enterprises and the Bank of America, was set up in 1983. In the early 1990s three more new banks were established, with the aim of boosting the regional economies and providing financial support for small- and medium-sized enterprises. These were the Donghwa Bank (established by Koreans originally from the northern part of the peninsula), the Dongnam Bank in Pusan, and the Taedong Bank in Taegu.

In 1991, a number of short-term finance companies were allowed to convert into banks or securities companies; two

TABLE 6 The three-stage financial liberalization plan

Stage 1 1992–3

- Expand certificate of deposit (CD) quota and extend CD maturity
- Treat foreign financial firms in South Korea as residents in stock investment
- Permit foreign securities firms to hedge foreign currency risk against operating capital
- Extend maturity of call money and loans to six months
- Relax underlying documentation requirements for forward currency deals
- Widen the wŏn–dollar fluctuation band to ± 0.8 per cent

Stage 2 1994–6

- Permit foreign banks to install ATMs outside branches
- Ensure regulatory transparency
- Permit foreign brokers to open additional branches
- Permit foreign fund managers to open liaison offices and make equity participation in local investment trust companies
- Lift control foreign exchange position for foreign banks
- Internationalize the wŏn
- Permit Koreans to make overseas portfolio investments

Stage 3 after 1997

- Review pace of interest rate deregulation
- Review mandatory allocation of liquidity control bonds to foreign banks
- Review whether to allow foreign banks and securities companies to set up subsidiaries
- Permit foreigners to invest in bonds
- Decide entry format for foreign fund management companies
- Implement short-term money market development plan
- Permit introduction of foreign commercial loans into South Korea

---

Source: Ministry of Finance.

short-term finance companies formed the Boram Bank, while another established the Hana Bank. (Five other short-term finance companies converted into securities companies.)

In 1992, the Peace Bank was established with paid-in capital of W300 billion (US$381 million); of this, W60 billion (US$76 million) was contributed by the Federation of Korean Trade Unions, W60 billion (US$76 million) by a number of special banks, W30 billion (US$38 million) by the Korean Employers' Federation and other employers, and W150 billion (US$191 million) through public offerings. Although classified as a commercial bank, the Peace Bank will function as a special bank, serving the interests of the South Korean labour force.

The Bank of Korea (BOK), established in 1950, is the sole note issuer within the Republic of Korea. The bank also regulates and supervises all other banks, and has responsibility for government lending and borrowing. In addition, the central bank is a major lender to financial institutions. The bank's monetary and credit policies are formulated by the Monetary Board, whose members include the Minister of Finance and the Governor of the Bank of Korea.

Commercial banks in South Korea include the nationwide city banks, the regional banks, and special banks. Although the commercial banks are now privately owned, the government still exerts considerable influence over their operations through the selection of key personnel and the issuance of guidelines for banking policy:

- The **nationwide city banks** operate branch networks throughout South Korea and overseas, and engage in both short-term and long-term financing business and a variety of other activities permitted by the Monetary Board, including investment in securities and foreign exchange business.

- The **regional banks** have their headquarters in provincial cities and specialize in serving their respective provinces. They are limited to operating just one branch office in the capital. Among the largest of the regional banks are the Bank of Pusan and the Bank of Taegu.

- The **special banks** include state-owned banking institutions established under their own particular statutes, to fulfil specific purposes. These banks are directed and supervised by the government rather than the Monetary Board, and receive some of their funds from the government, the rest coming from public deposits and debenture issues. The special banks engage in commercial banking business and in business activities related to their own specific area. Examples of special banks are the Industrial Bank of Korea, the Small and Medium Industry Bank, the Citizens' National Bank, the Korea Housing Bank, and the National Agricultural Cooperatives Federation. Also in this category are the development institutions: the Korea Development Bank, which supplies long-term credit for major industries and finances economic development; the Export–Import Bank of Korea, established to facilitate trade and external cooperation by providing medium- and long-term credit, underwriting export insurance and supporting overseas investment; and the Korea Long-Term Credit Bank, which offers banking services and medium- and long-term credit to business enterprises.

For more than three decades the role of the nation's banks has been to support the government's policy of promoting rapid economic growth and development. The government has used the state-owned commercial banks as a vehicle to channel cheap credit into strategic and productive sectors. The banks have offered low-interest policy loans to companies meeting certain government-set criteria, and the sectors targeted for development by the government. These policy loans accounted for 23.0 per cent of all loans extended between 1980 and 1990; this compares with 9.2 per cent in Taiwan, 2.4 per cent in Japan, 0.1 per cent in the United States, and 0.04 per cent in the United Kingdom during the same period.

Even after the privatization of the commercial banks in the early 1980s, the government has continued to give 'window guidance' or informal directives to banks in order to direct their policies and operations, and restricts the extension of their branch networks, both at home and overseas. The banks are also still required to offer policy loans, and to underwrite issues of Monetary Stabilization Bonds (MSBs), in line with the government's monetary policies.

While the government's development policies did result in spectacular economic growth, they also led to a distortion of the financial markets and rendered the nation's banks financially weak and uncompetitive. Safe in the knowledge that the government would not allow them to fail, the banks focused on working for the government rather than on boosting their profitability and enhancing their competitiveness. The policies also resulted in the commercial banks being saddled with non-performing assets in excess of W2 trillion (US$2.5 billion) – a result of providing loans to strategic industries in the 1970s and

1980s – and bad debts estimated at W2.1 trillion (US$2.7 billion) in 1991.

The banks remain heavily reliant on interest-bearing business such as loans and deposits, rather than fee-bearing business such as trade financing, foreign exchange transactions and securities. The banks have suffered from a lack of autonomy in managing their daily business activities and developing new financial products, but have also been accused of lacking imagination and initiative, and failing to develop many modern and sophisticated financial products and services which are available in other developing countries.

In a country with a savings rate in excess of 30 per cent, the banks have been experiencing increasing difficulty in attracting funds. The establishment of a number of new banks in the mid-1980s and early 1990s has forced competition among banking institutions. The old-established commercial banks, which previously enjoyed an oligopoly, now have to compete to survive – both with the new domestic banks, with their different management styles and greater freedom in setting deposit and loan rates, and with foreign banks, with their advanced know-how and wider range of products and services.

Savings have flowed to foreign banks and non-banking financial institutions (which are not as tightly regulated as regards the setting of interest rates) or into other investment vehicles. With the government controlling the supply of credit, companies unable to secure domestic bank loans likewise turn to foreign banks or alternative methods of financing, such as the curb market (see above). In 1991, the banks' share of the deposit market was 34.1 per cent, down from 34.3 per cent in 1990. Their share of the loan market also dropped, to 44.1 per cent from 45.6 per cent.

South Korean banks are being forced to change their role from one of government policy vehicle to one of global competitor, a transformation made much harder by the fact that they have not had to compete with anyone for the past three decades. In order to bring their competitiveness up to international standards, the banks have to undertake basic reforms in management, enhance their profitability, reduce their operating expenses, and streamline their operations by cutting manpower and closing non-performing branches.

Recently, banking institutions have been moving into new areas such as credit cards, the trust business, factoring, negotiable certificates of deposit, and high-yield deposit schemes for individual households, in order to increase their competitiveness *vis-à-vis* non-banking financial institutions and to meet the growing need for more diversified financial services.

In February 1991, the Five-Year Bank Reform Plan was

implemented to run through 1995. Local banks are making efforts to reduce their operating costs, trim manpower, enhance branch office management and increase computerization of banking operations. Since the implementation of the plan, the Office of Bank Supervision (OBS) has monitored the banks' progress towards the set goals, and awards grades accordingly. The grades are crucial for the banks when seeking loans from the central bank or an expansion of their branch networks.

Although South Korea is not currently a member of the Bank for International Settlements (BIS), there are plans to implement the bank's capital adequacy ratio standard in South Korea. The standard requires that member banks maintain a capital adequacy ratio (capital to risk-weighted assets) of at least 8 per cent, in order to be able to resolve international settlements.

South Korean banks with a capital adequacy ratio of less than 8 per cent will find it difficult to operate in BIS-member countries. The South Korean banks' average ratio has shown steady improvement in the last few years, rising from 6.6 per cent in 1990 to 10.5 per cent in June 1991, with only two banks falling below the 8 per cent level. Banks which fail to meet the requirement from 1994 onwards will face operating restrictions (such as on the opening of new branches) and will be required to increase their capital and/or reduce their risk-weighted assets.

FOREIGN BANKS

The history of foreign banks in the Republic of Korea goes back to the late 1960s, when Chase Manhattan, Citibank and the Bank of Tokyo opened branch offices in Seoul. By the end of 1991, there were 70 foreign bank branch offices and 24 representative offices in South Korea. (Branch offices are allowed to engage in a far broader range of activities than are representative offices.) The foreign banks provide financing to both multinational and Korean customers, and banking services to expatriates.

In the 1960s and 1970s, various privileges and incentives were offered to attract investment in South Korea by foreign banks, with the aim of mobilizing foreign capital to finance the nation's economic expansion. However, the privileges and incentives once offered to foreign banks are now slowly being phased out, at the same time as the regulations governing the operations of foreign banks are being eased.

'Swap' activities, in which foreign currency is traded for wŏn at the central bank on a fee-paying basis, have historically been a major source of local currency funding for foreign banks.

This preferential facility is now gradually being reduced, and the exclusion from policy loans previously enjoyed by foreign banks is being phased out. Moreover, foreign banking institutions are now required to underwrite Monetary Stabilization (liquidity control) Bonds, in common with their South Korean counterparts.

On the positive side, new sources of funding are being made available to foreign banks, such as the issuance of negotiable certificates of deposit (CDs), up to a specified limit of each bank's net worth. (CDs are short-term money market instruments, which are issued by banks to generate operating funds.) In addition, foreign banks are now allowed to use the Bank of Korea's rediscount facilities, and to operate in the trust business. The ban on the purchase of real estate by foreign banks has been eased, allowing major banks to buy their own buildings in Seoul.

The status of foreign banks in South Korea was greatly enhanced as a result of the ROK–US financial policy talks in the early 1990s. As a result of these talks, the South Korean authorities agreed to enhance the transparency of regulations pertaining to the supervision of banks, and to establish a channel of communication between the central banks and foreign banks to help avoid misunderstandings.

The meetings also resulted in an agreement that foreign and local banks should be subject to the same criteria and procedures for establishing networks of branch offices, and that foreign banks should be allowed to become members of the Korea Financial Telecommunications and Clearing Institute. Members of the KFTCI have access to electronic money transfer networks, such as automated teller machines and Giro accounts.

It was also agreed that the ceiling on foreign banks' in-country capital would be lifted, thus ensuring increased access to local currency funding. The limits on the issue of CDs would be raised, and foreign banks would be allowed to participate fully in the trust business. Foreign banks would be allowed to operate ATMs on a 24-hour basis, and install them outside their branches from July 1993. The regulations concerning the requirement for underlying documentation for spot and forward exchange transactions were also eased. (The requirement calls for documents proving the need for the transaction to be produced before it can be carried out.)

By implementing these measures, the South Korean authorities believed that they had dealt with the issue of national treatment for foreign banks. They had levelled the playing field for them and opened up the opportunities available to local institutions.

In fact, the authorities soon came under fire from local banks which claimed that, in certain respects, *they* are now discriminated against. Foreign banks have not been subject to the central bank's 'window guidance', they are less regulated in terms of setting interest rates, and they are not, in general, governed by direct credit controls and policy loan guidelines. Even though foreign banks are required to lend 25 per cent of their incremental lending funds to small- and medium-sized enterprises, this proportion is lower than the 35 per cent required of local banks.

The foreign banks' exemption from these regulations is cited by local banks as one of the reasons for their competitors' higher profitability. In fiscal year 1991, the average return on assets for the foreign banks was 1.08 per cent, compared with an average of 0.83 per cent for the top ten domestic banks, and 0.99 per cent for the top twenty banks. In the same year, the foreign banks' net profits increased by 36.9 per cent year on year; the average rate of increase for local banks was 12.0 per cent. Other reasons cited include the foreign banks' expertise in the lucrative foreign exchange business, and their cost-reduction programmes. Although the foreign banks' share of the domestic loan market is small (6 per cent in the year to March 1992), their presence is expected to expand with increasing liberalization and the growing use of hedging techniques for risk management and derivative products.

For their part, foreign bankers still maintain that access to local currency funds is quite limited. Even though foreign banks can now, in theory, establish nationwide networks of branch offices to match those of their domestic counterparts, in practice it is still difficult to do so. Whereas local banks may open branch offices without providing incremental capital, foreign banks must provide an additional W3 billion (US$3.8 million) for each new branch office opened, making the establishment of a nationwide network very costly. Without these networks, foreign banks will find it difficult to match the lending and funding capacity of local banks, and will have to raise funds by issuing CDs, or by purchasing funds in the inter-bank market.

NON-BANKING FINANCIAL INSTITUTIONS

Non-banking financial institutions include merchant banks, short-term finance companies, insurance companies, leasing companies and venture capital companies.

In 1991, there were six **merchant banks** operating in South Korea, all of which were joint ventures. These institutions, which were established to meet the demand from enterprises for a wide range of banking and financial services, engage in short-term local currency financing, short- and medium-term foreign currency loans, leasing, and capital markets transactions. The merchant banks enjoy a high degree of freedom in raising and utilizing their funds.

In early 1992, the Ministry of Finance (MOF) announced its plans to allow the establishment of two or three more joint venture merchant banks. However, criticism from the opposition parties and the media, and accusations that the MOF had offered licences to pre-selected conglomerates in return for funds for the ruling party's presidential campaign, forced the ministry to postpone the plan until after the elections.

Short-term finance companies were established in 1972 in order to develop the money markets and attract funds which would otherwise have flowed into the curb market (see above). The curb market had grown rapidly in the 1960s as the demand for funds exceeded supply; many of the companies which had been forced to borrow at high rates from it had subsequently suffered severe financial problems.

The short-term finance companies offer a variety of financial services to both industrial companies and private households. The fact that they are not subject to government restrictions on interest rates or business activities has enabled them to enter into direct competition with the banks, offering higher rates for deposits and a wider variety of financial services.

By the early 1990s there were concerns that the success of these companies was contributing to the downturn in the banks' performance. As part of its policy of restructuring and liberalizing the financial services industry, and also in a move to eliminate this excessive competition, the government implemented the Merger and Conversion of Financial Institutions Law in 1991. Under the provisions of this law, short-term finance companies were allowed to convert into banks or securities companies.

In 1991, the South Korean **insurance** market was the ninth largest in the world, with premium income amounting to W24.1 trillion (US$30.6 billion). The South Korean market ranked second in the world in terms of per capita premium income, which stood at W500,000 (US$635).

There are currently 30 life and 13 non-life insurance companies active in South Korea; the two areas are strictly separated, with life insurance companies prohibited from selling non-life products and vice versa. The life insurance sector is by far the larger – 80.4 per cent of the market in 1991 – and had a sixth-place world ranking in 1991. The non-life insurance sector ranked sixteenth in the world that year. In 1991, the combined assets of all the life and non-life insurance companies amounted to W44.7 trillion (US$56.8 billion).

In October 1991, a survey revealed that 37.8 per cent of the population had life insurance policies; this compares with a rate of more than 80 per cent in Japan at the same time. The average number of policies household was 1.4 in South Korea and 3.2 in Japan.

Among the policy-holders, 47 per cent said that they had taken out the policy to protect the family in case of death or injury. A further 39 per cent took out policies to finance their children's education and marriage, and 32 per cent took out insurance for their old age. (Some gave more than one reason for joining an insurance scheme.) Those with no policy commonly said that they had found non-insurance savings plans which gave a higher return than that available through insurance schemes. For many South Koreans, the high premiums demanded by local insurers are a powerful disincentive to take out cover.

For decades, the insurance sector has enjoyed government protection, enabling domestic insurers to focus on quantitative rather than qualitative growth. In the seller's market that has operated in South Korea there has been little incentive to develop new and competitive insurance products. However, the introduction of an insurance brokerage system and the opening of the insurance market to foreign companies will place South Korean companies in direct competition with foreign companies which can offer a wide variety of products.

In 1991, there were fourteen foreign companies with branch offices in South Korea, including six joint ventures; major players include: the Life Insurance Company of North America, the American Life Insurance Company, Nationale-Nederlanden (affiliated to the Georgia Life Insurance Company), and Prudential Korea. Although the foreign firms currently hold only a tiny market share – less than 2 per cent in 1991–2 – their performance showed steady improvement in the year to March 1992, in terms of policies sold, premiums received and assets held.

Foreign companies have found difficulties in carving a niche for themselves in the South Korean market. Some attribute this to cultural differences, such as the use by South Korean companies of personal connections to target customers, and the fact that South Koreans favour savings-oriented insurance schemes over protection-oriented schemes.

The Long-Term Insurance Development Plan, formulated by the Insurance Supervisory Board, aims to improve the competitiveness of domestic insurance companies while protecting the interest of policy-holders and allowing greater access for foreign firms. The plan calls for the deregulation of premium rates by the year 2000, and the abolition of inter-insurer agreements on the determination and collection of premiums.

There is currently no insurance brokerage system in South Korea; agents are tied to one company. However, a double agency system will be introduced in 1993–4, allowing agents to deal with the products of two insurers. A multiple agency system will be introduced in 1996–7, with agents permitted to handle three or more companies' products, and an insurance brokerage system may be introduced in the longer term. From 1993, cross-border trade for export marine cargo insurance will be liberalized, enabling South Korean exporters to buy insurance policies direct from insurers operating overseas. Cross-border trade on import marine cargo and aviation insurance will be liberalized in 1995.

The reinsurance market, in which the Korea Reinsurance Corporation currently enjoys a virtual monopoly, is scheduled to be deregulated on a gradual basis. The aviation and hull reinsurance sectors will be opened to foreign companies in 1993 and 1996 respectively, and all reinsurance products will be liberalized by 1998.

Foreign companies which meet certain criteria will be permitted to become full members of the Life and Non-Life Insurance Association. They will also be allowed to sell car insurance from 1993, provided that they have a nationwide claim service network in South Korea, or maintain a cooperative agreement with a domestic company having such a network.

The disclosure system will be strengthened, requiring insurers to make public information pertaining to dividends on premiums paid, premium refunding on policy surrender, etc. There are also plans to establish an Insurance Management Information Centre by 1994.

Domestic insurance companies will encouraged to develop new products, such as geriatric disease insurance and pollution insurance, and train actuaries and other specialists. New products already being offered in the market reflect changing lifestyles in South Korea: it is now possible to buy insurance against injuries suffered at health clubs; weekend insurance for fishermen, golfers and skiers; and even, as South Korea enters the satellite age, indemnity against a failed satellite launch or damage inflicted during the launch or in orbit.

Insurance companies will also be encouraged to change their marketing style from a soliciting system, based on the personal contacts of housewives and other part-time workers, to a professional salesforce with a more detailed knowledge of marketing. Some have already trained professional salespeople, called life planners or financial planners, who supply potential customers with information on both insurance products and investment instruments.

At US$10 billion, the South Korean **leasing** market was the second largest in Asia and the eighth largest in the world in 1991. Leasing was introduced to South Korea in 1972 in an effort to ease the financial burden of facility investment for domestic enterprises. The establishment of leasing companies would also, it was hoped, boost the domestic machinery industry by stimulating local demand. Although the industry has since expanded at an average annual rate of 60 per cent, scarcity of funds has been a perennial problem, and leasing companies remain heavily dependent on foreign borrowings. Leasing companies have been allowed to issue debentures since 1982.

In 1991, there were 34 companies engaged in full- or part-time leasing activities in South Korea, of which 6 were joint ventures. The main focus of the leasing companies' activities is the nation's small- and medium-sized enterprises, particularly those in the manufacturing sector.

In 1991, there were 53 **venture capital companies** in South Korea. These companies specialize in investing in and providing short-term, direct bridge financing for start-up businesses (both domestic and foreign) and enterprises in the early stages of development. The venture capital companies raise funds through the issue of bonds and the formation of venture investment partnerships; they are assisted by the government-run Start-Up Promotion Fund, which invests in and makes loans to venture capital companies and makes contributions to venture investment partnerships. In 1992, the fund stood at W100 billion (US$127 million).

THE LIBERALIZATION AND DEREGULATION OF THE FINANCIAL MARKETS

Although the liberalization of the financial sector is seen by the ROK government as an important element in the process of overall economic liberalization, it is also viewed as something that must be undertaken with extreme caution and with regard for its possible impact on the economy as a whole. This contrasts with the view put forward by some of South Korea's trading partners, that the country's economic situation will not improve until financial reforms are carried out.

The process of liberalization, which began in the 1980s, has accelerated in the early 1990s, due in large part to pressure from advanced nations in general and the United States in particular. In early 1992, the ROK government announced that it would draft a three-stage, medium- to long-term **financial liberalization** plan by the end of the year, covering the foreign exchange, capital and money markets, and the banking sector (see Table 6 above).

A four-phase **interest rate deregulation** plan was unveiled in August 1991. This was the second attempt to liberalize rates; previous efforts in 1988 were quickly abandoned as rates rose sharply following liberalization. The new plan calls for the liberalization of interest rates in four phases over a period of five years, with the liberalization of deposit rates proceeding more slowly than that of loan rates. The liberalization is to be undertaken on a step-by-step basis to mitigate possible negative effects on the economy.

Under the first phase, implemented in late 1991, only 10 per cent of bank deposit and loan rates were affected, along with 25 per cent of loan rates and 45 per cent of deposit rates at non-banking financial institutions. Although the second phase of interest rate liberalization has been postponed until 1993, the remainder of the nation's loan and deposit rates are due to be liberalized by 1997.

Even after the implementation of the first phase, there was little variety among the rates set by the older, well-established commercial banks on the liberalized accounts. This 'constructive cooperation' aimed to avoid cut-throat competition. However, the newer banks, which had been converted from short-term finance companies, and were therefore more used to competition and going for profits, were more daring. The more aggressive attitude of the newer banks and the foreign banks in setting rates should eventually break the interest rate cartel.

Although many foreign banks maintain that the rate of liberalization is too slow, the ROK government fears that overhasty deregulation could lead to the collapse of the nation's financial institutions. The government must also be aware, however, that too slow a pace could result in economic stagnation.

Key issues in the liberalization of the **foreign exchange** markets are the change to a 'negative system' for foreign exchange transactions, the widening of the daily fluctuation band for exchange rates, the easing of documentation requirements for foreign exchange dealings, and a reform of the foreign exchange concentration system.

The Foreign Exchange Control Act was revised in December 1991 – the first revision of the law in thirty years – to effect a change from a positive system (under which all transactions were prohibited unless expressly permitted by law) to a negative system (under which all are permitted unless expressly prohibited). Transactions subject to government approval and procedures for obtaining approval would be clearly defined, and approval would normally be given within 60 days.

In July 1992, the daily wŏn–dollar exchange rate fluctuation range was widened to 0.8 per cent of the previous day's average market rate, from the previous level of 0.6 per cent. The authorities will continue to widen the range ahead of the eventual adoption of a free floating currency *vis-à-vis* the US dollar.

In September of that year, forward exchange transactions up to the value of US$1 million were liberalized, and documentation requirements for local companies making foreign exchange deposits at domestic and foreign banks were relaxed. Although the concentration of foreign exchange has been eased to some extent, allowing banks and trading companies to hold larger amounts of foreign exchange at their own discretion, residents of South Korea are still not allowed to buy, sell or hold foreign currency freely. Similarly, the amount of money that can freely be brought into the country by foreigners is limited, and amounts in excess of the notified limit must be registered with the authorities.

Companies no longer have to seek approval for overseas investments of less than US$5 million, and financial institutions are permitted to make portfolio investments of up to US$100 million in financial markets overseas. The amount of money which Koreans travelling overseas can take with them, while still restricted, is being increased, as is the amount of money which can be sent to family members studying overseas.

However, the inflow of capital is still restricted, due to fears of an inflow of 'hot money', brought in to capitalize on South Korea's high interest rates. In principle, all incoming foreign exchange (cheques, traveller's cheques, cash or bank transfers) must be surrendered to the central bank or an authorized agent, such as a foreign exchange bank or hotel.

THE STOCK MARKET

Over the past three decades, the stock market has been a relatively minor source of financing for South Korean companies, which have tended to rely on loans from banks and non-banking financial institutions rather than on direct financing. This has resulted in notoriously high levels of debt among South Korean corporations; in 1991, the average debt-to-equity ratio for companies in the manufacturing sector was 239 per cent; the average for subsidiaries of the top thirty conglomerates was more than 400 per cent.

In 1991, the securities markets provided W15.4 trillion (US$19.6 billion) to South Korean corporations; a total of W2.7 trillion (US$3.4 billion) was raised in the equity market, whereas W12.7 trillion (US$16.1 billion) was raised through bond issues.

The government has been torn between encouraging companies to raise funds through the stock market and thus reduce their reliance on bank debt, and limiting the supply of new stocks when the market is performing badly. It has therefore alternated between encouraging companies to go public (often encountering considerable resistance from owners who fear a dilution of their control) and restricting the number of listings and rights issues.

The Korea Stock Exchange

The Korea Stock Exchange (KSE), which opened in 1956, is the only stock exchange in South Korea, and has a single trading floor located in Seoul. The KSE is a non-profit-making organization, whose shares are wholly owned by the nation's securities companies. The market is regulated by the Korea Securities Exchange Commission (KSEC) within the provisions of the Securities and Exchange Act of 1962. The Minister of Finance has the authority to impose additional restrictions on the market when these are deemed to be in the public interest.

The KSE has two sections; new listings are automatically assigned to the Second Section, where they remain for at least one year. The KSE conducts an annual review of the listed companies and determines the section assignment for each company on the basis of a number of factors, including trading, volume, dividends and return on capital stock. There is also a small over the counter (OTC) market operating for stocks not listed on the KSE. The OTC market prepares unseasoned companies for listing, and helps to obtain finance for medium-sized companies which are not eligible for listing on the KSE.

The stock exchange holds a morning session (09.40–11.40) and an afternoon session (13.20–15.20) from Monday to Friday, and a morning session on Saturdays. The market is closed on national holidays and at the end of the year (27–31 December).

Shares are traded on the KSE through securities companies which act as brokers and buy and sell as principals. Maximum and minimum commission rates are determined by the KSE and the KSEC. Shares in both sections can be purchased with cash; shares in the First Section can also be bought through margin transactions. (Margin requirements are set by the KSEC.)

Two indexes are published daily: the Korea Composite Stock Price Index (KOSPI) and the newer Revised Stock Price Average, which was introduced in 1992 in order more to reflect accurately the price movements of small- and medium-capital companies.

The KSE imposes limits on the movement of stock prices

in order to limit volatility. The daily stock price fluctuation limit currently stands at around 6 per cent of the previous day's closing price. The KSE also has the power temporarily to stop trading in order to protect the interests of the investors – for example, when there is an abrupt price movement during trading due to a rumour – or to ensure the widest possible dissemination of an important and relevant piece of corporate news.

In 1989, the year in which the Stock Price Index peaked at 1,007.77, market capitalization was W95.5 trillion (US$121.4 billion) and the share-holder population was 19 million. In that year, market capitalization was 79.8 per cent of GNP. At the end of 1991, market capitalization had shrunk to W73.1 trillion (US$92.9 billion), and the share-holder population had shrunk to 5.1 million. Market capitalization was 51.6 per cent of GNP.

In 1991, a total of 686 companies were listed on the KSE – 481 in the First Section and 205 in the Second Section. During the year, the exchange recorded an average daily volume of 14 million shares. In terms of both the number of listed companies and size of market capitalization, the South Korean market was second only to Japan among the Asian stock markets.

The recent history of the stock market

The 1980s saw a spectacular performance by the South Korean stock market. In the early 1980s, attempts to curb speculation in real estate resulted in an increase in funds flowing into the stock market, and towards the end of the decade, the market's performance was boosted by the economic boom, ample liquidity, democratic reforms, and the successful hosting of the Olympics. KOSPI soared to 1,007.77 in April 1989 from 279.67 at the end of 1986.

However, the stock market entered a prolonged slump as the economy began to show signs of slowing down. Market sentiment was depressed by poor economic prospects, political uncertainty, an oversupply of stock resulting from the government's promotion of supply-driven growth, and tighter monetary conditions which restricted investment activities. By the summer of 1992, the index had slumped to below 500.

The government has always exercised considerable influence over the growth and development of the equity markets. The result of the government's intervention has been a popular expectation that the authorities will not allow the index to fall too far in a bear market, to the extent that investors angered by falling prices will demonstrate and call on the government to take action to support the market.

Ironically, the more that the government intervenes to no effect, the lower both investor confidence and the index fall, and the louder the cries for official action become.

The slump in the late 1980s prompted the government to order certain financial institutions to invest heavily in an attempt to support the market with funds borrowed from the banks. The continuing fall in the index and the high interest rates on the bank loans brought three investment trust companies to the brink of bankruptcy. (Their combined losses amounted to W500 billion or US$635 million in 1991, while their total debts stood at more than W5 trillion or US$6.4 billion.) Their near-collapse necessitated a government bailout to the tune of almost W3 trillion (US$3.8 billion), and panicked investors into leaving the market.

Despite statements that there would be no further intervention in the market, the political consequences of a market crash ahead of the 1992 presidential elections prompted further action in the months before the December vote. In late August 1992, a W4 trillion (US$5.1 billion) aid package was announced, under the provisions of which both local and foreign financial institutions were required to buy stocks or contribute to the Stock Market Stabilization Fund. At the time, many analysts expressed concern that the package would save the stock market only at the expense of the financial sector.

Further government directives to institutional investors to remain net share buyers until the market recovered, and restrictions on the supply of new stocks, gave the market the boost it needed. By the end of the year, the index had recovered to around the 680 level from the low of 460 seen in August.

The liberalization of the stock market
The spectacular growth of the South Korean stock market in the 1980s inevitably led to foreign pressure upon the ROK authorities to open the market to foreign investors. Following the announcement of the Capital Markets Liberalization Plan in 1981, access for foreign investors was gradually increased, leading to a limited opening of the market in January 1992. At the same time, restrictions on investment by South Korean individuals and institutions in international markets have gradually been eased.

Until the early 1990s, foreign participation in the South Korean stock market was limited to a number of indirect investment vehicles. Between 1981 and 1991, international funds were established to allow indirect access to the South Korean market, by marketing units to non-resident investors. These included the Korea Fund Inc. (1984), the Korea–Europe Fund Ltd (1987) and the Korea Asia Fund (1991).

A limited number of South Korean corporations were allowed to raise funds in international markets through the issue of equity-linked securities, such as convertible bonds (CBs), bonds with warrants (BWs) and depositary receipts (DRs). In 1991, there were twenty such issues, which raised an aggregate principal amount of US$1.1 billion. In addition, a number of matching funds were made available to both South Korean and foreign investors in the early 1990s, which purchase both Korean and foreign securities.

Beginning in 1987, certain domestic financial institutions were allowed to make limited investments in overseas markets, as part of the government's plan to raise the institutions' international experience and enhance their competitiveness ahead of the full opening of the South Korean capital markets. Foreign securities companies established representative offices in Seoul, carrying out research and marketing activities in preparation for the market opening. Foreigners who had been resident in the Republic for more than six months were allowed to make direct investments in the stock market.

The fact that the government had made the execution of the liberalization timetable conditional on the fulfilment of certain economic goals and policies prompted a great deal of scepticism over whether liberalization would, in fact, go ahead as planned. However, in January 1990, the ROK government allowed foreigners to trade stocks converted from securities issued overseas in the OTC market, and foreign investors were subsequently permitted to reinvest in the stock market the proceeds from the sale of stocks acquired through conversion.

In September 1991, the ROK government published its 'Guidelines for the Opening of the Korean Stock Market', paving the way for the opening of what had been the largest closed stock market in the world. The opening was to be gradual, beginning in January 1992, with an initial limit of a 10 per cent aggregate foreign position in any class of shares for a single corporation, and a 3 per cent limit on holdings in a Korean company by any one individual. (Investment in 'sensitive' areas, such as utilities, transportation and communications, would be limited to 8 per cent.) Holdings by foreigners resident in the Republic of Korea, the various country funds, and stocks convertible from overseas issues were to be included in the limits.

Although, in principle, all transactions would be conducted through the KSE, foreign investors would be allowed to trade a company's shares through a securities company on the OTC market, once the company's aggregate foreign investment limit had been reached or exceeded, to prevent the development of an unregulated offshore market.

The market would be open to investment by foreign corporations and foreign individuals (defined as persons with permanent residence outside the Republic, including South Korean nationals overseas), who would have to obtain an ID card and a registration card. For this, they would be obliged to use their real names, a condition that does not apply to South Korean investors. This would enable the authorities to monitor the inflow and outflow of funds, and enforce the investment limits. Foreign investors would also be legally obliged to appoint a standing proxy and a custodian within the Republic. Foreign investors would not be allowed to trade on margin or engage in short selling, and foreign individuals would be required to make a good faith deposit equivalent to 40 per cent of the contract amount prior to placing a buy order.

After the market opening in January 1992, the foreign stock ownership limit was raised to 25 per cent for companies which had issued equity-related securities such as CBs and BWs overseas and for joint venture companies with foreign equity investment. The move aimed to give greater access to big-name stocks such as Samsung Electronics, Hyundai Motor and Goldstar, which are better known internationally and account for a larger portion of the stock market index.

In May 1992, the government announced that foreign investment would be permitted in the Korea Electric Power Corporation (KEPCO) and P'ohang Iron and Steel Company (POSCO), up to an 8 per cent aggregate and 1 per cent individual limit. Prior to this announcement, foreign investment in KEPCO and POSCO had been prohibited.

However, it is fair to say that the reasoning for the changes was based on the erroneous assumption that foreign investors would automatically target blue-chip companies for investment. In fact, the investment strategy of many foreign individuals and institutions focused more on small, less well-known stocks with growth potential than on the South Korean blue-chips.

The investor pool has also been gradually widened since the market opened to include foreign governments and pension funds, and the three offshore investment funds, which are allowed to invest up to a specified limit. In March 1992, the government announced that branches of foreign financial institutions which had been operational in South Korea for more than one year would be afforded the same treatment as domestic institutions, in terms of trading in stocks and bonds. The most important result of this was the waiving of the investment limits for these institutions.

Issued raised during the early days of direct investment

included taxation, proxy nomination, repatriation of funds, foreign exchange risks, and the availability of information in general and real-time information in particular.

Investors whose home country does not have a tax treaty with South Korea, including the Japanese, the Germans and residents of Hong Kong, must pay a capital gains tax equivalent to 26.875 per cent of their gains. The requirement that foreign investors nominate a securities company as proxy has excluded from the market certain institutional investors, such as Employee Retirement Income Security Act (ERISA)-regulated American pension funds, which are legally prevented from entering into standing agreements with securities companies.

Although foreign individuals are required to make a good faith deposit, there was no provision for the repatriation of unused deposits, and investors were therefore exposed to currency fluctuation risks. Investors also faced currency risks due to the lag between the placing and settlement of orders. Overseas investors complained about the quality of corporate accounting standards, the level of public disclosure, and the lack of real-time information on which to base their investment decisions.

In response to these concerns, the government permitted the repatriation of unused deposits, and allowed securities firms to enter into forward exchange rate contracts on behalf of their clients in order to reduce the risk of foreign exchange fluctuations. Flexible settlement deadlines are permitted for foreign investors, to allow for national holidays, etc., giving foreigners a few extra days to settle their accounts; South Korean investors who fail to meet the settlement deadline face a mandatory clearing of the account. The government plans to allow certain foreign press and/or news agencies to supply real-time information (including prices) to investors overseas, and will also tighten the requirements for corporate disclosure of information.

Although many expected the opening to breathe life into the flagging market, this optimism proved unfounded in the early stages. Equally, the prophets of doom who forecast a 'wall of Japanese money' entering the market, and a rash of foreign takeovers, appeared to have misjudged the attractions of their home market.

After the market opened, the index sank lower and lower throughout 1992, and after some initial interest, foreign investors adopted a wait-and-see attitude towards the market. As it weakened through the summer, the ROK authorities implemented measures to increase foreign investment (see above). The stock market rally in the autumn of 1992 and the increase in foreign investment which accompanied it triggered fears of 'hot money' flowing into South Korea. Whereas at the beginning of the year, foreign investors were looked on as potential saviours of a bearish market, they were now thought of as speculators looking to make a quick killing.

By the end of October in the first year of direct investment, foreign investment accounted for just 3 per cent of the market in terms of shares traded (184.8 million shares). The total value of shares traded was W3.3 trillion (US$4.2 billion), equivalent to 4.3 per cent of market capitalization.

In the medium to long term, the opening of the market will bring benefits to South Korean brokers and investors alike. South Korean securities companies will learn from their foreign partners and competitors, and there are already signs that investment practices are being affected by exposure to foreign investment strategies.

For a long time the South Korean market has had the reputation of being a speculative and theme-driven market in which investors focused more on rumours than a fundamentals. Thus, a news report of a breakthrough in North–South Korean relations could trigger a buying spree in the shares of companies that might be involved in trading with or investment in North Korea, regardless of the fundamentals of those companies.

A survey of investment practices conducted in the summer of 1992 revealed that more than half of the investors polled made their decision to invest on the basis of 'the possibility of an upward price movement', while only 17 per cent considered a company's fundamentals. Furthermore, the market was, in the past, regarded as a place to gamble in order to turn a quick profit, and as one could be manipulated by the major players or 'Big Hands'.

The approach adopted by many foreigners – the careful study of fundamentals and search for companies with low price–earnings ratio, low debt ratios and high growth potential – has given South Korean investors food for thought. Some analysts believe that in time this will result in a more rational and realistic approach to investment. The focus among foreign investors on smaller companies should please the ROK government, which is actively trying to promote the interests of small- and medium-sized enterprises.

The future development of the market

Although the stock market has experienced significant growth in terms of size and profit levels, in many respects it remains less developed than markets in advanced industrial nations. In response to this, medium- to long-term plans for the development of the securities industry include the strengthening of regulations (particularly those governing insider trading and the public disclosure of information), the increasing of levels of computerization within the industry, and introduction of derivative products such as futures and options.

One of the concerns expressed by foreign investors relates to the **transparency of regulations**: the ROK government has assured them that regulations will be gradually simplified and clarified. A major piece of legislation affecting foreign investors but not applied to South Koreans is that requiring registration under the investor's real name.

Attempts to implement the real-name system for financial transactions (including securities and real estate) in South Korea have so far proved unsuccessful. Although the proportion of investment transactions carried out under an alias is small – estimated at 3.5 per cent of total investment in August 1992 – fears remain that the implementation of a real-name system would lead to a substantial withdrawal of funds from the market.

The government is taking steps to counter **insider trading**, including monitoring trading activities to identify unusual patterns in price movement and trading volume. Those found guilty of insider trading will now face a three-year prison sentence, or a fine of up to W20 million (US$25,400) or three times the profits made. Officials, employees and major shareholders who sell shares in their company within six months of purchase must hand over the profits to the company, regardless of whether or not insider trading was involved. Foreign securities companies punished at home for violating insider trading laws will be stripped of their licence to do business in South Korea.

The plan to **computerize** KSE transactions was implemented in 1975; two years later the Korea Securities Computer Corporation (KOSCOM) was established as an electronic data-processing centre for the exclusive use of the securities industry. Within the KSE, the Stock Market Automated Trading System (SMATS) receives and sorts orders, and automatically matches them. SMATS currently handles 95 per cent of total daily trading volume. Market information service systems are becoming widely available, offering news reports, market and corporate information, and financial and economic indicators to terminals nationwide.

There are currently plans to establish a **futures exchange** by the mid-1990s, in order to reduce the financial risks associated with international business, such as currency movements and fluctuations in prices of raw materials. However, there is some debate as to whether a single exchange should be established or separate exchanges for commodity and financial futures.

Commodity futures were introduced to South Korea in 1974, following the first oil shock. In 1986, the value of futures transactions was just US$195 million, equivalent to 2.3 per cent of total imports that year. Just five years later in 1991, the value had increased to US$2.5 billion (11.3 per cent of total imports) and is forecast to rise even faster through the mid-1990s, reaching US$7.3 billion (13.1 per cent of total imports) by 1996. A total of ten companies (including four foreign firms) currently trade futures, the majority of the goods being agricultural products and raw materials.

A financial futures exchange would trade stock, foreign exchange, and financial futures products, to provide investors with the opportunity to hedge their risks in the face of liberalized interest and exchange rates. Some fear, however, that the establishment of such an exchange would give experienced and knowledgeable foreigners the opportunity to make a killing, and that it would become a gambling house for the wealthy. The establishment of a financial futures exchange presupposes the implementation of a number of reforms including the introduction of a real-name system for financial transactions, the deregulation of foreign exchange transactions, and the full liberalization of interest rates.

THE SECURITIES COMPANIES

In 1991, there were 31 domestic securities companies registered in South Korea, of which 19 were licensed to operate offices overseas. The securities business is divided into three areas – dealing, brokerage and underwriting. Applicants for a licence must meet a minimum capital requirement, which varies according to the scope of business to be undertaken. In addition, only securities companies with capital in excess of W20 billion (US$25.4 million) may engage in international business.

The total of 31 companies comprises 25 established securities companies and 6 relative newcomers, 5 of which came into being in 1991, following the government's decision to allow short-term finance companies to convert into banks or securities companies. The government also gave permission for the state-run Korea Development Bank to set up a securities arm, thus creating one of the few government-owned securities companies in the world, Korea Development Securities.

In 1991, the securities companies found themselves in a worsening position, with falling revenues and a stagnant market. During that year, their combined losses totalled more than W136 billion (US$173 million), compared with a combined profit of W23.5 billion (US$29.9 million) in 1990.

Rising interest payments, increasing operating expenses, and losses and bond transactions were also blamed for the poor performance.

In addition to worsening conditions in the domestic market, local brokerage houses face increasing competition from foreign securities houses, whose scope of operations is expanding with the liberalization of the capital markets. Although they will enjoy the advantage of being the local brokers in the short term, investors seeking more sophisticated products and services may well turn to the foreign competition if domestic firms are unable to come up with the goods.

By the end of 1992, 27 foreign securities companies had established representative offices in Seoul, and 10 foreign brokerage houses had received permission to establish branch offices in Seoul, including Merrill Lynch of the United States, Baring Brothers of the United Kingdom, and Jardine Fleming of Hong Kong. There was also one joint venture securities company.

Membership of the KSE is open to all securities companies which meet specified criteria. Both regular and annual memberships are available, the latter being offered to ease the financial burden of taking out a membership. (In 1991 the annual membership was W2.2 billion or US$2.8 million, compared with W9.7 billion or US$12.3 million for regular membership.) Annual membership can be converted to regular by making an application to the KSE. Foreign securities companies may also be admitted to the Korean Securities Dealers' Association as regular members, and will be subject to the same regulatory measures as South Korean members.

Like their colleagues in the banking sector, foreigners working in the securities industry have complained of discrimination against foreign securities companies. The government's decision in August 1992 not to allow foreign firms to handle CD brokerage business, which is open to all 31 domestic houses, added fuel to these complaints. The government justified its action on the grounds that the foreign branch offices should concentrate on their core business in the initial stages of their operations in South Korea.

Unlike their local counterparts, foreign securities companies operating in South Korea are required to set aside 10 per cent of their net profits as a legal reserve each business year until the reserve reaches 50 per cent of the company's capital base, and must make up for any losses within 60 days of recording them, bringing additional funds into South Korea from overseas for compensation.

FUND MANAGEMENT

The fund management market was closed to foreigners until June 1992, when the government offered liaison office licences to foreign fund management companies, on a selective basis. There are plans to permit foreigners to participate in the market through equity participation of no more than 5 per cent per foreign company and an aggregate of 10 per cent in one of the eight existing local fund management companies. However, many foreign companies may be wary of allying themselves with South Korean fund management companies, which include the three investment trust companies that came close to bankruptcy in 1991–2 as a result of government directives to support the flagging stock market.

THE BOND MARKET

In the 1950s, the ROK government issued bonds to raise funds for postwar rehabilitation. Although bank debentures and public bonds were floated in the 1960s, the government and domestic corporations still depended heavily on foreign borrowings and bank loans to finance economic growth and industrialization.

South Korea's first corporate bond was issued in 1963; five years later, the state-owned Korea Investment Corporation (KIC) was established to facilitate issuance, distribution, underwriting, brokerage, dealing, market making, the surveillance of public offerings, and the investment trust business. In 1972, KIC introduced a guarantee system for corporate bonds, which stimulated impressive growth in the market. Floating rate notes (FRNs) and long-term bonds were introduced in 1980, along with bond transactions under repurchase (repo) agreements.

Bonds are issued in the private sector by corporations and in the public sector by the Ministry of Finance, the Bank of Korea, government agencies and government-owned institutions.

Corporate bonds can be subdivided into non-guaranteed bonds, and bonds which are guaranteed by banks and other authorized institutions. Guaranteed bonds accounted for more than 90 per cent of outstanding bonds in 1991.

Government bonds include housing bonds, finance bonds, and Monetary Stabilization Bonds (MSBs), which are used as a means of controlling money supply. Financial institutions are required to underwrite a specified amount of MSB issues, which increase when the central bank wishes to absorb excess liquidity. In 1991, corporate bonds accounted for the majority of issues; a total of W29.2 trillion (US$37.1 billion) or 47.5 per cent of the total of W61.4 trillion (US$78.0 billion). MSBs accounted for a further W14.1 trillion (US$17.9 billion), or 22.9 per cent of the total.

As bond maturities are short, with more than half the new issues having maturities of three years or less and MSBs having maturities of less than one year, a large proportion of new issues is for refinancing. Although the bond market has in the past been characterized by a lack of variety (most corporate bonds have the same terms and maturity), the government has recently liberalized the issuing terms and types of bond, which now include convertible bonds, bonds with warrants, and mortgage-backed bonds.

According to the current liberalization plan, the bond market is due to be opened to foreign investment in the latter half of the 1990s.

37 Outward Investment

Outward investment by South Korean companies began in earnest after the recording of the nation's first significant current account surplus in 1986. Of the total of US$4.0 billion invested in almost 2,000 projects between 1968 and 1991, more than 70 per cent was invested after 1988.

By the end of 1991, the cumulative outstanding amount invested in 1,673 overseas projects by South Korean companies was US$3.4 billion. Although this represents a significant increase over 1985 levels – a total of US$500 million invested in 443 projects – the amount is still relatively small. In 1991, outward investment was just 1.2 per cent of GNP; this contrasts with 1990 figures of 6.8 per cent in Japan and 7.7 per cent in the United States.

Since the late 1980s, manufacturing projects have accounted for half the value and 46 per cent of the number of projects. In terms of number, 47 per cent of the projects have been located in Asia, 28 per cent in the United States, 8 per cent in Europe, and 16 per cent in the rest of the world. In terms of value, the largest share has been invested in the United States (46 per cent), followed by Asia (34 per cent) and Europe (7 per cent).

THE RATIONALE FOR OUTWARD INVESTMENT
In the late 1980s, the ROK government viewed overseas investment – the construction of production facilities overseas, the establishment of joint ventures abroad, and mergers with or acquisitions of foreign companies – as a useful means of managing the nation's current account surplus, which had swelled to US$14.2 billion in 1988 from US$4.6 billion in 1986. Although managing the surplus is no longer an issue (South Korea recorded deficits of US$2.2 billion in 1990 and US$8.7

billion in 1991), the government continues to view outward investment in a positive light. In encouraging it, the government aims to transfer overseas certain industries that have reached the limits of growth possible at home, facilitate technology transfer, strengthen cooperation with developing and developed countries, and promote the internationalization of small- and medium-sized companies.

For South Korean companies, the rationale behind the decision to invest overseas is threefold: to take advantage of supplies of raw materials and/or cheaper labour costs, to consolidate export positions and overcome trade barriers in major markets, and to acquire advanced technology. A further motive for companies in certain sectors might be to gain experience in a foreign business environment before the domestic market is opened up to foreign corporations.

The loss of the cheap labour advantage enjoyed by Korean manufacturers through the first twenty-odd years of the nation's development has prompted manufacturers, particularly in the textiles and footwear sectors, to relocate their labour-intensive production overseas. This leaves the production facilities at home available for the manufacture of high-value-added, capital- and technology-intensive goods. At the other end of the scale, the establishment of production facilities in advanced nations may result in access to advanced technology and skilled labour, as well as exposure to new management techniques.

Faced with the prospect of the emergence of trading blocs, such as the single European market, the European Economic Area, and the North American Free Trade Association, South Korean corporations wishing to break into or expand their presence in these markets must seriously consider direct investment in production facilities. However, the long-term considerations of investment in the western advanced nations are often overshadowed by the prospects offered by regions closer to home.

On the downside, there are fears that outward investment could create unemployment problems in South Korea, as labour-intensive production facilities are relocated overseas. Concerns have also been expressed over the conceivable 'leakage' of capital and foreign exchange out of the country, and the possibility of a boomerang effect, created when low-cost goods produced overseas are sold in and take a significant share of the domestic market.

PREFERRED FORMS OF INVESTMENT
It has tended to be the case that South Korean companies prefer to invest in wholly-owned subsidiaries rather than in joint

ventures with foreign partners; in the late 1980s, more than 60 per cent of investment approved was in subsidiary companies. In the joint ventures that have been established, the South Korean partner typically holds a majority share. The projects have also tended to be small in scale, with those invested at less than US$500,000 accounting for more than half of the total projects approved at the end of the 1980s.

Reports in the early 1990s that some South Korean companies were facing problems with their investments – unprofitable operations, excessive competition, and a variety of problems arising from the failure to make a thorough feasibility study prior to investing meant that almost 20 per cent of approved projects were withdrawn or abandoned – led some analysts to speculate that, in future, the South Koreans may look more closely at the benefits offered by joint ventures, mergers and acquisitions.

Although the majority of South Korean outward investment to date has been in the form of direct investment in manufacturing facilities, a small but growing number of companies are taking the M&A (mergers and acquisitions) route to establish a market presence or to leap-frog past the stage of developing advanced technology in house by acquiring proprietary technology. Two examples are the Hanjin group's acquisition of a hotel in Los Angeles, and Sammi Steel's purchase of Rio Algom's speciality steel divisions, Atlas and Al Tech.

PREFERRED LOCATION

In 1991, a total of US$1.1 billion was invested by South Korean companies in 453 overseas projects. Investment in the United States accounted for 41 per cent of the total (US$463 million), while investment in South-east Asia totalled US$431 million, or 38 per cent of the total. Investment in Europe remains small – a total of US$92 million, or 8 per cent of total investment in 1991.

Although the United States has long been a popular choice for South Korean companies looking to invest overseas, other nations closer to home are currently proving attractive to would-be investors.

The abundant natural resources and cheap labour available in the former Soviet Union and the north-eastern provinces of the People's Republic of China, combined with their sizeable communities of ethnic Koreans, make these areas particularly interesting to South Korean corporations. Although the initial frenzy for investment in the former Soviet Union and Eastern European countries has waned somewhat, the region still offers good long-term prospects, in terms both of resource development and of production bases for exports to Western Europe.

The establishment of diplomatic relations with Vietnam in December 1992 has opened up further investment opportunities for the South Koreans. In 1991, the Export – Import Bank's Overseas Investment Information Centre reported that enquiries about investing in China and Vietnam accounted for more than a third of all queries.

The geographical proximity of South-east Asia and its relatively low labour costs have been important factors in the decision by many South Korean companies to relocate production facilities to that region. However, recent months have seen a shift in interest away from the region, where labour costs are rising and investment in some sectors is reaching saturation point, to South Asian nations including India, Pakistan, Bangladesh, Myanmar (Burma) and Sri Lanka.

APPROVAL AND FINANCE

In order to promote outward investment, the ROK government has begun to simplify procedures for approval of projects, relax the nation's foreign exchange controls, and expand the sectors in which overseas investment is permitted.

From 1 September 1992, prior approval need only be sought for outward investment projects valued at more than US$5 million; all others may simply file a report with the Bank of Korea. (The previous ceiling for prior approval was US$2 million.) The ceiling on projects subject to prior government approval was also raised, to US$10 million from US$5 million, as was the investment ceiling on projects in the 'northern countries', including China and the former Soviet Union; the new ceiling is US$5 million.

The government may prohibit any project which, in its opinion, might prove detrimental to the nation, and may also deny approval in the interests of preventing excessive or duplicated investment. Projects which, in the government's view, might compromise the nation's internal affairs or prove harmful to its economy or its image are prohibited, and restrictions are imposed to guard against excessive competition among or duplicated investment by local companies. Although South Korea is not a member of the Coordinating Committee for Multilateral Export Controls (COCOM), the ROK government has agreed to abide by COCOM regulations.

In September 1992, the ROK government placed restrictions on overseas direct investment in the footwear, bags, toys and dolls, and ready-made suit industries, in an attempt to curb excessive competition among local companies. Restrictions were also placed on investments that might result in a boomerang effect and on certain real estate projects. However, the government actively continues to encourage investment in resource development projects, in projects that will secure export markets, and in the precision electronics, advanced materials and other high-tech sectors.

In most cases, finance for overseas investment projects is provided by the Export–Import Bank, although loans are also available from the Bank of Korea and the Korea Development Bank. In addition, companies meeting certain criteria are allowed to raise funds for an overseas project through equity-linked issues. One example of this method of financing was Saehan Media's issue of a convertible bond in 1988 to finance the construction of a videotape factory in Ireland.

However, as restrictions on the raising of funds in international markets currently force South Korean companies to rely on domestic sources, their ability to invest overseas can be restricted by a local credit squeeze, or a reversal in the balance of payments.

THE TUMEN DELTA PROJECT

A potential outward investment project which has attracted a great deal of interest in South Korea is the development of the Tumen Delta, an area of land bordered by Russia, the People's Republic of China and North Korea.

The project, which is being coordinated by the United Nations Development Programme (UNDP), aims to transform the 38,600 square miles (100,000 square kilometres) of forest and marshland into a Hong Kong-style free market and industrial metropolis of 500,000 people. The development of the area, which will cost an estimated US$30 billion over 15 to 20 years, will include the construction of duty-free shipping and processing zones, ports, air terminals, road and rail links, power supplies and other infrastructure.

For Russia, the project offers opportunities for links with the Asia-Pacific economy and access to foreign capital and technology. For China, there is the chance to boost its economic reform programme, and for North Korea an escape from diplomatic isolation and economic crisis.

In addition to the three nations which are directly involved, South Korea, Japan and Mongolia will also participate in the project. Japan and South Korea will provide the technology and part of the capital, while North Korea, Russia, China and Mongolia will contribute raw materials and labour. Additional financing will be sought from other advanced nations, including the United States, and from international financial organizations such as the World Bank and the Asian Development Bank.

The attractions of the project for South Korea are the consolidation and improvement of relations with its northern neighbours in general, and North Korea in particular, and the establishment of a foothold in what is being hailed as a new geoeconomic centre of north-east Asia. The South Koreans could look to gain a land route across central Asia to Europe – a modern-day Silk Road – as well as further penetration of the 'northern markets' of the People's Republic of China and the former Soviet Union. In addition, the project will also provide an opportunity to consolidate links with the one million ethnic Koreans living in north-east China.

Discussions began in earnest in July 1990 and continued through 1991, culminating in the adoption of an action plan, under which the initial investment phase would begin with a series of economic, technical, legal and financial feasibility studies. More concrete plans will be developed by 1995.

38 Exports and Imports

In 1991, exports from the Republic of Korea totalled US$71.9 billion on a customs clearance basis, an increase of 9.6 per cent from the previous year. In that year, South Korea's top ten export items were as shown in Table 7.

TABLE 7 Top ten exports, 1991

Item	US$	% of total
Electronics	20.1 billion	27.9
Textiles	15.5 billion	21.6
Steel products	4.5 billion	6.3
Ships	4.1 billion	5.7
Footwear	3.8 billion	5.3
Automobiles	2.5 billion	3.5
General machinery	2.3 billion	3.3
Petrochemicals	1.6 billion	2.3
Metal products	905 million	1.3
Toys	612 million	0.9

The United States was South Korea's largest export market in 1991, accounting for 25.8 per cent of the total. Japan took a 17.2 per cent share; Hong Kong, Germany and Singapore accounted for 6.6 per cent, 4.4 per cent and 3.8 per cent respectively.

Historical context

Throughout almost three decades, exports have been the engine of South Korea's economic growth and industrialization. In 1962 the Republic's exports totalled just US$55 million; three decades later, they were approaching the US$80-billion mark.

When President Park Chung-hee took power in 1963, he adopted an economic policy of export-led growth. The reasoning behind this was simple: the country lacked natural resources and the domestic market was small. Moreover, at that time, South Korea had only one available resource – its people and the value they could add to imported materials. The government therefore adopted a strategy of promoting exports of labour-intensive light manufactured goods, to provide a sound base from which the economy could develop further. In the 1970s, South Korea began to develop heavy and chemical industries, and, moving into the 1980s and 1990s, it stated to switch from labour-intensive to capital- and technology-intensive industries.

The success of South Korea's export-led policies was most clearly demonstrated in the late 1980s. Boosted by the so-called 'Three Blessings' – low interest rates, stable oil prices, and favourable rates of exchange – exports soared, producing the nation's first trade surplus in 1986. By 1988, the surplus had expanded to US$8.9 billion.

However, in the late 1980s, export performance began to flag. This was due to a number of factors, including rising labour costs, currency appreciation, and insufficient investment in R&D, quality enhancement and new product development (see: the Economy – General Overview). At the bottom end of the market, the South Koreans were struggling to compete with newly industrializing economies (NIEs) whose labour costs were still low. At the top end of the market, their efforts to compete with the Japanese were hampered by the comparatively low quality of their products.

Faced with a declining rate of export growth, the ROK government adopted a policy of encouraging domestic demand. The policy aimed to allow local demand to take up the slack created by sluggish exports, while a much-needed structural transformation took place. Export competitiveness was to be regained and enhanced by moving into more technology-intensive, high value-added production and boosting productivity.

The policy was, in effect, made possible by the rapid rise in wages and disposable income which had followed the implementation of democratic reforms and the formation of effective trade unions in 1987. At the same time, the gradual opening of the domestic market to foreign products gave consumers access to a wider range of goods than ever before. South Koreans had more money to spend, but many chose to spend their money on high-priced, brand-name imported goods rather than on locally produced merchandise.

Seeing the profits to be made from the import business, many trading companies (see below) switched their attention away from exports, where profit margins had become paper-thin, to the lucrative importing of luxury goods such as custom-made golf club sets, white goods, large screen televisions, rugs and carpets, and designer label clothes. Imports of foreign cigarettes, foods and beverages also saw rapid growth.

The annual rate of export growth, which had been as high as 36 per cent in 1987, dropped to 2.8 per cent in 1989, before recovering slightly to 4.2 per cent in 1990 and 10.5 per cent in 1991.

The general trading companies

In the late 1970s, the general trading companies (GTCs) were established with the specific aim of boosting the nation's exports. Trading companies which met certain requirements, including accounting for more than 2 per cent of South Korea's total exports, were designated GTCs and received benefits from the government, including tax and financial incentives and reduced tariffs on imports of raw materials for re-export.

In 1991, exports by the GTCs totalled US$30.3 billion, or 43 per cent of all South Korean exports. The *chaebŏl* trading houses led the way; the Hyundai Corporation with an export total of US$7.7 billion, Samsung Company Ltd with US$7.2 billion, and Daewoo Corporation with US$6.0 billion (see: The *Chaebŏl*).

Having been the key players in the government's export drive through the 1970s and early 1980s, the GTCs are now becoming trading companies in the true sense of the word. Until the late 1980s, they had little interest in imports and domestic sales; the imports that they did handle were largely raw materials and intermediate materials for re-export. However, developments in recent years have forced the GTCs to reappraise their business activities.

Since the late 1980s, an increasing number of companies have shown a preference for establishing their own overseas marketing and sales networks, rather than go through the GTCs. The rapid rise in disposable income seen in the late 1980s and early 1990s, the strong consumer preference for foreign brand-name goods, and the liberalization of the domestic market have combined to create excellent import and local sales opportunities for the GTCs. In addition to focusing more on imports and domestic sales, they are looking to diversify their business activities by moving into overseas resource development, joint venture investments, and information services.

IMPORTS

In 1991, imports to the Republic of Korea increased by 16.7 per cent year on year to reach US$81.5 billion on a customs clearance basis. The top ten import items that year are shown in Table 8.

TABLE 8 Top ten imports, 1991

Item	US$	% of total
General machinery	11.6 billion	14.1
Electronic parts	7.0 billion	8.6
Steel	5.4 billion	5.6
Organic chemicals	5.2 billion	6.3
Semiconductors	4.8 billion	5.9
Industrial electronics	3.5 billion	4.3
Petrochemicals	3.3 billion	4.0
Oil products	2.9 billion	3.6
Textiles	2.7 billion	3.3
Precision instruments	2.2 billion	2.7

Japan was South Korea's largest import market in 1991, accounting for 25.9 per cent of the total. The United States took a 23.2 per cent share of the total; Germany, China and Saudi Arabia accounted for 4.5 per cent, 4.2 per cent and 4.0 per cent respectively.

Historical context

Throughout its economic development, South Korea has been highly dependent on imports of raw materials, energy and capital goods. In 1991, imports of raw materials accounted for 43 per cent of all imports, while crude oil and capital goods took shares of 10 per cent and 37 per cent respectively. The remaining 10 per cent was accounted for by imports of consumer goods (8 per cent) and grains (2 per cent).

In recent years, imports have been further boosted by the

liberalization of the domestic markets, the lowering of import tariffs, and the consumption boom in South Korea. Over the past five years, imports of consumer goods have more than doubled, rising from US$2.7 billion in 1987 to US$6.2 billion in 1991. As the structural shift from labour-intensive, low-tech manufacture to capital- and technology-intensive production has continued, imports of capital goods have shown steady growth, rising from US$14.6 billion in 1987 to US$30.0 billion in 1991.

Although South Korea will continue to rely to a great extent on imported raw materials and energy, the rapid expansion seen in imports of capital goods should start to ease as companies move through and emerge from the current phase of restructuring. Imports of consumer goods may be expected to continue to rise, with the rate of growth limited by frugality campaigns and the like, but these so-called 'luxury' items will still account for a relatively small proportion of total imports.

THE TRADE ACCOUNT

In 1986, the Republic of Korea recorded the first significant trade surplus in its 38-year history; within two years, the surplus had swelled to US$8.9 billion on a customs clearance basis. However, the combination of increasing demand for imported consumer goods and the need for technology and equipment to upgrade and automate local production resulted in a swelling of imports, and, ultimately, a return to a deficit in the nation's trade account in 1990. The account went back into deficit in 1990, and then sank further into the red in 1991 with a record deficit of almost US$10 billion.

Over the past three decades, South Korea's trade account situation has largely been determined by its dealings with its two largest trading partners, the United States and Japan, which together accounted for 43 per cent of exports and 49 per cent of imports in 1991.

For the past three decades, the **United States** has been South Korea's largest export market, and until 1991 the balance of trade was always in the Republic's favour. During the boom years of the late 1980s, South Korean exports to the US market expanded rapidly – more than doubling between 1985 and 1988 – and South Korea's trade surplus swelled accordingly. The success of South Korean exports created friction between the ROK and US governments, and South Korean companies increasingly found themselves faced with trade barriers and protectionist measures in the United States. The trade surplus peaked in 1987 at US$9.5 billion; thereafter, as exports to the United States have flagged, the surplus has shrunk, falling to US$2.4 billion in 1990. In 1991, for the first time in its history,

South Korea recorded a deficit (US$335 million) in its trade with the United States.

South Korea has never recorded a trade surplus with **Japan**; the cumulative trade deficit recorded by South Korea between 1965 (when relations were restored after a 20-year hiatus following the end of Japanese colonial rule in Korea) and 1991 was US$66.5 billion. The trade deficit with Japan reached US$8.8 billion in 1991, equivalent to 90 per cent of South Korea's total trade deficit in that year.

Geographical proximity, good prices, fast delivery and efficient after-sales service have encouraged South Korean companies to look to Japan for capital goods and technology. The bulk of key components for major industries such as metal working, machinery, electronics, chemicals and textiles are still supplied by Japan. Although South Korean companies remain heavily dependent on Japanese capital goods and components, they face great difficulties in breaking into the Japanese market themselves.

As the deficit remains a contentious issue between the Japanese and the South Koreans, the ROK government is making concerted efforts to encourage companies to diversify their import sources away from Japan, and designates 'import diversification items' whose import from Japan is prohibited. Companies are encouraged to import items designated 'import source convertible items' from countries other than Japan. In the annual economic talks between South Korea and Japan, the ROK negotiators continue to ask for lower tariffs, the easing of non-tariff barriers (such as complicated and restrictive marketing channels), and increased technology transfer from Japan to South Korea.

TRADE FRICTION

The remarkable success of South Korean exporters in overseas markets in the late 1980s and the significant surpluses chalked up in some markets have led to an increase in trade friction between South Korea and its trading partners. Most vocal among South Korea's critics have been the Americans who take the view that the Republic has now developed to the point where greater access can be granted to foreign goods and services, and that, while progress is undeniably being made, it is not being made quickly enough. For its part, the ROK government points out the liberalization carried out in trade procedures and in the service and financial sectors, and accuse the Americans of insensitivity to South Korea's situation.

Among the most common complaints made by Korea's trading partners are: lack of enforcement of copyright and patent protection; overstrict testing and quarantine procedures for imported goods; restricted access to the financial, telecommunications, distribution and service industries; and the existence of a number of non-tariff barriers.

Perhaps the most contentious issue in recent years has been that of the frugality campaigns. Having encouraged domestic consumption, the ROK government found itself faced with a spending spree that was contributing to the deterioration in the nation's trade situation and aggravating inflationary pressures. Conspicuous or excessive consumption came to be blamed for a great many of South Korea's economic woes in the late 1980s and early 1990s. There were reports of tax investigations against those spending too ostentatiously and campaigns were launched to discourage the purchase of 'luxury' goods which usually meant imported consumer goods. The ROK government denied taking any role in the management of these campaigns, which it said merely aimed to encourage thrift among the South Korean people.

CURRENT TRADE POLICIES

The basic trade policies of the Republic of Korea are the balanced expansion of external trade, the internationalization and liberalization of the local economy, the diversification of markets, the development of brand names and product image, and the expansion of multilateral cooperation.

The balanced expansion of external trade

While it is true that exports have been the driving force behind South Korea's economic development over the past thirty years, the heavy reliance on overseas markets has left the economy vulnerable to any downturn in world markets. Efforts to boost domestic demand have been successful (even leading to an overheating of the economy), but such a solution can only be short-term in nature, and growth which is dependent largely on the small domestic market cannot be stable.

In the long term there needs to be greater balance between manufacture for export and production for the local market. Equally, the wide swings between a trade surplus of US$8.9 billion in 1988 and a deficit of nearly US$10 billion just three years later must be brought under control.

Government policies to boost exports can no longer rely on the artificial supports that were used to great effect in the past, as old-style export promotion drives will only incur the wrath of trading partners. Instead, the ROK government has to promote industrial restructuring and product quality enhancement in order to regain competitiveness.

The failure to invest in product innovation and quality

enhancement, and the neglect of quality control, marketing and after-sales service, have cost the South Koreans dear. For them to compete with the Japanese at the high end of the market, all of these issues must be addressed.

The internationalization and liberalization of the local economy

As South Korea moved into an era of trade and current account surpluses in the late 1980s, its success in export markets worldwide led to the raising of import barriers, an increase in protectionism and trade friction, and demands for greater access to the South Korean market for foreign companies.

Furthermore, with South Korea's graduation from General Agreement on Tariffs and Trade (GATT) balance of payments protection in October 1989, the provision allowing import restrictions under the condition of balance of payments deficit was revoked. South Korea must, therefore, remove the remaining import controls or conform to GATT provisions by 1997.

Accordingly, the ROK government has stepped up its efforts to liberalize the domestic markets, in an attempt to ease trade friction and comply with GATT requirements. The import liberalization ratio had risen to 97.3 per cent in 1990 from 68.6 per cent in 1980, and is forecast to rise further to reach 99.9 per cent in 1994.

Between 1983 and 1991, the average overall tariff rate fell to 11.4 per cent from 23.7 per cent, and tariffs on manufactured goods dropped to 9.4 per cent from 22.6 per cent. Although the overall rate is forecast to fall to 6.2 per cent by 1994, tariffs on agricultural products are expected to remain higher than those on manufactured goods, in line with the government's policy of protecting the interests of South Korea's farmers.

A three-phase, five-year plan for the liberalization of the domestic distribution system was launched in 1989, with the aim of improving access to the market for foreign·goods. In 1989 and 1990, foreign firms were allowed to invest in the wholesale distribution business; in July 1991, barriers to investment in retail distribution were eased, and the final phase will see the full liberalization of the retail distribution business.

The government is also promoting efforts to overcome the effects of trade friction and protectionism by encouraging 'strategic alliances' between South Korean and foreign companies, in fields as diverse as aerospace, semiconductors and automobiles.

The diversification of markets

As mentioned above, over the past three decades, South Korea has been heavily dependent on the United States for exports and on Japan for imports. The friction and problems caused by the virtually perennial surpluses with the United States and deficits with Japan have prompted efforts to diversify the nation's trade markets.

These efforts are paying off. In 1970, the United States accounted for 77 per cent of all South Korean exports; the diversification of markets has brought that share down to under 30 per cent in 1991. The success of President Roh T'ae-woo's 'Nordpolitik' and the opening up of former communist bloc markets has provided new opportunities for South Korean exporters; strenuous efforts have been made to promote exports to these markets as well as to South-east Asia, Africa and Latin America.

Although still heavily dependent on Japanese imports, South Korean companies have been sourcing more imports, notably of raw materials, from other countries, including the former Soviet Union, the People's Republic of China, and even North Korea.

The development of brand names and product image

South Korean companies still rely heavily on original equipment manufacture (OEM) exports, which accounted for 40 per cent of total exports, and as much as 80 per cent of shipments of home appliances, footwear and steel products in the late 1980s.

Although some South Korean names have achieved brand recognition overseas – most notably Samsung Electronics, Hyundai Motor and Goldstar – in the past, South Korean companies have tended to spend little on overseas advertising, looking on it as an expense rather than an investment. Expenditure on overseas advertising by the top ten conglomerates was estimated at just US$32 million in 1991.

However, many corporations in industries as diverse as footwear, textiles and toys are now recognizing the importance of getting their own names known overseas, and creating a new brand awareness of South Korean products that were previously sold on an OEM basis. This is particularly important as South Korea's new Asian rivals can now produce OEM goods at a much lower cost. The importance of investment in advertising, distribution channels, marketing networks and after-sales service facilities is also being realized.

The expansion of multilateral cooperation

South Korea is. active in trade diplomacy, participating in a number of international forums, and holding regular talks with major trading partners such as the United States and Japan. The ROK government is also taking an active role in the Uruguay Round negotiations, and is committed to cooperating with other trading nations in multilateral forums such as GATT. South Korea is seeking to join the Organization for Economic Cooperation and Development (OECD) by 1996 to boost the country's ties with the advanced nations of the world.

TRADE UNDER THE SEVENTH FIVE-YEAR PLAN (1992–6)

The Seventh Five-Year Plan calls for a 76 per cent increase in total trade volume during the period of the plan, to US$270 billion in 1996 from US$153 billion in 1991 (on a customs clearance basis). Exports should expand at an average annual rate of 13 per cent to reach US$136 billion, while imports will grow at a slower rate of 11 per cent, amounting to US$134 billion in 1996.

By 1995 a system of paperless trading will be operating in the Republic of Korea, with the establishment of an on-line computer network capable of handling all import–export procedures. Korea Trade Network (KTNet) will link 18,000 licensed South Korean traders and their overseas networks, domestic trade organizations, transportation companies, banks and customs houses. The standardization of all documents will enable traders throughout the country to process trades in an identical manner, and will reduce the average time taken to process export and import transactions to less than one week. The costs of processing will also be reduced, by an estimated 20 per cent.

39 Labour

The economic policies implemented by President Park Chung-hee in the early 1960s were formulated to gain full benefit from the one comparative advantage enjoyed by South Korea at that time – a good supply of literate, hard-working, low-cost workers, who could be employed in the mass production of cheap, light industrial goods for export.

However, thirty years later, the South Koreans can no longer compete on the basis of mass production and cheap prices. The implementation of democratic reforms in 1987, the subsequent increase in union activity and labour unrest, and the substantial wage increases won as a result of the collective bargaining process have forced a reappraisal of the traditional image of the South Korean workforce.

THE FORMATION OF TRADE UNIONS AND LABOUR UNREST

South Korea's labour problems began in earnest with the formation of effective and free trade unions after the implementation of democratic reforms in June 1987. Unions demanding a greater share of the benefits of South Korea's rapid and successful industrialization for their members clashed with company owners who had grown used to a compliant workforce and the backing of the government. Through the late 1980s, there were spates of labour disputes, stoppages and strikes, some of which became violent.

The impact of the unrest was far-reaching. Wage increases weakened the competitiveness of South Korean products in the domestic and international markets and foreign buyers, worried by the labour unrest, turned to South Korea's competitors as a more reliable and cheaper source of supply. The number of disputes peaked at 3,749 in 1987; two years later, production and export losses peaked at W4,199 billion (US$5.3 billion) and US$1.36 billion respectively.

By 1991, however, there were fewer and shorter labour disputes, and there were also signs that the unions were becoming less militant. The number of disputes dropped to 234, while production and export losses fell to W1,232 billion (US$1.6 billion) and US$238 million respectively. On 3 September 1991, South Korea experienced its first dispute-free day in four years. Furthermore, statistics showed that participation in union activities was declining to some extent. At the end of 1990, there were 7,698 unions in South Korea, a drop of 185 compared with the previous year. Membership had also fallen by 46,000 to 1.9 million members, and the unionization rate had slipped to 21.7 per cent from 23.4 per cent.

The improvement in labour–management relations in the early 1990s has been attributed to a number of factors, the most important of which is the accumulation of experience in negotiation by both sides. There also appears to be little sympathy from the middle class for the unions now, and their demands for extra bonuses and incentive pay are seen by many as inappropriate in view of the nation's current economic situation. The workers themselves, reading reports of increasing bankruptcies and hearing predictions of economic disaster, may also have come to the conclusion that a lower-paid job is better than no job at all.

However, critics of the government say that the decline in labour unrest is due to increased government suppression of union activities and its intervention in labour disputes. In February 1992, the government mobilized thousands of riot police to break up a month-long strike at the Hyundai Motor Company, and made it clear that it would not hesitate to intervene again in other damaging disputes.

WAGES

Wages have increased sharply in South Korea since the late 1980s, rising by an average of 21.0 per cent in 1989, 18.8 per cent in 1990, and 17.2 per cent in 1991, and making South Korean workers the second highest-paid in Asia, after Japan.

Average monthly wages in 1991 were W892,484 (US$1,134) for companies with more than 500 employees, W754,673 (US$959) for companies with fewer than 500 workers, W850,559 (US$1,081) for white-collar workers, and W618,640 (US$786) for blue-collar workers. Average wages for male employees were W881,980 (US$1,121); the average for female employees was W480,903 (US$611), just 55 per cent of the pay given to their male colleagues.

In 1992, the minimum monthly wage stood at W209,143

(US$266), up from W117,000 (US$149) in 1988. The minimum wage agreed upon for 1993 – W227,130 (US$289) – represents the smallest annual increase (8.6 per cent) since the minimum wage system was introduced in 1988. Increases in previous years were: 26.3 per cent in 1989, 15.0 per cent in 1990, 16.4 per cent in 1991, and 12.8 per cent in 1992. The 1993 rate applies to an estimated 75,000 workplaces and 5 million employees.

While it was, to a certain extent, possible to award substantial pay increases to workers during the boom years of the late 1980s, the economic slow-down and the deterioration in the financial condition of many companies have made it increasingly hard to meet union demands. In the early 1990s, the ROK government has attempted to set an example to the private sector by keeping a tight rein on wage increases in the public sector. The authorities now also use other, less direct methods to encourage wage restraint and smooth labour relations. These include offering tax and financial support for companies which suffer labour disputes as a direct result of complying with government guidelines on wage increases.

In 1992, companies awarding increases which fell below the official target of 5% received favourable treatment in the issue of corporate bonds and the application for policy loans, were exempted from tax inspections for a fixed period, and could be freed from credit controls on a limited basis. On the other hand, companies making settlements above the 5 per cent ceiling faced higher taxes, restrictions on entry to industrial estates and the use of state-owned property. (The Federation of Korean Trade Unions had called for an increase of 15 per cent in 1992, and the Council of Korean Trade Unions for a 25.4 per cent rise.)

A key factor in the success of the government's efforts to limit wage increases will be the degree to which it manages to curb inflation. The high rates of inflation experienced in the late 1980s and early 1990s worked against attempts at wage control as workers found that rises in certain key areas of the cost of living, such as housing and food, were outpacing the growth of their wages. However, the drop in consumer price inflation from 10 per cent in 1991 to 5 per cent in 1992 should aid the government's efforts to keep wage increases below 3 per cent in 1993.

Wage increases were showing signs of slowing during the first half of 1992, with an average increase of 9.9 per cent being recorded at 350 listed companies. The average, while almost double the government's target of 5 per cent, represented a substantial drop from the 17.2 per cent recorded in 1991. Just as important, the gap between wage increases and productivity increases had narrowed to just 0.1 per cent during the first six months of 1992.

A new problem for workers in the early 1990s was that of overdue wages. In May 1992, it was reported that 146 companies were late in paying wages to their employees due to the slump in business. The total amount overdue was W53 billion (US$67.3 million).

FUTURE LABOUR ISSUES

Key labour issues through the mid-1990s will include the easing of manpower shortages, the introduction of the 'total wage system', reforms of the labour laws, and changes in the Korean work ethic.

Manpower shortages

In contrast to the 1960s and 1970s, when South Korean manufacturing companies enjoyed easy access to a large pool of cheap, well-educated labour, the manufacturing sector in general and small- and medium-sized enterprises in particular are now facing manpower shortages.

At the beginning of 1992, the labour shortage in all industries was estimated at 250,000 persons, up from 190,000 in the previous year. By May, the shortfall had risen to 324,577, with particularly acute shortages in the electronics, apparel, furniture, mining and leather sectors, in small enterprises, and in low-paying jobs.

The shortages have been attributed to the increasing preference for employment in the service sector over jobs in the manufacturing sector and the growing dislike for the 'Three D' jobs (see: Human Resources). In 1992, the situation was aggravated by the presidential and local elections, which siphoned off an estimated 800,000 workers, including 400,000 from the manufacturing industry. The workers were attracted by the prospect of the higher wages paid to campaign workers.

There are also structural problems. Traditionally, the majority of people have found employment through informal networks of personal connections; far fewer have found jobs through advertisements, and only a tiny proportion through job centres. As a result there is no network of employment centres which can bring together potential employees and employers. The lack of crèches and nursery facilities, coupled with deep-rooted social attitudes, makes it difficult for women to return to the workplace after having children.

The worry for manufacturing companies is that, faced with a shortage of labour, wages must rise to attract those available for and willing to work. The increased production costs lead either to lower profits, if the company absorbs the increases, or to a further weakening of competitiveness, if the company passes the increases on to the consumer in the form of higher prices.

Although there have been calls from various sectors of the business community for the government to allow companies to employ foreign workers (see: Migrant Workers), the government has, so far, looked at other domestic sources of additional workers. In 1991, the government had plans to mobilize 12,000 undrafted reservists for work in the construction industry and the manufacturing sector.

In the early 1990s, there were an estimated 2.4 million retired workers, housewives and handicapped people in South Korea; the mobilization of just 10 per cent of this pool would, in theory, solve the manpower shortage problem. (However, it is hard to imagine that these people could be successfully employed in the difficult and dangerous jobs shunned by the young and healthy.) It is possible that the government may revise the relevant laws to allow part-time employment.

Government attempts to bring retired or, 'silver', workers back into the workforce have met with little success thus far, despite an increase in the number of elderly people looking for work. A government guideline calling for private enterprises to employ a certain proportion of people over the age of 55 (the official retirement age for South Korean men) has resulted in few job offers.

One of the targets of the Seventh Five-Year Plan (1992–6) is the development of a smooth supply of industrial manpower. The plan aims, therefore, to boost the training of technical workers and to intensify vocational training at middle-school level, where the focus has traditionally been on more academic subjects. Shortages in technical manpower have been attributed in part to the fact that the sciences still prove less attractive to South Korean students than do the arts and humanities. In the early 1990s, less than a third of all students registered for science and technology courses at higher education institutes.

The introduction of the 'total wage system'

The pay received by South Korean workers comprises a number of elements, including the basic wage, annual and special bonuses, pay for overtime and night work, and holiday allowances. Typically, the basic salary accounts for two-thirds of total remuneration, special allowances for almost a quarter, and overtime and holiday allowances for about a tenth.

In recent years, the government has found its efforts to keep wage increases below official targets frustrated by the practice of applying the limit only to the increase in the basic wages, (which is the figure reported to the authorities) and raising allowances and benefits in lieu of a large increase in basic pay. This means that the actual wage increase is often far higher than that reported to the government.

In 1992, the government introduced the total wage system for high-wage enterprises such as companies with more than 500 employees, businesses in the service sector with more than 300 workers, banks, and state-run companies. (This covers approximately 1,500 companies and 10 per cent of the workforce.)

Under the system, the ceiling set by the government each year applies to basic pay, allowances, regular bonuses and welfare subsidies on a total-sum basis. Overtime payments, night work and special bonuses are not affected. The unions are opposed to this on the grounds that it does not allow for flexibility in setting wage levels, and that it is another example of the government interfering in labour – management affairs. The public disclosure of basic wages, bonuses, allowances and fringe benefits required by the system is also opposed, on the grounds that it will lead to inter-company recruitment wars.

While not subject to the new system, medium-wage companies were encouraged to limit increases to 10 per cent, and small-wage companies were allowed to negotiate pay increases at their own discretion, but keeping pay rises in line with increases in productivity.

Reforms of the labour laws

Under the current labour laws, unions are banned from political activities – it is illegal for them even to endorse an election candidate. The unions want this law to be changed, along with those prohibiting more than one organization representing workers within a company or industry. Although the more radical unions are threatening to file a suit with the International Labour Organization, the fact that the ROK government did not, on becoming a member, ratify the 87th convention (which guarantees freedom of association) makes it unlikely that they would succeed in their demands for dual unions.

The work ethic

Concern has been expressed in recent years about a change in the South Koreans's legendary work ethic, citing the above-mentioned trend among young people to shun 'Three D' jobs, the decline in working hours and overtime, and the preference for family and leisure time rather than overtime, even at the expense of family earnings.

Whereas in the recent past, a university degree was seen

as a passport to a good job, the same can no longer be said in the early 1990s – graduates are finding it harder to obtain employment. In 1991, the unemployment rate for university and college graduates was 3.7 per cent, compared with a rate of 1.1 per cent for those having an elementary or middle-school education (see: Human Resources). Companies which plan to reduce their employment levels or recruitment typically cite the sluggish economy, increased automation of production processes, the relocation of production overseas, and high wages as the reasons for their decision.

At the same time, there have been reports that younger people are shunning work. In April 1992, out of a total of 4.7 million unemployed, 2.4 million were aged between 15 and 24 years. The high rate of unemployment among entrants to the workforce has been blamed on a change in the work ethic, dislike of the 'Three D' jobs, and higher household incomes, which ease the need to work.

The average working month for production employees has shown a steady decline since the mid-1980s, falling from 237.7 hours in 1986 to 234.6 hours in 1987, 228.6 hours in 1988, 220.0 hours in 1989, and 216.2 hours in 1991. In the first quarter of 1992 the average was 212.4 hours. From October 1991, the 44-hour work week was applied to all places of business with more than 300 employees; at that time, the ruling affected 114,000 businesses employing a total of 3.17 million people.

A survey carried out in 1991 by the Korean Chamber of Commerce revealed that more than 70 per cent of respondents valued leisure time more than overtime, and more than two-thirds felt that they could not sacrifice their family life for their company. The annual average number of holidays taken by South Koreans in 1992 was 20.3 days, including 19.8 days of paid holiday.

PART SIX

Doing Business in Korea

40 Market Entry: Investing in and Trading with South Korea

In the past, direct foreign investment in South Korea has focused on the manufacturing sector, in order to take advantage of the nation's low labour costs. Although South Korea can no longer offer cheap labour as an incentive for investment, it still offers significant opportunities to the foreign investor.

South Korea's geographical location gives easy access to South-east Asia and the Pacific Rim. An additional factor that should not be overlooked is the increased potential of the market in the event of reunification with North Korea.

As they move through the current period of industrial restructuring from low-tech, labour-intensive production to high-tech, capital- and technology-intensive production, South Korean companies need advanced technology, and the ROK government will actively support cooperative ventures that lead to technology transfer.

The increasing importance of the domestic market, and the rising demand for high quality consumer goods and sophisticated service industries, offer opportunities to foreign companies, which need a presence in the South Korean market in order to be able to service it well.

INVESTING IN KOREA
The government of the Republic of Korea is keen to attract direct foreign investment (DFI) in general, and in particular investment which brings with it the advanced technology needed for South Korea's industrial restructuring. The government's basic policy concerning foreign investment is 'to actively induce and protect foreign capital conducive to the sound development of the national economy and the improvement of the international balance of payments' (Foreign Capital Inducement Act).

The Foreign Capital Inducement Act, which replaced the Foreign Capital Inducement Promotion Act in 1966, is the primary law concerning direct foreign investment in South Korea. The provisions of the Act cover foreign equity investment, technology inducement and licensing, repatriation of capital and remittance of dividends, treatment of foreign-invested companies, and tax incentives.

The Ministry of Finance's 'Guidelines for Foreign Investment' are an important source of information concerning updates and revisions of the basic law. Other laws relating to DFI are the Foreign Exchange Control Act, the Commercial Code, the Tax Exemptions and Reductions Control Law, the Customs Law, and the Alien Land Acquisition Law.

THE HISTORY OF FOREIGN INVESTMENT IN KOREA

In the years immediately following the Korean War (1950–3) the focus of government economic policy was the substitution of imported intermediate and non-durable consumer goods with locally produced items. However, the effectiveness of this policy was constrained by the small size of the local market and the paucity of domestic savings. The lack of savings also forced the ROK government to seek funds overseas in order to finance the reconstruction projects that were needed after the war. During the late 1950s, the majority of the foreign capital entering South Korea was in the form of aid, grants and development loans, mostly from the United States.

In 1960, the Foreign Capital Inducement Promotion Act (FCIPA) was promulgated, with the aim of attracting foreign investment into South Korea, as an alternative to relying on overseas aid and loans. The Act provided for equal treatment for foreign companies operating in South Korea, offered them tax incentives, and guaranteed them the remittance of profits and the withdrawal of capital.

The year 1962 saw the first direct foreign investment in the Republic of Korea, with the establishment of a 50:50 joint venture nylon filament manufacturing company. The assets of the company, a venture between South Korea and the United States, totalled US$575,000. During the period of the First Five-Year Economic Development Plan (1962–6), the ROK government approved DFI totalling US$47.4 million, the majority of which was invested in large-scale projects in the manufacturing sector by American and British companies.

The FCIPA was replaced by the Foreign Capital Inducement Act (FCIA) in 1966. Subsequently, the ROK government has, at regular intervals, issued 'Guidelines for Direct Foreign Investment' (now called 'Guidelines for Foreign Investment'), which give notification of updates to or revisions of the FCIA.

Between 1967 and 1971, DFI more than quadrupled to reach US$219 million, of which 84 per cent was invested in the manufacturing sector. Japanese and American companies accounted for the lion's share of DFI over the five-year period, favouring the electronics, chemicals and textiles industries. Although there were only a small number of projects in which foreign equity participation exceeded 50 per cent, they tended to be the large-scale projects with substantial amounts of capital.

In 1973, concern over the possible impact of foreign companies holding majority stakes in joint enterprises led the ROK government to place an upper limit of 50 per cent on foreign equity participation in joint ventures. The limit was waived for projects which would boost exports from South Korea or introduce technology into the country, and for investments made in the free export zones at Masan and Iri or by South Korean nationals living overseas.

During the first half of the 1970s, DFI focused on the heavy and chemical industries, reflecting the priority given to these sectors by the ROK government. Foreign investment in the chemicals, metal products, machinery and transport sectors more than quadrupled between 1972 and 1976. There was also robust growth in investment in the service sector, the majority of which was accounted for by the construction of hotels. By the end of the five-year period, Japan was the largest foreign investor in South Korea.

The dependence of the South Korean manufacturing sector on imported energy left it extremely vulnerable to the oil shocks of the late 1970s. The adverse effects on the sector were reflected in a 28 per cent drop in DFI between 1977 and 1981, compared with the previous five-year period. However, investment in the service sector remained strong during the period of the fourth plan, increasing by 22 per cent compared with the period of the previous plan.

In the early 1980s, the adoption of new economic policies focusing on price stability, balanced growth and liberalization led to major revisions in the FCIA. The most significant change was that from a positive list system, under which the government made public a list of sectors in which DFI was prohibited, to a negative list system, under which automatic approval was given to all projects unless specifically prohibited. The regulations governing DFI were eased, and tax and financial incentives were offered to introduce advanced technology.

Between 1982 and 1986, DFI in the manufacturing sector almost doubled to approach US$1 billion. Approvals for investment in the service sector also saw a sharp increase, boosted by the special demand created by the holding of the 1986 Asian Games and the 1988 Summer Olympics in Seoul.

In 1986, the Republic of Korea recorded the first significant current account surplus in its 38-year history; in view of the improvement in the nation's balance of payments, the ROK government felt able to phase out the special measures and incentives designed to attract DFI, except in strategic or key industries and in projects which would introduce advanced technology. The moves also aimed to respond to complaints from local firms that foreign companies were operating with an unfair advantage. Nevertheless, DFI approvals continued to rise in 1986 and 1987, and still focused on the service sector.

On 19 May 1989, the Republic of Korea and the United States signed a trade agreement which set out a timetable for the complete liberalization of DFI in South Korea. This was in line with the growing worldwide trend towards greater liberalization, and increasing calls on South Korea, which had recorded trade and current account surpluses for three consecutive years, to open its markets to foreign goods and services.

The agreement called for sectors previously closed to DFI to be opened, investment approval procedures to be speeded up, and performance requirements, such as local content, the export of goods and services, and the transfer or licensing of technology, to be eliminated. Pharmaceuticals, cosmetics, travel, advertising businesses, alcoholic beverage wholesaling, retail sales, trucking services and international database and data-processing services were all due to be opened to DFI in the early 1990s.

The cumulative amount of direct foreign investment in South Korea between 1962 and May 1992 was US$9.7 billion in 3,865 projects. However, after reaching a peak of more than US$1 billion in 1988, the annual amount of DFI declined to US$803 million in 1990. In 1991, the amount jumped to US$1.4 billion, but this was thanks largely to Aramco's purchase of a 35 per cent equity stake in Ssangyong Oil. The number of new projects per year has also declined, falling from 362 in 1987 to 287 in 1991.

Although DFI has shown an overall decline, some sectors, such as finance, insurance and foreign trade, have experienced growth. In recent years, there has been a clear trend away from investment in the manufacturing sector towards investment in the service industries. Between 1987 and 1991, the number of investment projects in the manufacturing sector fell from 321 to 109 while projects in the service sector increased from 36 to 178.

South Korea is not as attractive a market as it once was,

due to high wages (now the second highest in Asia) and labour unrest, a reduction in financial incentives, high interest rates and funding difficulties, and problems in acquiring factory sites. Ironically, liberalization itself has also acted as a disincentive to DFI, as there is less motivation to invest in order to get round trade barriers if ready-made products can be freely imported.

Labour unrest following the formation of effective trade unions in the late 1980s, and the high wage increases that resulted from the sometimes violent disputes between labour and management, have made South Korea a less attractive manufacturing base in the late 1980s and early 1990s. The labour shortages which are currently being experienced in the manufacturing sector also act as a disincentive to DFI. The increasing availability of cheap labour in other countries in the region, such as the People's Republic of China, has led many potential and existing foreign investors to rethink their strategy.

The ROK government now takes the view that preferential treatment of foreign-invested companies is no longer appropriate, unless they introduce advanced technology or operate in the free export zones. The aim now is to afford foreign-invested firms the same treatment as domestic companies, by gradually removing both the incentives for and restrictions on investment in South Korea.

Historically, the government has controlled the amount of credit available to business from domestic and foreign banks. Foreigners may only bring in investment capital in the form of equity, and working capital must be raised locally at rates that are substantially higher than those in Japan, Europe and the United States. Furthermore, foreign banks in South Korea are short of local currency to loan to foreign companies and, like local banks, are under pressure to channel available funds to sectors favoured by the government.

Foreign banks and insurance companies, and foreign firms engaged in so-called 'pioneer' industries, have been allowed to acquire real estate since 1991. However, the shortage of land available for development in South Korea, and government restrictions on the construction of buildings for commercial purposes, make the acquisition of land both problematic and expensive.

REGULATIONS
Who can invest?
Residents of the Republic of Korea may apply for approval or submit notifications for DFI (see below); non-residents must do so through a proxy. South Korean nationals living overseas may

only make direct investments in the Republic if they have been resident overseas for more than ten years.

How much can be invested?
A minimum amount of W50 million (US$63,500) is required. Should two or more investors make a joint investment, each should invest at least W25 million (US$31,750). There are no restrictions on amounts for additional investment or the investment of dividend profits.

What sectors are open to investment?
Since 1984, the ROK government has operated a negative list system for DFI, under which foreign companies or individuals may invest in any industries which are not specified in the government's lists of restricted and prohibited projects.

In early 1992, there were 51 prohibited and 158 restricted projects, out of a total of 999 selected from the Korea Standard Industrial Classification. The manufacturing sector is more open to DFI than the service sector – in 1992, approximately 95 per cent of all manufacturing sectors were liberalized, compared with 61 per cent in the service sector, where liberalization is proceeding more slowly.

Prohibited projects are those which are currently operated by government or public organizations (such as broadcasting, public utilities, railway transportation), and those which are harmful to the health of the nation or to the environment, or contrary to public morals (such as gambling).

Industries on the restricted list include those which, in the government's opinion, are still at the development stage and are therefore in need of support and protection. Although these sectors are, in theory, closed to foreign investment, approval may be given by the Ministry of Finance on a case-by-case basis, when advanced technology can be introduced by foreign investors.

Restricted projects include those which consume excessive amounts of energy, cause pollution, or use unreasonable amounts of imported raw materials. Also restricted are projects which might encourage extravagance or excessive consumption. However, the restrictions on these projects will gradually be eased, as the economic situation of the nation changes.

Foreign companies and individuals may invest in certain sectors, including construction, non-life insurance, and alcoholic beverage production (distillation of ethyl alcohol, *soju*, *ch'ŏngju* and ginseng wine), provided that they do so through a joint venture with a company already licensed or authorized to do business in that sector. Finally, DFI is permitted in projects related to small- and medium-sized enterprises, under the provisions of the Small and Medium-Sized Industry (SMI) Adjustment Law and the SMI Systematization Promotion Law.

In November 1992, eight more areas were opened up to foreign investment, including aircraft leasing, the wholesale trade of alcoholic beverages, and the operation of harbour facilities. A limited opening of the wireless telegraph and telephone, cosmetic retailing, and quarrying businesses was also put into effect. Ten more industries are due for liberalization between 1994 and 1997. Joint venture requirements were lifted in certain sectors.

What are the procedures?

Notification, the simplest procedure, applies only to small-scale investments in 510 manufacturing sectors. The government plans gradually to increase the number of sectors converted to the notification system.

Plans for investment in projects with capital of less than US$3 million and foreign equity participation of less than 50 per cent can be sent to the Bank of Korea, provided that no tax exemptions or reductions are required. Acceptance is usually received within 20 days. If the foreign ownership exceeds 50 per cent, or if tax exemptions or reduction are requested, notification must be sent to the Ministry of Finance. In this case, acceptance will typically take 30 days. Should the MOF deem it necessary for the Foreign Capital Project Review Committee to review the proposal, the processing period will be extended to 60 days. The applicant will be notified in such cases, and in cases of unavoidable delay.

In exceptional cases, the relevant ministry may deny acceptance of the notification, should the project be deemed contrary to national security, public order or public morals. Acceptance may also be denied in the interests of fulfilling international, peace and security obligations, protecting the national health or the environment, preventing monopolistic practices, and upholding the Antitrust and Fair Trade Act.

Approval must be sought for larger-scale projects, and projects outside the manufacturing sector. Approval of a proposal for foreign investment is usually granted within 30 days of filing. However, projects with an investment amount of more than US$20 million will automatically be reviewed by the Foreign Capital Project Review Committee (FCPRC), in which case the processing period is extended to 60 days. (The ceiling for prior screening by the FCPRC was raised to US$20 million from US$5 million in October 1992.) Applications requiring coordination by the relevant ministries or requesting tax breaks will be screened by the FCPRC regardless of the investment amount. As is the case with notification, applicants will be informed of any additional and unavoidable delays in processing.

In order to be approved, projects must be reviewed and passed by the relevant authorities. The ministry concerned will review the contents of the project, and the Ministry of the Environment will screen projects that are potentially harmful to the environment.

The Fair Trade Commission is consulted in the case of investments of more than US$3 million, in order to determine whether the project violates any antitrust or fair trading laws. The Korea Development Bank reviews the funds for the project and sources of financing in cases where cash investment exceeds US$3 million or the amount of DFI exceeds US$5 million. The Economic Planning Board reviews proposals for investment in excess of US$10 million, in order to assess the likely impact of the project on internal and external trade policy.

Following the acceptance of notification or the granting of approval, the details of capital and induced goods are confirmed by the relevant ministry (if tax reductions or exemptions have been requested) or by a foreign exchange bank. Investment funds are deposited in a bank in South Korea, and a foreign capital inducement report is submitted to the Ministry of Finance or to the Bank of Korea.

The new corporation is established, and the foreign-invested enterprise is registered with the Ministry of Finance or the Bank of Korea. Investment in projects in the service sector, which are capitalized at less than US$1 million, must be completed within one year of approval of acceptance of notification. Investment in projects over US$10 million must be completed within three years; all other investment must be completed within two years.

According to the Capital Market Promotion Act, the Securities and Exchange Commission can require a foreign-invested enterprise, which was registered after 1 January 1989 and meets certain other criteria, to sell up to 30 per cent of its shares on the local stock market. Although this offers some advantages in respect of raising funds, problems also exist, such as the dilution of control over the company's activities, and the fact that the ROK government uses its own valuation system to determine the issue price for shares. Although this right has never been exercised, it would be a useful tool for the government to boost the supply of stock.

In 1992, the ROK government announced that it planned to formulate additional measures to attract more DFI to South Korea. These measures will include streamlining complicated administrative procedures, easing restrictions on equity holdings in some areas, reducing the number of foreign investment projects for which a joint venture with a local firm is mandatory, and placing all foreign investment projects in non-restricted areas on a notification basis. Performance requirements imposed on foreign-invested firms will gradually be eliminated.

In June 1992, equity restrictions on foreign partners in joint ventures were eased, allowing the foreign investor to increase its equity stake by making an additional investment or by buying the South Korean partner's stake and becoming the controlling share-holder. Equally, the foreign investor can reduce its equity stake by selling to the local partner, and can withdraw completely at will.

In November 1992, 24 businesses were added to the list of those qualifying for tax incentives. The number of tax-exempt technologies was increased from 71 to 101, and the number of industries qualifying for tax breaks from 58 to 80.

In December 1992, the Ministry of Finance removed all but one of 167 business requirements imposed on foreign-invested companies operating in South Korea. The requirements, which had been imposed as conditions of issuing licences to some 80 foreign-invested companies, related to production, sales, scope of business activity, foreign investment limits, and so forth.

In order to ease problems in acquiring land, the government also plans to offer production sites for foreign investors on a leased basis, and has designated 395,000 square yards (330,000 square metres) of the Asan Industrial Park, currently under construction, for use by foreign firms. In the meantime, the government plans to lease 39,500 square yards (33,000 square metres) of bonded warehouses for the use of foreign companies in export-oriented businesses. In addition, foreigners may be allowed to own land for use in certain types of manufacturing-related service sectors such as R&D centres, software development, and manpower training.

What types of business entity can be established?
Foreign companies will often make their first entry into the South Korean market through an agent, who can provide assistance and valuable local knowledge. However, in time, the company may wish to establish a presence in South Korea, through either a liaison office or a branch office. Other companies may wish to establish a joint venture with a local firm or set up a wholly-owned subsidiary in South Korea.

The activities of a liaison office are restricted by law to those which do not generate income, such as sales promotion, market research and client solicitation. As a liaison office is not deemed to be a distinct and separate entity under South Korean law, the funds for its operations must be provided by the foreign head office, and all its assets must be held in the parent company's name. Similarly, all employees are considered to be employees of the parent company or of its local representative.

Liaison offices are permitted to operate in virtually all business sectors, except those in which, in the government's opinion, an upgrading to branch office status is likely to occur within a short period of time. In these cases, the appraisal of the initial proposal will be very thorough. Great care must be taken to ensure that the liaison office does not engage in activities outside its remit. Should the office earn income, it will become liable for income tax, which could result in the head office being forced to close down the liaison office and open a branch office in its stead.

Although branch offices are permitted to earn income, it is possible to establish a branch office which will conduct liaison activities only – in this case, the office earns no income and pays no tax. Should the investor subsequently wish to move into areas where income will be generated, this can easily be arranged by obtaining approval and registering as a tax payer. There is no need in this case to close one office and open another. As a separate legal entity, the branch office can then conduct business under its own name, acquire assets and employ staff.

Sectors in which the establishment of an income-generating branch office is prohibited are specified on a negative list under which certain sectors are designated restricted or prohibited. Proposals for investment in restricted areas – often those in which it is deemed necessary to protect local industries from foreign competition – will be appraised on a case-by-case basis.

Branch offices may not be established for the purpose of manufacturing, the operation of wholesale or retail businesses, moneylending to residents of South Korea (unless permitted under the Bank Act or the Foreign Exchange Control Act), or the purchase of securities. Approval must be sought from the Ministry of Finance to engage in certain activities, such as the extension of credit, the underwriting of securities, the arrangement of insurance cover, or the provision of business management services.

The procedure for establishing an office in South Korea, while requiring government approval, is less complex than that required for other forms of DFI. A Korean translation of the standard report form and other necessary documentation are submitted to the Bank of Korea, outlining the proposed activities of the office. A business plan covering at least three years and a certificate of good standing (certifying that the parent company is legally and duly organized) must also be submitted to the central bank.

As in all matters relating to trade with and investment in South Korea, it is essential to obtain up-to-date information on procedures and documentation before proceeding. Approval is usually given within one week, unless the Bank of Korea feels that consultation with relevant ministries is required. Once approval is obtained, the tax office in whose jurisdiction the office will be located must be notified in order to obtain a tax number – a non-taxable number for liaison offices and a taxable one for branch offices.

Branch and liaison-type branch offices must also be registered in the commercial registry at the district court having jurisdiction over the area in which the office will be located. Offices which will be engaging in trading activities, for example, as an offer agent or importer, must obtain the necessary permits and licences before beginning operations.

Once the office has been set up, the operating capital specified in the business plan may be brought into the country. Additional approval from the central bank must be sought if the capital induced exceeds the equivalent of US$1 million in any one year. Quarterly reports on capital inducement must be submitted to the Bank of Korea.

There are two major types of business entity recognized by law and available to foreigners as investment vehicles. They are: the limited liability company (*yuhan hoesa*), which is similar to the *Gesellschaft mit beschranter Haftung* (GmbH) in Germany and the *Société à Responsabilité Limité* in France, and the joint stock company (*chushik hoesa*), which is similar to incorporated enterprises in the United States and Japan. There being no tax advantages to opting for a limited liability company in South Korea, the joint stock company is the most popular investment vehicle among foreigners.

Regulations concerning DFI are subject to change and amendment. Up-to-date information on procedures, documentation and the current extent of permissible activities can be obtained from the Korea desks of government agencies, the Korea Trade Promotion Corporation (KOTRA), or the commercial sections of foreign embassies in Seoul.

The Consultation Office for Overseas Companies (COOC) has been established within the Ministry of Trade and Industry in order to respond to queries from foreign companies setting up in South Korea. COOC provides practical information and advice on trade and investment procedures and related legislation. Enquiries can be made by telephone, fax or mail, and will be treated in strict confidence.

Also the Centre for Foreign Investment Services (CFIS) provides up-to-date information on investment opportunities in the Republic, and can act as a matchmaker between South Korean corporations and potential foreign investors. CFIS can be contacted direct or through South Korean embassies overseas, or through any branch of the Korea Trade Promotion Corporation (see: Who Can Help in Korea).

TAXATION

Joint ventures located in South Korea, wholly-owned subsidiaries of foreign corporations, and branches of foreign companies in South Korea are all treated as domestic corporations for tax purposes. Therefore, these enterprises are liable for both national and local taxes.

National taxes include income, corporation, inheritance and gift tax, as well as value added tax, liquor tax, and telephone and stamp tax. Customs duties, defence tax and education tax are also classified as national taxes. Local taxes, which are levied by provinces, counties and municipalities, include property tax, automobile tax, resident's tax, licence tax and registration tax.

Foreign corporations are liable for corporation tax only on income derived from sources within the Republic of Korea. This includes income from interests, dividends, real estate, royalties, capital gains, personal services, business, leasing aircraft, vessels etc., and the sale or other transfer of securities. The tax is assessed and collected in the same manner as with a local corporation. Corporation tax is not levied on income from liquidation.

The scope of tax incentives for foreign investors has been reduced in recent years. Previously, foreign-invested enterprises or investors were exempt from income tax, corporation tax and property acquisition tax for an initial period of five years, with a 50 per cent reduction for the following three years. Currently, tax concessions are available for projects which bring in advanced technology – 100 per cent exemption from corporate tax is offered for the first three years, and a 50 per cent reduction for the next two years. There is also a 50 per cent reduction in tax on dividend incomes, property and acquisition taxes for five years.

However, in practice, if the investment is sufficiently attractive, the ROK authorities will find a way to offer incentives, in the interests of reducing dependence on foreign loans and speeding up the process of technological development.

Foreign individuals who are not resident in South Korea, or who are resident for less than one year, are liable for tax only on income derived from sources within the Republic. Foreigners who are resident in South Korea for more than one year are liable for income tax on their ordinary income, that is salary, severance pay (if applicable) and money earned from dividends, interest, real estate.

Two types of taxation scheme are available: Class A and Class B. Individuals who register under Class A have tax on income earned in South Korea withheld at source on a monthly basis. The individual's employer pays the tax to the authorities, and the employee receives a certificate of payment at the end of the tax year. Tax due under the Class B scheme can be paid either in three four-month instalments or monthly, through a taxpayers' association.

A basic deduction of W300,000 (US$381) is made from the taxable income; further deductions can be made for dependants, insurance premiums paid, medical expenses, education expenses and donations. Exemptions are granted to individuals who are assigned to South Korea in accordance with a bilateral agreement between the two governments, employed as a result of a technology licensing agreement which has been approved for tax exemptions, working with South Korean corporations as specially qualified technicians, or working in a designated research institute as a technician with a doctoral degree.

A basic tax rate of between 5 per cent and 50 per cent is applied to individuals, plus a defence surtax of 10–20 per cent, and a resident's surtax of 7.5 per cent on the tax paid. Returns for a given tax year must be filed the following to the office which has jurisdiction over the individual's place of residence. A final return must be filed before finally leaving South Korea.

Up-to-date information about taxation in South Korea should be obtained from one of the local accountancy firms, many of which have affiliations with the 'Big Eight' international companies, or from an international law practice.

REPATRIATION OF PROFITS AND REMITTANCE OF FUNDS

Investments made under the provisions of the FCIA are guaranteed repatriation of investment capital and remittance of earnings. However, the remittance of profits and dividends must be approved in advance, as part of the investment approval process. Once approval is granted, dividends from stocks and shares, principal, interest and royalty payments may be repatriated. Approval must be given by the Bank of Korea for the repatriation of investments when a foreign-invested company ceases trading and closes down.

SETTLEMENT OF COMMERCIAL DISPUTES

The fastest and most confidential way to settle commercial disputes is through the Korean Commercial Arbitration Board (KCAB) which acts as an intermediary for the exchange of opinions in a commercial dispute. It should be noted, however, that a dispute should only be taken to court if it is intended that the relationship with the Korean partner be dissolved.

In its role as standing institutional arbitrator, KCAB makes suggestions and offers advice to effect a mutually acceptable agreement. The basic framework for arbitration is provided by the 1966 Arbitration Act; a three-person tribunal conducts the hearing and makes an award. Non-residents of South Korea may request that one member of the tribunal comes from a neutral country. KCAB has the authority to request sanctions, such as the revoking of import and export licences, against South Korean nationals who refuse to cooperate with or abide by its rulings.

KCAB also provides consultation services and offers advice on the prevention of disputes and the drafting of commercial contracts (see: Who Can Help in Korea).

TRANSFERRING TECHNOLOGY TO SOUTH KOREA

An agreement between a South Korean national and a foreign national to purchase industrial property rights or induce any technology from a foreign national constitutes a foreign technology inducement contract. Contracts in which the inducement period exceeds three years and the fixed payment exceeds US$100,000, the initial payment exceeds US$50,000, or royalties exceed 2 per cent of net sales of the products concerned are subject to the provisions of the FCIA.

The Act requires that the licensee receive authentication from a foreign exchange bank with regard to the contract of payment for the technology induced. If the inducement period is less than three years, the procedure is the same as for the technology inducement report under the FCIA. Contracts related to the defence industry also fall under the provisions of the Act.

The contract must be reported to the relevant ministry, and acceptance will generally be given within twenty days, unless the minister concerned requests additional information or requires that changes be made to the contract. The minister may refuse to accept the report if its main aim is simply to benefit from a monopoly sales right or to sell raw materials, parts or accessories. Contracts which violate the Antitrust and Fair Trade Act will also be rejected.

Under the Engineering Service Promotion Law (ESPL),

engineering services may be induced, including planning, development, design, procurement, testing, supervision and consultancy. Inducement of services under the ESPL are subject to the approval of the Ministry of Science and Technology.

Tax exemption on royalties is permitted for projects which are necessary for economic restructuring and the strengthening of international competitiveness. However, the projects must introduce advanced technology which would be difficult to develop independently in South Korea.

TRADING WITH KOREA

Foreign trade in the Republic of Korea is regulated by a number of laws, the most important of which are the Foreign Trade Act, the Foreign Exchange Control Act, and the Customs Act. Regulations relating to external trade are also published in the Ministry of Trade and Industry's 'Export and Import Notice', which is reviewed on a regular basis.

The most recent and detailed information concerning trade regulations and procedures, restrictions and the liberalization process, and tariff rates, can be obtained from the commercial sections of foreign embassies in Seoul, or from the Korea desks of government trade agencies, such as the Department of Trade and Industry in the United Kingdom and the Departments of Trade and Commerce in the United States (see: Who Can Help at Home).

The **1987 Foreign Trade Act (FTA)** regulates the flow of imports to and exports from the Republic of Korea. The basic aims of the FTA are to phase out restrictions on foreign trade (in line with the overall policy of reducing government intervention in economic activities), to facilitate the application of trade-related laws by making them simpler and easier to understand, to minimize friction with trading partners by ensuring that trade is carried out in a fair and ethical manner, and to soften the effects of import liberalization. The promulgation of the Foreign Trade Act in July 1987 marked a shift away from economic development through the promotion of exports and the regulation of imports towards development based on free and fair external trade.

The **Foreign Exchange Control Act (FECA)** governs matters such as foreign exchange transactions, the exchange rate system, and the payment and receipt of foreign exchange. It also controls the activities of exchange regulation authorities, including foreign exchange banks and money changers. The Ministry of Finance formulates policy relating to foreign exchange transactions, while the Bank of Korea holds and manages the nation's foreign exchange reserves.

Foreign exchange banks and foreign bank branches are

313

permitted to engage in international commercial banking and foreign exchange transactions. These institutions are also authorized to screen and approve most of the transactions governed by the FECA, and to issue import and export licences under the provisions of the FTA. Other institutions including customs houses and post offices carry out specific functions under the provisions of the FECA.

The **Customs Act** regulates customs systems and procedures, controls the entry of foreign goods and prevents smuggling. The Customs Tariff Schedule, which governs the valuation of goods and application of tariffs, has been based on the Harmonized Commodity Description and Coding System since 1988.

EXPORT AND IMPORT PROCEDURES
Trading Licences

Two types of trading licence are available in the Republic of Korea: Class A and Class B. Domestic and foreign-invested companies which meet specified paid-in capital requirements may apply for a Class A licence, which authorizes them to import and export goods either on their own behalf or for other companies. Trading agents having an agency agreement with two or more foreign exporters (one of which must be based outside Asia) can register with the Association of Foreign Trading Agents of Korea (AFTAK) as a Class A trader.

Domestic and foreign-invested companies in the manufacturing, mining, fishing and military goods supply sectors may apply for a Class B licence. With this, they can import raw materials and machinery for use at their own production facilities, and can export their own finished goods. They may not, however, engage in trading activities on behalf of other companies. Trading agents having an agency agreement with a foreign importer can register as a Class B trader with the Korea Export Buying Office Association. Registered branch offices of foreign companies and corporations designated by the Ministry of Trade and Industry may also apply for a Class B licence.

The fact that the Class A licence must be renewed each year and that licence holders are required to achieve a minimum annual level of export performance may cause problems for foreign companies wishing only to import goods into South Korea. This, combined with the fact that Class B licences only authorize the import of materials for production rather than sale, leads many foreign companies to export directly to the end-user or hire a local importer to handle the transactions on a fee-paying basis (typically 1–3 per cent of the value of the goods handled) rather than obtaining a trading licence themselves.

Foreign embassies in Seoul, Chambers of Commerce, the Korea Trade Promotion Corporation, domestic and foreign banks, accounting and consulting firms can all provide assistance in finding a suitable importer or agent. A visit in person can then be made to establish contact, and a business proposal can be forwarded to the company or individual in question. The business proposal should be clear and straightforward, stating exact requirements and specifications, technical or otherwise. It should also include information on the company's history, product lines and sales volume. Although there is usually no need to have the proposal translated into Korean as most companies employ translators, translation of the information is a polite gesture which will show goodwill.

It is worth noting that as many agents work with a small number of personal contacts, it may be better at first to engage a number of agents on a trial and (non-exclusive) competitive basis, in order to find a partner who can offer broad penetration of the market. It is possible to appoint one of the eight general trading companies (GTCs) as an agent; although appointing as agent (for example) the GTC Samsung Co. Ltd will not necessarily guarantee sales throughout the Samsung Group (because there is an increasing tendency for group-related companies to do their own sourcing, rather than operating through the group's trading arm), it will commonly result in the spread of information about the product throughout the group.

Once appointed the agent must register with AFTAK (see above), which requires a letter of appointment as agent from the principal, authenticated by the South Korean Embassy in the country in question or by a chamber of commerce. The letter should be written on the foreign company's letterhead and signed by both the foreign company and the South Korean agent. (It is perfectly acceptable for the letter to state that the arrangement is of a temporary, non-exclusive or trial nature.)

Selling into South Korea

All items currently on the Ministry of Trade and Industry's automatic approval list may be freely imported into the Republic of Korea. The import of restricted items is considered on a case-by-case basis, taking into consideration such factors as local supply and demand and the potential impact on domestic producers.

Details of restricted items are seldom made public and are subject to change without notice, and some items made be sold in hotels or duty-free outlets but not on the local market. The commercial departments of foreign embassies in Seoul and the

CASSELL BUSINESS BRIEFINGS **KOREA**

Korea desks of government agencies can best advise companies regarding restrictions currently in operation.

Once an import contract is concluded – on receipt of an offer based on a written agreement between a South Korean trading agent and a foreign supplier, or on acceptance of an offer issued overseas by a foreign exporter – an import licence must be obtained. Although the Ministry of Trade and Industry has responsibility for drafting regulations relating to trade, it is the foreign exchange banks and branches of foreign banks that issue import and export licences.

To import items on the automatic approval list, an agent simply has to submit an application form for an import licence together with the contract or firm offer sheet to a foreign exchange bank for approval. Should the item be on the restricted list, a certificate of recommendation for import must be obtained from the relevant ministry or trade association. Licences are valid for one year, and payment for and customs clearance of the goods must be completed within the term of the licence.

Items on the automatic approval list and items imported for government use can be imported for stock by traders, as can restricted items, provided that official approval is obtained prior to import. However, generally speaking, few South Korean traders stocks import goods for resale, so a more common line of distribution is straight from trading agent to end-user, thus eliminating the need for a stockist or distributor. (South Korean traders usually rely on being able to take rapid delivery of goods they need, rather than financing the storage of imported goods.)

The most common method of payments for imports into South Korea is 100 per cent unconfirmed letters of credit (L/C) drawing on a foreign branch of a South Korean bank. The L/Cs are usually opened between four and six weeks prior to shipment; since the expiry date will reflect the promised delivery date, delivery deadlines must be met if the L/Cs are not to expire. This method of payment has been found by most people to work faultlessly, and payment is usually extremely prompt. Long terms of credit are sometimes available for large, government-approved contracts, provided that some form of guarantee of payment is given.

Although the South Koreans usually prefer to deal in US dollars, it is possible to use sterling or other currencies. However, since these prices will usually be converted into US dollars for price comparison, it may be better to quote in dollars from the start. Prices should be quoted on a free-on-board (FOB) basis, as South Korean importers often prefer to arrange the shipping themselves.

When dealing with large South Korean customers, quotations will almost certainly be requested from other sources. For example, the potential client may contact a potential supplier's office in another region to see whether he or she can get a better price there. Similarly, a South Korean company based overseas may contact the supplier's home office direct to establish whether that office can offer a better deal than its Korean agent. It is essential, therefore, to inform branch offices that all requests for tenders from South Korea should be reffered to one office. Failure to do this can result in some very uncomfortable price negotiations.

When opening the L/C, the importer must use *exactly* the same information as provided on the import authorization form, and must express the amount in the currency specified on that form.

On receipt of the L/C, the foreign exporter or supplier ships the goods according to the conditions of the L/C, and obtains from his or her bank a documentary bill which is issued using the transport documents as security. The exporter or supplier's bank sends the transport documents to the South Korean bank that opened the L/C. The bank then verifies that the conditions of the L/C match those of the transport documents, settles the account and forwards the transport documents to the importer.

Once the importer has submitted the bill of lading to the shipping company and collected the goods, they are placed in a bonded area, and a report of import is made to the superintendent of the customs house. Should the freight arrive before the transport documents, the importer may obtain a letter of guarantee from his or her bank and collect the freight in advance.

The superintendent of the customs house checks the documentation and confirms that the goods match those described in the import authorization form. A customs tariff is then calculated and levied, usually on the basis of the cost, insurance and freight (CIF) price, but sometimes on the basis of the current domestic wholesale price. Value-added tax is levied on the duty paid, and additional taxes such as the special consumption tax may be levied. The importer is then free to remove the goods from the bonded warehouse.

Generally speaking, the settlement of debts is not a problem, as the South Koreans are prompt payers. However, should payment become overdue, settlement on an instalment basis can be arranged either inside or out of court, and court orders can be obtained for debt collection, which is carried out by a bailiff of the district court. Should these methods of debt collection fail or prove impossible to carry out, the relevant embassy may be willing to become involved in the matter. Disputes other than those concerning debt may be referred to the Korean Commercial Arbitration Board. It should be mentioned that the South Koreans themselves tend not to resort to litigation; taking a case to court, therefore, will usually mean the end of a business relationship.

Attention to detail in **paperwork** is extremely important when selling into South Korea. The smallest mistake can cause delays and even penalties, for which the buyer may well seek compensation from the supplier. A certificate of origin authenticated by a South Korean diplomatic mission abroad is required for GATT concessional tariff items and goods shipped from countries which are not import-restricted areas.

In addition, commercial invoices (showing place of shipment, port of origin and port of arrival), a full set of clean-on-board bills of lading (made out to the order of the importer's designated exchange bank), and packing lists are required. For plants, seeds, vegetable products and livestock, sanitary or health certificates must be furnished, and certificates of inspection are needed for shipments of cosmetics, pharmaceuticals, and medical and sanitary supplies.

The South Korean government is encouraging importers to arrange **insurance** for their goods with local firms and have the goods shipped CIF, as are government imports. However, most foreign companies still arrange for their goods to be shipped to South Korea CIF.

All goods must be labelled and marked in accordance with international practice. As losses can occur as a result of rough handling, damage and the elements, packing should be in sturdy boxes with waterproof coverings and secure metal straps.

Customs and private licensed bonded **warehouses** are available for storage, but at a price. Goods may be stored for up to six months, after which, following notification, they will be publicly auctioned. Different rules apply for live animals and perishable goods.

Samples and exhibition goods of no commercial value can be sent to the Republic of Korea by airmail, air freight or parcel post, and will be admitted free of duty. Samples carried into the country are noted in the bearer's passport and must be re-exported on departure. Duty-free samples may not be sold or used for other purposes and must either be defaced (so that they cannot be sold) or re-exported within six months. Foreign goods imported for display at an exhibition sponsored or authorized by the ROK government are also exempt from duty, provided that they are repatriated after the exhibition closes.

Other samples may be temporarily imported, duty-free, under the automatic temporary approval carnet system.

Although customs duties will be levied on samples not re-exported within six months of arrival in South Korea, it is possible to apply for an extension to one year.

Government purchases are generally put out to tender by the Office of Supply of the Republic of Korea (OSROK), which has responsibility for procuring foreign and local supplies requested by government organizations and enterprises. Requests are submitted to officials at the Ministry of Trade and Industry (MTI), who determine whether they can be supplied by domestic companies. Those which cannot be met locally are put out to tender.

Formal public invitations to bid are issued usually less than 40 days prior to closing, and details are provided on request. Only companies already registered with OSROK are eligible to take part in the bidding process; South Korean firms wishing to register with OSROK must already be registered with AFTAK. Although foreign companies are, in theory, able to register directly, it is far less complicated and the chances of success are greater if a foreign enterprise works through a local agent.

Terms of bid awards are very strict and must be complied with to the letter; they always include a harsh penalty clause for late delivery, and require that bids be held firm for a period of time, specified for each tender. A bid bond of at least 2 per cent of the bid value must be deposited with OSROK in the form of cash, underwriter's bond, bank cheque or letter of guarantee before the bid opening.

Contracts are awarded on the basis of the lowest prices, subject to quality and other terms specified in the invitation to bids. The successful bidder must deposit a minimum 5 per cent performance bond within a specified period of time after the contract is awarded; the bond will be forfeited should the bidder fail to comply with all the terms and conditions stipulated in the contract.

Additional information about OSROK and the procurement process is available from the Commercial Section of foreign embassies in Seoul.

Buying from Korea

On receipt of an L/C from a foreign importer, the South Korean exporter must determine, through an assigned export association, whether or not the goods in question may be freely exported, and secure authorization for every export transaction carried out. If the goods are restricted under the MTI Export and Import Notice, an export recommendation must be obtained from the relevant ministry or trade association before applying for export approval.

If the goods are restricted under special laws, such as the Law on Drugs, Cosmetics and Medical Instruments, a recommendation must be secured in accordance with that specific law. Once this is done, there is no need to apply for export approval.

Export approvals for items on the automatic approval list can be obtained from a foreign exchange bank, with the exception of plant exports and exports on deferred terms under which the collection period exceeds one year.

The ROK government carries out inspections of certain designated items prior to export, to ensure that the design, materials, manufacture, quality and packaging are of a sufficiently high standard to maintain the reputation of South Korean goods overseas. However, the inspection is waived if the L/C or contract stipulates that the goods be inspected by the buyer, and there are automatic exemptions for goods carrying the Korean Standard (KS) mark or similar international standards recognized by the Industrial Advancement Administration.

Having obtained export approval, the exporter places all the goods for shipment in a bonded warehouse and submits the documents to the superintendent of the customs house. An export authorization for customs clearance is given once the goods have been checked against the invoices and export approval certificates. The exporter than arranges insurance and shipment.

In order to collect the proceeds from the transaction, the exporter issues a bill of exchange, which is sent to a foreign exchange bank together with the shipping documents, the L/C and other documents as required. The proceeds must be collected within a period of time specified by the bank, that period not exceeding more than one year.

LIBERALIZATION

The ROK government's commitment to the liberalization of the domestic markets has led to an increase in the import liberalization ratio from 68.6 per cent in 1980 to 97.3 per cent in 1990. The aim of the government's policy is the gradual removal of items from the restricted lists (usually products of industries still considered to be in need of protection from international competition) and the reduction of tariff rates. The five-year tariff reduction programme introduced in 1988 calls for rates to fall to an average of 6.2 per cent in 1994 from 18.1 per cent in 1988. Tariffs on agricultural products will remain higher than those on manufactured goods, in order to cushion the impact of liberalization on the nation's farmers. However, access to the South Korean market for 'liberalized' items can be hindered by non-tariff barriers. Although the situation has been improving under pressure from major trading partners, notably the United States, problems still exist. Frequently cited examples are frugality campaigns aimed at discouraging the purchase of luxury goods (which, as often as not, means imported consumer goods), regulations on packaging, labelling and food additives, and quarantine and safety regulations (see: Exports and Imports).

DISTRIBUTION

The development of a modern, sophisticated infrastructure for marketing and distribution in South Korea began as late as the early 1980s. Until that time, retail merchandising was dominated by 'mom-and-pop' stores.

The distribution system comprises wholesale and open-air markets, department stores, supermarkets, chain stores, discount stores, underground shopping precincts, mom-and-pop stores and, most recently, convenience or 24-hour stores. (Franchising has been developing rapidly, with a number of joint venture convenience stores such as Lawson and 7-11 setting up operations in Seoul.) According to the Ministry of Trade and Industry forecasts, there will be more than 1,500 traditional and regular markets in South Korea by 1993, close to 20,000 supermarkets, 50 department stores, 405 large stores and 24 wholesale outlets.

The situation today is vastly different from even a decade ago when foreign goods were available mainly through foreigners' commissaries and on the black market. The range of foreign goods available in all retail outlets is increasing every year, and a large number of foreign retailers, including such well-known names as Laura Ashley, Aquascutum, Ralph Lauren and Gucci, have established a presence in Seoul, to cater to the South Korean consumer's taste for high-quality foreign brand-name goods.

Imported consumer goods are typically handled by department stores and shopping centres which have an 'imported goods corner'. Increasingly, large supermarkets, convenience stores and shops within apartment blocks are handling foreign consumer goods, particularly foods and beverages. Whereas almost all department stores will deal directly with the importer, the path to other outlets may involve exclusive purchasers of imported goods, wholesalers and retailers.

For the foreign supplier, department stores offer the advantages of access to a large, middle-class customer base, the ability to introduce new foreign goods quickly and easily, and the easy collection of tax data. However, foreign suppliers have found problems in recent years during frugality campaigns, when department stores have been among the first to remove foreign 'luxury' goods from their shelves.

There are three main routes for distributing imported industrial goods in the Republic of Korea. The first is from foreign supplier direct to end-user – this route is used by experienced, large-scale industrial consumers, who prefer to source their imports directly. The second brings in an import agent who acts as an intermediary – this is probably the most popular route for smaller-sized foreign suppliers and new entrants to the market. The third is from supplier via agent to user group, and then to the end-user – this would be the case for groups which make joint purchases, and then distribute the goods among group members.

The sector was partially opened to foreign competition in the early 1990s but has yet to be fully liberalized. The first phase of the liberalization plan, implemented in 1989–90, allowed foreign firms to invest in distribution projects. Under the second phase, regulations governing foreign investment in retail distribution were eased in July 1991, allowing foreign concerns to operate a maximum of ten stores each with a floor space of less than 1,200 square yards (1,000 square metres). Further liberalization of the retail sector will follow in the next few years.

ADVERTISING

In 1991, Korean firms spent a total of W2.3 trillion (US$2.9 billion) on advertising, a year-on-year increase of 16.5 per cent. In that year, the most popular medium for advertising was newspapers (44 per cent), followed by television (28 per cent), magazines and radio (5 per cent apiece). The largest spenders on advertising by sector were manufacturers of food and beverages (14.8 per cent), pharmaceuticals (10.9 per cent), service industries and entertainment (8.8 per cent apiece), apparel (8.5 per cent), and housewares, cosmetics and detergents (7.0 per cent). Together, these sectors accounted for almost 60 per cent of total revenue in that year.

Top corporate spenders on advertising in 1991 were Samsung Electronics (W33.6 billion or US$43 million), Goldstar (W25.7 billion or US$33 million), Lucky (W24.9 billion or US$32 million), Pacific Chemical (W23.3 billion or US$30 million) and Daewoo Electronics (W21.2 billion or US$27 million).

The rapid expansion seen in the industry in recent years partly reflects the growing awareness of the need for sophisticated marketing in the face of increasing competition from foreign goods. Growth has been apparent both in the number of agencies in Seoul, which rose to 140 in 1991 from 40 three years previously, and in the variety of advertising media available, including outdoor billboards and neon signs, signs along expressways and in the subway, and airport trolleys.

Since the opening of the market to foreign competition in the late 1980s, almost all the major South Korean advertising agencies have been seeking cooperative arrangements with foreign agencies, either through joint ventures or direct foreign investment. By 1991, Bozell, McCann-Erikson, Ogilvy and Mather Worldwide, and J. Walter Thompson had entered the market, with many more to follow.

Despite fears that foreign agencies would dominate the domestic market, billings by the top five foreign agencies amounted to just W51.2 billion (US$65 million) in 1991 – a market share of 2.2 per cent. However, their business is increasing rapidly in relative terms: the 1991 billings were almost double those of 1990, and the number of clients they serve jumped to 67 from 34 in the same one-year period.

An interesting, though perhaps not surprising, characteristic of the South Korean advertising business is that almost two-thirds of all advertising is handled by in-house agencies owned by the nation's conglomerates or chaebŏl (see: The Chaebŏl). For example, Cheil Communications, the in-house agency of the Samsung group, will manage all of that conglomerate's advertising. In 1991, eight of the top ten agencies handling broadcast advertising were owned by conglomerates. This clearly limits the extent to which foreign corporations can choose their own advertising agencies – for example, a company having links with the Samsung group would probably be expected to use Samsung's own in-house agency for advertisements in Korea.

Newspapers and magazines remain the dominant medium in South Korea. Of the total advertisements placed in the print media in 1991, 90 per cent were in newspapers. Advertising in newspapers and magazines has been boosted by the relaxation of government restrictions on publishing in 1987, and the subsequent surge in publications. In 1991, there were more than sixty newspapers – including nine national daily papers, five economic newspapers, three sports dailies and two English-language newspapers – and almost six thousand magazines.

Newspapers and magazines have published rate cards (rates are usually open to negotiation) and some offer contract rates with discounts for frequent advertisers. Occasionally, newspaper advertisements are not published on the agreed date, as they may be postponed, often over holiday periods, in order to make way for advertisements put in at higher rates.

In **radio and television**, the Korea Broadcasting Corporation (KOBACO) has exclusive rights for the sale of all advertising time for the three main broadcasting stations: Korea Broadcasting Service, Munhwa Broadcasting Corporation, and Seoul Broadcasting System.

KOBACO was established in 1981 to function as the exclusive sales agent for all television and radio advertising following the forced closures and mergers of newspapers and broadcasting stations at the beginning of the Chun administration. Before the establishment of KOBACO, the four privately-owned broadcasting stations handled their own advertising sales; once the state had taken control of radio and television, KOBACO became the exclusive advertising sales arm for the broadcast media.

KOBACO was established with the aim of collecting funds from the broadcast media, to be used for projects such as the production of programmes related to the mass communications industry and the enhancement of arts and culture, the hosting of events related to broadcasting and advertising, and the international exchange of information on the broadcast media.

The democratic reforms and easing of restrictions on the media implemented in 1987 brought into question the role of KOBACO and its 'public service fund'. Although there was criticism of KOBACO's activities, no alternative system has yet been proposed. However, the gradual liberalization and deregulation of the broadcasting media will inevitably weaken KOBACO's role within it.

At the time of writing, advertising time is still bought directly from KOBACO or through an advertising agent, who will approach KOBACO on the client's behalf. Instead of the commission being paid directly to the agency, a percentage is taken by KOBACO, and the remainder is passed on to the agency.

Commercial broadcasting is limited to 8 per cent of total broadcasting time. Both programme sponsorship and spot commercials by companies other than the programme sponsors are allowed; in the past, block advertising in the Western European style was also available, but this was recently abolished. Commercials are transmitted before or after but not during a programme, and last from 15 to 40 seconds, depending on the programme and the number of advertisers. The usual length of a television advertisement is 20 seconds. Typically, a prime-time programme is sponsored by twelve companies, each having a 15-second slot either before or after the show, with the order in which the advertisements are seen being rotated to give all equal exposure.

There are fixed rates for advertising on television or radio, calculated on the basis of a 30-second slot. Although, in theory, there are no restrictions on how much time you can buy, or the number of spots for the same product to be aired during a certain period of time, in practice demand far exceeds the supply of television and prime-time radio advertising space.

Fairs and exhibitions also provide excellent marketing opportunities. Seoul is one of the main centres in Asia for fairs, exhibitions and conventions, and, in the Korea Exhibition Centre (KOEX), has one of the finest venues in the region. In recent years, the focus of exhibitions in the Republic has broadened, from displaying South Korean products to foreign buyers, to introducing imported goods, technology and services to the South Korean market.

PATENTS, COPYRIGHTS AND TRADEMARKS

The Republic of Korea is a party to the World Intellectual Property Organization Convention, the Patent Cooperation Treaty, the Paris Convention for the Protection of Industrial Property, and the Budapest Treaty. The Republic of Korea recognizes foreign copyrights under the Universal Copyright Convention (UCC), and offers legal protection to computer programs and sound recordings under the Geneva Phonogram Convention.

Manufacturers and traders should patent their inventions and register their trade marks in South Korea through a patent or trade-mark agent. Although recent legislation has introduced harsher penalties for infringement, and the government conducts regular campaigns against the illegal use of foreign trade marks, loopholes still exist and violations do take place.

Product patents were introduced in South Korea in July 1987. The current law offers protection for fifteen years from the date of publication, plus a maximum of five years' waiting time. This is necessitated by the lengthy statutory testing procedures required under the law.

Application for a patent may be made to the Korea Industrial Property Office by the inventor, his or her assignee or his or her legal successor. In the case of United Kingdom nationals, written authority from the UK Patent Office is required before making a patent application, if an application for a UK patent for the same invention has not already been filed. A foreigner can apply for a patent in person or through a representative: in either case, the person filing the application must live or work in South Korea, unless the foreign country in question allows South Korean nationals to enjoy patent-related rights without a home or place of business in that country.

Application by a foreign person or company for a patent

should be made before the invention is publicly known or used in the Republic of Korea, and before the product has been so well described in South Korean publications that it could have been produced locally. Applications will be made public eighteen months from the date of filing.

Should two or more applications be made for the same invention, the earliest application is entitled to the patent. Opposition to the granting of a patent may be filed within two months of the publication date. Once the invention has been patented, the patentee may grant exclusive or non-exclusive licence in favour of other people.

Compulsory licences may be granted if the patented invention is not worked in South Korea to a reasonable extent within three years from the granting of the patent, or if the invention is not worked for three consecutive years without good reason. Should the invention not be worked for two consecutive years from the granting of a compulsory licence without good reason, the patent may be cancelled. The term of the patent can also expire early in the case of non-payment of annuities, abandonment of the right or invalidation.

Devices that fall outside the definition of 'invention' under patent law may be registered and protected for ten years from the date of publication under the Utility Model Act. As in the case of patents, only the earliest applicant will be granted the right, and opposition may be filed within two months of the publication date.

Trade marks are protected for ten years from the date of registration, and can be renewed for additional ten-year periods. Owners of foreign trade marks wishing to use or license them in the Republic of Korea must obtain approval from the Economic Planning Board, in accordance with the provisions of the Foreign Capital Inducement Law.

Owners of well-known trade marks would be well advised to register them even before entering the market, as prior use is not a requirement for registration and there have been cases of South Korean companies registering foreign trade marks for their own use. This is possible because the first applicant is entitled to registration of a trade mark and obtains exclusive rights to its use. However, if a well-known mark has been registered by an unauthorized company, the owner of the mark may go to court to have the registration invalidated. Should he or she so wish, the owner of a foreign trade mark may establish licensing agreements in the trade mark register, to allow the use of the mark within South Korea.

Opposition to the granting of a trade mark right may be filed within 30 days of the publication date. A trade mark right may be cancelled if the mark is not used in South Korea within one year of its registration, if the ownership of the mark is not transferred within one year of the owner's death, or if its owner ceases trading in the goods concerned. When applying for registration of a mark, the goods to which it will be applied must be specified. The cancellation of the mark may be requested if it is not used in South Korea for more than one year without good reason or if the owner discovers that the mark has been used illegally by a third party.

The **Copyright Act** came into effect in South Korea on 1 July 1987, and offers protection for 'works in which thoughts or sentiments are expressed in a creative way and fall within literary, scientific or artistic fields'. Protection is not given to works of a purely informative nature, such as news reports or official publications.

Copyrights, which must be registered with the Council of Copyrights, are effective until 50 years after the death of the author for written works, and for 20 years in the case of sound recordings. The ROK government is licensing copyright intermediary agents to assist in negotiations between copyright owners and potential users of copyright materials. An independent copyright deliberation council has been set up to help settle disputes out of court.

Computer software is protected under the Computer Program Protection Act for 50 years from the date of the program's creation, and unique designs are offered protection for eight years from registration under the Design Act.

41 Business Culture

Barriers to entry to any market can take a number of forms. The most basic is ignorance of the opportunities presented by the market, or failure to keep abreast of changes in a country's political and/or economic situation that would create new trading or investment opportunities. There can also be legislative or regulatory barriers – a particular government's policy towards the liberalization of the domestic markets, tariff and non-tariff barriers, for example. In addition, there are cultural obstacles ignorance of which can hinder or even prevent effect and profitable operations in a chosen market. Being both informed and culturally aware can help to overcome many of these barriers.

In the case of a rapidly developing country like South Korea, being informed about the economy makes obvious sense; the businessman or woman whose image of South Korea is rooted back in the days of cheap labour and low-tech mass production will be unaware of the opportunities for investment offered as the nation moves towards high-tech, capital-intensive production. Similarly, the businessman or woman who last visited Seoul ten years ago would probably be amazed at the explosion in consumerism in South Korea – a wealth of opportunities for foreign brand-name consumer goods. Keeping abreast of changes in government policy and legislation and being aware of which sectors are being opened up to foreign investment can also help to identify new opportunities.

In the case of South Korea, a knowledge of Korean history will help you appreciate the Koreans' pride in their cultural, political and economic achievements and understand their feelings towards their neighbours and trading partners. An understanding of even the most basic elements of Confucianism will explain the Koreans' liking for structure and

hierarchy, their respect for the elderly, their desire for education, and the low status afforded to women in the workplace.

A common error made by many businessmen and women
visiting the Far East in general, and South Korea in particular,
is to assume that doing business in such a truly foreign market
is simply a matter of western common sense. They play by
the same rules, apply the same logic, and expect the same
responses as they would back at home. Others simply assume
that, if you know one market, you know them all: does it really
matter, you may ask, if you mistakenly refer to South Korea
as Japan in a meeting, or walk into a Korean-style restaurant
with your shoes on? It does.

Clearly, there are differences of degree. Whereas being
unaware of the polite way to give and receive, or being unsure
of how to address your Korean counterpart correctly, is unlikely
to lose you a deal, getting it right will be appreciated. Showing
that you are informed about Korea and aware of Korean sen-
sibilities will create a lasting good impression.

It is unfortunately true that many South Koreans have a
preconception of westerners as pushy, brash and abrasive. The
most important attitude that you can convey in business is one
of sincerity – the conviction that you are in South Korea to
build a long-term relationship and not to make a quick killing.
It must be remembered that as much as the South Koreans
covet high technology and advanced products, they may also
fear dependence on the countries that can provide them.

There has been a growing sense of nationalism in recent
years, especially among younger South Koreans, and a businessman or woman who treats South Korea as a third-world,
second-rate nation is greatly reducing his or her chances of
success in the market. The South Koreans can be extremely
sensitive to real or perceived criticism or denigration of their
political, economic and cultural achievements.

The mistrust and hostility felt by many Koreans towards
the Japanese (See: History) means that comparisons with
Japan, the mistaken use of the word 'Japan' for 'Korea' in
meetings (explained away by jet lag or whistle-stop trips
around Asia – 'if it's Tuesday it must be Seoul' – but inexcus-
able nevertheless), or any implication that South Korea is
perceived as a second-rate Japan will win no friends.

Being culturally aware helps you to understand many factors that are key to doing business in South Korea, from the
way that South Koreans use language and silence, to the
importance of building and maintaining relationships.

ESTABLISHING CONTACT

Cold-calling on the telephone is rarely successful in South Korea. Equally, appearing suddenly and unannounced at a company on the off chance that someone will be available to see you is not advisable. This is because, when meeting new people, the South Koreans prefer the introduction to be effected by someone already known to them.

The South Koreans themselves are great networkers; westerners are often surprised that South Koreans seem to know who was in the classes above and below them at all levels of their education, who comes from their home town and so forth. The reason for this is simple: given that the most acceptable way to arrange a meeting is through a mutual friend or acquaintance, the wider one's circle of friends, relatives, alumni and co-workers, the easier it will be to open doors.

Foreign embassies in Seoul are usually prepared to act as go-betweens for businessmen and women visiting South Korea for the first time. A number of foreign companies in Seoul now employ 'fixers' – senior South Koreans with excellent contacts in business and government who can effect introductions with consummate ease. It is important to remember that, by introducing you to a mutual acquaintance, the go-between is acting rather like a sponsor, and is, to some extent, taking responsibility for your behaviour. Equally, if called upon to a effect an introduction, you should feel sure that the behaviour of your 'protégé' will not reflect badly on you.

Having established the contact, and set up a first meeting, it is a good idea to send a fax to the person or people you will be meeting, giving details of your company and the people who will be attending the meeting, and your proposed agenda. This enables the South Koreans to ensure that the relevant people from their side attend the meeting, and also gives them a chance to prepare mentally for what is to be discussed. As they will talking in their second language, English, any advance help with vocabulary or content will certainly be appreciated.

THE FIRST MEETING

Ideally, the first meeting should be limited to introductions and social niceties – getting to know you, rather than getting down to business. To a westerner it may seem that an inordinate amount of time is taken up in small talk during meetings with South Koreans: as far as they are concerned, this is a way of establishing trust, judging sincerity and commitment, and building relationships. In practice, time constraints during a busy visit may make it necessary to combine introductions and business at the first meeting. This is fine, provided that you devote a reasonable amount of time at the beginning of the meeting to introductory formalities.

When meeting South Koreans for the first time, it is best, as a rule, to limit direct physical contact to a handshake. As far as bowing is concerned, among South Koreans the depth of the bow indicates the degree of respect felt for the person being greeted: it is very difficult for westerners to judge this, and a simple, dignified inclining of the head will usually suffice. These days, handshakes are widely used in South Korea, and may even be combined with a bow; when visiting, wait for your host to extend his hand to you first, in case he is not comfortable with the practice of shaking hands.

Name cards are essential for doing business in South Korea. Your name card is your company passport and should clearly show your place in the company hierarchy. For this reason, it is advisable to have your cards printed in English and Korean, with a Korean title which accurately reflects your place in the company hierarchy. For example, the owner of a company who uses the title of 'Director' at home should use the Korean for 'Company President' rather than 'Director' on his or her name cards, to give an accurate picture of his or her place in the company hierarchy.

South Koreans will often supplement scrutiny of a name card with questions which may seem blunt, if not impertinent. But the answers to these questions – 'How old are you?', 'Are you married?', 'How many children do you have?', or even, 'How much do you earn?' – are useful in slotting the foreigner into their frame of reference. Bear in mind that it is often quite difficult for Koreans to tell how old westerners are, and they may, in addition, be confused by some western job titles. It may, for example, seem odd that a person in his or her thirties could be the deputy to the company president – a vice president – when, in fact, the title is used in many American firms to denote the first level of management.

You should always take with you far more name cards than you would ever imagine it possible to use. Name cards should be given and received with both hands (preferably) and *never* with the left hand. The most respectful way to give or receive in South Korea is with both hands. Watching South Koreans you will see that, when giving and receiving, most people rarely use just one hand even if the left hand appears just to be reaching towards the middle of the right forearm.

When given someone's name card, you should treat it with respect, study it carefully and then either place it on the table in front of you, if seated, or in your name-card holder if standing. Do *not* give it a quick glance and pop it into your pocket. Placing the card in front of you has a practical benefit in meetings as it helps you remember who is who, and which Mr Kim is seated where.

Generally speaking, it is discourteous to write on someone's name card in their presence, although it is often invaluable to jot a few notes down on the back after the meeting. And remember: never write a person's name in red ink. Red ink is used exclusively for recording deaths in a family's genealogical record.

When addressing Koreans, it is considered polite to use their family name plus their title. In most cases a simple 'Mr', 'Mrs', 'Doctor' or 'Miss' will suffice. A Korean name usually comprises three syllables – for example, Kim Hae-gŭn. The first name, in this case Kim, is the family name or surname. These are fairly easily identified as they are relatively few in number, the most common being Kim, Lee and Park. The second syllable, Hae, is the generation name, given to all brothers and cousins, and sometimes to the sisters as well. The final syllable, gŭn, is the personal name.

First names, as they would be considered in the west – in this case, Hae-gŭn – are generally for use by family and intimate friends only and should not be used by westerners, unless specifically invited to do so. When writing their names in the roman alphabet, Koreans sometimes try to westernize them by inverting the word order and placing the family name last, thus: Hae-gŭn Kim. The fact that women do not take their husband's name when they marry can also cause confusion.

It may seem awkward to westerners to keep referring to a Korean whom one knows quite well as Mr Kim or Miss Lee. Many Koreans will adopt western names or initials (such as 'David' Park or 'K.S.' Kim) to circumvent this problem, and it may take some time for them to feel comfortable using a western colleague's first name.

An understanding of the South Koreans' use of language and silence in meetings or negotiations is crucial. In the vast majority of meetings between foreign and South Korean businessmen and women in Seoul, English will be used as the common language. It is a good rule of thumb that, unless your South Korean counterpart is very competent in English, no more than half of what you say is actually communicated. It is also well worth bearing in mind that, working in a second language, the South Koreans will always be at a disadvantage. Foreign businessmen and women should, therefore, make every effort to meet their Korean counterparts part-way.

The use of simple, clear, easily understood English (with no slang or jargon), delivered at a speed that is readily comprehensible without being patronizing, will be greatly appreciated. Given the general exposure to American English, some

South Koreans may be confused at first by a British accent or unfamiliar vocabulary and expressions. For many South Koreans, the loss of face that would follow admitting that they have lost the thread of a discussion may lead them to continue nodding, apparently in agreement, when they are in fact totally lost. Remember that skill in making small talk in English does not automatically mean ability to conduct a discussion about technical matters: reinforce key points and try to be sensitive to the comprehension ability of your counterpart.

Providing handouts and visual aids such as charts, diagrams and bullet points is also useful in getting a message across. It is advisable to send a written outline of the points to be covered ahead of any meeting, and to follow up with a summary of the decisions made. Given the limited opportunities for regular practice of English conversation with a native speaker, and the use of English-language textbooks at schools and colleges, a great many South Koreans are more comfortable reading English than they are speaking it.

Although the effort taken by a westerner to learn just a few simple Korean phrases is always greatly appreciated, throwing odd words of Korean into a conversation in an attempt to impress will only lead to confusion. Unless they are very good, save your Korean skills for social niceties and entertaining.

Silence is often used to great effect by the South Koreans. Whereas westerners tend to feel uncomfortable and try to fill a silence, South Koreans will often simply wait in silence for further clarification – or a better offer. The use of the simple word 'yes' may differ too: a South Korean nodding and saying, 'Yes . . . yes' while a westerner is talking is more likely to mean, 'I hear what you are saying' than, 'I agree with what you are saying'. He may even be thinking, 'I don't understand what he is saying, but I'll keep nodding anyway' – a point worth remembering when seeking agreement or approval.

As a blunt refusal or negative is considered rude in South Korea, local businessmen may find other ways to put the same message across – 'That may be a problem', 'I will have to ask my colleagues about that', etc. – and western businessmen and women would be well advised to do the same.

Perhaps the greatest cause of confusion lies in the answering of negative questions:

Question:	Didn't Mr Kim call?
Answer (Korean):	Yes (he didn't call).
Answer (western):	No (he didn't).

It is useful, therefore, to remember the song title, 'Yes, we have no bananas' – or better still, always to ask questions in the affirmative: 'Did Mr Kim call?'.

When taking your leave, however pressed you may be to get to your next appointment, you should not let your South Korean counterpart know that his was just one of several offices to be visited that afternoon. It is even worse to cut short the meeting so that you can rush off to the next client on the list. It is better to allow more time for each meeting and build in an extra allowance for the time inevitably spent in Seoul traffic jams.

On a business trip to South Korea, it is advisable to take a supply of small, wrapped gifts for the people whom you visit for the first time. On receiving a gift, it is polite to ask if you may open it there and then – etiquette requires that the giver apologizes for the humble gift, no matter what the price tag.

If there is one cardinal rule for doing business in South Korea it is that business begins and ends, stands or falls on the strength of relationships. A great deal of time and effort must be put into maintaining a relationship – by meetings and entertaining when in Seoul, and by regular contact when back in the office. It is important to get to know your partner well and to personalize all relationships – for example, sending small gifts for family celebrations and Christmas or New Year cards.

MAINTAINING THE RELATIONSHIP

Maintaining a business relationship in South Korea requires time and effort, a fair amount of entertaining plus a degree of sensitivity to cultural issues. Once formed, a good relationship will last a lifetime; South Koreans tend to be extremely loyal and will go to great lengths to assist their friends. Equally, once a relationship is marred – for example, by a show of lack of faith or an act which results in a loss of face (see below) – a great deal of hard work will be required to get the relationship back on the right track.

Entertaining forms an essential part of any business relationship: probably as much entertaining is done over a bottle of whisky in South Korea as round a boardroom table. Invitations can come at short notice, and entertaining usually takes place in restaurants rather than in the home. Although Karaoke evenings, games of golf and picnics in the mountains may seem to have no connection to the business in hand, it is all part of the relationship-building process. Entertaining should not be regarded as irksome; it should be accepted when offered and reciprocated in due course.

Wives are seldom invited to after-work functions, and then only to meals, for example, when a foreign businessman is travelling with his wife. At other times, it is 'boys only', the female company usually being provided by the drinking establishment visited after the meal. Whether or not western businesswomen attend these functions is a matter of personal choice, unless it is made clear that their presence would rather dampen the proceedings. Some South Korean men may feel ill at ease drinking with western women present.

As a rule when dining and drinking, wait for your hosts to take the lead as far as etiquette is concerned. Some general rules: when entering a traditional Korean restaurant or someone's house you will be required to take off your shoes and wear slippers, which will be provided. To avoid embarrassment, try to make sure that there are no holes in your socks or stockings and, for convenience's sake, wear slip-on shoes rather than lace-ups.

It is best to wait to be seated, as one's place at a formal meal is determined by status. At most meals the eating implements are a spoon and chopsticks. The chopsticks may be wooden or metal – eating with these takes some skill, as it is rather like eating with knitting needles! The spoon should be used for the soup, and may be used for the rice. Fingers are seldom used (watch your hosts to see when using them is appropriate), and fruit served at the end of a meal is usually picked up with a small fork or toothpick provided.

When eating, do not stick your chopsticks upright in your rice (this is only done at funerals); rest them across your bowl if you pause while eating, and lay them on the table beside your bowl when you have finished. It is also considered impolite to talk a great deal during a meal, and to finish all the food, as this implies that the amount was insufficient.

South Korean male colleagues will be only to pleased to introduce you to the intricacies of drinking rituals – you will have to be very insistent to avoid drinking and, once a firm 'No thank you, I don't drink' is given, you will have to continue abstaining. A meal is generally followed by a drinking session, which is almost always accompanied by singing; it is a far greater social *faux pas* to refuse to sing at all than to struggle, tone deaf, through 'Old MacDonald Had a Farm'!

The lavish entertainment laid on by some South Korean hosts may leave westerners feeling emotionally and financially unable to reciprocate. In Seoul, the best approach may be to offer lunch at a good western restaurant, and back at home, a game of golf or a meal at a traditional restaurant would fit the bill very well.

An official dinner, hosted by a company or its president, will be discreetly paid for by the hosts, while, after an informal lunch out near the office, a great deal of discussion may occur around the cash register as everyone tries to pay the bill. It is important to be seen to be pushing and shoving as much as the next man; should you lose, you can pay next time.

FACE AND *KIBUN*

When doing business in South Korea, it is essential to be sensitive to the importance of 'face' and *kibun*. Face is a person's social and professional position, whereas *kibun* is a person's feelings, mood, frame of mind. Both must be maintained, and great care must be taken not to cause loss of face or damage to *kibun*. Showing anger or hostility in public, or openly criticizing incompetence or mistakes, is distasteful to South Koreans. Equally important is the need to offer a way out of a tricky situation which will enable one to save face and prevent shame and embarrassment.

The lengths to which South Koreans will go to preserve good *kibun* are illustrated by what is referred to among expatriates as the 'Friday Afternoon Syndrome', where bad news is withheld until late on Friday afternoon in order not to upset the boss's *kibun*. The South Koreans are skilled in reading non-verbal reactions and sensing whether or not the *kibun* is right, and they may assume that foreigners are equally able to read situations and act accordingly. The byword is 'harmony', which must be preserved at all costs.

The basic message when doing business in Seoul is to bear in mind that the way that South Koreans think, act and do business has been conditioned over decades if not centuries. These are well-established modes of social behaviour and personal relations; railing against things that seem illogical or irrational will not change them.

A good and frequently cited example of the differences in western and South Korean business practices is that of our respective attitudes towards contracts. Whereas westerners look on the signing of a contract as a legally binding end to a series of negotiations, to the South Koreans a contract is a personal agreement which symbolizes the beginning of a relationship. For a South Korean, the content of the contract may not be as important as who signed it and the fact that it exists. Should one of the signatories change jobs or leave the company, the terms of the contract may be considered invalid or in need of renegotiation. The dialogue and the relationship must continue after the contact is signed, enabling both sides to respond to changes and adjust the contract accordingly.

It is more diplomatic to try to understand the reasons behind South Korean business practices and adapt your own ideas and attitudes to suit the local conditions than to try to force your standards on your Korean counterpart. It is also worth remembering that there may well be aspects of western business practices that South Koreans find infuriating or distasteful.

MANAGEMENT

There have been three important influences on the South Korean management style – those of Confucianism, Japan and the United States – all of which are reflected to some degree in modern management practices in South Korea.

The traditional Chinese Confucian scorn for commerce and trade meant that there were no large-scale private enterprises in Korea at the end of the nineteenth century to which management principles could have been applied. During the Japanese colonial period (1910–45), the Koreans were exposed to Japanese management practices, but were generally excluded from managerial posts.

After Korea was liberated from Japanese rule, many Koreans went to the United States to study and brought back with them American theories of management. Koreans who worked closely with the United States Military Government between 1945 and 1948, and latterly with the US armed forces stationed in South Korea, studied American military and business management systems. After being discharged from military service, they applied their new skills to their work in the private sector.

Some important characteristics of South Korean management style are:

- **The influence of Confucian traditions**. It is still generally true to say that when South Koreans organize and manage enterprises, they do so according to the same principles that govern their private lives. In other words, many South Korean companies resemble large families, with a paterfamilias exercising almost total authority over the family members (see also: Introduction to Society; The Chaebŏl). The head of the company has absolute rights and responsibilities – he must be obeyed and, in return, must provide for the people in his charge.

  The influence of Confucianism can also be seen in the dedication exhibited by South Korean workers, their respect for seniority, and their loyalty. Promotion within a company is commonly on the basis of length of service rather than skills and ability, making it difficult or even impossible to promote a young high-flyer over the heads of his seniors. Once again, this is in the interests of group harmony.

Unlike in Japan, loyalty is more often to an individual than to the company as a whole. As a large proportion of recruitment is still carried out on personal recommendation, there are strong feelings of loyalty on the part of employees to the person who brought them into the company.

- **Top-down decision making**. Although in theory, principles of consensus formation apply in South Korean companies, in more cases than the South Koreans may care to admit, decision making is highly centralized. In many companies and business groups, the chairman or top executives (often family members) tend to make decisions unilaterally or in small groups after consultation with the parties involved. However, the South Koreans may pretend that decisions are built on a consensus view, and the delays in decision making which can arise from this can cause frustration to a westerner who does not understand what is really going on.

- **The treatment of women as temporary workers**. Many companies still require women to resign on marriage or retire at 30, even if they are single. It is common to see women with university degrees and excellent foreign language skills working as secretaries in South Korean companies, as they are perceived to be marking time until they get married and start a family.

  Women seldom get the chance to rise to managerial positions in 'traditional', male-oriented sectors, although they have more chance to use their skills in areas not dominated by men, such as the media, advertising and public relations. Women still tend to get lower pay than their male counterparts, with small increments and poor promotion prospects (see: Introduction to Society).

The coming years should see significant changes in South Korean management style. The government is actively encouraging a change to professional management – that is, replacing family member executives in corporations with professional managers. While the concept of paternalistic management is unlikely to disappear completely, it will be modified to recognize the increasing maturity and capabilities of the workers.

Changes like this could also bring in employment and promotion on the basis of ability rather than connections. The labour shortage facing many sectors of the economy should bring greater opportunities for women, although it remains to be seen how far they will advance into managerial posts.

PART SEVEN

Directory

42 Who Can Help at Home

As a general rule, advice on trading with or doing business in the Republic of Korea can be obtained from: trade-related government agencies, trade representatives and commercial staff attached to South Korean foreign missions, local offices of the Korea Trade Promotion Corporation (KOTRA), commercial consultancies, and companies already active in the South Korean market.

The international divisions of many banks prepare economic reports on overseas markets, and chambers of commerce usually collect market information, which is available to members.

UNITED KINGDOM-GOVERNMENT ORGANIZATIONS

**Department of Trade and Industry
  – Export Market Information
  Centre**
Ashdown House
123 Victoria Street
London SW1E 6RB

(T) 071-215 5444/5445
(F) 071-215 4231

The Centre provides research materials, statistics, directories, and access to databases.

**Department of Trade and Industry –
  The Korea Desk**
Kingsgate House
66–74 Victoria Street
London SW1E 6SW

(T) 071-215 4809/4747
(F) 071-215 4701

The Desk handles enquiries on trading with South Korea, and provides information and advisory services.

Department of Trade and Industry –   (T) 071-276 2414
   Overseas Promotions Supports
Dean Bradley House
52 Horseferry Road
London SW1P 2AG

This branch of the DTI provides information on trade missions to South Korea and Korea-related promotional events and trade fairs within the United Kingdom.

Regional DTI offices also offer information on overseas markets and assist companies in their efforts to break into new markets.

Export Credits Guarantee   (T) 071-512 7000
   Department   (F) 071-512 7649
2 Exchange Tower
Harbour Exchange Square
London E14 9GS

ECGD provides export insurance and helps exporters to obtain access to cheap export finance.

The Korea Trade Action Committee
c/o The Korea Desk
(as above)

The Committee comprises businessmen and women with experience in the Korean market, who offer advice to exporters on a voluntary basis. The Department of Trade and Industry (DTI) Korea Desk is the KTAC secretariat.

UNITED KINGDOM – PRIVATE SECTOR ORGANIZATIONS

Export Marketing Research Scheme   (T) 0203 694484
The Association of British Chambers
Of Commerce
4 Westwood House
Westwood Business Park
Coventry CV4 8HS

The Institute of Export   (T) 071-247 9812
Export House   (F) 071-377 5343
64 Clifton Street
London EC2A 4HB

The Institute offers technical assistance to exporters and provides training on export-related topics for specific markets.

Korea Business Services   (T) 0742 682800
PO Box 760   (F) 0742 666063
Sheffield S11 8GH

KBS is a commercial consultancy which offers a comprehensive range of services designed to help British companies develop successful and profitable links with Korea.

UNITED KINGDOM – OTHER ORGANIZATIONS

Technical Help for Exporters (THE)   (T) 0908 220022
British Standards Institution   (F) 0908 225080
Linford Wood
Milton Keynes MK14 6LE

THE was established by Royal Charter to offer help with technical requirements in overseas markets.

KOREAN GOVERNMENT ORGANIZATIONS

The Embassy of the Republic of   (T) 071-581 0247
    Korea   (F) 071-581 8020
4 Palace Gate
London W8 5NF

The Korea Trade Centre   (T) 071-834 5082
Vincent House   (F) 071-630 5233
Vincent Square
London SW1P 2NB

UNITED STATES OF AMERICA – GOVERNMENT ORGANIZATIONS

The Korea Desk   (T) (202) 482 4957
Room 2308   (F) (202) 482 4453
Office of the Pacific Basin
US Department of Commerce
14th and Constitution Ave NW
Washington DC 20230

The Desk assists other US government trade-related agencies in the formation of trade policy.

The Korea Desk   (T) (202) 647-7717
Room 5313   (F) (202) 647-7350
Office of East Asia and the Pacific
US Department of State
2201 Constitution Ave NW
Washington DC 20520

The Desk is responsible for broad policy formation and economic relations.

New-to-Export Information   (T) 1-800-USA TRADE
                                            1-800-872 8723

This service, which is located in the Trade Information Centre of the Commerce Department in Washington, also publishes 'Export Programs: A Business Directory of US Government Resources'.

United States Trade Representative   (T) (202) 395-4755
Winder Building   (F) (202) 395-3911
600 17th Street NW
Washington DC 20506

The USTR has responsibility for generic trade policy and market access issues.

UNITED STATES OF AMERICA – PRIVATE SECTOR ORGANIZATIONS

The US-Korea Business Council   (T) (202) 842-0567
1023 15th Street NW   (F) (202) 842-3275
Washington DC 20005

The Council is a high-level, private-sector forum, which hosts an annual US–Korea Business Conference.

UNITED STATES OF AMERICA – KOREAN ORGANIZATIONS

The Embassy of the Republic of   (T) (202) 939-5600
  Korea   (F) (202) 797-0595
2450 Massachusetts Ave NW
Washington DC 20008

The Korean Embassy has Consulates General in Anchorage, Atlanta, Boston, Chicago, Honolulu, Houston, Los Angeles, Miami, New York, San Francisco and Seattle.

The Korea Economic Institute of   (T) (202) 371-0690
  America   (F) (202) 371-0692
1030 15th Street NW #662
Washington DC 20005

The Institute promotes economic relations through public information programmes, handles enquiries about Korea, and acts as a link with Korean corporations.

The Korea Foreign Traders' Association (KFTA) has offices in New York and Washington; the New York office also houses the Korea Chamber of Commerce and Industry.

The Korea Trade Promotion Corporation (KOTRA) has offices in Chicago, Dallas, Los Angeles, Miami, New York, San Francisco and Washington.

AUSTRALIA AND NEW ZEALAND

Australian Trade Commission (T) 276-5111
  (Austrade) (F) 276-5105
GPO Box 2386
Canberra City NSW 2601

Austrade aims to facilitate and encourage trade with foreign countries, represents the trading and commercial interests of Australia overseas, provides information, and assists indirectly and directly in trade negotiations.

Austrade has offices in Adelaide, Brisbane, Darwin, Geelong, Melbourne, Newcastle, Perth, Sydney, Townsville, Wollongong, and Hobart, Tasmania.

Export Guarantee Office (EXGO) (T) 720-265
The State Insurance Building (F) 725-824
Waring Taylor Street
Wellington
Also at:
The Parkview Building (T) 394-706
200 Victoria Street
Auckland

Export Institute of New Zealand Inc. (T) 605-296
PO Box 47
Auckland

The Institute is a private-sector, non-profit-making organization, which aims to encourage and develop foreign exchange earnings, and encourage export expertise. It has branch offices in Bay of Plenty, Canterbury, Manawatu, Nelson, Otago, Southland, Taranki, Waikato and Wellington.

Ministry of Foreign Affairs (MOFA) (T) 728-877
Business Contacts Programme
MOFA Economic Division
Private Bag
Wellington

Exporters can register with the Ministry and receive a selection of current reports from overseas posts.

New Zealand Manufacturers'   (T) 473-3000
  Federation Inc.   (F) 473-3004
Enterprise House
3 Church Street
Wellington

Technical Help to Exporters (THE)   (T) 842-108
Standards Association of New
 Zealand
Private Bag
Wellington

THE assists with overseas standards, regulations, codes of practice, product approval procedures, certification and testing. It helps in negotiations with overseas approval authorities and translates documents from and into foreign languages.

Tradenz   (T) 499-2244
Pastoral House   (F) 733-193
25 The Terrace
Wellington 6001

Tradenz offers advice and assistance to exporters, by providing ongoing monitoring of overseas markets and preparing marketplace assessment (MPA) reports on prospects for exports of goods and services. Trade commissioners based overseas can also offer assistance through Tradenz, which has offices in 35 cities worldwide.

    Tradenz has regional offices in Auckland, Lower Hutt, Christchurch and Dunedin, which take primary responsibility for serving exporters in their region. In the regional offices, export consultants liaise with manufacturers, producers and suppliers to develop the most effective marketing strategy for overseas activities.

43 Who Can Help in South Korea

KOREAN GOVERNMENT DEPARTMENTS AND ORGANIZATIONS

Consultation Office for Overseas Companies (COOC)

1st Floor	(T) 551-6781
KOEX Main Building	(F) 551-6784
159 Samsŏng-dong	
Kangnam-gu	
Seoul 135-731	

COOC serves as an ombuds office for foreign businessmen and women on trade and investment matters.

Economic Planning Board (EPB)

2nd Government Integrated Building	(T) 503-9032
1 Chungang-dong	(F) 503-9033
Kwach'ŏn-shi	
Kyŏnggi-do	
Seoul	

The EPB has responsibility for the overall planning of the economy, the formulation and execution of the national budget, and the coordination of inward and foreign investment, as well as for research and technical development, and economic cooperation with foreign countries and international organizations. The Minister concurrently serves as one of the nation's two deputy prime ministers. The EPB incorporates the Fair Trade Commission and the Office of Supply.

Export–Import Bank of Korea   (T) 784-1021
  (Exim Bank)   (F) 784-1030
16-1 Yŏŭido-dong
Yŏngdŭngp'o-gu
Seoul

The Exim Bank is a special government financial institution established to promote the sound development of the South Korean economy and to foster economic cooperation with foreign countries. The bank administers financing programmes to facilitate the export of capital goods and services, overseas investments and major resource developments, and operates export insurance schemes on behalf of the ROK government. The bank also operates and manages the government's Economic Development Cooperation Fund (ECDF).

Korea Broadcasting Advertising
  Corporation (KOBACO)
Press Centre Building   (T) 731-7114
1-25 T'aepy'ŏng-no   (F) 731-7110
Chung-gu
Seoul 100-745

Founded in 1971, KOBACO is the exclusive sales agent for television and radio advertising.

Korea Commercial Arbitration Board
  (KCAB)
43rd Floor   (T) 551-2000
Korea World Trade Centre   (F) 551-2020
159 Samsŏng-dong
Kangnam-gu
Seoul 135-729

KCAB selects South Korean and foreign arbitrators for the formal settlement of disputes which have not been resolved during the mandatory 90-day 'private resolution' period. It is a member of the International Commercial Arbitration Association.

Korea Customs Administration (KCA)
Seoul Headquarters   (T) 512-2309
   (F) 512-2322

Seoul Main Customs House   (T) 544-3711
   (F) 516-1882

Kimp'o Airport Customs House	(T) 660-5612
	(F) 660-5399

Pusan Main Customs House	(T) 051-426 0011
	(F) 051-523 0852

The KCA levies customs duties, permits customs clearance for goods entering and leaving the Republic, and controls smuggling.

Korea Industrial Property Office (KIPO)

823-1 Yŏksam-dong	(T) 568-6077
Kangnam-gu	(F) 553-9584
Seoul 135-785	

Originally the Bureau of Patents, KIPO now has responsibility for issuing patents and registering trade marks.

Korea Trade Promotion Corporation (KOTRA)

Korea World Trade Centre
159 Samsŏng-dong
Kangnam-gu
Seoul

President's Office	(T) 551-4100
	(F) 551-4475

Senior Vice-President	(T) 551-4105

Director of Trade Fairs and	(T) 551-4400
Exhibitions	(F) 557-5784

KOTRA, which maintains more than 80 centres in 65 countries, is primarily responsible for the promotion of South Korean exports. It also handles trade enquiries, assists visiting trade delegations, organizes outward missions, trade fairs and exhibitions, and promotes industrial and international cooperation.

Ministry of Finance (MOF)

1 Chungang-dong
Kwach'ŏn-shi
Kyŏnggi-do
Seoul

The MOF is responsible for the government's financial affairs, including finance-related legislation, currency and foreign exchange, national accounts, control of state-owned properties, taxation and customs. It controls the Office of National Tax Administration, the Office of Monopoly, the Office of

Customs Administration, and the Securities and Insurance Bureaux, and it directs and supervises the special banks and those banks in which the government holds the majority share.

The Ministry has established a Foreign Investment Information Centre (tel: 503-9259, fax: 503-9260) to help local and foreign investors by distributing information on investment and technology inducement. There is also a One-Stop Service Office within the MOF (tel: 503-9258, fax: 503-9324), which aims to speed up the procedures for foreign investment approval.

Ministry of Trade and Industry (MTI)

1 Chungang-dong
Kwach'ŏn-shi
Kyŏnggi-do
Seoul 427-760

(T) 503-9410
(F) 503-9496

The Ministry has responsibility for commerce, foreign trade (including import and export regulations), industry, trade marks and patents, and industrial standards.

Office of National Tax Administration

108-4 Susong-dong
Chongno-gu
Seoul

(T) 739-6768

ONTA handles all matters relating to the levying and collection of taxes.

Seoul Immigration Office

1st Floor
Shin-Ah Building
39-1 Sŏsomun-dong
Chung-gu
Seoul

(T) 776-8984/7

This government office handles matters relating to the Republic of Korea, including residence permits, and re-entry permits for foreign residents.

Small and Medium Industry Promotion Corporation (SMIPC)

27-2 Yŏŭido-dong
Yŏngdŭngp'o-gu
Seoul

(T) 783-9611
(F) 784-9230

The SMIPC is a non-profit-making organization which promotes the interests of small- and medium-sized industries, providing training services, and modernization and cooperation programmes. It also collects, processes and disseminates information, and operates and manages the Small and Medium Industry Promotion Fund.

SMIPC has established a Centre for Foreign Investment Services (tel: 783-9466, fax: 782-9702) to promote foreign investment in small enterprises.

KOREAN PRIVATE-SECTOR ORGANIZATIONS

**Association of Foreign Trading Agents
in Korea (AFTAK)**
AFTAK Building
218 Han'gang-no 2-ga
Yongsan-gu
Seoul

Trade Promotion Department   (T) 792-1581
                                  (F) 785-4373

The Association currently comprises over 8,000 members, who represent more than 40,000 foreign manufacturers and suppliers of goods and services.

Federation of Korean Industries (FKI)
28-1 Yŏŭido-dong   (T) 780-0821
Yŏngdŭngp'o-gu   (F) 782-6425
Seoul 150-756

The FKI is a private, independent, non-profit-making federation of nearly 500 companies which account for the lion's share of the nation's foreign trade. It is the major lobby group for big business in South Korea, and has its own research arm, the Korea Economic Research Institute (KERI).

**Korean Chamber of Commerce and
Industry (KCCI)**
45 Namdaemun-no 4-ga
Chung-gu
Seoul 100-743

International Affairs   (T) 316-3523
                                  (F) 757-9475

As the national federation of local chambers of commerce, KCCI aims to develop commerce and industry, promote and protect the interests of those engaged in business, and strengthen international business relations. It also provides counselling on business management, certifies trade documents, trains workers, managers and executives, and holds seminars on trade-related topics. It operates bilateral economic cooperation committees with more than 30 countries, and maintains cooperative relationships with chambers of commerce in over 60 countries.

Korea Federation of Small Businesses
(KFSB)

16-2 Yŏŭido-dong	(T) 785-0010
Yŏngdŭngp'o-gu	(F) 785-0199
Seoul 150-010	

KFSB is the counterpart of the Federation of Korean Industries for small businesses (those with twenty or fewer employees), providing information and business education services, organizing research projects, and managing the Small Business Fund. It also conducts international cooperation projects and promotes exports on behalf of small businesses.

Korean Foreign Trade Association
(KFTA)
702 Korea World Trade Centre
159 Samsŏng-dong
Kangnam-gu
Seoul

Trade Inquiry Office	(T) 551-5267
Trade Cooperation Department	(T) 551-5301
	(F) 551-5100

KFTA provides trade information and business counselling services, conducts market research and surveys, organizes trade and buying missions, and sponsors seminars and workshops related to trade and the economy. All businesses wishing to export or import on their own account must join KFTA.

In July 1992, KFTA launched the Korea Trade Network (KTNet) on a trial basis. The system will allow the exchange of trade-related, standard-format documents between computers – a significant step towards paperless trading. KFTA is also operating a Korean-language trade database called KOTIS.

FOREIGN GOVERNMENT DEPARTMENTS AND ORGANIZATIONS

Australian Embassy, Austrade

11th Floor	(T) 730-6490
Kyobo Building	(F) 734-5085
1 Chongno 1-ga	
Chongno-gu	
Seoul	

British Embassy, Commercial Section
4 Chung-dong   (T) 735-7341/3
Chung-gu   (F) 733-8368
Seoul

Mailing address from the United
Kingdom:
British Embassy Seoul
BFPO3
Forces Airmail

British Consulate in Pusan
1201 Yoochang Building   (T) 051-463 4630
25-2 Chungang-dong 4-ga
Chung-gu
Pusan 600-014

Delegation of the Commission of the
European Community in Korea
109 Changch'ung-dong   (T) 271-0781/3
Chung-gu   (F) 271-0786
Seoul

Embassy of the United States of
America, Foreign Commercial
Service
82 Sejong-no   (T) 397-4356
Chongno-gu   (F) 739-1628
Seoul

Mailing address from the United States:
American Embassy Seoul
Unit 5550

APO AP 96205-0001

Consulate of the United States of
America in Pusan
American Consulate Building   (T) 051-246 7791
24 2-ga Taech'ang-dong
Chung-gu
Pusan

New Zealand Embassy, TradeNZ
18th Floor   (T) 730-7794
Kyobo Building   (F) 737-4861
1 Chongno 1-ga
Chongno-gu
Seoul

FOREIGN PRIVATE SECTOR ORGANIZATIONS

American Chamber of Commerce in Korea (AmCham)

Room 307	(T) 752-3061
Westin Chosun Hotel	(F) 755-6577
87 Sogong-dong	
Chung-gu	
Seoul 100-070	

AmCham is a private, non-profit-making association comprising business executives from the United States, the Republic of Korea and other countries. AmCham lobbies the Korean government, briefs visiting businessmen and women, and organizes seminars.

British Chamber of Commerce in Korea

392-11 Hongǔn 3-dong	(T) 303-4058
Sǒdaemun-gu	(F) 376-3337
Seoul 120-103	

Korea–American Business Institute (KABI)

Room 808	(T) 753-7750
Paik Nam Building	(F) 752-6921
188-3 Ŭlchi 1-ga	
Chung-gu	
Seoul 100-191	

KABI provides consultative services, research, training and administrative support to the American business community in Seoul.

Korea–US Economic Council Inc. (KUSEC)

Suite 4304	(T) 551-3366
Trade Tower	(F) 551-3365
159 Samsǒng-dong	
Kangnam-gu	
Seoul	

KUSEC is a private, non-profit-making organization which maintains close links with the American business community in Seoul and promotes economic cooperation between the two nations.

44 Contact Addresses in South Korea

ACCOUNTANTS
The following are among the local companies associated with international accountancy firms:

Anjin Accounting
17-3 Yŏŭido-dong   (T) 784-6901
Yŏngdŭngp'o-gu   (F) 785-4753
Seoul 150-010
Associated with Arthur Andersen
  & Co.

Sae Dong & Co.
15th Floor   (T) 785-3600
63 Building   (F) 784-8362
60 Yŏŭido-dong
Yŏngdŭngp'o-gu
Seoul 150-763
Associated with Touche Ross.

Samil Accounting Corporation
20th and 21st Floors   (T) 796-7000
Kukje Centre Building   (F) 796-7027
191 Han'gang-no 2-ga
Yongsan-gu
Seoul
Associated with Coopers & Lybrand.

San Tong & Co.
7th Floor   (T) 733-2345
Koreana Building   (F) 733-5317
61-1 T'aepy'ŏng-no 1-ga
Chung-gu
Seoul
Associated with KPMG Peat Marwick.

Seihwa Accounting Corporation
9th Floor   (T) 745-5671
Samwhan Building   (F) 738-0447
98-5 Uni-dong
Chongno-gu
Seoul
Associated with Price Waterhouse.

Young Wha Accounting Corporation
11th-14th Floors   (T) 783-5261
Dae Yu Building   (F) 785-6991
25-15 Yŏŭido-dong
Yŏngdŭngp'o-gu
Seoul
Associated with Ernst & Young
  International.

AIRLINES: DOMESTIC

Korean Air
KAL Building   (T) 751-7114
41-3 Sŏsomun-dong   (F) 751-7386
Chung-gu
Seoul

Asiana Airlines
10-1 Hoehyŏn-dong 2-ga   (T) 774-4000
Chung-gu   (F) 758-8090
Seoul

AIRLINES: FOREIGN

Air France
6th Floor   (T) 773-3151/5
Samwha Building   (F) 774-4533
21 Sogong-dong
Chung-gu
Seoul

British Airways
Room 210   (T) 774-5516
Westin Chosun Hotel   (F) 757-5427
87 Sogong-dong
Seoul

Cathay Pacific Airways
Room 701   (T) 773-0321/10
Kolon Building   (F) 756-0170
45 Mugyo-dong
Chung-gu
Seoul

Continental Airlines
25th Floor   (T) 775-1500
Lotte Building   (F) 774-4555
1 Sogong-dong
Chung-gu
Seoul

Delta Airlines
Room 1402   (T) 754-3694/5
Dongbang Plaza   (F) 755-6961
150 T'aep'yŏngno 2-ga
Chung-gu
Seoul

KLM Royal Dutch Airlines
9th Floor   (T) 753-1093
Samwha Building   (F) 774-4677
21 Sogong-dong
Chung-gu
Seoul

Lufthansa German Airlines
Room 601   (T) 757-4381
Centre Building   (F) 756-8244
91-1 Sogong-dong
Chung-gu
Seoul

Northwest Airlines
10th Floor   (T) 733-4191
Northwest Building   (F) 736-8007
111-1 Sŏrin-dong
Chongno-gu
Seoul

Quantas
Room 801   (T) 777–6871/5
Dong Min Building   (F) 774–8514
95 Mugyo-dong
Chung-gu
Seoul

Swiss Air
Room 301   (T) 757–8906/7
Oriental Chemical Building   (F) 753–2644
50 Sogong-dong
Chung-gu
Seoul

United Airlines
Room 1501   (T) 757–8911/5
Ankuk Insurance Building   (F) 752–2970
87 Sogong-dong
Chung-gu
Seoul

BANKS: DOMESTIC

Bank of Korea
110 Namdaemun-no 3-ga   (T) 759–4114
Chung-gu   (F) 752–6548
Seoul

Bank of Pusan
830–38 Pomil-dong   (T) 051–67 3151
Tong-gu
Pusan

The Export–Import Bank of Korea
16–1 Yŏŭido-dong   (T) 784–1021
Yŏngdŭngp'o-gu   (F) 784–1030
Seoul

The Industrial Bank of Korea
50 Ŭlchiro 2-ga   (T) 729–6114
Chung-gu   (F) 729–6305
Seoul

Korea Development Bank
10–2 Kwanch'ŏl-dong   (T) 398–6114
Chongno-gu   (F) 733–4768
Seoul

Korea Exchange Bank
181 Ulchiro 2-ga   (T) 729–0114
Chung-gu
Seoul

BANKS: FOREIGN

Upwards of sixty foreign banks are currently represented in Seoul; of these more than ten have branches in Pusan. For addresses and contact numbers, see the Korea Yellow Pages.

BOOKS AND MAGAZINES (INCLUDING FOREIGN PUBLICATIONS)

The Kyobo Book Centre
8–9 Chongno 2-ga   (T) 732–2331
Chongno-gu
Seoul

CHURCHES

Church services are held for a variety of faiths; the Saturday edition of the *Korea Times* lists the times of services in Seoul.

COMMUNICATIONS

DACOM
Planning and Coordination Division   (T) 796–6601
65–228 Han'gang-no   (F) 796–8500
Yongsan-gu
Seoul

DACOM provides data communication and international telephone services.

Korea Telecom
Overseas Cooperation Department   (T) 750–3810
100 Sejong-no   (F) 750–3830
Chung-gu
Seoul

Korea Telecom enjoys a monopoly on all basic telecommunications services, with the exception of international telephone calls.

CONFERENCE CENTRES

The Korea World Trade Centre

159 Samsŏng-dong	(T) 551–5114
Kangnam-gu	(F) 557–7414
Seoul 135–731	

The 50-acre (20-hectare) complex comprises a 55-storey Trade Tower, home to many of the nation's trade-related associations, the Korea Exhibition Centre (KOEX), a convention centre, the Korea City Air Terminal, the Intercontinental Hotel, and a branch of the Hyundai department store. KOEX is the largest trade-show venue in South Korea, and hosts over 80 shows per year in its two halls and annex (total display area of more than 300,000 square feet, or 28,000 square metres). The World Trade Centre is served by the Number 2 subway line.

All deluxe and super-deluxe hotels have conference and convention facilities.

CONSULTANTS

Andersen Consulting

Room 1600	(T) 739–9000
Kyobo Building	(F) 739–6999
1 Chongno 1-ga	
Chongno-gu	
Seoul	

S. H. Jang & Associates

Suite 1409	(T) 753–4531
The Korea Herald Building	(F)
1-2 3-ga Hoehyŏn-dong	
Chung-gu	
Seoul	

Samil Coopers & Lybrand Consulting Ltd.

10th Floor	(T) 796–7000
Kukje Centre Building	(F) 790–4251
191 Han'gang-no 2-ga	
Yongsan-gu	
Seoul	

Seoul Business Consultants Services Inc.

Suite 802   (T) 555–9242
BYC Building   (F) 555–9243
648–1 Yŏksam-dong
Kangnam-gu
Seoul 135–080

COURIER SERVICES

DHL (Uni-Ocean Express Co. Ltd.)
Map'o   (T) 716–0001
PO Box 139   (F) 719–6454
Seoul

Federal Express (Airway Express)
158–11 Tonggyo-dong   (T) 333–8000
Map'o-gu   (F) 335–0180
Seoul

CREDIT CARDS

American Express International
181–1 Puam-dong   (T) 398–0114
Chongno-gu
Seoul

Diners Club International
2–191 Han'gangno   (T) 796–4100
Yongsan-gu
Seoul

Visa International
50 Sogong-dong   (T) 752–6523
Chung-gu
Seoul

HOSPITALS

Asan Medical Centre
388–1 P'ungnap-tong   (T) 480–3025/6
Songp'a-gu
Seoul

Asia Emergency Assistance   (T) 790–7561
Asia Emergency Assistance provides a 24-hour emergency referral service for foreigners, acting as a link between foreign patients and Korean hospitals. Fees are payable for this service.

International Clinic
5-4 Hannam-dong   (T) 796-1871
Yongsan-gu
Seoul

Seoul Adventist Hospital
29-1 Hwigyŏng-dong   (T) 244-0191
Tongdaemun-gu
Seoul

**Severance Hospital, International
  Clinic**
134 Shinch'on-dong   (T) 392-3404
Sŏdaemun-gu
Seoul

LEGAL ADVICE/PATENT ATTORNEYS

Numerous firms are listed in the Korea Yellow Pages; check
these listings for contact addresses and numbers, and seek
advice on which firms have experience in dealing with foreign
clients.

PUBLIC RELATIONS

Burson-Marsteller Korea Inc.
9th Fl. Daio Building   (T) 782 7151/7
26-5 Yŏŭido-dong   (F) 782 7158
Yŏngdŭngp'o-gu
Seoul

Burson-Marsteller handles corporate, financial and marketing
communications for companies located in South Korea.

TOURIST INFORMATION

Korea National Tourism Corporation
10 Ta-dong   (T) 757-6030
Chung-gu   (F) 757-5997
Seoul 100-180

Lost and Found
Citizens' Room of Seoul Metropolitan (T) 754-7000
Police Bureau
201-11 Naeja-dong
Chongno-gu
Seoul

Tourist Complaint Centre
CPO Box 903   (T) 735-0101
Seoul 100-609

TRANSLATORS AND INTERPRETERS
The staff at the Korea Exhibition Centre can arrange the hiring
of interpreters to work at trade shows.

Star Communications
Suite 306   (T) 756-0761
Westin Chosun Hotel   (F) 756-0755
CPO Box 8541
Seoul 100-685

The company provides personnel, language, secretarial, liaison
and representation services.

PART EIGHT

Appendix

45 Top-performing Conglomerates and Companies

TABLE 9 Top ten conglomerates in sales (millions of wŏn), 1991

Group	1991 Sales (actual)	1992 Sales (projection)	% Change year on year
Samsung	W31,051	W40,000	28.8
Hyundai	29,889	44,000	47.2
Lucky-Goldstar	18,971	23,200	22.3
Daewoo	13,373	19,400	45.1
Sunkyong	9,384	12,000	27.9
Ssangyong	6,976	8,950	28.3
Kia	4,686	6,800	45.1
Hanjin	4,589	6,050	31.8
Lotte	4,384	4,800	9.5
Korea Explosives	3,440	4,500	* 30.8

Source: Respective groups.

TABLE 10 Debt ratio of the top ten conglomerates (listed subsidiaries only), 1990–1

Group	Number of listed companies	Debt ratio	
		1990	1991
Daewoo	7	269.4	298.1
Hanjin	5	571.0	693.9
Hyundai	10	391.0	446.1
Kia	5	273.6	328.7
Korea Explosives	5	245.7	274.8
Lotte	4	273.1	330.9
Lucky–Goldstar	12	294.8	350.6
Samsung	9	348.1	322.2
Ssangyong	9	220.9	197.8
Sunkyong	3	378.4	244.2
Total/average	*69*	*326.6*	*348.7*

Source: Korea Times, 17 March 1991.

TABLE 11 Top twenty corporations in sales (millions of wŏn), 1991

Rank	Company	Sales	% change year on year	Net profit	Debt ratio
1	Samsung Co.	10,199,070	28.3	15,045	261.9
2	Hyundai Corp.	9,361,204	47.9	9,031	174.9
3	Daewoo Corp.	6,398,085	22.0	30,152	189.2
4	Pohang Iron and Steel Co. (POSCO)	5,827,412	21.3	145,680	918.6
5	Korea Electric Power Co. (KEPCO)	5,702,157	13.3	719,049	174.3
6	Hyundai Motor	5,605,244	20.4	56,762	223.7
7	Samsung Electronics Co.	5,227,130	15.9	68,628	320.3
8	Yukong Ltd	4,020,142	26.2	24,524	563.7
9	Goldstar Co.	3,682,800	23.4	18,542	89.9
10	Lucky–Goldstar International Corp. (KEIC)	3,567,767	18.6	3,888	109.5
11	Hyundai Motor Service	2,751,691	32.0	29,756	527.9
12	Kia Motors	2,744,777	8.0	15,785	181.7
13	Hyundai Engineering & Construction	2,541,903	28.5	25,291	102.6
14	Sunkyong Ltd.	2,352,245	15.6	8,674	194.7
15	Ssangyong Corp.	2,071,794	18.1	5,012	205.7
16	Korean Air	2,008,809	21.8	15,951	129.3
17	Lucky Ltd	1,837,919	15.9	43,784	133.1
18	Ssangyong Oil Refining	1,813,924	120.7	40,320	234.4
19	Daelim Ind.	1,676,064	38.5	8,828	315.4
20	Daewoo Electronics	1,576,733	20.3	13,605	81.4

Data based on 510 of the 528 companies that ended their 1991 operations on 31 December 1991. Figures were not available from the remaining 18 companies.

Source: Coryo Research Institute.

TABLE 12 Top twenty corporations in net profits (millions of won), 1991

Rank	Company	1990	1991
1	Korea Electric Power Corp.	605,831	719,049
2	Pohang Iron & Steel Co.	79,025	145,680
3	Samsung Electronics	73,019	68,628
4	Hyundai Motor Co.	67,511	56,762
5	Life Housing & Construction	1,490	45,196
6	Lucky Ltd.	61,851	43,784
7	Korea Mobile Telecom Corp.	19,597	42,749
8	Ssangyong Oil Refining	25,946	40,320
9	Kukje Corp.	(6,195)	34,644
10	Inchon Iron & Steel	31,868	30,893
11	Daewoo Corp.	53,084	30,152
12	Hyundai Motor Service	31,944	29,756
13	Ssangyong Cement	30,420	29,253
14	Woosung Ind.	1,793	28,524
15	Hankook Tire Manufacturing	23,839	27,756
16	Dongkuk Steel Mill	24,418	26,907
17	Samsung Electron Devices	30,322	26,058
18	Daehan Synthetic Fibre	4,272	25,472
19	Hyundai Engineering & Construction	17,298	25,291
20	Samsung Engineering & Construction	24,448	25,078

Banks are not included.
Source: Coryo Research Institute.

TABLE 13 Top ten exporters (millions of dollars, per cent), 1991

Rank	Company	1991	% change year on year
1	Hyundai Corp.*	7,679	32.8
2	Samsung Co.*	7,233	15.2
3	Daewoo Corp.*	6,032	27.0
4	Lucky–Goldstar International Corp.*	3,625	24.4
5	Ssangyong Corp.*	2,192	28.5
6	Sunkyong Ltd.*	1,967	21.5
7	Hyosung Corp.*	1,601	6.6
8	Anam Industrial	1,317	4.5
9	Kolon International Corp.	544	6.9
10	H.S. Corp.	522	(5.2)

Exports by top ten companies	$32,712 million
1991 total exports	$71,870 million
As a percentage of total exports	45.5

* *General Trading Company.*
Source: Korean Foreign Trade Association.

TABLE 14 Top ten investors in R&D (billions of wŏn, millions of dollars), 1991

Ranking	Company	R&D investment	
		W billion	US$ million equivalent
1	Samsung Electronics	473.7	601.9
2	Samsung Aerospace	107.4	136.5
3	Hyundai Motor	84.9	107.8
4	Goldstar	76.7	97.5
5	Kia Motors	73.8	93.8
6	Asia Motors	53.8	68.3
7	Hyundai Electronics	49.7	63.2
8	Goldstar Electron	49.7	63.1
9	Daewoo Electronics	43.7	55.6
10	Ssangyong Motor	43.3	55.1

US dollar equivalents calculated at W787/US$1.
Source: Korea Industrial Research Institute.

46 Miscellaneous

AIR RAID DRILLS AND NATIONAL SECURITY

Continuing concern over national security and the possibility of infiltration by spies results in a number of security practices which may seem excessive or irritating to foreign visitors. Although the security measures are far less strict than even a decade ago, when there was a nightly curfew and monthly air raid practices, the drills *are* taken seriously by the South Koreans and should be respected by foreigners. There may also be roadblocks and restrictions on entry and photography in some areas of Seoul, for example, in the area around the President's residence, and access to hills and mountains throughout the country may be also be restricted for military reasons.

During the civil defence drills, everyone is required to get off the streets (leaving their cars if they were driving at the beginning of the exercise) when the air-raid siren sounds, and take shelter inside a building until the all-clear sounds about twenty minutes later. Less frequently, there are black-out exercises at night, during which all lights must be extinguished. Advance notification is usually given of the black-out drills on the American Forces Korea Network (AFKN) television and radio stations, but the civil defence drills are less widely publicized.

Foreign nationals planning to live and work in the Republic should register with their embassy on arrival. The embassies will usually provide information on procedures in the unlikely event of evacuation being necessary due to military conflict. Once again, AFKN radio and television will provide information in an emergency.

CURRENCY

The unit of currency is the wŏn, which is not an international currency and therefore cannot usually be exchanged outside the Republic of Korea. Denominations currently in circulation are W1,000, W5,000 and W10,000 notes, and W10, W50, W100 and W500 coins. Bank cheques are widely used for large amounts of money, typically in W100,000 denominations.

Above a publicized set limit (currently $5,000), details of foreign currency holdings must be entered on a customs declaration form on entering the Republic of Korea. Below that limit no registration of foreign currency is required, but it is necessary to keep receipts when money is changed into wŏn, as they will be required as documentary evidence when converting back on departure. (It is worth noting that it is often difficult to convert back into less frequently used currencies at the airports. The five most frequently used foreign currencies are pounds sterling, US dollars, yen, German marks and Hong Kong dollars.)

Foreign currency can be converted into wŏn on entry at Kimp'o airport, at designated local banks, at branches of foreign banks and at any registered tourist hotel in Seoul, if one is a guest there.

Major credit cards are accepted at many hotels, at department stores and larger restaurants. However, payments by credit card may be subject to a 5 per cent handling surcharge.

ELECTRICITY SUPPLY

Although the official policy of switching to a universal 220 volts AC/60 cycles supply by 1996 is well under-way, many houses in Seoul still have both 110- and 220-volts outlets. Plug fittings are generally two-pin square, and light-bulb fittings are the screw type rather than bayonet-style.

Supply for industrial use is 3,300, 5,700, 6,600, 22,000, 22,900 and 150,000 volts AC.

EMERGENCIES

The emergency numbers in South Korea are 112 for the police, 129 for the ambulance service, and 119 for the fire department; however, these are of little use unless you speak Korean. There are police boxes on every major street, but again, reporting any incident can be a problem unless you have a Korean speaker with you. It is often better to contact the staff of your hotel or office, or notify a staff member at your embassy. Foreign missions will usually have a recorded message giving an emergency number for out-of-office hours.

In case of medical emergency, Asia Emergency Assistance (tel: 790-7561) provides a 24-hour fee-based emergency service for foreigners, and acts as an essential link between foreign patient and local doctor.

HEALTH CARE

The sicknesses which most commonly afflict foreign visitors are respiratory and eye problems (due to the air pollution), and stomach upsets and diarrhoea (due to the change in diet if eating Korean food).

Most brand-name medicines can be bought over the counter without a prescription, and many of these are manufactured under technical licensing agreements or in joint ventures with well-known foreign pharmaceuticals companies. However, care should be taken, as dosage strengths vary, and South Korean pharmacists when dispensing medicine often treat the symptoms rather than the illness – for example, giving a three-day course of antibiotics, which will clear up the symptoms without removing the infection as will a full seven-day course will.

As a general rule, it is advisable to avoid tap water, unless marked 'potable', and drink bottled water, which is widely available. In the summer, be wary of seafood (especially raw fish) and ice cubes, as outbreaks of hepatitis are possible.

LOCAL TIME

Korean Standard Time (KST) is nine hours ahead of Greenwich Mean Time (GMT) and eight ahead of British Summer Time (BST). Seoul is fourteen hours ahead of New York, one hour ahead of Hong Kong, and one hour behind Sydney. There is no time difference between South Korea and Japan.

Attempts to introduce summer time in South Korea, most recently in 1988 for the Olympics, were unsuccessful. The country operates on KST throughout the year.

NATIONAL HOLIDAYS

The Republic of Korea currently celebrates fourteen official public holidays. Three festivals – Lunar New Year, Buddha's Birthday and Ch'usŏk – are movable feasts in that the date of their celebration is set according to the lunar calendar. Although Korean Alphabet Day was celebrated on 9 October, the holiday was recently abolished due to government concern over the increase in the number of holidays taken by South Korean workers.

1 January (2,3) – New Year's Day The first three days of the new year are public holidays.

The 1st day of the 1st lunar month – Lunar New Year   This holiday is officially known as Folk Customs Day, in order to avoid confusion with the solar New Year's celebrations. The holiday was reinstated in 1985 in response to calls for the restoration of traditions. One of the biggest holidays of the year, it is the time to call on parents and aged neighbours to pay New Year's greetings.

1 March – Independence Movement Day   The anniversary of the national movement against Japanese colonial rule in 1919 in which hundreds of demonstrators were killed or injured (see: History). Memorial services are held in Seoul for the deceased patriots.

10 March – Labour Day   Although this is not an official holiday, many banks and most businesses are closed.

5 April – Arbor Day   Concern for the deforestation of the countryside during and immediately after the Korean War prompted the declaration of an annual festival, during which people could plant saplings throughout the country.

The 8th day of the 4th lunar month – Buddha's Birthday   The day is marked by rituals at Buddhist temples throughout the country and a spectacular lantern procession through the streets of Seoul.

5 May – Children's Day   A holiday since 1975, Children's Day is an opportunity for parents to spend the day with their children. The trend towards excessive consumption, notably on lavish parties and entertainment at top-class hotels, has incurred official displeasure in recent years.

6 June – Memorial Day   The war dead are remembered in ceremonies and wreath-layings at the National Cemetery.

17 July – Constitution Day   This holiday commemorates the promulgation of the Republic's first Constitution in 1948.

15 August – Liberation Day   A celebration both of the liberation from Japanese colonial rule in 1945 and of the anniversary of the establishment of the Republic of Korea in 1948.

The 15th day of the 8th lunar month – Ch'usŏk (Harvest Moon Festival)   Along with Lunar New Year, this is one of the biggest festivals in the year, a cross between Christmas and

Thanksgiving. It is a time for harvest celebrations, ancestor-worship ceremonies, feasting, gift-giving and traditional games.

1 October – Armed Forces Day   This national holiday is celebrated with military parades and honour guard ceremonies.

3 October – National Foundation Day   The holiday marks the founding of Korea in 2333 BC by the nation's mythical progenitor, Tan'gun (see: History).

25 December – Christmas Day   Christmas is observed as a national holiday, as in the west.

Foreign embassies in Seoul generally observe certain of their own national holidays (such as Easter, Labour Day and Thanksgiving) in addition to selected Korean holidays.

OFFICE AND BANKING HOURS
Businesses are generally open from 09.00 to 12.00 and 13.00 to 19.00 between Monday and Friday, and between 09.00 and 13.00 on Saturday. Although these are the official working hours, it is not uncommon to find offices opening at 08.30 and remaining open late into the evening.

Government offices are open from 09.00 to 12.00 and from 13.00 to 18.00 between Monday and Friday, and between 09.00 and 13.00 on Saturday. The offices close one hour early, at 17.00, on weekdays between November and February.

Local banks are open from 09.30 to 16.30 from Monday to Friday, and between 09.30 and 13.00 on Saturdays.

Foreign diplomatic missions usually maintain strict business hours, opening between 09.00 and 17.00 on weekdays, and closing at weekends.

SHOP HOURS
Major department stores, such as the Lotte, Shinsegae and Hyundai, are open between 10.30 and 19.30 six days a week. These stores will usually open on a Sunday, and close on one weekday.

Smaller shops and the newer convenience stores tend to be open from early in the morning until late in the evening every day. Many have regular days off, for example, the first and third Sundays in a month.

TAX
Value-added tax (VAT) is levied on most goods and services at a standard rate of 10 per cent, and is included in the selling

price. In tourist hotels this 10 per cent tax is chargeable on rooms, meals and services and is added to the bill along with the service charge of 10 per cent.

TELEPHONES

There are three types of public telephone currently in use: orange for local calls only, grey for local and long distance calls, and card phones for local, long-distance and international calls. The orange telephones cost W20 for a three-minute call (with an automatic cut-off after three minutes), while the grey telephones take W10, W100 and W500 coins. Telephone cards are available in W3,000, W5,000 and W10,000 denominations from banks and from shops near telephone booths.

The international dialling code is 001 or 002 + country code + district code (minus the initial 0) + individual number. International calls can also be made through the international operator (dial 007). The code 001 is used for calls made through the Korea Telecom, and 002 for calls made through DACOM. Information on international calls can be obtained by dialling 004.

Telegrams can be sent by dialling 115, or (possibly easier and less prone to misunderstandings and misspellings) by filling out a telegram form at the telephone office.

TIPPING

Although this is not a traditional Korean custom, it has been catching on in recent years, especially among taxi drivers. As a service charge of 10 per cent is automatically added to hotel bills, there is no need to tip, nor is it necessary to tip taxi drivers unless they help you with luggage or have been particularly helpful.

WEIGHTS AND MEASURES

Three systems of measurement – Korean, metric and inch-pound – are used in South Korea. The metric has now become the official system, except for certain purposes relating to land and buildings, where the old Korean system is still in use. The use of Korean units of weight in shops and markets will probably survive for many years to come.

1 *p'yŏng* = 35.6 square feet = 3.3 square metres

1 *kwan* = 8.3 lb = 3.8 kg

1 *kŭn* = 1.32 lb = 0.6 kg

47 Further Reading

GENERAL
A Handbook of Korea (8th edition). Seoul: Hollym, 1990.

Korea Annual 1992 (29th edition). Seoul: Yonhap News Agency, Annual.

BUSINESS AND THE ECONOMY
Amsden, Alice. *Asia's Next Giant*. New York: Oxford University Press, 1989.

De Mente, Boye. *Korean Etiquette and Ethics in Business*. Chicago: NTC Business Books, 1988.

Jang, Song-hyon. *The Key to Successful Business in Korea*. Seoul: Yong Ahn Publishing Co., 1988.

Korea Trade Promotion Corporation. *How to Trade with Korea: A Guide to Trade and Investment* (5th edition). Seoul: Korea Trade Promotion Corporation, 1991.

Song, Byung-nak. *The Rise of the Korean Economy*. Hong Kong: Oxford University Press, 1990.

Steers, Richard M. *et al*. *The Chaebŏl: Korea's New Industrial Might*. New York: Harper and Row, 1989.

CULTURE
Adams, Edward B. *Korea Guide: A Glimpse of Korea's Cultural Legacy* (7th edition). Seoul: Seoul International Publishing House, 1988.

Kim, Che-won and Lee, Lena Kim. *Arts of Korea*. Tokyo: Kodansha International, 1974.

Lee, Peter H. *Anthology of Korean Literature from Early Times to the 19th Century*. Hawaii: University of Hawaii Press, 1981.

Pratt, Keith. *Korean Music: Its History and Its Performance.* Seoul: Chong Um Sa, 1987.

HISTORY

Eckert, Carter J. et al. *Korea Old and New: A History.* Seoul: Ilchogak, 1990.

Lee, Ki-baik. *A New History of Korea.* Trans. Edward W. Wagner and Edward J. Schultz. Seoul: Ilchogak, 1984.

Nahm, Andrew C. *Korea: Tradition and Transformation.* Seoul: Hollym, 1988.

LANGUAGE

Barron's Talking Business in Korean. New York: Barron's Bilingual Business Guides, 1988.

Chang, Suk-in. *Modern Conversational Korean* (revised). Seoul: Seoul Press, 1992.

Park, Francis Y. *Speaking Korean I–III.* Seoul: Maryknoll Fathers and Brothers, 1980.

SOCIETY AND CUSTOMS

Current, Marion E. and Choi, Dong-ho. *Looking at Each Other: Korean and Western Cultures in Contrast.* Seoul: Seoul International Publishing House, 1989.

Hoare, James and Pares, Susan. *Korea: An Introduction.* London: Kegan Paul International, 1988.

TOURIST GUIDES

Insight Guides: The Republic of Korea (5th edition). Hong Kong: APA Publications, 1988.

Popham, Peter. *The Insider's Guide to Korea.* Seoul: Seoul International Publishing House, 1987.

Rucci, Richard B. (ed.). *Living in Korea* (6th edition). Seoul: American Chamber of Commerce, 1992.

Steenson, Gary. *Coping with Korea.* Oxford: Blackwell, 1987.

DIRECTORIES AND STATISTICS

1992 Korea Directory. Seoul: The Korea Directory Company, annually.

American Embassy, Foreign Commercial Service. *American Business in Korea, Guide and Directory, 1992–1993.* Seoul: Association of Foreign Trading Agents of Korea, 1992.

Business Korea Yearbook. Seoul: Business Korea Co. Ltd, annually.

Directory of Foreign Companies in Korea 1992. Seoul: World Media Inc., 1992.

Directory of Korean Trading Agents. Seoul: Association of Foreign Trading Agents in Korea, 1992.

Economic Statistics Yearbook. Seoul: Bank of Korea, annually.

Korea Business Directory. Seoul: Korean Chamber of Commerce and Industry, annually.

Korea Company Handbook. Seoul: Asia Pacific Infoserv Inc., bi-annually.

Korea Statistical Yearbook. Seoul: Korean Statistical Association, annually.

Major Statistics of the Korean Economy. Seoul: Korean Statistical Association, annually.

NEWSPAPERS, MAGAZINES AND JOURNALS

Daily in English: *Korea Herald, Korea Times.*

Weekly in English: *The Korea Economic Weekly.*

Monthly in English: *Business Korea, Korea Business Review, Korea Business World, Korea Economic Review, Korea News Review, Korea Post.*

48 Key Phrases

A NOTE ON PRONUNCIATION
Vowels
For vowels, a general pronunciation (based on 'British English')
is given, unless the vowel's position in a syllable affects its
pronunciation. The vowels **a**, **ya**, and **i** are pronounced as short
vowels at the beginning or in the middle of a syllable, and as
long vowels at the end of a syllable.

	General pronunciation	Beginning or middle syllable	End of syllable
a		cat	father
ya		yam	yard
ŏ	not		
yŏ	yacht		
o	or		
yo	your		
u	to		
yu	you		
ŭ	ability		
i		see	it
ae	energy		
yae	yet		
e	edelweiss		
ye	yale		
oe	earn		
wa	soirée		
wae	wet		
we	waver		
wi	we		
wŏ	want		
ŭi	oeil		

Consonants

The pronunciation of the consonants **k′, t′, p′** and **ch′** is aspirated; that is, the pronunciation should be accompanied by a puff of breath.

The pronunciation of the consonants **kk, tt, pp** and **tch** is possibly the most difficult for westerners to master. There is a very slight pause and build-up of tension before the consonant is pronounced, as in the English:

> book **k**eeper
>
> head **d**own
>
> top **p**erson
>
> that **j**udge

The consonant **ng** must be distinguished from the combination of two consonants **n** and **g**, which is written as **n′g**. For example:

> yŏ**ng**o
> ha**n′g**ungmal

GREETINGS AND COURTESIES

Annyŏng hashimnikka?	Formal general greeting used at any time of the day (and when conducting business transactions) (Lit.: Are you at peace?)
Ne, annyŏng hashimnikka?	Reply to the above greeting (Lit.: Yes, are you at peace?)
Annyŏng haseyo?	Informal general greeting used at any time of the day (Lit.: Are you at peace?)
Ne, annyŏng haseyo?	Reply to the above greeting (Lit.: Yes, are you at peace?)
Ch'ŏŭm poepkesssŭmnida	It's a pleasure to meet you (When meeting someone for the first time)
Mannasŏ pangapsŭmnida	Pleased to meet you
Che myŏnghami yŏgi isssŭmnida	Here is my name card
Che irŭmi . . . imnida	My name is . . .

Sŏnghami ŏttŏk'e toeshimnikka?	What is your name? (Formal)
Irŭmi muŏshieyo?	What is your name? (Informal)
Chŏnŭn miguk saramimnida	I'm American
Chŏnŭn yŏngguk saramimnida	I'm British
Annyŏnghi kashipshio	Saying a formal goodbye to someone who is departing (Lit.: Go in peace)
Annyŏnghi kaseyo	Saying an informal goodbye to someone who is departing (Lit.: Go in peace)
Annyŏnghi kyeshipshio	Saying a formal goodbye to someone who is staying where he or she is (Lit.: Stay in peace)
Annyŏnghi kyeseyo	Saying an informal goodbye to someone who is staying where he or she is (Lit.: Stay in peace)
Tto poepkesssŭmnida	See you again
Kamsa hamnida	Thank you
Ch'ŏnmaneyo	You're welcome
Mian hamnida or *Choesong hamnida*	I'm sorry
Kwaench'ansŭmnida	That's all right
Sillye hamnida	Excuse me
Chamkkanmanyo	Just a moment, please
Toessŭmnida	That's OK (Polite refusal of food, etc.)
Yŏboseyo	Answering the telephone, attracting one's attention (Lit.: Please look here)

YES AND NO

Ye or *Ne*	Yes (Both are used)
Animnida	No (formal)
Aniyo	No (informal)

COMMUNICATING

Yŏngŏrŭl hashimnikka?	Do you speak English?
Han'gungmarŭl morŭmnida	I don't speak Korean
Han'gungmarŭl chogŭm hamnida	I speak a little Korean
Morŭgesssŭmnida	I don't understand/I don't know

ASKING DIRECTIONS

. . . *ŏdi isssŭmnikka?*	Where is the . . . ?
chŏnhwa	telephone
hwajangsil	toilet
ŭnhaeng	bank
chihach'ŏl	subway
ipku	entrance
ch'ulgu	exit

GETTING AROUND

T'aekshirŭl pullŏjuseyo	Please call me a taxi
. . . *kapshida*	Take me to . . .
(Name) *Hot'el*	. . . Hotel
Kimp'o konghang	Kimp'o airport
Shich'ŏng	City Hall
Miguk taesagwan	American Embassy
Yŏngguk taesagwan	British Embassy
. . . *paekhwajŏm* e.g. *Lotte paekhawjŏm*	. . . department store Lotte department store
Yŏgisŏ sewŏjuseyo	Please stop here (To taxi driver)

ASKING AND TELLING THE TIME

Myŏtshi?	When, at what time?
Myŏtshiimnikka?	What time is it?
Korean number + *shi*	. . . o'clock

Korean numbers:

han	1		*ilgop*	7
tu	2		*yŏdŏl*	8
se	3		*ahop*	9
ne	4		*yŏl*	10
tasŏt	5		*yŏrhan*	11
yosŏt	6		*yŏldu*	12

Chinese number + *pun* or . . . minutes past
bun

obun	5 past	*samshibobun*	25 to
shippun	10 past	*sashippun*	20 to
shibobun	quarter past	*sashibobun*	quarter to
ishippun	20 past	*oshippun*	10 to
ishibobun	25 past	*oshibobun*	5 to
samshippun (or . . . *shi ban*)	half past		

For example:

1.10 *hanshi shippun*
5.30 *tasŏtshi samshippun* or *tasŏtshiban*
6.50 *yŏsŏtshi oshibobun*
9.25 *ahopshi ishibobun*

ojŏn and *ohu* go before the time: *ojŏn* a.m; *ohu* p.m.; *ojŏn* *yŏlshi* 10 a.m.

DAYS OF THE WEEK

onŭl	today	*suyoil*	Wednesday
ŏje	yesterday	*mogyoil*	Thursday
naeil	tomorrow	*kŭmyoil*	Friday
wŏryoil	Monday	*t'oyoil*	Saturday
hwayoil	Tuesday	*iryoil*	Sunday

SHOPPING

... *chuseyo*   Please give me ...

Ŏlmaimnikka!   How much is it?
or *Olmaeyo!*

Chinese number + *wŏn*   ... *wŏn*

il	1	*yuk*	6	*paek*	100
i	2	*ch'il*	7	*ch'ŏn*	1,000
sam	3	*p'al*	8	*man*	10,000
sa	4	*ku*	9		
o	5	*ship*	10		

numeral + *ship*	tens
numeral + *paek*	hundreds
numeral + *ch'ŏn*	thousands
numeral + *man*	tens of thousands
numeral + *paengman*	millions

Above 9,999 Koreans count in units of ten thousand, so:
24,000 is two ten thousands + four thousand: *iman sach'ŏn*
153,000 is fifteen ten thousands + three thousand: *shiboman samchŏn*
For example:

W15,000	*man och'ŏn wŏn*
W3,700	*samch'ŏn ch'ilbaek wŏn*
W295,500	*ishipkuman och'ŏn obaek wŏn*

NB. The pronunciation of 'sixteen' is irregular: *ship* + *yuk* = *shimnyuk*

and similarly for compounds of ten: *ishimnyuk*, 26;
oshimnyuk, 56

49 Index